IMAGES OF WOMEN IN CHINESE THOUGHT AND CULTURE

Writings from the Pre-Qin Period
through the Song Dynasty

ROBIN R. WANG

Indianapolis/Cambridge

D0322868

Everything embodies yin and embraces yang. Through blending these vital energies they attain harmony. 萬物負陰而抱陽，中氣以為和

Daodejing 42

For Kelly 海利 and Mindy 明蒂 two strong women to be.

Copyright © 2003 by Hackett Publishing Company, Inc.

08 07 06 05 04 03   1 2 3 4 5 6 7

For further information, please address:

Hackett Publishing Company, Inc.
P.O. Box 44937
Indianapolis, IN 46244-0937

www.hackettpublishing.com

Cover photograph: Detail from Princess Yongtai's Tomb, Qianxian County, Shaanxi Province, Tang Dynasty. Photograph by Robin R. Wang.

Cover design by Abigail Coyle
Interior design by Jennifer Plumley
Composition by SNP Best-set Typesetter Ltd., Hong Kong
Printed at Sheridan Books, Inc.

Library of Congress Cataloging-in-Publication Data
Wang, Robin.
    Images of women in Chinese thought and culture : writings from the pre-Qin period through the Song dynasty / Robin R. Wang.
        p. cm.
    Includes bibliographical references.
    ISBN 0-87220-652-1—ISBN 0-87220-651-3 (pbk.)
    1. Women–China–History.   I. Title

HQ1767.W384 2003
305.4'0951—dc21

2003047768

∞

CONTENTS

Part Five: Tang and Song 唐宋 (618–1279 C.E.)   265

LIST OF ILLUSTRATIONS

ACKNOWLEDGMENTS

Many minds, hearts, and hands have contributed to the development of this book. In particular I wish to thank the following individuals for their intellectual insights and heartfelt generosity in assisting me in this project. At an early stage in its development, Bryan Van Norden provided indispensable advice and support. Paul R. Goldin throughout this process has been for me a living "encyclopedia" helping me to resolve some obscure difficulties. Ping Yao, Sherry Mou, and Suzanne Cahill have provided many constructive suggestions from their expertise in history and literature. I have also benefited much from discussions with Philip J. Ivanhoe, Roger Ames, Patricia B. Ebrey, Kenneth Inada, and Susan Mann. Special thanks are also due to Victor Mair for his critical and detailed evaluation of the whole manuscript, and to my graduate student, Sean Heismann, for his careful reading of it. Loyola Marymount University is to be thanked for providing a Summer Research Grant, but also a Rain Research Assistant, Matthew Morgan, whose mastery of computer technology has saved me a lot of time and anguish over the fine points of digital publication. My appreciation and gratitude go to Dennis P. McCann for his invaluable editorial assistance.

Finally, I wish to take this opportunity to thank Deborah Wilkes, the philosophy editor, and Jenevieve Maerker at Hackett Publishing Company, for their unconditional faith in me and in this project. They have always been there for me with timely advice and kindly support.

TRADITIONAL CHRONOLOGY

Pre-Qin

Xia	ca. 2000–1500 B.C.E.
Shang	ca. 1600–1045 B.C.E.
Zhou	1045–256 B.C.E.
Western Zhou	1045–771 B.C.E.
Eastern Zhou	770–221 B.C.E.

Dynasties of Imperial China

Qin	221–206 B.C.E.
Han	202 B.C.E–220 C.E.
Wei, Jin, Nan-Bei Chao	220–581 C.E.
Sui	581–618 C.E.
Tang	618–907 C.E.
Five Dynasties	907–979 C.E.
Song	960–1279 C.E.
Yuan	1279–1368 C.E.
Ming	1368–1644 C.E.
Qing	1644–1912 C.E.

INTRODUCTION

This anthology of Chinese texts from the earliest writings (ca. 1200 B.C.E.) to the Song dynasty (1279 C.E.) illustrates and explores Chinese perspectives on women and gender, cosmology and human nature, as well as women's social roles and virtue. It includes a variety of texts—many translated especially for this volume and some available in English for the first time—that might be classified as historical, philosophical, religious, and literary. All the texts collected here have contributed to and shaped the larger moral and philosophical vision of Chinese thought, culture, and tradition for thousands of years.

China possesses a long, rich textual history. Many ancient texts were followed as a blueprint of the Way (*Dao*), a sacred, cosmic vision of the natural order and the perfect model for living in the human world. Numerous selections presented here have been regarded throughout Chinese history as canonical—in the sense that they were either accepted as foundational for a person's moral and literary education or were thought to exemplify the teachings in foundational texts. Thus this collection furnishes readings from classics, such as *The Book of Odes* (*Shijing*), *The Classic of Changes* (*Yijing*), Confucius' *Analects* (*Lunyu*), and Laozi's *Daodejing*, while also featuring various less familiar works, such as *The Comprehensive Discussions in the White Tiger Hall* (*Baihutong*), Tang dynasty *Examination Essays* (*Panbacui*) and *Epitaphs* (*Muzhiming*), meant to commemorate the success of deceased mothers, wives, and daughters in living virtuous lives.

This anthology brings together some astonishing and usually scattered materials that specifically convey women's basic identities, their distinctive virtues, their ultimate purpose in life, and the social roles and responsibilities they might anticipate. Wherever possible, the writings that Chinese women have produced to instruct their daughters and sisters in the Way proper to women have been highlighted. For example, two complete texts from the so-called *Four Books for Women* (*Nü sishu*)[1] are included here: Ban Zhao's *Lessons for Women* (*Nüjie*) and

---

[1] The *Four Books for Women* (*Nü sishu*) include *Lessons for Women* (*Nüjie*) by Ban Zhao, *The Analects for Women* (*Nü lunyü*) by the Tang female scholar Song Ruoxi, *The Instructions for*

the Tang sisters' *Analects for Women* (*Nü lunyü*). Not surprisingly, women's writings that have achieved canonical status are relatively rare. Nevertheless, even in antiquity Chinese women who had access to a classical education did create works that were just as noteworthy as those authored by their male counterparts.

The volume is divided into five sections and organized chronologically, that is, the readings are arranged in the order in which they are commonly believed to have been written. There is a brief introductory note at the beginning of each selection, which is intended to facilitate the reader's own effort at textual analysis. The chronological arrangement also underscores that the evolution of attempts to discern and explicate the proper Way for women has been inseparable from the development of the Chinese philosophical view of a moral person, family, and state. If the state is ultimately an extension of the relationships of men and women in the family writ large, then the vicissitudes in Chinese experience of both statecraft and family life will inevitably shape and reshape women's lives and society's expectations of them.

Reading these texts in historical sequence provides a reliable map of the development of the Chinese understanding of women and gender, starting with highly specific images, more or less protean, ad hoc, and unsystematic, to a more ordered, deliberate, ideologically driven, and comprehensive ideal, in which the various images are made into highly structured sex roles. This pattern of historical development may raise critical questions regarding the ways in which the Chinese primordial vision of a cosmically grounded complementarity between the sexes was transformed into something rather different. As readers proceed through the selections, they may note an increasingly rigid pattern of gender division, one in which female submissiveness, in the narrowest sense, became the norm for women. A careful and sympathetic reading of the texts presented here may suggest that the all-too-familiar pattern of female subordination and restriction is a departure—sometimes subtle, sometimes blunt—from the richer and more open-ended estimation of women found in the Chinese classics.

Seeking to be rigorously fair in presenting the Chinese primary

---

the *Inner Court* (*Neizhe*) by Empress Ren Xiao (1362–1418), wife of the Ming emperor Chengzu (r. 1403–1424), and *The Short Records of Models for Women* (*Nüfan jielu*) by Liu Shi the mother of the late Ming Confucian Wang Xiang (1624). These four books were first published as a collection in 1624. They were assigned reading for women through many centuries.

writings, this collection supplies readers with ample resources for comprehending traditional images of women and how those images have been fostered over two thousand years. It ends roughly with the fall of the Song dynasty (1279 C.E.), before the oppression of women was fully implemented. If Western feminist critiques of Chinese patriarchy have any merit, they are most on target in denouncing the abuses of women legitimated by late Ming-Qing Neo-Confucianism. But even here two caveats must be kept in mind. The first is that in the modern period of Chinese history, beginning with the attempts to reform Chinese society toward the end of the Qing dynasty and culminating in the May 4th Movement (1919), Chinese women and men were themselves the most perceptive critics and uncompromising foes of socially oppressive institutions and the decadence into which the aristocratic Chinese family had fallen. The second is that the Ming-Qing Neo-Confucian views of women and their institutionalization cannot be well understood or effectively criticized apart from an appreciation of the earlier perspectives on women illustrated in the ancient texts. Thus the writings selected here present a vision that could assist in constructing a well-informed and balanced view of the identity and roles of women.

The interpretation and exploration of these influential writings may help readers appreciate how women have played a crucially important part in the development of Chinese thought, culture, and tradition. Indeed, Chinese thought and culture would be unthinkable without the contribution of women—unthinkable, that is, for anyone who truly comprehends the Chinese view of the complementarity of women and men, which is described in these texts as an ideal possibility and, astonishingly often, as a lived experience. Although the problems of sexism and all other forms of social oppression are significant, the reader may hesitate to identify these problems as either the inevitable result or the essential implication of the cosmic vision animating Chinese thought and culture. One will experience how these textual discussions of women are situated in the conceptual constructions of philosophy, morality, and the meaning of human life.

One important key to interpreting the complexities of images of women emerging in these writings is a general appreciation of women's philosophical and cosmological identity. Take an example from the Appended Statements (*Xici*) in *The Classic of Changes* (*Yijing*):

> How profound is the *Dao* of the *Changes* (*Yi*)! When using it to foretell
> fathomless events, it has no boundary. When using it to clarify the events
> at hand, it is stable and proper. When using it to explain the events

between *tian* (the sky, the heavens) and *di* (earth), it can cover them in detail and not leave anything behind.

Qian is productive because when it is still, *qian* is pure and focused, and when in motion, it is straight without limitation. *Kun* is procreative because when it is quiet, *kun* is closed, and when in motion, it is open into a vast field.

That is why we correlate the functions of both *qian*'s productivity and *kun*'s procreativity with *tian* (the sky, the heavens) and *di* (earth); their change and continuity (*biantong*) with the four seasons; the significance of *yin* (female) and *yang* (male) with the sun and the moon; and beauty and goodness, which are easy and simple with the highest excellence (*de*).[2]

This passage identifies the complementarity of female and male with the familiar pattern of *yin* and *yang*. But the elementary forces of *yang* and *yin* are themselves embodied as *tian* and *di*, the heavens and the earth, and rendered symbolically in the first two of the *Yijing*'s hexagrams, *Qian* and *Kun*. The social roles proper to men and women are yet another expression, on the human level, of the dynamic complementarity of *yang* and *yin*. As complementary archetypes, *yin* and *yang* give cosmic meaning to the range of social interactions possible for human beings. Each has its distinctive role to play without which the other ceases to exist, indeed, without which the whole cosmos ceases to exist. Among human beings, then, male and female are merely the highest animate embodiment of *yin* and *yang*. Though each human being is gendered as either male or female, both males and females concretely possess a specific synthesis of *yang* and *yin*. No female being is exclusively *yin*, any more than any male is exclusively *yang*. Such a being, indeed, would be unbalanced!

The cosmological identity of woman, however, is not simply an important fact defining her physical appearance, or psychological dispositions, any more than it is for man. Her cosmological identity, as is also true for the man, is first of all her *Dao*, the Way by which she is to achieve her own distinctive fulfillment as a human being. Chinese women's social roles as daughter, wife, and mother are the embodiment of their *Dao*. Each role has its own specific virtues, and the task of self-cultivation proceeds differently in each of these clusters of relationships. It is through the practice of self-cultivation that women, like men, make valuable contributions to human life and society. The cosmic vision thus entails a systematic and conceptual negation of the

---

[2] See the selection from *The Classic of Changes*, pp. 29–30.

kind of dualistic thinking that has warranted misogynistic prejudice, as if woman were merely an incomplete man, and hence his biological and social inferior in most important respects. In the context of Chinese conceptual understanding, woman's cosmological identity guarantees that women are equal and complementary to men, at least at the metaphysical level.

Each of the social roles laid out for Chinese women—daughter (*nü*), wife (*qi*), and mother (*mu*)—is suffused with this cosmological identity. One primal pattern is woman as mother. Since the *Dao*, to the extent that it can be named, is fittingly named "Mother" (cf. *Daodejing* 25), motherhood is seen as a privileged way of following the *Dao*. Another primal pattern is woman as wife. Marriage is the appropriate institution in which the complementarity of *yin* and *yang*, woman and man, is lived out. The third primal pattern is woman as daughter. Within the family a woman cultivates the central virtue of filial piety, out of respect for her parents and ancestors and in preparation for her entry into her husband's family. Taken together, these three roles are the source of a woman's power through which she achieves her own metaphysical dignity.

Though from a Western point of view women's identification with the family or the inner quarters (*nei*) may seem unduly restrictive, the social significance of these three roles should not be underestimated. In Chinese tradition, the family is the model for the Empire, and the most necessary part of the social structure. Women's role in the family, therefore, is essential to their role in public life. It also serves as a model for the King, whose success depends on responding to the needs of the people in much the same way that a woman must respond to the needs of her family. Chinese culture envisions the wise and virtuous woman empowering her husband and her children for social leadership, from which the whole family and state will benefit. The selections that follow will allow readers to investigate these roles in detail and see how both Chinese women and men have actually perceived them. It is left to the reader to decide how successful these writings have been in remaining faithful to the promise of complementarity and equality given in the cosmic vision of the *Dao*.

Implicit in all three roles is yet another pattern that can usefully be explored here. This is the aesthetic image of woman as lover, the inexhaustible source of artistic inspirations. In many Chinese writings, women are not identified with lust, or blamed as the root of evil in the world. In diverse ways women were admired as aesthetic objects and cherished for their intrinsic beauty. Beauty is honored and cultivated as an expression of virtue. Women's beauty ultimately resides in virtue, but beauty itself is a sign of virtue. Beauty and goodness, following the *Dao*, are intertwined, and the relationship is one of complementarity. Beauty is simply an externalization of a woman's inward goodness.

The primary Chinese texts presented here thus celebrate different female virtues; they show the way in which women contribute to the overall harmony of the family and, through the family, to society as a whole. What is noteworthy about these virtues, as the reader will soon discover, is that there is no sharp distinction among them of spiritual, moral, intellectual, emotional, or indeed aesthetic concerns. All are seamlessly woven into a single fabric, one in which there is no room for a patronizing dichotomy between women's "beautiful" virtues versus the "noble" virtues reserved for men (as Immanuel Kant claimed). While the ensemble of women's virtues remains socially significant, women and men will both follow the path toward self-cultivation, but each in their own unique ways.

It has been an enjoyable and rewarding experience for me to have the opportunity to revisit these intellectual works. As a woman who was brought up in China, I have a special attachment to these texts. Many of these writings are, in fact, a part of public education as well as the way of life. They have been integrated into the language we speak, the code of conduct we follow, and the living ideal we strive for. This collection is ostensibly centered on women's experience as reflected in these primary texts, but its conceptual depth and historical breadth also distinguish it as a unique study of Chinese philosophy, literature, history, religion, gender, and above of all, the wisdom of life. This work, in addition to creating an intellectual space for a philosophical analysis of Chinese primary texts, is also dedicated to furthering an appreciation of the legacy of Chinese thought, culture, and tradition.

Robin R. Wang
Los Angeles, Spring 2002

PART ONE

SHANG
商

AND

WESTERN ZHOU
西周

(1600–771 B.C.E.)

1

ORACLE BONE INSCRIPTIONS
ON WOMEN

甲骨文

The earliest Chinese dynasty for which we have contemporary historical records is the
Shang. When the rulers of the Shang dynasty wished to predict the future or communicate with, or influence, the spirits of their ancestors and other powers, they used
"oracle bones." These bones were cracked by heating and then, in some manner
unknown to us, their cracks were interpreted. After Shang rulers read the cracks, they
often carved inscriptions into the bones, using the earliest known forms of Chinese
characters.

The information found in a complete oracle bone inscription included the date on
which the divination was performed, the name of the person who performed it, the
topic about which the divination was conducted (frequently in both positive and negative forms: "There will be . . . ," "There will not be . . ."), an interpretation of the
cracks by the King, and a report on what had actually resulted. Unfortunately, most
inscriptions did not include all these items. Nevertheless, the Shang people have left us
a number of pieces of text that give us a fascinating glimpse into the lives of the Shang
nobility, including the lives of noble women.

It is often said that the subordination of women is indicated in the earliest form
of the Chinese character for "woman," seen in the oracle bone inscriptions, which
appears to show a kneeling figure. However, the significance of this character is unclear,
since kneeling was common to men and women prior to the introduction to China
of the chair centuries later. It does seem clear, nevertheless, that in the Shang period
women already had a subordinate status to men in Chinese society. This is indicated,
for example, by the more luxurious burial that males typically received in comparison to females.

Such subordination did not prevent some women from achieving a certain measure
of importance, however. One such woman was Fu Hao or "Lady Hao," the consort
of King Wu Ding, who lived around 1200 B.C.E. Lady Hao's tomb has been dis-

From David N. Keightley, "At the Beginning: The Status of Women in Neolithic and
Shang China," Nan Nü I : I (Brill, 1999): I–6I. Reprinted by permission of David N.
Keightley and Brill Academic Publishers. Modified by Bryan Van Norden.

covered, and it includes an impressive array of burial goods in her honor: 468 bronze items (weighing a total of 1.5 metric tons), 755 jades, and over 6,880 cowries shells, all of which were of significant value in the Shang period and long thereafter). In addition, at least sixteen people were buried with her. Following are some oracle bone inscriptions referring to Lady Hao, interspersed with explanatory comments (in italics).

Bryan Van Norden

It appears that, during her life, Lady Hao had some control over military units: Crack-making on the day *yiyou*. Que divined: "Call upon Lady Hao to first raise men at Pang."

Crack-making on the day *xinsi*. Zheng divined: "In the present season, if the King raises men and calls upon Lady Hao to attack the Tufang,[1] we will receive abundant assistance."

The subordination of women is evident in the preference for male offspring: Crack-making on the day *jiashen*. Que divined: "Lady Hao's child-bearing will be good." The King read the cracks and said, "If the child-bearing be on a *ding*-day, it will be good; if the childbearing be on a *geng*-day, there will be prolonged luck." After thirty-one days, on the day *jiayin*, she gave birth. It was not good; it was a girl.

Lady Hao was important even after her death. She was given the honorific posthumous title "Ancestress Xin" and was given ritual sacrifices by later rulers: Crack-making on the day *xinsi*. We divined: "The King hosts Wu Ding's consort, Ancestress Xin, and performs the *zai* ritual; there will be no fault."

Lady Hao's posthumous psychic influence is also evident in the following divination: We divined: "That the King dreamed of Lady Hao does not mean that there will be harm."

---

[1] The Tufang were a people who lived on the border of, and frequently raided, the Shang state.

2

THE BOOK OF ODES
(Shijing)
詩經

The Book of Odes (Shijing) *is a collection of 305 poems dating from probably 1000–600* B.C.E. *According to Sima Qian (known as "the grand historian," 145–90* B.C.E.*), Confucius was the editor of the* Shijing, *and he selected the poems from an original body of about 3,000. The* Shijing *was the text Confucius used to teach his students to give expression to their feelings and thoughts and was also an essential part of aristocratic education. In Book 17.9 of the* Analects, *Confucius acknowledges the value of the* Shijing: *"The Mater said, 'My young friends, why don't any of you study the Songs (Odes)? Reciting the Songs can arouse your sensibilities, strengthen your powers of observation, enhance your ability to get on with others, and sharpen your critical skills. Close at hand it enables you to serve your father, and away at court it enables you to serve your lord. It instills in you as a broad vocabulary for making distinctions in the world around you.'"*[1] *It was probably because of Confucius' appreciation of these Odes that gave rise to an extraordinary literary craze to this book through Chinese history. It is one of the five Confucian Classics* (Wujing).[2]

The Odes contain many different images of Chinese women. The position of women generally seems to bear greater similarity to that of the present day, especially in rural communities, than it does to the quite different conditions characteristic of the imperial period (221 B.C.E.*–1911* C.E.*). Several of the Odes, such as Odes 23, 42, 94, 95, and 99, without inhibition celebrate the joys of sex outside of mar-*

From *The Chinese Classics*, 2nd ed., 5 vols., translated by James Legge (Oxford: Clarendon, 1893–1895). Modified by Robin R. Wang.

[1] *The Analects of Confucius*, translated by Roger T. Ames and Henery Rosemont, Jr. (New York: Ballantine Books, 1998), Book 17.9, p. 206.

[2] The other four of the five Confucian Classics (*Wujing*) includes *The Classic of Changes* (*Yijing*), *The Canon of Documents* (*Shujing*), *The Record of Rites* (*Liji*), and *The Spring and Autumn Annals* (*Chunqiu*).

riage, while others, such as Odes 1, 12, 139, 143, 145, and 218, celebrate passionate love between the sexes in the context of courtship and marriage. In both instances, women are praised for their beauty and intelligence, but only the latter also praise them for their virtue. Odes 2, 28, 29, 30, 35, 58, 62, and 94, purport to give a woman's perspective. Although some of these may actually have been composed by women, their general purpose seems to have been to offer moral exhortations to men, specifically to shame them for not living up to society's expectations for their relationships with women. Odes 29, 30, and especially Ode 35, give vivid expression to the complaints of wives who feel they have been mistreated by their husbands. On the other hand, Ode 62 memorializes a wife's longing for her husband, absent in military service, a sentiment that is mirrored by Ode 31, in which husbands absent in military service express their fear that fate may not allow them to survive the war and return safely home to their wives. In addition to celebrating female joys and sorrows, the Odes also project images of women that are cosmic in their significance. Ode 245, for example, recalls how the legendary ancestor Jiang Yuan gave birth to the people (shengmin). *More importantly, it describes how she brought the god of grains* (Houji) *into being. The birth of Houji to Jiang Yuan is one of the earliest mythological tales.*

Taken together, the Odes presented here give readers a chance to savor directly the feelings (imagined or otherwise) *of Chinese men and women living out their often complex and sometimes perplexing relationships with one another. Consistent with what came to be the Confucian tradition, the Odes testify to the fundamental importance of marriage and family in society, and to how these institutions work in their distinctive ways. The Odes memorably render, for example, a glimpse of a first wife's attitude toward her husband's taking a second wife or concubine* (Ode 35), *and the suffering that some widows have to endure in not being allowed to remarry* (Ode 32). *Despite such sufferings, however, the Odes generally confirm a basic cultural commitment to the underlying complementarity of male and female gender roles, and the cultivation of emotions appropriate to that complementarity. The final selection* (Ode 290), *a work song celebrating the labor of peasants in the fields, suggests that the ideal of harmonious solidarity between men and women runs deep in the Chinese soul, and that it is an aspiration shared by all social classes at all times throughout China's history.*

Robin R. Wang

Part One
Lessons from the States (*Guofeng*)

Book 1: The Odes of Zhou and the South (Zhounan)

Ode 1

"*Guan! Guan!*" go the ospreys,
On the islet in the river.
The modest, retiring, virtuous, young lady—
For our prince, she is a good mate.

Here long, there short, is the duckweed,
To the left, to the right, borne about by the current.
The modest, retiring, virtuous, young lady—
Waking and sleeping, he sought her.

He sought her and found her not,
And waking and sleeping he thought about her.
Long he thought—oh! long and anxiously;
On his side, on his back, he turned, and back again.

Here long, there short, is the duckweed;
On the left, on the right, we gather it.
The modest, retiring, virtuous, young lady—
With lutes, small and large, let us give her a friendly welcome.

Here long, there short, is the duckweed;
On the left, on the right, we cook and present it.
The modest, retiring, virtuous young lady—
With bells and drums let us show our delight in her.

Ode 2

How the dolichos[3] spreads itself out,
Extending to the middle of the valley!
Its leaves were luxuriant;
The yellow birds flew about,
And collected on the thickly growing trees,
Their pleasant notes resounding far.

How the dolichos spread itself out,
Extending to the middle of the valley!

---

[3] Dolichos is a species of vines found primarily in tropical areas, from whose fibers a kind of cloth is made.

Its leaves were luxuriant and dense.
I cut it and boiled it,
And made both fine cloth and coarse,
Which I will wear without getting tired of it.

I have told the matron,
Who will announce that I am going to see my parents.
I will wash my private clothes clean,
And I will rinse my robes.
Which need to be rinsed, and which do not?
I am going back to visit my parents.

Book 2: The Odes of Zhao and the South (Zhaonan)

Ode 12

The nest is the magpie's;
The dove dwells in it.
This young lady is going to her future home;
A hundred carriages are meeting her.

The nest is the magpie's;
The dove possesses it.
This young lady is going to her future home;
A hundred carriages are escorting her.

The nest is the magpie's;
The dove fills it.
This young lady is going to her future home;
These hundreds of carriages complete her array.

Ode 15

She gathers the large duckweed
By the banks of the stream in the southern valley.
She gathers the pondweed
In those pools left by the floods.

She deposits what she gathers
In her square baskets and round ones;
She boils it
In her tripods[4] and pans.

---

[4] The tripod supports the pan over the cooking fire. Duckweed is slightly boiled and pickled in order to be presented as a sacrificial offering. The young wife here is being praised for her diligence in fulfilling her familial responsibilities.

She sets forth her preparations
Under the window in the ancestral chamber.
Who superintends the business?
It is this reverent young lady.

Ode 23

In the wild there is a dead antelope,
And it is wrapped up with the white grass.
There is a young lady with thoughts natural to the spring,
And a fine gentleman would lead her astray.

In the forest there are the scrubby oaks;
In the wild there is a dead deer,
And it is bound round with the white grass.
There is a young lady like a gem.

She says, "Slowly; gently, gently;
Do not move my handkerchief;
Do not make my dog bark."

Book 3: The Odes of Bei (Beifeng)

Ode 28

The swallows go flying about,
With their wings now high, now low.
The lady was returning to her native state,
And I escorted her far into the country.
I looked till I could no longer see her,
And my tears fell down like rain.

The swallows go flying about,
Now up, now down.
The lady was returning to her native state,
And far did I accompany her.
I looked till I could no longer see her,
And long I stood and wept.

The swallows go flying about;
From below, from above, comes their twittering.
The lady was returning to her native state,
And far did I escort her to the south.
I looked till I could no longer see her,
And great was the grief of my heart.

Lovingly confiding was the lady Zhong;
Truly deep was her feeling.
Both gentle was she and docile,
Virtuously careful of her person.
In thinking of our deceased lord,
She stimulated worthless me.

Ode 29

O sun, O moon,
Which enlighten this lower earth!
Here is the man,
Who treats me not according to the ancient rule.
How can he get his mind settled?
Would he then not regard me?

O sun, O moon,
Which overshadow this lower earth!
Here is the man,
Who will not be friendly with me.
How can he get his mind settled?
Would he then not respond to me?

O sun, O moon,
Which come forth from the east!
Here is this man,
With virtuous words, but he is really not good.
How can he get his mind settled?
Would he then allow me to be forgotten?

O sun, O moon,
Which come forth from the east!
O father, O mother,
There is no sequel to your having nourished me.
How can he get his mind settled?
Would he then respond to me, contrary to all reason?

Ode 30

The wind blows and is fierce.
He looks at me and smiles,
With scornful words and dissolute—the smile of pride.
To the center of my heart I am grieved.

The wind blows, with clouds of dust.
Kindly he seems to be willing to come to me;

But he neither goes nor comes.
Long, long, do I think of him.

The wind blew, and the sky was cloudy;
Before a day elapses, it is cloudy again.
I awake, and cannot sleep;
I think of him, and gasp.

All cloudy is the darkness,
And the thunder keeps muttering.
I awake and cannot sleep;
I think of him, and my heart is full of pain.

Ode 31

Hear the roll of our drums!
See how we leap about, using our weapons!
Others do the fieldwork in the State, or fortify Cao,
While we alone march to the south.

We followed Sun Zizhong,
Peace having been made with Chen and Song;
But he did not lead us back,
And our sorrowful hearts are very sad.

Here we stay; here we stop;
Here we lose our horses;
And we search for them,
Among the trees of the forest.

For life or for death, however separated,
To our wives we pledged our word.
We held their hands—
We were to grow old together.

Alas for our separation!
We have no prospect for life.
Alas for our promises!
We cannot make them good.

Ode 32

The genial wind from the south
Blows on the heart of the jujube tree,

Till that heart looks tender and beautiful.
What toil and pain did our mother endure!

The genial wind from the south
Blows on the branches of the jujube tree,
Our mother is wise and good;
But among us there is no one good.

There is the cool spring
Below the city of Jun.
We are seven sons,
And our mother is full of pain and suffering.

The beautiful yellow birds
Give forth their pleasant notes.
We are seven sons,
And cannot compose our mother's heart.

Ode 35

Gently blows the east wind
With cloudy skies and with rain.
Husband and wife should strive to be of the same mind
And not let angry feelings arise.
When we gather the mustard plant and earth melons,
We do not reject them because of their roots.
While I do nothing contrary to my good name,
I should live with you till our death.

I go along the road slowly, slowly,
In my inmost heart reluctant.
Not far, only a little way,
Did he accompany me to the threshold.
Who says that the sow thistle is bitter?
It is as sweet as the shepherd's purse.[5]
You feast with your new wife,
Loving as brothers.

The muddiness of the Jing appears from the Wei,
But its bottom may be seen about the islets.
You feast with your new wife,

---

[5] Legge translates "*qi*" as a shepherd's purse (*capsella bursa pastoris*), a common weed bearing pouch-like seed pods. It was considered a very sweet plant.

Figure 1. Youyu's wife and concubine bring him a refreshing lunch as he labors
Zhuan) by Chou Ying (1509–1552).]

in the field. [From *Chou's Illustrations of the Biographies of Woman (Chou Hua Lienu*

And think me not worth being with.
Do not approach my dam,[6]
Do not move my basket.
I am rejected—
What avails it to care for what may come after?

Where the water was deep,
I crossed by a raft or a boat.
Where it was shallow,
I dived or swam across it.
Whether we had plenty or not,
I exerted myself to be getting.
When among others there was a death,
I crawled on my knees to help them.

You cannot cherish me,
And you even count me as an enemy.
You disdain my virtues—
A peddler's wares that do not sell.
Formerly, I was afraid our means might be exhausted,
And I might come with you to destitution.
Now, when your means are abundant,
You compare me to poison.

My fine collection of vegetables
Is but a provision against the winter.
Feasting with your new wife,
You think of me as a provision only against your poverty.
Cavalierly and angrily you treat me;
You give me only pain.
You do not think of the former days
And are only angry with me.

Ode 42

How lovely is the retiring girl!
She was to await me at a corner of the wall.
Loving and not seeing her,
I scratch my head, and am perplexed.

---

[6] The river is pictured as being crossed by a stone dam, with open spaces, through which fish might pass, only to be caught in a fisherman's baskets. Here the old wife is warning the new wife to stay away from her property——the dam she had used to supply fish for her family——but then thinks the better of it, since she has no further interest in anything that had belonged to her before.

How handsome is the retiring girl!
She gave me a red tube.[7]
Bright is the red tube—
I delight in the beauty of the girl.

From the pasturelands she gave me shoots of the white grass,
Truly elegant and rare.
It is not you, O grass, that is elegant—
You are the gift of an elegant girl.

Book 4: The Odes of Yong (Yongfeng)

Ode 49

Boldly faithful in their pairings are quails;
Vigorously so are magpies.
This man is all vicious,
And I consider him my brother!

Vigorously faithful in their pairings are magpies;
Boldly so are quails.
This woman is all vicious,
And I regard her as marchioness![8]

Book 5: The Odes of Wei (Weifeng)

Ode 57

Large was she and tall,
In her embroidered robe, with a plain single garment over it:
The daughter of the marquis of Qi,
The wife of the marquis of Wei,
The sister of the Crown Prince of Qi,
The sister-in-law of the marquis of Xing,
The viscount of Tan, also her brother-in-law.

Her fingers were like the blades of young white grass;
Her skin was like creamy lotion;
Her neck was like the tree grub;

---

[7] Legge translated *tongguan* in Chinese as a red tube. *Tong* refers the color red and *guan* is a small piece of decorated bamboo, whose specific use is unknown.

[8] A marchioness is a woman of the rank and dignity of a marquis. The point is that the aristocratic couple being denounced in this ode are still, despite the author's complaint, regarded with proper affection and respect.

Her teeth were like melon seeds;
Her forehead lovely; her eyebrows beautiful;
What dimples, as she artfully smiled!
How lovely her eyes, with the black and white so well defined!

Large was she and tall,
When she halted in the cultivated suburbs.
Strong looked her four horses,
With the red ornaments so rich about their bits.
Thus in her carriage, with its screens of pheasant feathers,
She proceeded to our court.
Retire early, you great officers,
And do not tire the marquis!

The waters of the He, wide and deep,
Flow northwards in majestic course.
The nets are dropped into them with a splashing sound,
Among shoals of sturgeon, large and small,
While the rushes and sledges are rank about.[9]
Splendidly adorned were her sister ladies;
Brave looked the attending officers.

Ode 58

A simple-looking lad you were,
Carrying cloth to exchange it for silk.
But you came not to purchase silk;
You came to make proposals to me.
I accompanied you through the Qi,
As far as Dunqiu.
"It is not I," I said, "who would protract the time;
But you have had no good go-between.
I pray you, be not angry,
And let autumn be the time."

I ascended that ruinous wall
To look towards Fuguan;
And when I did not see you coming,
My tears flowed in streams.
When I saw you coming from Fuguan,

---

[9] Legge's use of the term "sledge" seems idiosyncratic, and corresponds to no much conventional meaning. From context, it is clear that Legge is referring to the tall reeds among which the shoals of sturgeon are lurking.

I laughed and I spoke.
You said you had consulted the tortoise shell and the yarrow
    stalks,
And there was nothing unfavorable in their response.
"Then come," I said, "with your carriage,
And I will leave with my goods."

Before the mulberry tree has shed its leaves,
How rich and glossy are they!
Ah! dove,
Eat not its fruit to excess.
Ah! young lady,
Seek no licentious pleasure with a gentleman.
When a gentleman indulges in such pleasure,
Something may still be said for him;
When a lady does so,
Nothing can be said for her.

When the mulberry tree sheds its leaves,
They fall yellow on the ground.
Since I went with you,
Three years have I eaten of your poverty.
And now the full waters of the Ji
Wet the curtains of my carriage.
There has been no difference in me,
But you have been double in your ways.
It is you, Sir, who transgress the right,
Thus changeable in your conduct.

For three years I was your wife,
And thought nothing of my toil in your house.
I rose early and went to sleep late,
Not ceasing my labors for even a morning.
So on my part our promise was fulfilled,
But you have behaved cruelly.
My brothers will not know all this,
And will only laugh at me.
Silently I think of it,
And feel sorry for myself.

I was to grow old with you—
Old, you give me cause for sad repining.
The Qi has its banks,
And the marsh has its shores.

In the pleasant time of my girlhood, with my hair simply
Gathered in a knot,
Harmoniously we talked and laughed.
Clearly we were sworn to good faith,
And I did not think the engagement would be broken.
That it would be broken I did not think,
And now it must be over!

Ode 62

My noble husband is mighty and strong!
The hero of the country!
My husband, grasping his halberd,[10]
Is in the leading chariot of the king's host.

Since my husband went to the east,
My hair has been like the flying cattail.
It is not that I could not anoint and wash it;
But for whom should I adorn myself?

O for rain! O for rain!
But brightly the sun comes out.
Longingly I think of my husband,
Till my heart is weary, and my head aches.

How shall I get the plant of forgetfulness?
I would plant it on the north of my house.
Longingly I think of my husband,
And my heart is made to ache.

Book 7: The Odes of Zheng (Zhengfeng)

Ode 94

On the moor is creeping grass,
And how heavily is it loaded with dew!
There was a beautiful man,
Lovely, with clear eyes and fine forehead!
We met accidentally,
And my desire was satisfied.

On the moor is the creeping grass,
Heavily covered with dew.
There was a beautiful man,

---

[10] Legge translated Chinese *shu* as Halberd. *Shu* is an ancient weapon that is like a spear.

Lovely, with clear eyes and fine forehead!
We met accidentally,
And he and I were happy together.

Ode 95

The Zhen and the Wei[11]
Now present their broad sheets of water.
Ladies and gentleman
Are carrying flowers of valerian.[12]
A lady says, "Have you been to see?"
A gentleman replies, "I have been."
"But let us go again to see.
Beyond the Wei,
The ground is spacious and fit for pleasure."
So the gentlemen and ladies
Make sport together,
Presenting one another with small peonies.

The Zhen and the Wei
Show their deep, clear streams.
Gentlemen and ladies
Appear in crowds.
A lady says, "Have you been to see?"
A gentleman replies, "I have been."
"But let us go again to see.
Beyond the Wei
The ground is spacious and fit for pleasure."
So the gentlemen and ladies
Make sport together,
Presenting one another with small peonies.

Book 8: The Odes of Qi (Qifeng)

Ode 99

The sun is in the east,
And that lovely girl

---

[11] The Zhen and Wei are two rivers in Zheng.

[12] The plant identified as valerian grows in marshy places and near rivers. It is also known as "the fragrant grass." Among the Zheng the plant was used in baths, and to drive away pestilential influences, as well as a stimulant on festive occasions, such as the picnic described in this ode.

Is in my chamber.
She is in my chamber;
She treads in my footsteps, and comes to me.

The moon is in the east,
And that lovely girl
Is inside my door.
She is inside my door;
She treads in my footsteps, and hastens away.

Book 12: The Odes of Chen (Chenfeng)

Ode 139

The moat at the east gate
Is fit to steep hemp in.
That beautiful, virtuous lady
Can respond to you in songs.

The moat at the east gate
Is fit to steep the boehmeria in.[13]
That beautiful, virtuous lady
Can respond to you in discourse.

The moat at the east gate
Is fit to steep the rope-rush in.[14]
That beautiful, virtuous lady
Can respond to you in conversation.

Ode 143

The moon comes forth in her brightness;
How lovely is that beautiful lady!
O to have my deep longings for her revealed!
How anxious is my heart!

The moon comes forth in her splendor;
How attractive is that beautiful lady!
O to have my anxieties about her relieved!
How agitated is my heart!

---

[13] The plant identified as boehmeria is a species of hemp, or nettle, from which grass cloth is made.
[14] The plant identified as rope-rush is another hemp-like plant from whose leaves fibers were obtained for making string and/or rope.

The moon comes forth and shines;
How brilliant is that beautiful lady!
O to have the chains of my mind relaxed!
How miserable is my heart!

Ode 145

By the shores of that marsh,
There are rushes and lotus plants.
There is the beautiful lady;
I am tortured by her, but what avails it?
Walking or sleeping, I do nothing;
From my eyes and nose water streams.

By the shores of that marsh
There are rushes and the valerian.[15]
There is the beautiful lady,
Tall and large, and elegant.
Walking or sleeping, I do nothing;
On my side, on my back, with my face on the pillow, I lie.

Part Two
Minor Odes of the Kingdom (*Xiaoya*)

Book 7: *Decade of the Sanghu*

Ode 218

"*Roll, roll*" went the axle ends of my carriage,
As I thought of the young beauty, and went to fetch her.
It was not that I was hungry or thirsty,
But I longed for one of such virtuous fame to come and be
With me.
Although no good friends be with us,
We will feast and be glad.

Dense is that forest in the plain,
And there sit the long-tailed pheasants.

---

[15] See the footnote of Ode 95 for an explanation of valerian.

In her proper season that well-raised lady,
With her admirable virtue, has come to instruct me.
We will feast, and I will praise her.
"I love you, and will never be weary of you."

Although I have no good spirits,
We will drink what I have, and perhaps be satisfied.
Although I have no delicacies,
We will eat what I have, and perhaps be satisfied.
Although I have no virtue to impart to you,
We will sing and dance.

I ascend that lofty ridge,
And split the branches of the oaks for firewood.
I split the branches of the oaks for firewood,
Amid the luxuriance of their leaves.
I see you whose match is seldom to be seen,
And my whole heart is satisfied.

The high hill is looked up to;
The great road is easy to travel on.
My four steeds advanced without stopping;
The six reins made music in my hands like a lute.
I see you, my bride,
To the comfort of my heart.

Part Three

The Greater Odes of the Kingdom

(Daya)

Book 2: Decade of Shengmin (Shengmin)

Ode 245

The first of our people born
Was from Jiang Yuan.
How did she give birth to our people?
She had presented a pure offering and sacrificed,
That her childlessness might be taken away.
She then trod on a toe-print made by God, and was moved,
In the large place where she rested.

She became pregnant; she dwelt quietly;
She gave birth to and nourished a son,
Who was Hou Ji.

When she had fulfilled her months,
Her first-born son came forth like a lamb.
There was no bursting, nor rending,
No injury, no suffering—
Showing how wonderful he would be.
Did not God give her comfort?
Had he not accepted her pure offering and sacrifice,
So that easily she brought forth her son?

Part Four
Odes of the Temple and the Altar
(SONG)

Book 1: Sacrificial Odes of Zhou

Ode 290

They clear away the grass and the bushes;
And the ground is laid open by their ploughs.

In thousands of pairs they remove the roots,
Some in the low wetlands, some along the dykes.
There are the master and his eldest son;
His younger sons, and all their helpers, and their hired
    servants.
How the noise of their eating brought to them
Resounds!
The husbands think lovingly of their wives;
The wives keep close to their husbands.
Then with their sharp plough-shares,
They set to work on the south-lying acres.

They sow their different kinds of grain,
Each seed containing in it a germ of life.

In unbroken lines rises the blade,
And well-nourished the stalks grow long.

The young grain looks luxuriant,
And the weeders go among it in multitudes.

Then come the reapers in crowds,
And the grain is piled up in the fields,
Myriad, and hundreds of thousands, and millions of stacks;

For spirits and for sweet spirits,
To offer to our ancestors, male and female,
And to provide for all ceremonies.

Fragrant is their aroma,
Enhancing the glory of the State.
Like pepper is their smell,
To give comfort to the aged.

It is not here only that there is this abundance;
It is not only now that there is such a time:
From ancient times it has been so.

3

THE CLASSIC OF CHANGES
(Yijing)
易經

The Yijing (The Classic of Changes) *is generally regarded as the first and most important Chinese philosophical text and is cherished in both the Confucian and Daoist traditions. The* Yijing, *also known as the* Zhouyi (The Changes of Zhou), *was developed from two older books, the* Guicang *and the* Lianshan. *The* Yijing *is a collection of the wisdom of generations of sages, as it came into being over a period of thousands of years. Originally, it was a manual of divination, which, according to tradition, was devised by* Fu Xi, *who invented the eight trigrams* (ba gua), *or three-lined figures consisting of combinations of solid and broken lines. King Wen* (Wen Wang) *combined these eight trigrams into sixty-four six-lined figures, known as hexagrams* (gua).

Though people still usually regard the Yijing *as a book of divination, its philosophical profundity is by no means limited to divination. The text is divided into four parts: images* (xiang), *numbers* (shu), *patterns* (li), *and divination* (zhan). *Its main aim is to clarify the* dao (way, path, course) *of* tian (the heavens, the sky, nature) *and* di (earth), *or the* dao *of the sages, and draw out its practical applications. Because of its important contribution to the development of a theory of* dao, *the* Yijing *is a significant source for all of the Chinese philosophical schools that came after it.*

What exactly is the dao *that the* Yijing *reveals to human beings? One part of the answer to this question is the* dao *of yin and yang, which are considered to be the two basic fluctuating patterns of all things in the world. The* Yijing *sets up a system of broken and solid lines that represent, respectively, yin* (female, soft, weak, etc.) *and yang* (male, hard, strong, etc.), *and thus form the trigrams. These two symbols reflect the Chinese understanding of the world as a complementarity of movement processes and events* (wu), *which can be characterized as dominated by yin or yang at any given moment.*

Translated By Hai-ming Wen and John Trowbridge. The translators would like to thank Professors Ma Hengjun, Roger T. Ames, and Chung-ying Cheng.

The sixty-four hexagrams that are composed of various combinations of yin *(broken) and* yang *(unbroken) lines form the basis for the philosophical reflections recorded in the text of the* Yijing. *The hexagrams are followed by commentaries explaining the symbolic and philosophical significance of the situations described by the particular hexagrams that are cast in the process of divination. Each of the eight tri-grams, of which the sixty-four hexagrams are composed, represent a power in nature, either active or passive: the heavens* (tian), *earth* (di), *fire* (huo), *water* (shui), *mountains* (shan), *wind* (feng), *thunder* (lei), *and lake* (ze). *The sixty-four hexagrams elaborate on these eight images as they occur in various combinations with one another. The commentaries* (Yizhuan), *transmitted along with the text* (Yijing), *became the basis for the development of the cosmological and metaphysical speculation emergent in the early Han dynasty. In addition to their philosophical significance, the ideals of the* Yijing *have also been employed in the areas of politics, literature, and daily life.*

A word about the chronology of the composition of both the text and the Yizhuan *is in order here. The sixty-four hexagrams, along with the hexagram judgments (the text given under each hexagram), represent the earliest layer of the text. The* Yizhuan *consists of the Ten Wings* (Shi Yi), *which were composed much later than the hexa-gram judgments. The Ten Wings are:*

1. Tuanzhuan (Commentary on the Dominant Meanings), *Part 1.*[1] (*Also called* Tuan)

2. Tuanzhuan (Commentary on the Dominant Meanings), *Part 2.*[2] (*Also called* Tuan)

3. Xiangzhuan (Commentary on the Images), *Part 1.*[3] (*Also called* Xiang)

4. Xiangzhuan (Commentary on the Images), *Part 2.*[4] (*Also called* Xiang)

5. Wenyan (The Words of the Classic Text)[5]

6. Xicizhuan (Commentary on the Appended Statements), *also known as the* Dazhuan (Great Commentary), *Part 1.* (*Also called* Xici)

7. Xicizhuan (Commentary on the Appended Statements), *also known as the* Dazhuan (Great Commentary), *Part 2.* (*Also called* Xici)

8. Shuogua (Explaining the Trigrams)

---

[1] Commentaries that correspond to Part 1 of the hexagrams (hexagrams 1–30).

[2] Commentaries that correspond to Part 2 of the hexagrams (hexagrams 31–64).

[3] Commentaries that correspond to Part 1 of the hexagrams (hexagrams 1–30).

[4] Commentaries that correspond to Part 2 of the hexagrams (hexagrams 31–64).

[5] Commentaries on the first two hexagrams only.

9. Xugua (The Order of the Hexagrams)
10. Zagua (The Hexagrams in a Mixed [Miscellaneous] Order)

Portions of the Ten Wings that relate to the role and function of yin are translated here. The two parts of the Tuan, the two parts of the Xiang, and the Wenyan (the first Five Wings) appear immediately after the selected hexagram judgments. Although this arrangement joins strata of the text from radically different time periods, the commentaries on the hexagrams are best understood when read together with the hexagram judgments. The relevant selections from the Xici, Shuogua, and Xugua are translated in separate sections. Contrary to tradition, but following Ma Hengjun,[6] these commentaries are presented before the hexagrams and their associated judgments because without the commentaries it is nearly impossible to make sense of the hexagrams.

Hexagrams 1, 2, 11, 31, 32, 37, 54, 63 in particular are relevant for under-standing both the cosmic significance of gender and its influence on shaping traditional Chinese moral and social expectations. Each of the hexagrams selected here provides an image of the significance of yin from different perspectives. Some of them, notably, hexagram 37, make explicit the significance of yin within the family. Indeed, this hexagram contains within it the quintessence of traditional Chinese morality, for it describes the proper ordering of all human relationships relative to the exigencies of tian and di (earth), all within an overarching pattern of complementarity. Wives, for example, will act in ways proper to their role when husbands act in ways that are proper for a husband. The roles, though complementary, are asymmetrical, in that the woman's place is naturally within the home while the man's place is naturally outside it.

Taken together, the hexagrams also suggest the possibility of movement or even friction within the family. As changes are indicated by the subtle shifting of the yin and yang balance in each trigram, they signal the presence of various forms of instability in cosmic and human relationships. Such possibilities, nevertheless, only reinforce the validity of the dao of tian and di, by providing the opportunity for moral exhortations that warn of the consequences of proceeding toward one's goals in an improper way. The asymmetrical character of these exhortations is vividly represented in the following piece of advice from the Xiang commentary on hexagram 32 (heng): "Six in the fifth place: In making one's excellence long-lasting (heng), persevere. It is good fortune for a woman, but misfortune for a man. The Xiang commentary says: It is good fortune for a woman to persevere because she follows her husband all her life. The behavior of a man should be regulated by the appropriateness (yi) of things. It is misfortune for him simply to follow his wife." If one can begin to appre-

---

6 Ma Hengjun is the leading scholar in the study of *Yijing* in China. His work includes *Zhouyi Bianzheng* (Shijiazhuang: Hebei People's Press, 1995) and *Zhouyi* (Beijing: Huaxia Press, 2001).

ciate how and why such an observation would be cherished as salutary moral wisdom, one may also come to know how and why Chinese people still regard the Yijing *as one of the most ancient and profound resources on women's identity available in their cultural tradition.*

Hai-ming Wen and John Trowbridge

Xici
Appended Statements

I.1

That *tian* (sky, heavens, nature) is high and *di* (earth) is low is a natural phenomenon.[7] This is why *qian* (creativity) is high up and *kun* (formation) is low down. High and up is noble; low and down is base. The up and down is displayed, so the noble and mean in the lines of the trigram are fixed in different places.

Moving is the characteristic of *tian* and being static is that of *di*. If one is in motion, one is strong and vigorous; if one stands still, one is soft and submissive. There is constant regulation in the movement of *tian* and *di*.

The strong and vigorous and the soft and submissive can then be distinguished. Therefore, the strong line and the weak line are stipulated in the *Yijing*. The myriad things in nature gather together according to their different classifications, so the advantages and disadvantages among them produce good fortune and misfortune.

The changing of *yin* and *yang* is represented as the various changes of the movements of the sun and the moon and the stars in *tian* (the heavens), and as the formation and maturity of the myriad things on *di* (earth). The *Yijing* can reflect this kind of change because it models the images in *tian* and the forms of *di*.

Because the *yang* line and the *yin* line of the *Yijing* model the changing movements of nature, the strong and weak lines will come into contact and exert friction with one another. By the same token, the

---

[7] The philosophical basis that is applied in the creation of the *Yijing* understands *tian* (the sky, the heavens, nature) as the representation of *yangqi*, and *di* (earth) as that of *yinqi*. *Qi* (animating energy, vital energy, hylozoistic vapors) is considered to be the basis of all sixty-four hexagrams (*gua*) in the *Yijing*. All of these hexagrams change and arise from *qian* and *kun*. *Qian* is the imitation of *tian*, and *kun* is the imitation of *di*. The movements of *qian* and *kun* are the imitation of the movements of *yin* and *yang*.

eight trigrams will agitate each other. The trigram *zhen* is thunder. The trigram *xun* is wind. The trigram *dui* is rain. The trigram *li* is the sun. The trigram *kan* is the moon. The movements of the eight trigrams are like the thunder aroused in nature, or like the nourishing of the wind and rain, or like the changes of winter and summer—and the four seasons during the processes of contact, movement, revolution, and formation of the sun and the moon.

The movements of *qian* [*yang*] create the male, and the movements of *kun* [*yin*] complete the female. The function of the trigram *qian* is to take charge of the origination of the myriad things, and the function of the trigram *kun* is the formation and maturity of the myriad things.

The trigram *qian* functions in an easy way, and the trigram *kun* functions in a simple way. What is easy causes people to understand it easily; what is simple easily causes people to follow it. If something is easily comprehended, there will be some people who approach it closely, and when what is easy follows, it creates achievements. Those who approach it closely are able to last long. If one can last long, this is the way and excellence (*de*) of the worthy person (*xian ren*). If one can develop his strengths and make greater his talents, these are the undertakings of the worthy person. For a worthy person, it is easy and simple to grasp the theory of the whole world. After he grasps the theory of the whole world, he is able to achieve his own position in the world.

1.5

The correlation of one *yin* and one *yang* is *dao*. The succession of *dao* is *shan* (good); the formation of the *dao* is *xing* (natural tendencies).

When a humane person sees *dao*, he calls it humanity. When a wise person sees *dao*, he calls it wisdom. The common people use *dao* everyday, but they are never aware of it. Therefore, the *dao* of the exemplary person is understood by almost nobody.

1.6

How profound is the *dao* of the *Changes* (*Yi*)! When using it to foretell fathomless events, it has no boundary. When using it to clarify the events at hand, it is stable and proper. When using it to explain the events between *tian* (the sky, the heavens) and *di* (earth), it can cover them in detail and not leave anything behind.

Qian is productive because when it is still, *qian* is pure and focused, and when in motion, it is straight without limitation. *Kun* is procreative because when it is quiet, *kun* is closed, and when in motion, it is open into a vast field.

That is why we correlate the functions of both *qian's* productivity and *kun's* procreativity with *tian* (the sky, the heavens) and *di* (earth); their change and continuity (*biantong*) with the four seasons; the significance of *yin* (female) and *yang* (male) with the sun and the moon; and beauty and goodness, which are easy and simple with the highest excellence (*de*).

2.1

When the eight trigrams are displayed in a line, the images are already among them. When the eight trigrams are overlapped and combined with one another, the six lines are already among them. When the *yang* (strong, hard) line and the *yin* (weak, soft) line evolve into one another, the changes are already among them. In appending judgments to the different hexagrams and lines, movement is already there.

Good fortune, misfortune, regret, and danger all come from the movements of the lines. The *yang* (strong, hard) line and the *yin* (weak, soft) line are the basis of the changes. Change and continuity (*biantong*) are adaptive to the time and space. Good fortune and misfortune are based on achieving victory when following the proper way (*dao*). The *dao* of *tian* (the heavens) and *di* (earth) is the great manifestation of the proper way (*dao*). The *dao* of the sun and the moon releases light by means of the proper way (*dao*). All movement under *tian* can converge because each is practicing the proper way (*dao*).

2.4

The *yin* (female) lines are greater in number than the *yang* (male) lines [in the three son trigrams, *zhen, kan,* and *gen*], and the *yang* lines are greater in number than the *yin* lines [in the three daughter trigrams, *xun, li,* and *dui*]. What is the reason for this? It is because *yang* is represented by the odd numbers, and *yin* is represented by the even numbers.

What about their moral conduct? [In the son trigrams,] one *yang* (male, strong) line is the ruler, and two *yin* (female, weak) lines are the subordinates. This is the *dao* of exemplary persons (*junzi*). [In the daughter trigrams,] two *yang* (male, strong) lines are the rulers, and one *yin* (female, weak) line is the subordinate. This is the *dao* of petty persons (*xiaoren*).

2.5

It is because of the intercourse of the *yangqi* of *tian* and the *yinqi* of *di* that the myriad things are produced. The myriad things are propagated when the seminal essence of the male is mixed with the blood of the female. It is said in the *Yijing*, "If three persons walk along together, one of them will be lost in the end. If a person walks alone, he will find his friend." This is talking about the required balance between the *yinqi* and *yangqi*.

2.6

The master [Confucius] said, "*Qian* and *kun* should be the entrance to the *Changes* (*Yi*)!" *Qian* represents the *yang*-things-and-events (*yang wu*), and *kun* represents the *yin*-things-and-events (*yin wu*). The excellence (*de*) of the *yang* (strong, hard) and the *yin* (weak, soft) converge, so the *yang* and the *yin* manifest their form and structure. These representations and manifestations are the embodiment of the changing, transforming, and generating events of *tian* and *di* (the heavens and earth). These embodiments are correlated with a penetrating and spiritually illumined understanding of the excellent achievements of processes and events. The names [based on these two trigrams] that are given to the myriad events (*wanwu*) are numerous but not disorderly. This work must be carried out in an era of decline, because the different situations represented by the trigrams were carefully examined!"

Shuogua
Explaining the Trigrams

In ancient times, when the sages invented the *Changes* (*Yi*), they followed these procedures: They subtly created the method of using yarrow stalks to divine in order to help the spiritual beings (*shen*). They formulated the principle [of the *Yijing*] based on the interweaving of the three numbers of *tian* as odd and the two *di* numbers as even.[8] They set up the trigrams (*gua*) based on their observations of the changing of *yin* and *yang* forces in nature. They invented the lines (*yao*)

---

[8] For an explanation of the method of divination using yarrow stalks, see Richard Wilhelm and Cary F. Baynes, trans., *The I Ching or Book of Changes* (Princeton: Princeton University Press, 1950, 1967) 721–723. Among the five productive numbers (*sheng shu*), numbers 1, 2, 3, 4, and 5, there are three *tian* numbers, which are 1, 3, and 5, and two *di* numbers, which are 2 and 4.

based on the changing and moving of the *yang* (strong, hard) and the *yin* (weak, soft). They established the theory (*li*) in appropriateness (*yi*) according to the continuity of human excellence (*de*) and the *dao* of *tiandi* (the heavens and earth) and *yin* and *yang*. They were able to explain the destinies of all the processes and events by exhausting their patterns (*li*), and by getting the most out of their natural tendencies.

In ancient times, when the sages invented the *Changes* (*Yi*), they formulated their own system of divination in order to have it follow the theories of natural tendencies (*xing*) and the propensities (*ming*) of all processes and events. In this system, they established that *yin* and *yang* belong to the *dao* of *tian* (*tiandao*), that the weak/soft (*yin*) and the strong/hard (*yang*) belong to the *dao* of *di* (*didao*), and that humanity (*ren*) and appropriateness (*yi*) belong to the *dao* of people (*rendao*). Therefore, they used six lines to formulate a hexagram (*gua*) so as to include each of the two aspects (*yin* and *yang*) of the three powers (*sancai: tian, di,* and *ren*). There are six lines circulating in each hexagram that represent the six positions in which the sages assigned the *yin* and the *yang* lines. They alternated the application of the strong/hard (*yang*) and the weak/soft (*yin*) lines, based on the nature of their positions.

Qian is the representation of *tian*, which belongs with *yang* (male), so *qian* is also the representation of the father. *Kun* is the representation of *di*, which belongs with *yin* (female), so *kun* is also the representation of the mother. *Kun* (earth) receives the first *yang* (strong, hard) line from *qian* and gives birth to *zhen* (thunder), therefore *zhen* is the representation of the first son. *Qian* receives the first *yin* (soft, weak) line from *kun* and gives birth to *xun* (wind), therefore *xun* is the representation of the first daughter. *Kun* receives the second *yang* (strong, hard) line from *qian* and gives birth to *kan* (water), therefore *kan* is the representation of the middle son. *Qian* receives the second *yin* (weak, soft) line from *kun* and gives birth to *li* (fire), therefore *li* is the representation of the middle daughter. *Kun* receives the third *yang* (strong, hard) line from *qian* and gives birth to *gen* (mountain), therefore *gen* is the representation of the youngest son. *Qian* receives the third *yin* (weak, soft) line from *kun* and gives birth to *dui* (lake), therefore *dui* is the representation of the youngest daughter.[9]

---

[9] This passage presents an analogy between parents giving birth to the six children (three sons and three daughters) and *qian* and *kun* giving birth to the six trigrams.

Xugua
The Order of the Hexagrams

The ten thousand processes and events (*wanwu*) come into being only after *tian* and *di*. The male and female exist only after the ten thousand processes and events. The relationship of husband and wife is possible only after there are male and female. There is the relationship of father and son only after there is husband and wife. The difference of superior and inferior between the ruler and ministers is possible only after the superior and inferior relationship between the father and son becomes manifest. The difference in ranking between the upper and the lower comes only after the relationship of superior and inferior between the ruler and ministers is established. The system of rites (*li*) will be diversified because of the difference in ranking between the upper and the lower. The proper way between husband and wife should not fail to last long. Hence, *heng* (long-lastingness) comes after *xian* (responding emotionally), because *heng* means persistence and eternity. Nothing can remain in one place forever and not develop or change. Therefore, *tun* (retreating) comes after *heng*, since *tun* means to retreat and withdraw.

Hexagram 1: Qian *(Creativity)*
Qian *is* tian **(qian,** *the heavens, below;* **qian,** *the heavens, above)*
Qian (Creativity):[10] Originality, flourishing, harmony, and perseverance.[11]

Qian (Creativity)

---

[10] Each hexagram has a different diagram, which is called *"guatu"* or *"guahua"* (diagram of a hexagram). ☰ is the diagram of the hexagram *qian*. In the *Yijing*, the name of the hexagram comes after each diagram of the hexagram. This hexagram's name is *qian*.

[11] The name of each hexagram is followed by the judgment that applies to it, which is called *"guaci"* (the judgment of the hexagram). Here "originality, flourishing, harmony, and perseverance (*Yuan heng li zhen*)" is the judgment of the hexagram *qian*.

The *Tuan* (*Commentary on the Dominant Meanings*) says:[12] So great is the origin of *qian* (*yang*),[13] that the myriad processes and events (*wanwu*) come into being because of it, and it has the function of controlling all the celestial bodies.[14]

Qian [*yang*] arranges the clouds and the rain. Because of its movements, all things have their own forms. The sun continues to move from morning till night, so the daytime is divided into six different stages, which are represented as six different line positions in the hexagrams. It leads the movement of the celestial bodies by controlling the six stages of *yang* lines like driving six dragons according to the proper time.[15]

The celestial bodies move and transform according to the way of *qian* (*qian dao*) so that the myriad processes and events have their proper *xing* (natural tendencies, dispositions) and *ming* (propensities, destinies). That is, the myriad processes and events come to their proper state of harmony (*he*). It keeps the *yuanqi* (original vital energy) from *qian* [*yang*] and never allows it to scatter. In this way *xing* and *ming* come into existence. In this way things can exist in their proper situation and live constantly. First, it creates all things and events (*shuwu*) so that all the states[16] are at peace.

The *Wenyan* (*The Words of the Classic Text*) says: *Qian*'s "originality" starts to proceed smoothly. "Harmony and perseverance" concerns natural tendencies (*xing*) and reality and responses (*qing*). Only *qian* [*yang*] has the ability to harmonize the world by means of beauty and harmony, and does not claim that it has done anything harmonious. It is so great! *Qian* is great indeed! The *dao* of *tian* moves forward in the proper way; its perseverance never deviates. It is composed purely of *jingqi* (seminal essence and vital energy) [*yangqi*]. The function that developed from the changing of the six lines of *qian* can be correlated with the natural tendencies and reality-and-responses of the ten thousand processes and events: "Driving six dragons according to the proper time" to "harness the motions of the celestial bodies";

---

[12] All of the following passages that begin with the expression, "The *Tuan* (*Commentary on the Dominant Meanings*) says:" are from the *Tuanzhuan* (*Commentary on the Dominant Meanings*), which is said to be Confucius' explanation of the *guaci* (the judgments of the hexagrams).

[13] *Qian* consists of six *yang* lives, so it is often understood with reference to *yang*.

[14] This passage explains *yuan* (originality).

[15] This passage explains *heng* (flourishing).

[16] This passage explains *li zhen* (harmony and perseverance).

"arranging the clouds and rain," so that peace will be attained throughout the world.

The exemplary person takes the accomplishment (or achievement) of excellence as his own practice. This practice should be manifested in his everyday life.

Hexagram 2: Kun *(Formation)*
Kun *is* di, *earth* (kun, *earth,* above; kun, *earth,* below)

Kun (Formation): Proceeding smoothly at the beginning. Gaining advantage through the perseverance of the mare.[17] When the exemplary person moves forward, he will first lose his way, and afterwards he will follow a lord. It is advantageous for him to find friends in the southwest [because the *yinqi* grows up in that direction]. It is also advantageous for him to lose his friends but follow their lords in the northeast [because the *yangqi* grows up in that direction]. They peacefully persevere in their proper way with good fortune.

The *Tuan* commentary says: Great is the potency of the inchoate formation of *kun* [*yin*]. The ten thousand processes and events have to rely on it to complete their forms. The movement of *kun* (formation) follows that of *qian* (creativity). *Kun* is the representation of *di*, which sustains the ten thousand things and events (*wanwu*). It is boundless when the formation of *kun* cooperates with the creativity of *qian*. *Kun* encompasses expansively without limitation, and all processes and events proceed smoothly. The mare is of a kind with *di* (*kun*). It runs all over the earth and has no boundaries. It is advantageous for it to preserve a submissive character. The exemplary person moves forward after he casts the hexagram *kun*. He will lose his way if he wants to lead others at the beginning [e.g., before casting the

Kun (Formation)

---

[17] The mare is a representation of *yin* (female) things.

hexagram], and he will find his constant way (*chang*) after he follows *kun*. He will find his friends in the southwest because he associates with those of his own kind. He will lose his friends in the northeast because he associates with *qian* [*yang*], [which is of the opposite characteristic to him]. However, since *yin* follows *yang*, it results in great happiness. The good fortune of peacefully persevering in his proper way responds to the character of *di*, which has no boundary.

The *Xiang* commentary says: The propensity of *di* (earth) corresponds to the formation of *kun*. The exemplary person uses his profound excellence to support the ten thousand things and events (*wanwu*) like the character of *di*.

Six in the first place:[18] The hard ice will form soon after you step on the snow.

The *Xiang* commentary says: "The hard ice will form soon after you step on the snow" because the *yinqi* has begun to condense. The hard ice will definitely come about if one is developing smoothly along this way.

The *Wenyan* (*The Words of the Classic Text*) says: The character of *kun* (formation) is the most submissive in its softness, but it will become very strong if it is activated with *qian* (creativity). The character of *kun* is quiet and still, but its excellence is upright. It always follows *qian*, is guided by it, and travels along its constant way (*chang*). It can contain the ten thousand things (*wanwu*) and has the power to complete the [trans]formation of them. Isn't it the character of *kun* (formation) to follow *qian* (creativity)? It always moves according to its proper time and follows the creativity of *tian*.

The family that accumulates good deeds will surely have excessive blessings [which it will pass on to its descendants]. The family that accumulates evil deeds will surely have excessive disasters [which it will pass on to its descendents]. When the ministers are about to kill their ruler, or the sons are about to kill their father, it is never carried out in a single day and night. It must result from gradual accumulation. This occurs because there is no discernment of the evil while it is still accumulating to find ways to prevent it. When the *Changes* (*Yi*) says, "The hard ice will form soon after you step on the snow," it is talking about the result that comes from the gradual accumulation of this kind of tendency.

"Uprightness (*zhi*)" is proper and centered because the six in the

---

[18] Six indicates a *yin* line and nine indicates a *yang* line. "In the first place" means it is the first line of the hexagram, which is the bottom line.

second place is in the middle position of the lower trigram.[19] "Appropriateness (*fang*)" means doing things appropriately.

Though the *yin* things have beauty, they cannot show off when they want to achieve something by following a ruler, and they do not dare to consider themselves to be in a position of completion. This is the *dao* of *di* (earth), the *dao* of a wife, and the *dao* of a minister. The *dao* of *di* is not to claim its own completion, but to represent *tian* and give form to its creativity.

The movement and change brought about from the communication of the creativity of *tian* and the formation of *di* will cause the grass and trees to flourish. When the creativity of *tian* and the formation of *di* cease to communicate, the result is the withering away and dying of the ten thousand things (*wanwu*). Under this circumstance, the worthy person should seclude himself. It is said in the *Changes* (*Yi*) [in "six in the fourth place"]: "A pouch tied up, there is no blame and no praise." This means that we should be careful in our behavior when the creativity of *tian* and the formation of *di* cease to communicate.

The exemplary person thoroughly understands the patterns of events when preserving the yellow central propriety,[20] and locates his body in its proper place. The beautiful character inside him will fully express itself through his four limbs. Forming his excellence according to his enterprises is the utmost of beauty.

[When *yin* grows to the six at the top, the hexagram, *qian* has changed into the hexagram *kun*.] *Yinqi* is disliked by *yangqi*; hence the fight between them is inevitable. It is suspected that *yangqi* might disappear from the top position, so the "dragon (*long*)" is mentioned because it is a hint to the existence of *yangqi*. The "blood (*xue*)" is mentioned because there is no deviation from the class of *yin*, for which blood is a representation. Black-and-yellow is the color of the mixture of *tian* and *di*, because *tian* is black and *di* is yellow.

Hexagram 11: Tai (*Peaceful Communication*)
Earth, tian (qian, *the heavens, below;* kun, *earth, above*)

Tai (Peaceful Communication): Lose less and gain more, good fortune, flourishing.

---

[19] This means that the *yin* line remains in the second place. The second place or the middle position of the lower trigram is the proper place for *yin*.

[20] This sentence explains the fifth line, which is centered in the upper trigram. Yellow is the color of the earth and of royalty. Exemplary persons (*junzi*) try to keep their proper places, and understand all the things and events in the world.

Tai (Peaceful Communication)

The *Tuan* commentary says: "*Tai*, lose less and gain more, good fortune, flourishing," because *tian* and *di* interact and the myriad things communicate. Also, the upper and the lower are attracted to each other and share the same purposes. The *yangqi* is inside and the *yinqi* is outside, socially speaking, thus the inner trigram is strong and steadfast, and the outer trigram is submissive. Therefore the whole image describes a situation where one is internally an exemplary person and externally a petty person. The *dao* of exemplary persons is growing, and the *dao* of petty persons is in decline.

The *Xiang* commentary says: The upper trigram, *qian* as *tian*, and the lower trigram, *kun* as *di*, communicate with each other. This is *tai* (peaceful communication). The ruler of the state regulates the patterns of communicating between *yin* and *yang* by examining the *dao* of *tian* and *di*. The ruler facilitates the proper movement of the *dao* of *tian* and *di* in order to teach his people.

Six in the fifth place: Emperor Yi[21] had his daughter married, so great good fortune followed.

The *Xiang* commentary says: "Great good fortune followed" because his wishes had been realized.

Hexagram 31: Xian *(Responding Emotionally)*
Lake, mountain (gen, *mountain, below;* dui, *lake, above*)

Xian (Responding Emotionally): Proceeding smoothly. It is prosperous to persevere. Marrying a woman will bring good fortune.

The *Tuan* commentary says: The meaning of *xian* is feeling and response. When changing from *pi*, the nine at the top and the six in the

---

21 Emperor Yi was one of the emperors of the Shang dynasty and is usually considered to be the father of Emperor Zhou. Emperor Yi had his daughter married to Wang Ji of the Zhou dynasty, and she gave birth to King Wen of Zhou (Zhou Wen Wang) who was regarded as the founder of the *Yijing* system and Chinese culture. Wang Ji was a vassal, so it was "great good fortune" for him to marry the daughter of the Emperor.

Xian (Responding Emotionally)

third place of *pi* change places and become *xian*.[22] The soft *yin* line moves up and the strong *yang* line moves down. This is a symbol of the feeling and response of the *yinqi* and *yangqi* coming together. The upper trigram *dui* means happiness, and the lower trigram *gen* means stopping. The combined meaning is stopping at happiness. In the process of the hexagram changing, the strong *yang* line as the male descends and the soft *yin* line as the female ascends. This is just like the common situation of a young man, full of humility, begging for marriage from a young woman. Therefore, "proceed smoothly. It is prosperous to persevere. Marrying a woman will bring good fortune . . ." [In *pi*, the upper trigram *qian* is *tian*, and the lower trigram *kun* is *di*. During the process of the hexagram changing,] the *yangqi* of *tian* interacts with the *yinqi* of *di*, so the ten thousand processes and events are transformed and generated. The sage moves the hearts-and-minds (*xin*) of the people and the world is at harmony and peace. Looking at the feelings and responses among the people, one is able to see the reality and responses (*qing*) of all the processes and events between *tian* and *di*.

The *Xiang* commentary says: The lower trigram *gen* is mountain, and the upper trigram *dui* is lake. The combined image is the hexagram *xian* (responding emotionally). The exemplary person sees the great lake on the top of the mountain and determines to follow the character of the great mountain, and supports other people with open-mindedness.

Hexagram 32: Heng *(Long-Lastingness)*
Thunder, wind (xun, wind, below; zhen, thunder, above)

Heng (Long-Lastingness): Proceeding smoothly. No blame. It is prosperous to persevere. It is prosperous to move forward.

---

[22] According to the system by which hexagrams change, the hexagram *xian* is changed from the hexagram *pi*. Specifically, the nine, being a *yang* line, in the top place of *pi*, changes places with the six, being a *yin* line, in the third place, and thus becomes *xian*.

Heng (Long-Lastingness)

The *Tuan* commentary says: The meaning of *heng* is long-lasting. *Heng* is developed from *tai*, from which the nine in the first place changes places with the six in the fourth place. The strong *yang* line moves up, and the soft *yin* line moves down. The upper trigram *zhen* signifies thunder, and the lower trigram *xun* signifies the wind. The combined image is that of the wind strengthening the power of the thunder. The lower trigram *xun* is smooth, and the upper trigram *zhen* is moving. The combined image is proceeding smoothly. The six in the first place responds to the nine in the fourth place; the nine in the second place responds to the six in the fourth place; and the nine in the third place responds to the six at the top. All six lines respond to one another in their proper places.[23] This is why the hexagram *heng* should be long-lasting. "*Heng*: proceeding smoothly. No blame. It is prosperous to persevere. It is prosperous to move forward." This is because the situation is moving in the proper way for a long duration. The *dao* of *tian* and *di* keeps on moving without end. "It is prosperous to move forward," because the things and events are continually moving forward as they complete a former process. The sun and the moon can shine forever because they continue to move according to their proper ways. The times of the year and months come into being because the four seasons keep on coming and going. The sage follows the proper way of *tian* and *di*, and continues to move along his proper course (*dao*). In this way, all the people under *tian* will be cultivated, and the civilization will be guided properly. The sage observes his long-lastingness (*heng*), the reality and responses (*qing*) of the ten thousand processes can be seen.

---

23 We translate the word, "*ying*" as "respond." In this context, "respond" refers to the respective *yin* lines in each trigram responding to their corresponding *yang* lines in the other trigram. *Yin* and *yang* are commonly understood to "respond" to each other in this manner.

The *Xiang* commentary says: The upper trigram *zhen* signifies thunder and the lower trigram *xun* signifies wind. The combined image is the hexagram *heng* (long-lastingness). The exemplary person will not change his standpoint when cultivating himself and influencing others.

Six in the fifth place: In making one's excellence long-lasting (*heng*), persevere. It is good fortune for a woman, but misfortune for a man.

The *Xiang* commentary says: It is good fortune for a woman to persevere because she follows her husband all her life. The behavior of a man should be regulated by the appropriateness (*yi*) of things. It is misfortune for him simply to follow his wife.

Hexagram 37: Jiaren *(Family)*
Wind, fire *(li, fire, below; xun, wind, above)*

Jiaren (Family): It is prosperous for women to persevere.

Jiaren (Family)

The *Tuan* commentary says: In *jiaren* (family), the proper place for the woman is inside the family, and the proper place for the man is outside the family. When both man and woman are in their proper places, this is the great appropriateness (*yi*) of *tian* and *di*. There should be strict rulers of the family. These are called father and mother. When the father behaves according to the proper way of being a father; the mother behaves according to the proper way of being a mother; the elder brother behaves according to the proper way of being an elder brother; the younger brother behaves according to the proper way of being a young brother; the husband behaves according to the proper way of being a husband; and the wife behaves according to the proper way of being a wife, the *dao* of the family is proper. The whole world is stable when all its families are properly ordered.

The *Xiang* commentary says: The lower trigram *li* is fire, and the upper trigram *xun* is wind. The combined image is the wind appearing from the fire. This is *jiaren* (family). The exemplary person observes the image of the wind appearing from the fire and understands that the wind is developed from the fire, just as words are developed from the heart-and-mind and the behavior is developed out of following a course of excellence (*daode*). Therefore, when speaking, his words should have some content; when acting, his routine should be constant.

Nine in the first place: It is good to prepare for anything that will happen when you are in the family. Remorse diminishes.

The *Xiang* commentary says: "It is good to prepare for anything that will happen when you are in the family." This is because the intentions of the family's members are not yet changed for the worse.

Six in the second place: The wife does not do everything according to her own purposes [she also follows the opinions of her husband]. She is in charge of the meal for the whole family. It is good fortune for her to persevere.

The *Xiang* commentary says: The good fortune of the six in the second place comes about because she follows her husband and makes everything go smoothly.

Nine in the third place: The leaders of the family use a loud voice to blame family members. Though this is a strict style in which to rule the whole family, it is better than that of those who are not responsible to their family members. The women and children in the family are chattering and laughing excessively, so there will be danger and regret in the end.

The *Xiang* commentary says: "The leaders of the family use a loud voice to blame family members." This is because the regulation of the family has not yet been lost. "The women and children in the family are chattering and laughing excessively." This is because the regulation of the family has been lost.

Nine in the fourth place: The family is becoming wealthier. It is great good fortune.

The *Xiang* commentary says: "The family is becoming wealthier. It is great good fortune." This is because the six in the fourth place as a soft *yin* line is properly situated.

Nine in the fifth place: The ruler of the family uses utmost sincerity to reform and move his own family. Don't worry. Good fortune.

The *Xiang* commentary says: "The ruler of the family uses utmost sincerity to reform and move his own family." All the members of the family love one another.

Nine in the top place: Full of sincerity and reverence, there will be good fortune in the end.

The *Xiang* commentary says: The good fortune indicated by "full of sincerity and reverence" means that the husband, as the ruler of the family, is able to turn and examine himself.

Hexagram 54: Guimei (*Marrying Maiden*)
Thunder, lake (dui, lake, below; zhen, thunder, above)

Guimei (Marrying Maiden): It is dangerous to move forward. There is nothing that would be advantageous.

Guimei (Marrying Maiden)

The *Tuan* commentary says: *Guimei* (marrying maiden) is the great appropriate (*yi*) pattern of *tian* and *di* [because *guimei* is changed from *tai*. This means that the *yangqi* of *tian* changes places with the *yinqi* of *di*]. The ten thousand processes and events (*wanwu*) will never arise when *tian* and *di* do not interact. *Guimei*, as the marriage of a man and a woman, is both the starting and ending points of human relationships. The lower trigram *dui* stands for happiness, and the upper trigram *zhen* represents activity. The combined image is happily active. This is the maiden that is waiting for marriage. "It is dangerous to move forward" because the nine in the second place, the six in the third place, the nine in the fourth place, and the six in the fifth place are not in their proper places.[24] "There is nothing that would be advantageous," because the soft *yin* line is immediately above the strong *yang* line.

The *Xiang* commentary says: The lower trigram *dui* signifies lake, and the upper trigram *zhen* stands for thunder. The combined image is the hexagram *guimei* (marrying maiden). The exemplary person perseveres in the proper way for a long time and understands the shortcomings of stopping halfway.

Nine in the first place: When the younger sister accompanies the marrying maiden, the cripple is able to walk. It is a good time to move forward.

---

[24] The proper places for a nine, or a *yang* line, are the first, third, and fifth places. The proper places for a six, or a *yin* line, are the second, fourth, and sixth places.

The *Xiang* commentary says: "The younger sister accompanies the marrying maiden" because the intention to keep the marriage endures. "The cripple is able to walk" because the good fortune of the marriage can be passed on.

Nine in the second place: It is possible for a man who is nearly blind to see. It is good for people in the dark to persevere.

The *Xiang* commentary says: "It is good for people in the dark to persevere," because they have not yet changed the ordinary situation.

Six in the third place: when a concubine accompanies the marrying maiden, [it is easy for there to be trouble between them], so it becomes suitable to have her younger sister accompany her.

The *Xiang* commentary says: "Having a concubine accompany the marrying maiden" is not yet fitting.

Nine in the fourth place: The date of the marriage has been postponed. There will be a new date for the marriage.

The *Xiang* commentary says: The purpose behind "postponing the marriage" is to wait for a good husband.

Six in the fifth place: When the Emperor Yi of the Shang dynasty had his daughter married, her clothes were not as good as those of the maiden who accompanied her. The moon is nearly full. Good fortune.

The *Xiang* commentary says: "When the Emperor Yi of the Shang dynasty had his daughter married, her clothes were not as good as those of the maiden who accompanied her." The six in the fifth place is in the central position in the upper trigram, which is a noble place. Therefore, the meaning of this line is to be married in a noble status.

Six at the top place: For the marriage or the sacrifice to the ancestors, if the woman has an empty basket in her hand or there is no blood when the man is killing the sheep, there is nothing advantageous.

The *Xiang* commentary says: The six at the top is a soft *yin* line, not a strong *yang* line. Therefore, the basket is empty.

Hexagram 63: Jiji (Completing)
Water, fire (li, fire, below; kan, water, above)

Jiji (Completing): It proceeds smoothly in small aspects. It is advantageous to persevere. It is good fortune at the beginning, but disorder in the end.

The *Tuan* commentary says: "*Jiji*, it proceeds smoothly," but in small aspects. "It is advantageous to persevere," because the strong *yang* lines and the soft *yin* lines are all in their proper positions. "It is good

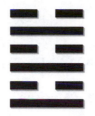

Jiji (Completing)

fortune at the beginning," because the soft *yin* lines are in the central position of the lower trigram. "It is disorder in the end," because the *dao* of this process has reached its limits.

The *Xiang* commentary says: The upper trigram *kan* represents water, and the lower trigram *li* stands for fire. The combined image is *jiji* (completing). The exemplary person observes this and reflects on anxieties yet to come in order to prepare for them.

Six in the second place: The woman lost the headdress. There is no need to look for it. It will be found again after seven days.

The *Xiang* commentary says: "It will be found again after seven days," because it always travels along the central way.

4

THE CANON OF DOCUMENTS
(Shujing)
書經

The text known as The Exalted Documents (Shangshu) *or* The Canon of Documents (Shujing) *is made up of speeches attributed to some of the most famous men in the earliest epochs of China's long history. The authenticity of the materials contained in the* Documents *has often been questioned. Mencius, for example, is said to have declared that one cannot believe much of the collection (Mencius 7B3). More recent scholarship has made great strides in applying philological and historical evidence to separate the genuine core of the* Documents *from later accretions, thus largely bearing out Mencius' skepticism. Longstanding concerns about the purity of the text, however, have not prevented it from attaining a place among the most authoritative works in the Confucian tradition. As early as the fourth century* B.C.E., *lists of normative scriptures regularly include the* Documents.

The following selection masquerades as the speech delivered by King Wu of Zhou to his troops on the morning of the fateful battle of Muye (ca. 1040 B.C.E.*), when the Shang host was destroyed and its cruel overlord deposed. Although the text, as it has come down to us, almost certainly does not record the genuine words of King Wu, it must still be regarded as one of the earliest examples of a prolific early Chinese genre: discussions of the dangers that come about when women are not kept in their place. The Shang King, we are told, has disregarded the ancient dictum: "The hen does not announce the morning." In other words, he has listened too much to his wife, abandoning his religious, familial, and political obligations. The implication is that social chaos will be the inevitable result when women usurp authority.*

Paul R. Goldin

Translated by James Legge, Introduction by Paul R. Goldin.

The Speech at Mu

The time was the gray dawn of the day *jiazi*. On that morning the King came to the open country of Mu in the borders of Shang and addressed his army. In his left hand he carried a battle-axe, yellow with gold, and in his right he held a white ensign, which he brandished, saying, "Far are ye come, ye men of the western regions!" He added, "Ah! Ye hereditary rulers of my friendly States; ye managers of affairs, the ministers of instruction, of war, and of public works; the many officers subordinate to them; the master of my bodyguards, the captains of thousands, the captains of hundreds; and ye, O men of Yong, Shu, Jiang, Mao, Wei, Lu, Peng, and Pu—lift up your lances, join your shields, raise your spears—I have a speech to make."

The King said, "The ancients have said, 'The hen does not announce the morning. The crowing of a hen in the morning indicates the subversion of the family.' Now Shou, the King of Shang, follows only the words of his wife. He has blindly thrown away the sacrifices which he should present and makes no response for the favors which he has received; he has blindly thrown away his paternal and maternal relatives, not treating them properly. They are only the vagabonds of the empire, loaded with crimes, whom he honors and exalts, whom he employs and trusts, making them great officers and nobles, so that they can tyrannize over the people, exercising their villainies in the city of Shang.

"Now I, Fa,[1] am simply executing respectfully the punishment appointed by Heaven. In today's business do not advance more than six or seven steps; and then stop and adjust your ranks—my brave men, be energetic! Do not exceed four blows, five blows, six blows, or seven blows; and then stop and adjust your ranks—my brave men, be energetic! Display a martial bearing. Be like tigers and panthers, like bears and grizzly bears—here in the border of Shang. Do not rush on those who fly to us in submission, but receive them to serve our western land—my brave men, be energetic! If you are not thus energetic, you will bring destruction on yourselves."

---

[1] Fa is his personal name.

5

THE RECORD OF RITES
(Liji)
禮記

The Record of Rites (Liji) *is said to have been compiled in the early part of the first century* B.C.E. *by two cousins, known as the Elder and the Younger Dai, from various texts of the late Zhou, Qin, and Han Dynasties. The Elder Dai prepared a work in eight-five sections, known as* Dadai liji *or* The Ji of the Elder Dai. *The Younger Dai reduced these to forty-nine sections, known as* Xiaodai liji *or* The Ji of Younger Dai, *which is the text of the* Liji *in its present form. Although this book later became one of the five Confucian Classics, it is known as* Ji *(Record) and not as* Jing *(Classic). The reason might be that all four of the other books are believed to have come to us directly from the hand of Confucius.*

The Liji *puts together a comprehensive account of all the rules of propriety* (li) *that were codified during the Warring States period and the early Han dynasty, ranging from government regulations to detailed instructions on how to manage a household, or even how to behave at a dinner or funeral. Most of these rules were formulated by the early disciples of Confucius, and thus are expressed or illustrated in the form of anecdotes about Confucius and his disciples.*

Not surprisingly, the Liji *contains much legislation on the roles and virtues of women. It is believed that this text contains the earliest formulation of the Confucian code for women, what later became known as the* sancong side *(three obediences and four virtues). A woman's life was to unfold within the family and involved the expectation of loyal submission to her father as his daughter, to her husband as his wife, and to her grown son—the father's heir—as his mother (Book IX, Jiao Te Xing, Section III, Number 10). The rules required for living faithfully by the* sancong, *as the reading will demonstrate, could become quite complicated. They consist of detailed prescriptions for how to behave toward one's in-laws and the husband's concubines, while observing the strict separation in the household between*

From *The Sacred Books of China: The Texts of Confucianism*, 4 vols., Sacred Books of the East 3, 16, and 27–28, translated by James Legge (Oxford: Clarendon, 1879–1895). Modified by Robin R. Wang.

the outer (wai) and inner (nei) quarters assigned to males and females, respectively. The rules also cover exceptional situations where the expected norms had already been violated, such as how, or indeed whether, a filial son should mourn his mother who died after being divorced from his father (cf. Book II, Zhang Gong, Section I, Part I, Number 4). The apparent harshness of such rules is relieved somewhat by the knowledge that divorce was virtually unheard of, and that the point of the sancong side is to preserve the integrity of the family. By the same token, the side (four virtues) instructs women in proper etiquette that displays the excellence of women's virtue (fude), women's speech (fuyan), women's appearance (furong), and women's work (fugong) (Book XLI, Hun Yi, Section X). Though each of these are comprehensive and detailed, they do define boundaries on what can and cannot legitimately be demanded by way of faithful service from one's daughter, wife, or mother. These four virtues (side) became the important core of the teachings for women through Chinese history.

Interspersed with these crucial expectations for womanly propriety the reader will also find certain rules suggesting the evolution of Chinese morality that the disciples of Confucius hoped to support. Notable among these are rules meant to discourage the practice of burying living persons, mainly wives, concubines, and other servants, along with the deceased male. Though such persons were to be dispatched in order to cater to the needs of the deceased in the afterlife, the Liji condemns such care as beyond the bounds of propriety. It recommends that those who advocate burying living persons ought to have themselves dispatched rather than impose this sacrifice on others (Book II, Zhang Gong, Section II, Part II, Numbers 15 and 19). This is but one of the ways in which the various rules of the Liji seek to remain faithful to the Confucian "Golden Rule."

Robin R. Wang

Book One
Qu Li

Section I. Part III. Number 6

Male and female should not sit together (in the same apartment), nor have the same stand or rack for their clothes, nor use the same towel or comb, nor let their hands touch in giving and receiving.

A sister-in-law and brother-in-law do not interchange inquiries (about each other). None of the concubines in a house should be employed to wash the lower garment (of a son).

Outside affairs should not be talked of inside the threshold (of the women's apartments), nor inside (or women's) affairs outside it.

When a young lady is promised in marriage, she wears the strings (hanging down to her neck); and unless there be some great occasion, no (male) enters the door of her apartment.

When a married aunt, or sister, or daughter returns home (on a visit), no brother (of the family) should sit with her on the same mat or eat with her from the same dish. (Even) the father and daughter should not occupy the same mat. Male and female, without the intervention of the matchmaker, do not know each other's name. Unless the marriage presents have been received, there should be no communication or affection between them.

Hence the day and month (of the marriage) should be announced to the ruler, and to the spirits (of ancestors) with purification and fasting; and (the bridegroom) should make a feast, and invite (his friends) in the district and neighborhood, and his fellow officers— thus giving due importance to the separate positions (of male and female). He must not marry a wife of the same surname as himself. Hence, in buying a concubine, if he does not know her surname, he must consult the tortoise-shell about it. With the son of a widow, unless he is of acknowledged distinction, he should not associate himself as a friend.

Book Two
The Zhang Gong

Section I. Part I. Number 4

When Zi Shang's mother died, and he did not perform any mourning rites for her, the disciples of (his father) Zi Si[1] asked him, saying, "Did your predecessor, the superior man, observe mourning for his divorced mother?" "Yes," was the reply. (And the disciples went on), "Why do you not make Pai also observe the mourning rites (for his mother)?" Zi Si said, "My progenitor, a superior man, never failed in pursuing the right path. When a generous course was possible, he took it and behaved generously; and when it was proper to restrain his generosity, he restrained it. But how can I attain to that? While she was my wife, she was Pai's mother; but when she ceased to be my wife, she was no longer his mother." It was in this way that the Kong family

---

[1] Zi Si is Confucius' grandson.

came not to observe mourning for a divorced mother; the practice began from Zi Si.

Section II. Part II. Number 5

On the death of the mother of Guo Zhaozi, he asked Zi Zhang,[2] saying, "At the interment, when (all) are at the grave, what should be the places of the men and of the women?" Zi Zhang said, "At the mourning rites for Situ jingzi, when the Master directed the ceremonies, the men stood with their faces to the west and the women stood with theirs to the east." "Ah!" said the other, "that will not do;" adding, "All will be here to see these mourning rites of mine. Do you take the sole charge of them. Let the guests be the guests, while I (alone) act as the host. Let the women take their places behind the men, and all have their faces towards the west."

Section II. Part II. Number 15

Chen Ziche having died in Wei, his wife and the principal officer of the family consulted together about burying some living persons (to follow him). When they had decided to do so, (his brother), Chen Zikang arrived, and they informed him about their plan, saying, "When the master was ill, (he was far away), and there was no provision for his nourishment in the lower world; let us bury some persons alive (to supply it)." Zikang said, "To bury living persons (for the sake of the dead) is contrary to what is proper. Nevertheless, in the event of his being ill, and requiring to be nourished, who are so fit for that purpose as his wife and steward? If the thing can be done without, I wish it to be so. If it cannot be done without, I wish you two to be the parties for it." On this the proposal was not carried into effect.

Section II. Part II. Number 19

When Chen Qianxi was lying ill, he assembled his brethren, and charged his son Zun Ji, saying, "When I am dead, you must make my coffin large, and make my two concubines lie in it with me, one on each side." When he died, his son said, "To bury the living with the dead is contrary to propriety; how much more must it be so to bury them in the same coffin!" Accordingly, he did not put the two ladies to death.

---

[2] Zi Zhang is one of Confucius' immediate disciples.

Section II. Part III. Number 15

When the mother of Zi Si died in Wei, and news of the event was brought to him, he wailed in the ancestral temple. His disciples came to him and said, "Your mother is dead, after marrying into another family; why do you wail for her in the temple of the Kong family?" He replied, "I am wrong, I am wrong." And thereon he wailed in one of the smaller apartments of his house.

Section II. Part III. Number 30

Confucius said, "The people of Wei, in burying husband and wife together (in the same grave and shell), leave a space between the coffins. The people of Lu, in doing the same, place them together, which is the better way."

Book Five
The Question of Zengzi

Section I. Number 20

Confucius said, "The family that has married a daughter away, does not extinguish its candles for three nights, thinking of the separation that has taken place. The family that has received the (new) wife for three days has no music; thinking her bridegroom is now in the place of his parents. After three months she presents herself in the ancestral temple, and is styled 'The new wife that has come.' A day is chosen for her to sacrifice at the shrine of her father-in-law; expressing the idea of her being (now) the established wife."

Section IV. Number 13

When there is generous affection between father and son, harmony between brothers, and happy union between husband and wife, the family is in good condition. When the great ministers are observant of the laws, the smaller ministers pure, officers and their duties kept in their regular relations, and the ruler and his ministers are correctly helpful to one another, the state is in good condition.

Book Eight
The Li Yun

Section III. Number 7

By the united action of heaven and earth all things spring up. Thus the ceremony of marriage is the beginning of a (line that shall last for) myriad ages. The parties are of different surnames; thus those who are distant are brought together, and the separation (to be maintained between those who are of the same surname) is emphasized. There must be sincerity in the marriage presents; and all communications (to the woman) must be good. She should be admonished to be upright and sincere. Faithfulness is requisite in all service of others, and faithfulness is (specially) the virtue of a wife. Once mated with her husband, all her life she will not change (her feeling of duty to him), and hence when the husband dies she will not marry (again).

Book Nine
Jiao Te Xing

Section III. Number 10

The woman follows (*cong*) the man: in her youth, she follows (*cong*) her father and elder brother; when married, she follows (*cong*) her husband; when her husband is dead, she follows (*cong*) her son.

Book Ten
The Nei Ze

Section I. Number 3

(Sons') wives should serve their parents-in-law as they served their own. At the first crowing of the cock, they should wash their hands and rinse their mouths; comb their hair, draw over it the covering of silk, fixing this with the hair-pin, and tie the hair at the roots with the fillet. They should then put on the jacket, and over it the sash. On the left side they should hang the duster and handkerchief, the knife and whetstone, the small spike, and the metal speculum to get fire

Figure 2. The faithful wife, Jin Gonggong, pleads with Duke Yao to execute *Woman (Chou Hua Lienu Zhuan)* by Chou Ying (1509–1552).]

her in place of her captive husband. [From *Chou's Illustrations of the Biographies of*

with; and on the right, the needle-case, thread, and floss, all bestowed
in the satchel, the great spike, and the borer with which to get fire
from wood. They will also fasten on their necklaces, and adjust their
shoestrings.

Section I. Number 12

The men should not speak of what belongs to the inside (of the
house), nor the women of what belongs to the outside. Except at sacrifices and funeral rites, they should not hand vessels to one another.
In all other cases when they have occasion to give and receive anything, the woman should receive it in a basket. If she has no basket,
they should both sit down, and the other put the thing on the ground,
and she will then take it up. Outside or inside, they should not go to
the same well, nor to the same bathing-house. They should not share
the same mat in lying down; they should not ask or borrow anything
from one another; they should not wear similar upper or lower garments. Things spoken inside should not go out; words spoken outside
should not come in. When a man goes into the interior of the house,
he should not whistle nor point. If he has occasion to move in the
night, he should use a light; and if he have no light, he should not
stir. When a woman goes out at the door, she must keep her face
covered. She should walk at night (only) with a light; and if she have
no light, she should not stir. On the road, a man should take the right
side, and a woman the left.

Section I. Number 16

If a son have two concubines, one of whom is loved by his parents,
while he himself love the other, yet he should not dare to make this
one equal to the former whom his parents love, in dress, or food, or
the duties that she discharges, nor should he lessen his attentions to
her after their death. If he very much approves of his wife, and his
parents do not like her, he should divorce her. If he does not approve
of his wife, and his parents say, "she serves us well," he should behave
to her in all respects as his wife, without fail even to the end of her
life.

Section I. Number 18

When a wife's father-in-law is dead, her mother-in-law takes the place
of her mother's; but the wife of the eldest son, on all occasions of
sacrificing and receiving guests, must ask her directions in everything,

while the other sons' wives must ask directions from her. When her parents-in-law employ the eldest son's wife, she should not be dilatory, unfriendly, or impolite to the wives of his brothers (for their not helping her). When the parents-in-law employ any of them, they should not presume to consider themselves on an equality with the other; walking side by side with her, or giving their orders in the same way, or sitting in the same position as she.

Section I. Number 19

No daughter-in-law, without being told to go to her own apartment, should venture to withdraw from that (of her parents-in-law). Whatever she is about to do, she should ask leave from them. A son and his wife should have no private goods, nor animals, nor vessels; they should not presume to borrow from, or give anything to, another person. If anyone gives the wife an article of food, or dress, a piece of cloth or silk, a handkerchief for her girdle, an iris or orchid, she should receive and offer it to her parents-in-law. If they accept it, she will be glad as if she were receiving it afresh. If they return it to her, she should decline it, and if they do not allow her to do so, she will take it as if it were a second gift, and lay it by to wait till they may want it. If she wants to give it to some of her own cousins, she must ask leave to do so, and that being granted, she will give it.

Section II. Number 13

The observances of propriety commence with a careful attention to the relations between husband and wife. The husband and wife built the mansion and its apartments, distinguishing between the exterior and interior parts. The men occupied the exterior; the women the interior. The mansion was deep, and the doors were strong, guarded by porter and eunuch. The men did not enter the interior; the women did not come into the exterior.

Section II. Number 14

Males and females did not use the same stand or rack for their clothes. The wife did not presume to hang up anything on the pegs or stand of her husband; nor to put anything in his boxes or satchels; not to share his bathing-house. When her husband had gone out (from their apartment), she puts his pillow in its case, rolled up his upper and under mats, put them in their covers, and laid them away in their proper receptacles. The young served the old, and the low served the noble, also in this way.

Section II. Number 15

As between husband and wife, it was not until they were seventy that they deposited their things in the same place without separation. Hence, even if a concubine were old, until she had completed her fiftieth year, it was the rule that she should be with the husband (once) in five days. When she was to do so, she purified herself, rinsed her mouth and washed, carefully adjusted her dress, combed her hair, drew over it the covering of silk, fixed her hair-pins, tied up her hair in the shape of a horn, brushed the dust from the rest of her hair, put on her necklace, and adjusted her shoestrings. Even a favorite concubine was required in dress and diet to come after her superior. If the wife were not with the husband, a concubine waiting on him would not venture to remain the whole night.

Section II. Number 16

When a wife was about to have a child, and the month of her confinement had arrived, she occupied one of the side apartments, where her husband sent a messenger twice a day to ask for her. If he were moved and came himself to ask about her, she did not presume to see him, but made her governess dress herself and reply to him.

When the child was born, the husband again would send twice a day to inquire for her. He fasted now, and did not enter the door of the side apartment. If the child were a boy, a bow was placed on the left of the door; and if a girl, a handkerchief on the right of it. After three days the child would to be carried, and some archery would be practiced for a boy, but not for a girl.

Section II. Number 19

A special apartment was prepared in the palace for the child, and from all the concubines and other likely individuals there was sought one distinguished for her generosity of mind, her gentle kindness, her mild integrity, her respectful bearing, her carefulness and freedom from talkativeness, who should be appointed to be the boy's teacher; one was chosen next who should be his indulgent mother, and a third who should be his guardian mother. These all lived in his apartment, which others did not enter unless they had some (special) business.

Section II. Number 20

At the end of the third month a day was chosen for shaving off the hair of the child, excepting certain portions—the horn-like tufts of a boy, and the circlet on the crown of a girl. If another fashion were adopted, a portion was left on the left of the boy's head and on the right of the girl's. On that day the wife with the son appeared before the father. If they were of noble families, wife and son were in full dress. From the commissioned officer downwards, all rinsed their mouths and washed their heads. Husband and wife rose early, bathed and dressed as for the feast of the first day of the month. The husband entered the door, going up by the steps on the east, and stood at the top of them with his face to the west. The wife with the boy in her arms came forth from her room and stood beneath the lintel with her face to the east.

Section II. Number 36
A girl at the age of ten ceased to go out (from the women's apartments). Her governess taught her (the arts of) pleasing speech and manners, to be docile and obedient, to handle the hempen fibers, to deal with the cocoons, to weave silks and form fillets, and to learn (all) women's work: how to furnish garments, to watch the sacrifices, to supply the liquors and sauces, to fill the various stands and dishes with pickles and brine, and to assist in setting forth the appurtenances for the ceremonies.

Section II. Number 37
At fifteen, she assumed the hair-pin; at twenty, she was married, or if there were occasion (for the delay), at twenty-three. If there were betrothal rites, she became a wife; and if she went without these, a concubine. In all salutations of females, the upper place was given to the right hand.

Book Forty-One
Hun Yi

Section III
The respect, the caution, the importance, the attention to secure correctness in all details, and then (the pledge of) mutual affection—these were the great points in the marriage ceremony, and served to establish the distinction to be observed between man and woman, and the righteousness to be maintained between husband and wife. From the distinction between man and woman came the righteousness between husband and wife. From that righteousness came the affec-

tion between father and son; and from that affection, the rectitude between ruler and minister. Whence it is said, "The ceremony of marriage is the root of the other ceremonial observances."

Section X

Therefore, in ancient times, for three months before the marriage of a young lady, if the temple of the high ancestor (of her surname) were still standing (and she had admission to it), she was taught in it, as the public hall (of the members of her surname); if it were no longer standing (for her), she was taught in the public hall of the Head of that branch of the surname to which she belonged—she was taught women's virtue (*fude*), women's speech (*fuyan*), women's appearance (*furong*), and women's work (*fugong*). When the teaching was accomplished, she offered a sacrifice (to the ancestor), using fish, and soups made of duckweed and pondweed. So was she trained in the obedience of a wife.

Section XI

It is therefore said, "From the son of Heaven there were learned the lessons for men; and from the queen, the obedience proper to women." The son of Heaven directed the course to be pursued by the masculine energies, and the queen regulated the virtues to be cultivated by the feminine receptivities. The son of Heaven guided in all that affected the external administration (of affairs); and the queen, in all that concerned the internal regulation (of the family). The teachings (of the one) and the obedience (inculcated by the other) perfected the manners and ways (of the people); abroad and at home harmony and natural order prevailed; the states and the families were ruled according to their requirements; this is what is called "the condition of complete virtue."

Section XIII

The son of Heaven attends to the lessons for men—that is the function of the father. The queen attends to the obedience proper to women—that is the function of the mother. Therefore it is said, "The son of Heaven and the queen are (to the people) what father and mother are." Hence for him who is the Heaven (appointed) King they (the people) wear sackcloth with jagged edges, as for a father; and for the queen, they wear sackcloth with even edges, as for a mother.

PART TWO

EASTERN ZHOU
東周

(770–221 B.C.E.)

6

ANALECTS OF CONFUCIUS
(Lunyü)
論語

The Analects (lunyü—*literally, the "Classified Sayings"*) purports to be a record of the teachings of Kongzi or "Confucius" (551–479 B.C.E.) and his disciples. Although traditionally read as a coherent text recorded by Confucius' immediate disciples, in more recent times scholars have begun to question this picture of the Analects. Various attempts have been made to identify distinct strata in the text. The most plausible of these determinations sees Books 1–10 (or sometimes 3–9) as the earliest stratum, recorded not long after Confucius' death, which is followed by Books 11–15 and (last of all) 16–20. Despite the heterogeneous nature of the text, internal philosophical and terminological evidence suggests that no portion of the Analects was written after the early fourth century B.C.E. We can thus take the text as a whole as representing the state of the early Confucian school as it existed prior to the philosophical explosion of the fourth century B.C.E. and the Mencian innovations demanded by this increasingly sophisticated intellectual milieu. In the discussion that follows, "Confucius" should be understood as a shorthand reference to the author(s) and editor(s) who compiled the Analects.

Women feature only rarely in the Analects, and are primarily portrayed indirectly as temptations to men—the "physical beauty" (se) or object of lust that leads men away from Confucian morality. The only direct references to women are notoriously unflattering: the discounting of the woman who served King Wu in passage 8.20 as not counting as a ren, that is as a "person" (normally gender-neutral); and the infamous remark about women and servants in 17.25. To be fair to Confucius, it is not entirely clear in 8.20 whether his discounting is due to misogyny or simply to the fact that, in his time, a woman would not be found serving as a minister. Passage 17.25 suggests the former, but as it is from a probably later stratum of the text we might not be justified in reading these two passages together. Passages such as 6.28 suggest that at least some women had succeeded in acquiring a measure of informal political influence and power in Confucius' age, although this apparently rare

From Confucius, *Analects*, translated by Edward Slingerland. Copyright © 2003 Hackett Publishing Company, Inc. Reprinted by permission of Hackett Publishing Company, Inc.

phenomenon was channeled through male connections and was evidently viewed with suspicion and disapproval.

Edward Slingerland

6.28

The Master had an audience with Nanzi, and Zilu was not pleased. The Master swore an oath in Zilu's presence, saying, "Heaven prevent me from having done otherwise! Heaven prevent me!"

Commentary

Nanzi was the consort of Lord Ling of Wei, and a woman of bad repute. Zilu, a disciple of Confucius, is not pleased that Confucius would seek an audience with such a person. As many commentators point out, however, it is likely that ritual dictated that when arriving in a state one request an audience with the "orphaned little lord"— that is, the wife or consort of the local ruler. In having an audience with Nanzi upon arriving in Wei, Confucius was therefore suppressing his personal distaste for Nanzi, overcoming the disapproval of his disciples, and risking more general opprobrium in order to observe an important dictate of ritual propriety. He thus thanks Heaven for his having had the moral strength to do his ritual duty. Alternate interpretations of the passage see Zilu's displeasure as resulting from suspicion—either that illicit activity may have occurred during Confucius' audience with the notoriously lascivious Nanzi, or that the Master was seeking some sort of questionable political advantage in seeing her—and have Confucius defending his innocence ("If I have done anything wrong, may Heaven punish me!"). This, however, seems unlikely.

8.20

Shun had five ministers and the world was well governed. King Wu said, "I have ten ministers in charge of establishing order." The Master commented, "The saying, 'Talent is difficult to find'—is it not true? Virtue flourished as never before after the reigns of Tang and Yu, and yet [even among King Wu's ten people] there was a woman included, which means he really only had nine good men."

Commentary

This is a rather difficult passage, and many commentators suggest that important connecting text is missing. There is a great deal of commentarial controversy concerning the identity of the ten ministers of King Wu, who were most likely his nine brothers and then either his mother or wife. What the meaning may be beyond the sentiment that "good men are hard to find" is difficult to say with certainty.

9.18

The Master said, "I have yet to meet a man who loves Virtue as much as he loves female beauty."

Commentary

There are two slightly different ways to take this passage. He Yan sees it as a criticism of Confucius' contemporaries: "The Master is complaining that his contemporaries viewed Virtue lightly and instead focused upon the pursuit of female beauty." This is how Sima Qian understands it as well, claiming that 9.18 was inspired by an event in Confucius' life when he was publicly humiliated by Duke Ling of Wei, who honored his consort—the infamous Nanzi—over Confucius himself. Li Chong, on the other hand, sees the passage as more of a general statement about self-cultivation, a claim that "if people simply loved Virtue as much as they love female beauty, then they would discard immorality and return to rectitude." Most likely both points are intended: if only people could love the Way in the same spontaneous, effortless fashion that they love the pleasures of the flesh, Confucius' job would be done, but he was not optimistic about this happening anytime soon with his contemporaries.[1]

16.7

The Master said, "The gentleman guards against three things: when he is young, his blood and vital essence are still unstable, and there-

---

[1] Both points are also clearly intended in the very similar, but slightly more explicit, 15.13 (also cf. 9.24, 15.16).

fore he is on guard against [the temptation of] female beauty; when he reaches his prime, and his blood and vital essence have become unyielding, he is on guard against being contentious; when he reaches old age, and his blood and vital essence have begun to decline, he is on guard against acquisitiveness."

Commentary

A similar passage in the second century B.C.E. syncretic text *Huainanzi* reads, "It is the general nature of human beings that, when young, they are prone to be wild and undisciplined; when in their prime, they are prone to be violent and aggressive; and when old, they are prone to be greedy." Confucius' comment therefore probably reflects common wisdom of the time. This passage is interesting because it is the only place in the *Analects* where human vices are explicitly linked to psycho-physiological factors, and it represents the first evidence we see in the text of the influence of medical theories concerning the blood and vital essence (*xueqi*) that later had such a large impact on the thought of Mencius, Zhuangzi, and Xunzi. This may be an indication of a relatively late date for this passage.[2]

16.14

With regard to the official wife of the lord of the state, the lord himself refers to her as "Lady," while the Lady refers to herself as "little child." The people of the state refer to her as "our Lord's Lady," but when they are abroad, refer to her as "Our Orphaned Little Lord." People of other states refer to her as "the Lord's Lady."

Commentary

This passage is stylistically quite anomalous for the *Analects*, and sounds very much like an excerpt from a ritual text such as *The Record of Rites* that somehow found its way into the *Analects*. This impression is reinforced by the fact that it comes at the end of the chapter—a likely location for textual additions. It has thus been dismissed by many modern Chinese and Western scholars as a later interpolation. Han dynasty commentators treat it as part of the text, however, explaining it as an attempt on the part of Confucius to correct the ritual improprieties of his contemporaries. For our purposes, it is

---

[2] Compare 9.18, selected here, and 15.13.

included to indicate the manner in which women were intended to humble themselves verbally in ritually dictated ways.

17.25

The Master said, "Women and servants are particularly hard to manage: if you are too familiar with them, they grow insolent, but if you are too distant they grow resentful."

Commentary

An infamously misogynous passage that some later commentators have sought to soften. The use of the word *yang* (manage, care for, raise) suggests the context of aristocratic household management, which is why *xiaoren* (elsewhere generally rendered as "petty people") is translated in its more concrete social sense of "servants" or lower-class people. Some claim that, considering the context of household management, "women" (*nüzi*) is meant only to refer to slave women or female servants. Such women were certainly still being kept in aristocratic households in Confucius' age, but so were male slaves and servants, which means that even with this interpretation we have the problem of why women in particular are being singled out. In the *Zuo Commentary* for Duke Xi, Year 24, we read, "Female attractive power (*nüde*) is infinite, and there is no end to the resentment of women." Du Yu's commentary on this passage paraphrases 17.25: "The disposition of women is such that if one is familiar with them they do not know when to stop or when is enough, whereas if one is distant with them their resentment knows no bounds." The danger of "female power" is a constant theme in traditional Chinese texts from the earliest times, and usually manifests itself in two ways: more generally, as a force analogous to alcohol that intoxicates men and leads them into immorality, and more specifically, in the form of the deleterious influence of concubines or dissolute wives who hold the ear of the ruler and thereby lead the state into moral and political ruin. We have already seen examples of the former sense in *Analects* 9.18, and 16.7, and the latter in the person of the infamous Nanzi of Wei in 6.28. With this in mind, the sense of 17.25 is probably that, considering their potentially dangerous sexual power and inability to control themselves, household women (i.e., wives and concubines), like servants, need to be managed firmly, but with respect, if they are to remain obedient and not overstep their proper roles.

7

DAODEJING
道德經

The Book of Laozi or Daodejing *(traditionally assigned to the sixth century* B.C.E., *but possibly dating from as late as the third century* B.C.E.*) has only about 5,250 Chinese characters yet is known as the foundation of* Daoism. *It consists of eighty-one brief sections or paragraphs and is divided into two parts:* Dao *and* De. *Throughout Chinese history Laozi's teaching has been considered the philosophy of yielding. One important aspect of yielding is being* rou *(soft, gentle, supple). Not surprisingly, the female and femininity have enormous significance for Laozi. The metaphors by which the Secret of Life is variously expressed presuppose an under-standing of the primal relationship of* yin *and* yang *in all things. Unlike other inter-pretations of* yin/yang *complementarity, the* Daodejing *suggests the primordiality, indeed the superior power, of* yin *in general and the female in particular. Thus women are portrayed as the* yin, *soft* (rou) *force of the universe, and their images resonate with the mystical meanings of, for example, valley, water, and mysterious gate. From the perspective of the* Daodejing *women are not excluded, shunned, frozen out, dis-advantaged, rejected, unwanted, abandoned, dislocated, or otherwise marginalized. Instead, their basic identity, as complementary and necessary to men, is recognized as embodying the Secret of Life.* Yin *(female) and* yang *(male) embrace each other and blend into a state of harmonious balance (42). If any name can be given to the* Dao *in all things, it is "Mother" (25). The "Door of the Mystic Female"* (xuancizimen) *is "the root of Heaven and Earth" (6). Just as "the softest substance of the world goes through the hardest" and "that-which-is-without-form penetrates that-which-has-no-crevice," so "the Female overcomes the Male by quietude, and achieves the lowly position by quietude" (61). Success in human affairs depends upon taking no action* (wuwei), *as in the lowly position.*

Robin R. Wang

From *The Simple Way of Laotzu,* translated by Walter Gold Orn (Philadelphia: David McKay Co., 1913). Modified by Robin R. Wang.

Book 1: Mother of All Things

The *Dao* that is the subject of discussion is not the true *Dao*.
The quality that can be named is not its true attribute.
That which was before Heaven and Earth is called the
    Nonexistent.
The Existent is the mother of all things.
Therefore doth the wise people seek after the first mystery
    of the Nonexistent, while seeing in that which exists the
    Ultimate thereof.
The Nonexistent and Existent are identical in all but name.
This identity of apparent opposites I call the profound, the
    great deep, the open door of bewilderment.

Book 6: The Mystic Female

The spirit of the valley never dies.
I call it the mystic female.
The motion of the mystic female is the root of Heaven and
    Earth.
Forever it endures and moves without design.

Book 10: Play the Part of Female

By conserving the natural and spiritual powers
it is possible to escape dissolution.
By retraining the vital energy to achieve gentleness
it is possible to continue as the newborn child.
By purging the mind of impurities
it is possible to remain untainted.
By governing the people with love
it is possible to rule without interference.
By opening and shutting the Gate of Heaven
it is possible to play the part of female.
By comprehending all sides
it is possible to remain unrecognized.
To bring forth and preserve, to produce without possessing,
    to act without hope of reward, and to expand without
    waste, this is the supreme virtue.

Book 25: Mother of Heaven and Earth

Before Heaven and Earth existed there was in Nature a
    primordial substance.
It was silent, it was boundless.

It was self-existent, it was unchanging.
It was omnipresent, nor suffered any limitation.
It is to be regarded as the mother of heaven and earth.
I do not know its name, but I call it *Dao*.
If forced to qualify it, I call it the great.
Being great, I call it the inscrutable.
Being inscrutable, I call it far-reaching.
Being far-reaching, I call it returning.
Dao is supreme, Heaven is supreme, Earth is supreme, the
King is supreme.
There are in the universe four kinds of supremacy, and their
rulership is one.
Man models himself after the Earth, the Earth models itself
after Heaven, Heaven models itself after *Dao*, *Dao* models
itself after nature.

Book 28: Know the Male But Preserve the Female

He who, being a man, remains a woman, will become a
universal channel.
As a universal channel the eternal virtue will never forsake
him. He will become a newborn child.
He who, being in the light, remains in obscurity, will become
a universal model.
As a universal model the eternal virtue will not pass him by.
He will go back to the all-perfect.
He who, being glorious, continues in humility, will become a
universal valley.
As a universal valley the eternal virtue will fill him. He will
revert to the first essence.
The first essence is that which, being differentiated, gives rise
to innumerable vessels of life.
A wise man, by embracing it, becomes the wisest of
governors.
A liberal government is that which neither disregards nor
hurts anyone.

Book 42: Everything Embodies Yin *and Embraces* Yang

Dao emanated the One; the one emanated the Two; and the
two emanated the Three.
From the Three all things have proceeded.
Everything embodies *yin* and embraces *yang*, through the union
of the pervading principles it reaches harmony.

70 Part Two: Eastern Zhou

Book 43: Non-Action

The gentlest thing in the world will override the strongest.
The Nonexistent pervades everything, though there be no inlet.
By this I comprehend how effectual is non-action.
To teach without words and to be useful without action, few among men are capable of this.

Book 51: Sublime Virtue

Dao (Way) brings forth, and De (virtue) nourishes.
All things take up their several forms, and natural forces bring them to perfection.
Therefore all things conspire to exalt Dao and to cherish De.
But this regard of Dao and De is not in deference to any mandate.
It is unconstrained, and therefore it endures forever.
For Dao produces all things, and De nourishes, increases, feeds, matures, protects, and watches over them.
To produce without possessing; to act without expecting; to enlarge without usurping; this is the sublime virtue.

Book 52: To Remain Gentle Is to Be Invincible

That from which the universe sprang may be looked upon as its Mother.
By knowing the Mother you have access to the child.
And if, knowing the child, you go back to hold the Mother, though your body perish, yet you will come to no harm.
Keep your mouth shut, and close up the doors of sight and sound, and as long as you live you will have no vexation.
But open your mouth, or become inquisitive, and you will be in trouble all your life long.
To perceive things in the germ is intelligence.
To remain gentle is to be invincible.
Follow the light that guides you homeward, and do not get lost in the darkness.
This I call using the eternal.

Book 54: Cultivate the Dao

He who plants rightly never uproots.
He who lays hold rightly never relinquishes.
His posterity will honor him continually.

Whoever cultivates the *Dao* in himself will be rooted in
  virtue.
Whoever cultivates the *Dao* in his family will cause his virtue
  to spread.
Whoever cultivates the *Dao* in his village will increase
  prosperity.
Whoever cultivates the *Dao* in the kingdom will make good
  fortune prevalent.
Whoever cultivates *Dao* in the world will make virtue
  universal.
I observe myself, and so I come to know others.
I observe my family, and all others grow familiar.
I study this world, and others come within my knowledge.
How else should I come to know the laws that govern all
  things, save thus, that I observe them in myself?

Book 55: Harmony

Those who are saturated with Virtue are like newborn
  children.
Scorpions will not sting them, wild beasts will not seize them,
  nor will birds of prey pluck at them.
Their young bones are not hard, neither are their sinews
  strong, yet their grasps are firm and sure.
They are full of virility, though not knowing of the union of
  male and female.
Though they should cry out all day, yet they do not become
  hoarse.
In this is shown their harmony with Nature.
To know this harmony is called constancy.
To know this constancy is called discernment.

Book 61: The Case of Woman

The kingdom, like a river, becomes great by being lowly; it is
  thereby the center to which all the world tends.
It is similar in the case of woman:
She conquers man by continual quietness.
And quietness is the same as submission.
Therefore a great state, by condescension to those beneath it,
  may gain the government of them.
Likewise a small state, by submission to one that is greater,
  may secure its alliance.

Thus the one gains adherence, and the other obtains favors.

Although the great state desires to annex and to nourish others, yet the small state desires to be allied to and serve the greater.

Thus both will be satisfied, if only the greater will condescend.

Book 76: Softness and Gentleness Are Companions of Life

People are supple and tender when living, but rigid and strong when dead.

It is the same with everything.

Trees and plants are pliant and soft when living, but they are withered and tough when dead.

Thus rigidity and strength are companions of death, but softness and gentleness are companions of life.

Therefore the warrior who relies on his strength cannot conquer death, while the powerful tree becomes a mere timber support.

For the place of the strong and the firm is below, while that of the gentle and yielding is above.

Book 78: The Weak Can Conquer the Strong

Nothing on earth is so weak and yielding as water, but for breaking down the firm and strong it has no equal.

This admits of no alternative.

All the world knows that the soft can wear away the hard, and the weak can conquer the strong; but none can carry it out in practice.

Therefore the Sage says: He who bears the reproach of his country is really the lord of the land. He who bears the woes of the people is in truth their king.

The words of truth are always paradoxical!

8

THE ZUO COMMENTARY

(*Zuozhuan*)

左傳

The Zuo Commentary (Zuozhuan) *is a large complex of interconnected narratives arranged in the form of a commentary to* The Spring and Autumn Annals (Chunqiu), *an archaic chronicle covering the years 722–483* B.C.E. *Because the significance of the terse entries in* The Spring and Autumn Annals *can be unclear, the text is often read in conjunction with the* Zuozhuan, *which provides elaborate background information and exegesis. The* Zuozhuan, *like* The Spring and Autumn Annals, *is organized according to the calendar of the state of Lu: dates are identified by the name of the duke of Lu who was in power at the time, and by the year of that duke's reign. (For example, the first selection is dated "Xi 22," or the twenty-second year of the reign of Duke Xi of Lu, which corresponds to 638* B.C.E.*) Scholars rarely dispute the authenticity of* The Spring and Autumn Annals *as a document contemporary with the events that it records. The date of the* Zuozhuan, *on the other hand, has been the subject of contentious discussions for several centuries. Most specialists today agree that the* Zuozhuan *dates to the fourth century* B.C.E. *at the latest, and may include passages that are substantially older.*

The general purpose of the Zuozhuan *is to demonstrate the normative patterns of human conduct on a grand historical canvas. Many of the tales in the work deal with the folly of rash or tyrannical rulers, and their subsequent chastisement at the hands of more virtuous lords. Women often play pivotal roles in these stories as the objects of licentious desire. One of the text's favorite themes is the social disintegration wrought by powerful men who pursue their lustful impulses beyond all prudent measure. But women are not presented simply as passive figures around whom wars are kindled and fought. Sometimes they appear as counselors to their husbands or agents with political influence whose foresight can save entire nations. These representations in the* Zuozhuan *are important in view of the text's later standing as a revered historical source. Chinese literati of all subsequent periods turned to its pages for guidance in matters pertaining to relations between men and women.*

Paul R. Goldin

From *The Chinese Classics*, 2nd ed., 5 vols., translated by James Legge (Oxford: Clarendon, 1893–1895).

Xi 22, 638 B.C.E. [*A passage expressing disapproval of a weak state's willingness to entertain a mighty lord with its noblewomen, and of that lord's eagerness to enjoy himself in such company.*]

Canon:[1] In winter, in the eleventh month, on *jisi*, the first day of the moon, the duke of Song fought with an army of Chu near the Hong, when the army of Song was disgracefully defeated.

Commentary: . . . Early in the morning of *bingzi*, the ladies Mi and Jiang, the wives of Wen, earl of Zheng, went to congratulate the viscount of Chu and feast his troops at the marsh of Ke, when the viscount made the band-master Jin display to them the captives and the ears of the slain. The superior man will pronounce that this was contrary to rule. A woman, when escorting or meeting a visitor, does not go beyond the gate; when seeing her brothers, she does not cross the threshold. The business of war has nothing to do with the employment of women.

On *dingchou*, the viscount entered the city of Zheng and was feasted. Nine times the cup was presented to him; the courtyard was filled with a hundred different objects; six kinds of food were set forth in the dishes more than ordinary. He left the city at night after the feast, Wen Mi [i.e., Lady Mi] accompanying him to the army; and he took the earl's two daughters with him to Chu. Shuzhan said, "The King of Chu will not die a natural death! The ceremonies shown on his account have ended in his breaking down the distinctions regulating the intercourse between the sexes, and where this is done, there can be no propriety. How should he die a natural death? The prince may know that he will not attain to the presidency of them."

Xi 23, 637 B.C.E. [*The famous peregrinations of Chong'er, the exiled prince of Jin, are punctuated by several encounters with insightful women.*]

Commentary: When Chong'er first met with misfortune, a body of men from Jin attacked him in the city of Pu, the men of which wanted to fight with him. Chong'er, however, would not allow them to do so, saying, "By favor of the command of my ruler and father, and through possession of the emolument he has assigned me, I have got the rule over these people, and if I should employ them to strive with him, my crime would be very great. I will fly."

He then fled to the Di, and there followed him Hu Yan, Zhao Cui,

---

[1] This is a quotation from the *Chunqiu* (*The Spring and Autumn Annals*). All later references to "Canon" are quoted from the same source.

Dian Xie, Wei Wuzi, Jizi, minister of Works [with many others]. In an invasion of the Jianggaoru, the Di captured the two daughters of their chief, Shu Wei and Ji Wei, and presented them to the prince. He took Ji Wei to himself as his wife, and she bore him Bochou and Shuliu. Her elder sister he gave to Zhao Cui, who had by her his son Dun. When he was about to go to Qi, he said to Ji Wei, "Wait for me five and twenty years, and if I have not come back then, you can marry another husband."

She replied, "I am now 25, and if I am to marry again after another 25, I will go to my coffin. I had rather wait for you."

The prince left the Di after residing among them twelve years. Traveling through Wei, Duke Wen treated him discourteously; and as he was leaving it by Wulu, he was reduced to beg food of a country-man, who gave him a clod of earth. The prince was angry, and wished to scourge him with his whip, but Zifan [Hu Yan] said, "It is Heaven's gift [a gift of soil, a happy omen]." On this he bowed his head to the earth, received the clod, and took it with him in his carriage.

When he came to Qi, Duke Huan gave him a wife,[2] and he had twenty teams of four horses each. He abandoned himself to the enjoyment of his position, but his followers were dissatisfied with it, determined to leave Qi, and consulted with him about what they should do under the shade of a mulberry tree. There happened to be upon the tree a girl of the harem, employed about silkworms, who overheard their deliberations and reported them to the lady Jiang, the prince's wife. Her mistress put her to death and said to the prince, "You wish to go again upon your travels. I have put to death one who overheard your design." The prince protested that he had no such purpose, but his wife said to him, "Go. By cherishing me and reposing here, you are ruining your fame." The prince refused to leave; and she then consulted with Zifan, made the prince drunk, and sent him off, his followers carrying him with them. When he awoke, he seized a spear, and ran after Zifan.

When they came to Cao, Duke Gong, having heard that the prince's ribs presented the appearance of one solid bone, wished to see him naked, and pressed near to look at him when he was bathing. The wife of Xi Fuji said to her husband, "When I look at the followers of the prince of Jin, every one of them is fit to be chief minister of a State. If he only used their help, he is sure to return to Jin and be its marquis; and when that happens, he is sure to obtain his ambition and become leader of the States. He will then punish all who have been discourteous to him, and Cao will be the first to suffer. Why should you not

---

2 That is to say, Duke Huan made Chong'er his son-in-law.

go quickly and show yourself to be a different man from the earl and his creatures?" On this, Fuji sent the prince a dish of meat with a *bi*[3] of jade also in it. The prince accepted the meat, but returned the *bi*.

When they came to Song, the duke presented to the prince twenty teams of horses, but when they came to Zheng, Duke Wen there was another to behave uncivilly. Shuzhan remonstrated with him, saying, "I have heard that men cannot attain to the excellence of him whose way is opened by Heaven. The prince of Jin has three things which make it likely that Heaven is going to establish him as king—I pray your lordship to treat him courteously. When husband and wife are of the same surname, their children do not prosper and multiply. The prince of Jin [himself a Ji] had a Ji for his mother, and yet he continues till now—this is one thing. During all his troubles, a fugitive abroad, Heaven has not granted quiet to the State of Jin, which would seem as if it were preparing the way for his return to it—this is a second thing. There are three of his officers sufficient to occupy the highest places, and yet they adhere to him—this is the third thing. Jin and Zheng, moreover, are of the same stock. You might be expected to treat courteously any scions of Jin passing through the State, and how much more should you so treat him whose way Heaven is thus opening?" To this remonstrance the earl of Zheng would not listen.

When they came to Chu, the viscount of Chu was one day feasting the prince, and said, "If you return to Jin and become its marquis, how will you recompense my kindness to you?"

The prince replied, "Women, gems, and silks your lordship has. Feather, hair, ivory, and hides are all produced in your lordship's country; those of them that come to Jin are but your superabundance. What should I have with which to recompense your kindness?"

"Nevertheless," urged the viscount, "how would you recompense me?"

The prince replied, "If by your lordship's powerful influence I shall recover the State of Jin, should Chu and Jin go to war and meet in the plain of the Middle Land, I will withdraw from your lordship three stages [each of 30 *li*[4]]. If I then do not receive your commandments to cease from hostilities, with my whip and my bow in my left hand, and my quiver and my bow-case on my right, I will maneuver with your lordship."

On this, Ziyu begged that the prince might be put to death, but the viscount said, "The prince of Jin is a grand character, and yet distinguished by moderation, highly accomplished and yet courteous.

---

[3] A jade disk.

[4] A unit of distance; one *li* is roughly one-third of a mile.

His followers are severely grave and yet generous, loyal and of untiring ability. The present marquis of Jin has none who are attached to him. In his own State and out of it he is universally hated. I have heard, moreover, that the Jis of Jin, the descendants of Tang Shu, though they might afterwards decay, yet would not perish—may not this be about to be verified in the prince? When Heaven intends to prosper a man, who can stop him? He who opposes Heaven must incur great guilt."

After this, the viscount sent the prince away with an escort to Qin, where the earl presented him with five ladies, Huai Ying [the earl's daughter] among them. The prince made her hold a goblet and pour water from it for him to wash his hands. When he had done, he ordered her away with a motion of his wet hands, on which she said in anger, "Qin and Jin are equals; why do you treat me so, as if I were mean?" The prince became afraid and humbled himself, putting off his robes and assuming the garb of a prisoner.

Another day, the earl invited him to a feast, when Zifan said, "I am not so accomplished as Cui; pray make him attend you." The prince sang the *Heshui*, and the earl the *Liuyue*.[5]

Zhao Cui said, "Chong'er, render thanks for the earl's gift." The prince then descended the steps and bowed with his head to the ground. The earl also descended a step and declined such a demonstration. Cui said, "When your lordship laid your charge on Chong'er as to how he should assist the son of Heaven, he dared not but make so humble an acknowledgement."

Xuan 9, 600 B.C.E. [*An officer is murdered for objecting to Duke Ling's outrageous conduct with Lady Xia, a* femme fatale.]

Canon: Chen put to death its great officer Xie Ye.

Commentary: Duke Ling of Chen, with [his two ministers] Kong Ning and Yi Hangfu, all had an intrigue with Lady Xia, and each of the three of them wore an article of her underclothing, with which they made game with one another in the court. Xie Ye remonstrated with the duke, saying, "When ruler and ministers proclaim their lewdness, the people have nothing good to imitate. The report of such things is not good—let your lordship put that article away." The duke said

---

[5] *Heshui* and *Liuyue* are both titles of traditional songs. The reference of the former is disputed; the latter is found in *The Book of Odes*, Mao 177. Singing *Liuyue* was understood as an implicit compliment to Chong'er.

he would change his conduct, but he told the other two what Xie Ye
had said, and when they asked leave to kill him, he did not forbid
them. Ye was thereon killed.

> Confucius said, "The words of the ode,
> 'When the people have many perversities
> Do not set up your own perversity before them,'
> are applicable to the case of Xie Ye."

Xuan 10, 599 B.C.E. [*Duke Ling himself is murdered after he impugns the legitimacy of Lady Xia's son by jesting that he resembles one of her lovers.*]

Canon: On *guisi*, Xia Zhengshu of Chen murdered his ruler, Pingguo
[i.e., Duke Ling].

Commentary: Duke Ling of Chen, with Kong Ning and Yi Hangfu,
was drinking in the house of the Xia family, when the duke said to
Hangfu, "Zhengshu [the son of Lady Xia, and Head of the Family,
as his father was dead] is like you."
   "He is also like your lordship," was the reply.
   Zhengshu [overheard these remarks and] was indignant at them,
and when the duke was [trying to] escape from the house by the stable,
he shot and killed him. The two officers fled to Chu.

Xuan 11, 598 B.C.E. [*The King of Chu enters Chen with his host and exe-
cutes the regicide Xia Zhengshu. He then annexes Chen, but is later persuaded to
return the territory to its people.*]

Canon: In winter, in the tenth month, the people of Chu put to death
Xia Zhengshu of Chen. On *dinghai*, the viscount of Chu entered [the
capital of] Chen. He restored Gongsun Ning [i.e., Kong Ning] and
Yi Hangfu to Chen.

Commentary: In winter, the viscount of Chu, because of the deed per-
petrated by the head of the Xia family, invaded Chen, publishing a
notice to the people that they should make no movement, as he wished
to punish only the head of the Shaoxi.[6] Forthwith he entered [the
capital of] Chen, and put to death Xia Zhengshu, having him torn in
pieces by chariots at the Li Gate. He then proceeded to make Chen
a district [of Chu].

Cheng 2, 589 B.C.E. [*The King of Chu and his foremost councilor both wish
to take the beautiful Lady Xia for themselves, but a certain Wuchen dissuades both
of them. Eventually, the crafty Wuchen manages to marry her for himself.*]

---

[6] That is, the house of Xia.

Commentary: When Chu punished the Head of the Xia family in Chen, King Zhuang wanted to take Lady Xia to his harem, but Wuchen, duke of Shen, said to him, "Do not do so. You called out the States to punish a criminal. If you now take Lady Xia to your harem, it will be through desire of her beauty. Such desire is lewdness, and lewdness is a great crime. One of the Books of Zhou says, 'He illustrated virtue and carefully abstained from wickedness'—it was thus that King Wen made Zhou [what it became]. 'He illustrated his virtue'—that is, he did his utmost to exalt it. 'He carefully abstained from wickedness'—that is, he did his utmost to put it away. If, having roused the States to this expedition, you go on to commit a great wickedness, that is not careful abstinence from it. Let your lordship well consider this matter." The King on this desisted in his purpose.

Zifan then wished to take her, but Wuchen said to him, "She is a woman of evil omen. She brought [her brother] Ziman to an early death; proved the death of [her husband] Yushu; occasioned the murder of the marquis Ling, the execution of [her son] Xia Nan, the expulsion of Kong and Yi, and the ruin of the State of Chen. What more inauspicious a woman could there be? Man's life is encompassed with difficulties—is there anyone who cannot [naturally] find death? There are many beautiful women in the world—why must you have this one?" Zifan on this [likewise] gave up his purpose.

The King then gave her to the *lianyin*, Xiang Lao, who died at the battle of Bi,[7] though his body had not been found. His son Heiyao then had a connection with her, but Wuchen sent a message to her, saying, "Return and I will make you regularly my wife." He further brought it about that they should send from Zheng to call her there, on the ground that the body [of her husband, Xiang Lao] could be found, and that she must come and meet it.

Lady [Xia] informed the King of this message, who asked Qu Wu [i.e., Wuchen] about it. Wuchen replied, "The thing is true. The father of Zhi Ying [a prisoner in Chu since the battle of Bi] was a favorite with Duke Cheng [of Jin], and is the youngest brother of Zhonghang Bo. He has recently been made assistant-commander of the army of the center, and is very friendly with Huang Xu of Zheng. He is much attached to this son, and is sure, through Zheng, to offer to restore our King's son [a prisoner, since the same battle, in Jin] and the body of Xiang Lao in exchange for him. The people of Zheng are afraid [of Jin] in consequence of the battle of Bi, and anxious to conciliate its favor, so that they will agree to the wishes of Zhi Ying's father."

[On hearing this], the King sent Lady Xia back to Zheng, and as she

---

7 A famous battle between the mighty states of Chu and Jin.

was about to commence the journey, she said to those who were escorting her, "If I do not get the body [of my husband], I will not return here." [Thus she went to Zheng, and by and by] Wuchen made proposals of marriage with her to the earl of Zheng, who accepted them.

Cheng 11, 580 B.C.E. [*A vignette of family strife caused by rigid hierarchies.*]

Canon: The marquis of Jin sent Xi Chou to Lu on a friendly mission, and on *jichou*[8] the duke made a covenant with him.

Commentary: Xi Chou came to Lu on a friendly mission, and to make [on the part of Jin] the covenant [which the duke had requested].

The mother of Shengbo had been without [the regular ceremony of] betrothal, and Lady Mu [her sister-in-law] said: "I will not acknowledge a concubine as my sister-in-law." After the birth of Shengbo, his father sent away the mother, who was afterwards married to Guan Yuxi of Qi. She bore him two children, and was then left a widow, when she came back with the children to Shengbo. He got his half-brother made a great officer [of Lu], and married his half-sister to Shi Xiaoxu.

When Xi Chou came on his friendly mission, he applied for a wife to Shengbo, who took his half-sister from Shi Xiaoxu and gave her to him. She said [to her husband], "Even birds and beasts do not consent to lose their mates; what do you propose to do?"

He said, "I am not able to die for you."

On this she went [to Jin], where she bore two children to Chou. After his death, they sent her back from Jin [to her former husband] Shi, who met her at the Yellow River and drowned in it her two children. She was angry, and said to him, "You could not protect me when I was your wife, and let me go away from you, and now you are not able to cherish another man's orphans and have killed them— what death do you expect to die?" She then swore that she would not live again with him.

Zhao1, 541 B.C.E. [*Two suitors contend over a desirable woman, with disastrous consequences.*]

Commentary: Xuwu Fan of Zheng had a beautiful sister who was betrothed to Gongsun Chu [designated Zinan]. Gongsun Hei [Zixi], however, also sent a messenger who violently insisted on leaving a goose at the house [a ceremony of espousal]. Fan was afraid, and reported the matter to Zichan, who said, "This is not your sorrow

---

[8] A day in the sexagemary cycle.

[only]; it shows the want of government in the State. Give her to which of them you please." Fan then begged of the two gentlemen that they would allow him to leave the choice between them to the lady, and they agreed to it.

Zixi then, splendidly arrayed, entered the house, set forth his offerings, and went out. Zinan entered in his military dress, shot an arrow to the left and another to the right, sprang into his chariot, and went out. The lady saw them from a chamber, and said, "Zixi is indeed handsome, but Zinan is my husband. For the husband to be the husband and the wife to be the wife is what is called the natural course." So she went to Zinan.

Zixi was enraged, and by and by went with his bow-case and in his buff-coat to see Zinan, intending to kill him and take away his wife. Zinan knew his purpose, seized a spear, and pursued him. Coming up to him at a cross road, he struck him with the weapon. Zixi went home wounded and informed the great officers, saying, "I went in friendship to see him, not knowing that he had any hostile purpose, and so I received the wound."

The great officers all consulted about the case. Zichan said, "There is a measure of right on both sides, but as the younger, and lower in rank, and chargeable with an offense, we must hold Chu [i.e., Zinan] to be the criminal." Accordingly he [caused] Zinan to be seized and enumerated his offenses, saying, "There are the five great rules of the State, all of which you have violated—awe of the ruler's majesty; obedience to the rules of the government; honor to the nobler in rank; the service of elders; and the kindly cherishing of relatives. These five things are necessary to the maintenance of the State. Now you, while the ruler was in the city, presumed to use your weapon—you had no awe of his majesty. You violated the laws of the State—not obedient to the rules of government. Zixi is a great officer of the first degree, and you would not acknowledge your inferiority—you have not honored the nobler in rank. Younger than he, you showed no awe of him—not serving your elder. You lifted your weapon against your cousin—not kindly cherishing your relative. The ruler says that he cannot bear to put you to death, and will deal gently with you in sending you to a distance. Make an effort and take your departure quickly, so as not to incur a second offense."

In the fifth month, on *gengchen*, Zheng banished You [Zinan's clan-name] Chu to Wu. When he was about to send him away, Zichan consulted with Taishu[9] on the subject. Taishu said, "I cannot protect

---

[9] A relative of Zinan.

myself; how should I be able to protect the members of my clan? The affair belongs to the government of the state and is not any private hardship. If you have planned for the benefit of the State, carry out your decision. Why should you have any hesitancy? The duke of Zhou put to death Guanshu and banished Caishu not because he did not love them, but because it was necessary for the royal House. If I were to be found in any crime, you would send me away; what difficulty need you have in the case of any other You?"

Ding 14, 497 B.C.E. [*A crown prince conspires to kill his debauched mother.*]

Canon: Kuaiwai, heir-son of Wei, fled from that state to Song.

Commentary: The marquis of Wei, to gratify his wife Nanzi, had invited Song Chao [her brother] to his court. At the meeting at Tao, Kuaiwai, the eldest son of the marquis, had presented [the city of] of Yu to Qi, and as he was [returning] through the country of Song, the country-people sang to him,

> Since you have allayed the heat of your sow,
> Why not send back our old boar?

The prince was ashamed, and said to Xiyang Su, "Follow me, when I visit the duchess, and when she sees me, and I look round, do you kill her." Su agreed to this. The prince accordingly went to the court of the marchioness, who saw him, but though he looked round thrice, Su did not advance.

The marchioness observed his countenance, burst into tears, and ran off, crying, "The prince is going to kill me." The marquis took her by the hand and went up with her to a tower. [On this] the prince fled to Song, and all belonging to his party were driven out of the state. It was in consequence of this that Gongmeng Kou fled to Zheng, and from Zheng to Qi.

The prince said to people that Xiyang Su had been the occasion of his calamity, but Su told people that the prince had brought calamity on him. "Contrary to all principle," he said, "the prince wanted me to kill his mother, and said that if I did not consent he would kill me. If I had killed the marchioness, he would have thrown the blame on me. I agreed to do it, therefore, but did not do it, wishing to defer my death. The common saying is that people preserve themselves by good faith. I hold that the good faith must be in regard to what is righteous."

9

DISCOURSES OF THE STATES
(*Guoyü*)
國語

Discourses of the States (Guoyu) *is a collection of* speeches and narratives
similar to the Zuozhuan. *The form, content, language, and didactic orientation of
the two texts are comparable; they are both set in the same period, and were probably composed (if one disregards certain later additions to the* Discourses) *within a
century of each other. Sometimes the* Discourses of the States *and the*
Zuozhuan *provide alternate versions of the same historical event. The major difference is that the* Discourses *are not arranged chronologically and were not transmitted as a commentary to* The Spring and Autumn Annals. *The selections
presented here center on two of the most prominent women in the* Discourses of
the States: *Bao Si and Lady Jing. The former was the favorite concubine of King
You of Zhou (r. 781–771* B.C.E), *the last ruler of the Western Zhou dynasty, whose
demise is directly attributed to the "dissipation of his virtue" that Bao Si causes. Lady
Jing, by contrast, is one of the most respected women in ancient Chinese literature.
She is the mother of Gongfu Wenbo (also known as Gongfu Chu), an eminent statesman in Lu and a contemporary of Confucius. In the* Discourses of the States,
*she is praised for her industry, decorum, and knowledge of ritual principles. Although
her behavior and opinions do not always accord with our notions about the role of
women in society, she remains a crucial figure in that she refutes simplistic charges of
misogyny that are sometimes leveled at the Confucian tradition. The stories about
Lady Jing embody the belief that all men, including those at the apex of society, can
learn from a wise woman.*

Paul R. Goldin

Translated by Paul R. Goldin.

Historian Su Argues that Lord Xian's Attack on the Li-Rong Will Bring about Victory, but Will Still Be Inauspicious

[*Lord Xian of Jin (r. 676–652 B.C.E.) defeats the Li Rong, a non-Chinese enemy, and takes one of the tribe's noblewomen as his own queen. The Court Historian, a man named Su, has warned Lord Xian against this campaign, and, gloating in apparent success, Lord Xian humiliates Su at a banquet by allowing him to drink but not eat.*]

He drank his liquor and went out. Historian Su said to the grand masters: "There are male warriors and there are female warriors. Now that Jin has defeated the Rong with male warriors, the Rong will surely use female warriors to defeat Jin. What should be done about that?"

Li Ke said: "What does that mean?"

Historian Su said: "In the past, Jie of Xia attacked the You-Shi, and the men of You-Shi sent Mei Xi to [Jie] as a wife. Mei Xi attained his favor, and thus her part in the annihilation of Xia was comparable to that of Yi Yin.[1] Xin of Yin attacked the You-Su, and the clan of You-Su sent Da Ji to [Xin] as a wife. Da Ji attained his favor, and thus her part in the annihilation of Yin was comparable to that of Jiao Ge.[2] King You of Zhou attacked the You-Bao, and the men of Bao sent Bao Si to [King You] as a wife. Bao Si attained his favor, gave birth to Bofu, and thus her part in chasing away Crown Prince Yiqiu and installing Bofu [as Heir Apparent] was comparable to that of Shifu of Guo.[3] The Crown Prince fled to Shen,[4] and the men of Shen and Zeng summoned the Western Rong to attack Zhou. Thus Zhou was annihilated.

"Now [the Lord of] Jin has paltry virtue and takes pleasure in a captive woman, increasing his favors towards her; would it not be appropriate to associate him with those three Kings, the last [of their respective dynasties]?"

[*No one challenges the assumption that the woman of the Li Rong, like the wicked consorts to whom she has been compared, must have evil intentions. The narrator concludes the story by observing that the state of Jin did not enjoy stability until five suc-*]

---

[1] Yi Yin was the famous minister of King Tang of Shang, who vanquished the Xia dynasty.

[2] An officer of Shang who defected and aided King Wu of Zhou, who conquered the Shang dynasty.

[3] A treacherous minister.

[4] The fief of his maternal grandmother.

cessive rulers had taken the throne; these facts are supposed to verify Historian Su's prediction that attacking the Li Rong would be "inauspicious."]

Historian Bo Discusses Flourishing and Decay for Lord Huan

[*Part of a long discussion between Lord Huan of Zheng (r. 806–771 B.C.E.) and his historian. In the following discourse, Bo explains to Lord Huan why the Zhou dynasty is about to fall.*]

Shifu of Guo is a slandering, fawning, and craftily obsequious man, yet he has been raised as a minister; this is because the king[5] focuses on those who are similar to himself. [The king] has abandoned his legitimate queen and raised a concubine from his harem [as his chief consort]; this is because he is fond of turpitude. Indeed, dwarves and hunchbacks serve [as entertainers] by his side; this is because he allows the churlish to draw near. He does not let the standards of Zhou shine, but carries out the words of a woman; this is because he makes use of the slanderous and nefarious. He does not establish [meritorious] ministers, but employs [the advice] of his bewitching [wife] and installs his favorites; this is because he carries out machinations. Such a state of affairs cannot continue long.

Moreover, in the time of King Xuan [r. 827–782 B.C.E.], there was a children's song: "A bow of *yan*-wood and a quiver of *ji*-grass—these indeed will annihilate the state of Zhou." Thereupon King Xuan heard this, [and learned] that a man and wife were selling such implements. The king sent guards to arrest them and humiliate them publicly. [At the same time,] a minor concubine in the seraglio gave birth to a daughter, but as it was not the king's child, she abandoned it in fear. These people [i.e., the husband and wife being humiliated in the streets] collected [the girl] and fled to Bao.

Heaven mandated this long ago; what more can one do? It is said in the *Speeches of Instruction*:[6]

When Xia was in decay, some spirits of Bao transformed into two dragons. They went together to the royal palace and said: 'We are the two

---

[5] That is, the aforementioned King You.

[6] Commentators identify this as a chapter of the *Yi Zhoushu* (*Lost Writings of Zhou*, a collection of materials similar to the *Canon of Documents*), but no such legend is to be found in the received text.

lords of Bao.' The ruler of Xia divined as to whether he should kill them, get rid of them, or stop them, but none of the results were auspicious. Then he divined as to whether he should request their spittle and store it; the result was auspicious. So he laid out ritual offerings for them and exorcised them with inscriptions on bamboo. The dragons departed, but their spittle remained. [The king] had it stored in a box, and regularly sacrificed to [the dragons] in the suburbs.

Down to the Yin and Zhou Dynasties, [the box] had not been opened. In the last years of King Li,[7] the people opened it and watched. The spittle flowed throughout the palace and could not be removed. The king sent women without undergarments to chant at [the spittle]; it transformed into a black turtle and entered the royal seraglio, where a young maidservant who had not lost her milk teeth came upon it. When she received her hairpin,[8] she became pregnant, and gave birth in the time of King Xuan. Since she had given birth without a husband, she was afraid and abandoned [the child]. The couple that had made the bows and quivers happened to be suffering their humiliation in the street. They were aggrieved as [the baby] cried at night, so they took it, hid it, and fled to Bao.

Xu of Bao [the ruler of Bao] had committed a crime, so he offered [this girl] to King [You], and the king subsequently excused him. [The king] came to dote on the girl and made her his queen; she gave birth to Bofu. Heaven engendered this [disaster] long ago. The poison of [the girl from Bao] is great; [she] was granted to the king in order to bring about the dissipation of his virtue.[9] When poison is well stewed, it kills even more quickly. Shen, Zeng, and the Western Rong are now mighty, and the royal house is in disarray; since the king continues to indulge his desires, is [the situation] not all the more difficult? The king wishes to kill the crown prince in order to secure Bofu; he will surely request [the crown prince] from Shen. The men of Shen will not consent to [handing over the crown prince], and the king will surely attack them. If he attacks Shen, and Zeng and the Western Rong unite to attack Zhou, then Zhou cannot be defended. Zeng and the Western Rong treat Shen kindly, and Shen and Lü are mighty, their warm love of the Crown Prince well known. If the king's army

---

[7] A wicked king whose reign ended when he was exiled in 841 B.C.E.

[8] A girl received her hairpin at the age of fifteen *sui* (thirteen or fourteen years of age, by our reckoning).

[9] This line in the original is difficult to construe, and the translation offered here represents a plausible guess.

should arrive, it is certain that [Shen's allies] would rush to its assistance. The king's heart is angry; the lord of Guo obsequious. The existence or destruction of Zhou will be determined within three years. Lord, if you wish to avoid these difficulties, will you not quickly design some hiding place; if you wait for an opportunity once this affair comes to pass, I fear that it will be too late!

[*Lord Huan of Zheng was killed in the climactic battle of 771 B.C.E., when the Marquis of Shen and his allies attacked King You and put an end to the Western Zhou dynasty.*]

Gongfu Wenbo's Mother Responds to Ji Kangzi's Questions

Ji Kangzi[10] asked Gongfu Wenbo's mother: "Madam, do you have something else to say to me?"

She replied: "I have been able to become old and nothing more; what would I have to say to you?"

Kangzi said: "Though that is the case, I wish to hear from you."

She replied: "I have heard my former mother-in-law say: 'If a noble man is able to toil, his posterity will continue.'"

Zixia heard this, and said: "Well spoken! I have heard it said: 'When a woman was married in ancient times, if her mother-in-law had already passed away, it was considered unlucky.' A wife can learn from her mother-in-law."

Gongfu Wenbo Feasts Nangong Jingshu with Liquor

Gongfu Wenbo feasted Nangong Jingshu with liquor and had Lu Dufu as his [premier] guest. When the turtle soup was brought to them, [Dufu's portion] was small. Dufu was enraged, and as the others were passing around the turtle soup and eating it, he declared: "I shall wait for this turtle to grow before I eat it!" Then he went out.

Wenbo's mother heard of this, and said angrily [to Gongfu Wenbo]: "I heard your grandfather say: 'At a sacrifice, one tends to the medium; at a banquet, one tends to the premier guest.' What [ceremony] did you use with your turtle soup? And you made him angry!"

---

[10] The great-nephew of Gongfu Wenbo's mother. He died in 468 B.C.E.

Then she banished him. Five days later, the grand masters of Lu apologized for him, and she allowed him to return.

Gongfu Wenbo's Mother Discusses the
Inner Court and The Outer Court

Gongfu Wenbo's mother went to the Ji clan. Kangzi was in the courtyard. He spoke to her, but she did not respond to him. He followed her to the door of her bedroom, but she did not respond to him and entered. Kangzi left the courtyard and entered [her apartment] to see her, saying: "I have not heard your command; have I offended you?"

She said: "You have not heard it? The Son of Heaven and the feudal lords tend to the affairs of the people in the outer court; they tend to the affairs of the spirits in the inner court. From the chamberlains down, they tend to official duties in the outer court; they tend to affairs of the household in the inner court. Within the doors of her bedroom is where a woman conducts her business. This is the same for superiors and inferiors. The outer court is where you should take the lord's official duties as your business; the inner court is where you should regulate the governance of the Ji clan. These are all matters on which I dare not speak."

Gongfu Wenbo's Mother Discusses Toil and Indolence

Gongfu Wenbo withdrew from court and greeted his mother in the morning as she was spinning thread. Wenbo said: "Madam, you spin thread even in a household as [comfortable] as mine. I fear the resentment of the Jisun clan, who may consider me unfit to take care of you."

His mother sighed and said: "Oh, Lu is doomed! Are its offices not filled by uninformed children? Sit, and I shall speak to you. In the past, when the Sage Kings settled the people, they would select barren lands for [the people] to settle on. They would work their people and use them, thus emerging as kings of the world. When people toil, they think; when they think, their good minds are born. When they are indolent, they become licentious; when they are licentious, they forget the good; when they forget the good, their evil minds are born. People of fertile soil are not talented; they are indolent. People of barren soil never fail to direct themselves towards righteousness; they toil.

"Therefore the Son of Heaven salutes the sun in the morning in his five-colored robes. With the Three Dukes and Nine Chamberlains, he studies and comes to know the potency of Earth. At midday he examines the government and participates in the governmental affairs of the many officials. The grand masters direct the troops, regional representatives, and counselors; they set in order all the affairs of the people. [The Son of Heaven] sacrifices to the moon in the evening in his three-colored robes. With the Grand Scribe and Director of Records, he investigates and reveres the laws of Heaven. When the sun has set, he oversees the Nine Concubines; he commands them to clean and present the millet vessels for the *di* and *jiao* sacrifices. Only then does he rest.

"In the morning, the feudal lords execute the undertakings and commandments of the Son of Heaven. During the day, they examine the administration of their own fiefs. In the evening, they reflect on the codices and laws. At night, they admonish the many artisans, lest they become insolent and licentious. Only then do they rest.

"In the morning, the ministers and grand masters examine their administrative duties. During the day, they see to their regular offices. In the evening, they put undertakings in order. At night, they arrange their family affairs. Only then do they rest.

"In the morning, the scholar-officials receive the [command to carry out] affairs of state. During the day, they see to their studies. In the evening, they review. At night, they tally their transgressions, so that they have no regrets. Only then do they rest.

"The common men and those below them work during daylight hours and rest when it is dark; there is not one day when they are idle.

"The royal queens weave [the king's] black hat-tassels with their own hands. The ladies of the dukes and marquises add hat-strings and cloth ornaments. The concubines of the ministers make the great girdles [worn at sacrifices]. The wives of the grand masters complete the sacrificial vestments. The wives of the scholar-officials add court vestments. The common women and those below them clothe their husbands.

"At the spring sacrifice, one prepares for [agricultural] work; at the winter sacrifice, one offers of the harvest. Men and women both exercise their duties, and if they are remiss, they are punished. These are the ancient institutes. That gentlemen should work with their minds, and lesser men with their strength, is the instruction of the former kings. From superiors down to inferiors, who dares to slacken with a licentious heart? Now I am but a widow, and you are in an inferior position [at court]. Even if we devote ourselves to our affairs from morning to evening, we should still fear that we may be forgetting our

ancestors' industry. How much less should we expect to avoid
punishment if we loaf in idleness? I have hoped that you would
encourage me from morning to evening by saying: 'You must not be
the ruin of our ancestors.' But now you say: 'Why do you not take
your ease?' An official who serves his lord in this manner—I fear that
Mubo's legacy will be cut off."[11]

Confucius heard of this, and said: "Disciples, take note: the woman
of the Ji clan is not licentious."

Gongfu Wenbo's Mother Observes Rituals Separating Male and Female

Gongfu Wenbo's mother was the great-aunt of Ji Kangzi. When
Kangzi went to her, she would open the door to speak to him, but
would never step beyond the threshold. When they sacrificed to
Daozi,[12] Kangzi would participate, but she would not receive any of
the sacrificial meat. When the sacrificial vessels were cleared away, she
would not take part in the ensuing banquet. If the officiant were not
on hand, she would not take part in the [customary] sacrifice on the
second day. Before the standing libation ritual after the second sacrifice had ended, she would retire. Confucius heard of these [habits],
and considered them part of the ritual of separating male and female.

Gongfu Wenbo's Mother Wishes to Find a Household for Wenbo

Gongfu Wenbo's mother wished to find a household for Wenbo.[13] She
invited the clan's ritual servants to a feast and recited the third stanza
of "Green Vestments" for them.[14] The servants requested that a

---

[11] Mubo is Gongfu Wenbo's deceased father.

[12] Kangzi's great-grandfather.

[13] That is to say, she wished to find a wife for him.

[14] Mao 27 in *The Book of Odes*. The third stanza, in Legge's translation: "[Dyed] green
has been the silk—/It was you who did it./[But] I think of the ancients,/That I may
be kept from doing wrong." This is to be understood as an elegant expression of her
desire not to make a mistake in finding a wife for Wenbo.

scapulimancer[15] carry out a divination regarding the future wife's clan. Music-Master Hai heard of this, and said: "Well done! At a banquet for the union of male and female, members of one's clan are not to be included; in planning a marriage for the clan, one cannot fail to include the ritual servants. She did not err in her plans, and [her designs] were subtle but clear. The *Odes* are used to express one's intentions; songs are used to chant the *Odes*. She used an ode to express [her designs] regarding marriage; she used a song to chant [the ode]. This conforms with ritual standards."

When Gongfu Wenbo Died, His Mother Warned His Concubines

When Gongfu Wenbo died, his mother warned his concubines, saying: "I have heard that if a man loves the inner, women die for him; if he loves the outer, men die for him. Now my son has died young; I would hate for others to hear of him on account of his love of the inner. Women, when you serve at the sacrifice to his spirit, bear your sorrow. I request that you not scratch your face, sob softly, beat your breast, or bear a distressed countenance. Wear mourning vestments one grade lower than what is prescribed, not one grade higher. Be silent during the rites; this will reflect well on my son."

Confucius heard of this, and said: "A girl's knowledge is not like that of a woman; a boy's knowledge is not like that of a man. The woman of the Gongfu clan is wise! She wished to make clear her son's estimable virtue."

Confucius Refers to Gongfu Wenbo's Mother as One Who Knows Ritual

Gongfu Wenbo's mother would weep for Mubo in the morning and Wenbo in the evening. Confucius heard of this, and said: "One can refer to the woman of the Ji clan as one who knows ritual. She loved unselfishly and observes the regulations of superior and inferior."

[*She earns this praise because she wept for her husband before her son.*]

---

[15] A diviner who used the scapula of an ox or a plastron of a turtle.

10

THE CLASSIC OF MOUNTAINS AND SEAS

(Shanhaijing)

山海經

The Classic of Mountains and Seas (Shanhaijing), *compiled in the third to second century* B.C.E., *survives as the definitive collection of ancient Chinese myths and legends. Throughout Chinese history it was classified either as a work on omens, portents, and prodigies, or as an important record of geographical and cosmological lore. Divided cartographically into eighteen volumes, this narrative surveys the territories inside and outside pre-imperial China, and maps the vibrant landscape of the ancient Chinese imagination. Fantastic kingdoms are peopled with bizarre creatures and a curious pantheon of gods and goddesses.*

In this text, so rich with imaginary landscapes and mythological figures, female images abound. The following selections highlight three major goddesses, certain traits of whom recur in episodes featuring other female deities in the Shanhaijing. *The Queen Mother of the West* (Xiwangmu),[1] *with feral features reminiscent of the tiger and leopard and her command over celestial catastrophes, is the most prominent example of these female deities who demonstrate both power and the determination to use it.* Chang Yi *and* Yi He, *the wives of the supreme god,* Di Jun, *are representative of the role many female deities played in the ancient calendar and cosmology. The bathing motif common to* Chang Yi, *the solar goddess, and* Yi He, *the lunar goddess, suggests their fertility as well as their ritual purity. Another series of images celebrating female power is found in the stories of* Jing Wei *(Spirit Guard),* Nüji *(Woman Sacrifice),* Nüqi *(Woman Warrior), and* Nümie *(Woman Destroyer). These spirits are powerful in specific geographical locations and must be placated. Finally, there is* Huangdi Nüba *(Goddess of Drought) who is fated to move from place to place, as she is continually exhorted to do by apprehensive northern peasant families. These*

Translated by Robin R. Wang.
[1] See pp. 346–365 for more stories about Queen Mother of the West (*Xiwangmu*).

mythological figures, some beneficent and some menacing, suggest the irreducible otherness involved in the full range of mythological images of woman.

Robin R. Wang

Part One
The Classic of the Mountains (*Shanjing*)

Book 3: The Classic of the Northern Mountain

The Mountain of Fajiu (*Fajiu shan*): Two hundred *li* further north is the mountain of Fajiu.[2] Most of the trees on the top of the mountain are mulberry trees (*zheshu*).[3] In the mountain there is the bird that looks like a crow but has a beautiful design on its head (*wenshou*), a white beak, and red feet. This bird is called Jing Wei (Spirit Guard). Its singing sounds like she is calling out her name. Jing Wei was the daughter of Yandi[4] and named Nüwa. One day, Nüwa was swimming toward the Eastern Sea and drowned there. She never came back and was transformed into Jing Wei (Spirit Guard). For eternity she carries wood and pebbles in her beak from the West Mountain to fill in the Eastern Sea.[5]

Book 2: The Classic of the Western Mountains

Jade Mountain (Yushan): Three hundred and fifty *li* to the west stands a mountain called Jade Mountain. This is the dwelling place of the Queen Mother of the West (*xiwangmu*). The Queen Mother of the West takes human form, yet she has the tail of a leopard and the teeth of a tiger. She is good at whistling. In her disheveled hair, she wears

---

[2] It is located in Changezi County, Shanxi province. It is known today as Fanbao shan, Lugu shan, or Lainshan and is part of Taihang shan.

[3] Three-bristle cudrania, a small tree with multiple uses: the leaves can be used for feeding silkworms; the seeds can be eaten or used for making the wine; the trunk can be extracted as medicine or yellow pigment.

[4] A legendary ruler of ancient China. According to mythology, Yandi was the leader of the Jiang tribe and was defeated by Huangdi, another legendary ruler. The Chinese people often identify themselves as *Yan Huang zisun*: descendants of Yandi and Huangdi.

[5] This became a popular story: "Jin Wei fills in the East Sea (*Jing Wei tianhai*)" to celebrate the power of woman.

a crown symbolic of victory (*sheng*). She takes charge of the heavenly calamities (*tianzili*), and the five destructive forces (*wucan*).

Part Two
The Classic of Seas (*Haijing*)

Book 2: The Classic of Beyond the Western Seas

Woman Sacrifice (Nüji) *and Woman Warrior* (Nüqi): Woman Sacrifice and Woman Warrior live to the north of the battle ground that lies between two rivers. Warrior (*qi*) holds an eel, and Sacrifice (*ji*) holds the meat utensil (*zu*).[6]

The Country of Women (Nüzi guo): The Country of women[7] lies north of the country of Wuxian. Two women live there. They are surrounded by water. It is said that these two women live at the same gate.

Book 7: The Classic of Within the Northern Seas

Queen Mother of the West (Xiwangmu): The Queen Mother of the West stands upright upon her platform, wearing her jade victory crown and carrying her staff. There are three green birds from the south bringing food for her. This is at the northern side of Kunlun Mountain.

Book 10: The Classic of the Great Southern Wilderness

Yi He Gives Birth to the Suns (Yi He shengri): Beyond the Southeast sea, next to the sweet river, lies the country of Yi He, where there lives a woman named Yi He. Presently, she is bathing the sun in the sweet waters of the reservoir. Yi He is the wife of Di Jun, the supreme god. She gave birth to the ten suns.

Book 11: The Classic of the Great Western Wilderness

Chang Yi Gives Birth to the Moons (Chang Yi shengyue): There is a woman who is just now bathing the moon. She is Chang Yi, the wife of Di

---

[6] *Zu* is an ancient sacrificial utensil.
[7] The Chinese word here is *Nüzi*, which can refer to women or girls.

Jun. She gave birth to all the moons, ten plus two of them, and she was the first to bathe them here.

Woman Sacrifice (Nüji) *and Woman Destroyer* (Nümie)[8]: There is a cold and desolated country. It has two people: Woman Sacrifice *(Nüji)* and Woman Destroyer *(Nümie)*.

Book 12: The Classic of the Great Northern Wilderness

The Goddess of Drought (Huangdi Nüba): Here is the mountain of Xikun. A common altar lies in this mountain no archers dare to face in its direction. There is a person, wearing green clothes and named Huangdi Nüba (Goddess of Drought).[9] Once Chiyou[10] brought soldiers to attack Huangdi, then Huangdi ordered Responding Dragon (*yinglong*) to battle Chiyou in the wild place of Jizhou. Responding Dragon attempted to hoard all the water, but Chiyou asked the Lord of Winds and the Master of Rains to release strong wind and heavy rain. Huangdi sent the sky woman, (*tiannü*) called Ba[11] to help Responding Dragon. She stopped the rain and killed Qiyou, but she could not go back to the sky again.[12] There is no more rain in her dwelling place in the earth. The deity Shujun reported this to Huangdi, and Huangdi restricted the Goddess of Drought (Nüba) to the north of the river of Chi. The deity Shujun became the charger of the field. The Goddess of Drought (Nüba) often flees from place to place. Every place she goes people want to chase her away. They command her: "Goddess, go back north!"[13] The peasants also cleaned up the water path, connecting the ditches and channels so that she could readily return to the north.

---

[8] It is said that these two women, *Nüji* and *Nümie*, are the same women as *Nüji* and *Nüqi* in Book 2.

[9] Haungdi has been translated as Yellow Emperor or the Great God Yellow. Nüba literally means Goddess of Drought. Anne Birrell translated Huangdi Nüba as the daughter of the Great God Yellow in *The Classic of Mountains and Sea* (New York: Penguin Books, 1999), p. 186.

[10] Chiyou was believed to have invented weapons and became the god of war.

[11] Ba is the legendary god of drought.

[12] According to one interpretation, she could not return to the sky because she had used up all her power.

[13] That is, north of the river Chi, the place Huangdi sent her.

11

NÜ GUA

女娲

From Liezi

列子

Liezi, *a book that supposedly consists of stories, sayings, and essays by and about the Master, can be dated as late as 300 C.E., though some portions go back as far as 400 B.C.E The book, consisting of eight chapters, is considered to be an important work on philosophical Daoism after the* Daodejing *and* Zhuangzi. *It is significant because it contains the earliest recorded tradition of the mythological figure Nü Gua (Nü Wa).*[1] *Nü Gua's identity in ancient Chinese history can be seen in a dual light: as a ruler and as a goddess. As the former, Nü Gua is a popular figure involved in the dawn of Chinese history. Her name is often connected to Fu Xi and Shen Nong, all three of whom are responsible for the betterment of ancient people's lives. Nü Gua is sometimes referred to as "an ancient empress who is surnamed Feng (Wind)." Making use of reeds, she creates a musical instrument. The establishment of marriage laws in which no union will be allowed between man and woman with identical last names is also attributed to her.*

As a goddess, it is said that Nü Gua possesses a human face and a snake's body. One of her great accomplishments is saving the world from natural disasters like earthquakes and floods. Being a powerful goddess, she creates humankind with yellow earth. And as described in The Classic of Mountains and Seas, *even her guts turn into ten deities and gods.*

To present a full picture of Nü Gua, the selections from the Liezi *have been supplemented with some discussions from* Master Huainan (Huainanzi) *by*

Translated by Fatima Wu.

[1] Scholars such as Anne Birrell regard Nü Gua and Nü Wa as separate mythological figures, yet there are other critics and translators who interpret them as the same person, with Nü Gua as the antique nomenclature and Nü Wa a the later and more popular name. This selected translation concentrates on the figure of Nü Gua found in the classics. Nü Wa, who drowned in the ocean and turned into a bird, is not included here. (For this story see the selection in *The Classic of Mountains and Seas*, p. 93.)

Liu An (179–122 B.C.E.) and A General Discussion of Customs (Fengsu tongyi).

Fatima Wu

Selections From
Liezi

Chapter 2: *The Yellow Emperor* (Huangdipian)

Fu Xi,[2] Nü Gua, Shen Nong,[3] and Xia Hou[4] had bodies of snakes and faces of human beings. They had heads of oxen and noses of tigers. Although they did not possess the looks of humans, they certainly harbored the virtues of the great sages.

Chapter 5: *Tang's Questions* (Tangwenpian)

In a way heaven and earth are also things, and things are sometimes imperfect. That is why in ancient times we have Nü Gua smelting five-colored stones to fill the holes in heaven, and breaking the legs of a turtle to support the four corners of the earth. Later, when Gong

---

[2] Fu Xi (ca. 2852 B.C.E. traditional date) was one of the three ancient emperors; the other two were Shen Nong and Suiren. Fu Xi, surnamed Feng, was considered to be a sage king, because it was believed that he invented the eight trigrams (*ba gua*), writing, fishing, and trapping. According to legend, he set his capital at Chen and ruled for 165 years.

[3] Shen Nong (ca. 2737 B.C.E. traditional date) literally means "God of Agriculture." The legendary emperor was also surnamed Jiang because he was born in Jiangshui. He made the first plough and taught people to farm. Sometimes he was referred to as Yandi (God of Fire), for it was believed that he brought fire to the people. After he became king, he tasted various herbs in order to find out about their potency in curing diseases. From his first capital at Chen, he moved to Lu. He was buried at Changsha after ruling for 120 years.

[4] Xia Hou or Xia Yu (ca. 2205 B.C.E. traditional date), the founder of the Xia dynasty, was the grandson of Zhuan Xu. His father Gun was killed by King Shun when he failed to prevent the flood. Succeeding his father, Xia Yu worked hard and finally was able to control the waters. For this, he received gifts of praise from the people. Seeing this, King Shun abdicated and offered him the throne. Xia Yu named his reign Xia after his first fief and set his capital at Anyi. He died in Huiji during a trip to the south after having ruled for eight years.

Gong[5] and Zhuan Xu[6] engaged in a battle for the title of emperor, in a fit of anger Gong Gong hit upon Mount Buzhou.[7] For that the heavenly pillar was broken and the earth's balance was upset. As a result, heaven tipped toward the northwestern direction, followed by the decline of the sun, moon, and stars. The earth did not fill in the southeast. That is why hundreds of rivers and rain waters gather there.

Selection On
Nü Gua from *Huainanzi*

Chapter 6: A Survey on Old Teachings (Lanmingxun)

During the time of antiquity, the four corners of the earth were destroyed while the nine continents crashed. Heaven was unable to cover everything, and the earth was not managing to contain all. Scorching fires burned hot without going out, while floodwaters flowed incessantly like oceans. Ferocious animals preyed on the common people, and fierce birds attacked the old and the weak. Hence Nü Gua smelted five-colored rocks to patch up the sky and broke the turtle's legs to support the four corners of the earth. In order to save Jizhou, she killed the black dragon. With the ashes of reeds she was able to dam the flood. When the sky was patched up, the four corners balanced, the floods controlled, Jizhou pacified, and the monstrous dragon eliminated, the common people survived.

■■

Fuxi and Nü Gua did not make up rules and regulations. They only left their best virtues to posterity. Why is that? They would rather be abstract and pure than being harsh, specific, and bothersome.

---

[5] According to *Liezi*, Gong Gong was a powerful lord living between the times of Fu Xi and Shen Nong. Later, Zhuan Xu, grandson of the Yellow Emperor, engaged in war with Gong Gong in a territorial fight.

[6] Zhuan Xu was grandson of the Yellow Emperor and the son of Chang Yi. He ascended to the throne at the age of twenty and set his capital at Gaoyang, hence he was also named Gaoyang. Later he moved the capital to Dichiu and, according to legend, ruled for a total of seventy-eight years.

[7] Mount Buzhou is a legendary mountain at the northwestern pole of the earth.

Selection On
Nü Gua from *A General Discussion of Customs* (*Fengsu tongyi*)

Chapter 1: On Emperors and Rulers (Huangdi diyi)

Fuxi, Nü Gua, and Shen Nong were the three emperors.

The virtues of Suiren[8] exceeded those of Zhu Rong[9] and Nü Gua. It was he who brought beauty and prosperity to earth.

Chapter 6 On Sounds (Shengyin diliu)

Nü Gua created the reed organ.

Chapter 26: The Lost Chapters (Yiwen)

According to legend, at the beginning of heaven and earth, human beings did not exist. Nü Gua kneaded the yellow earth to create men. Working hard, soon she felt tired. Hence she used a rope and dipped it into mud. The earth that dripped from the rope became men. As a result those made from the yellow earth by hand became the rich while those from the rope were among the common and the poor.

Nü Gua, Fu Xi's younger sister, prayed to the venerable gods. She established the system of marriage, uniting man and woman.

---

[8] In antiquity people ate raw food, which hurt their stomachs and caused health problems. Suiren used flint stones to procure fire, which cooked the raw food and rid it of its unwanted smells and flavors. The people were so happy that they hailed him king and gave him the name "Suiren," which means "man who invented the fire apparatus."

[9] Zhu Rong, the son of Zhuan Xu, was also one of the legendary emperors of China. In some classical books, he was listed as one of the "Three Emperors" with Shen Nong and Fu Xi. Later the name Zhu Rong was used to refer to the God of Fire and also to the title of the count officer in charge of business concerning fire.

12

MOZI

墨子

Mo Di or Mozi (ca. 480–390 B.C.E.) was born shortly after the death of Confucius and died a few years before the birth of Mengzi (Mencius). Mozi had great faith in argumentation, which led him to develop a systematic analysis and criticism of both Confucian and Daoist teachings. His arguments were focused on shaping behavior rather than developing virtue. The Han dynasty version of the book Mozi *is composed of seventy-one sections, of which eighteen are now lost. Some of the chapters are in the form of dialogues between Mozi and various contemporaries, and others are essays dealing with particular topics. The selection here discusses women in terms of human nature, and points to the union of men and women as a fundamental aspect of life.*

Eirik Harris

Chapter Five

If a mother while carrying her child on her back and drawing water from a well dropped her child into the well, she would certainly follow [to try to retrieve her child]. Now, when the harvest suffers calamity and the people experience catastrophe leading to starvation, this sorrow is more serious than dropping a child into a well; shouldn't it be examined?

Chapter Ten

Among those who live between heaven and earth and within the four seas, none lack the nature of heaven and earth and the harmony of *yin* and *yang*. Even the ultimate of sages cannot change this. How do

Translated by Eirik Harris.

we know that this is so? When the sages taught about heaven and earth, they spoke about the upper and the lower and the four seasons, then they spoke about *yin* and *yang*. When they spoke about the nature of humans, then they spoke about men and women. When they spoke about the beasts and birds, then they spoke about the male and female.

As for the fundamental nature of heaven and earth, even the former kings could not change this. The private interests of the sages of earlier generations did not adversely affect their behavior, and therefore the people were not resentful. The palaces did not accumulate women inside its walls and thus there were few unmarried men. Since women were not accumulated inside [the palace walls], and outside there were few unmarried men, the population of the kingdom was great.

Now, the present lords of large states accumulate thousands of women in their palaces and lords of small states accumulate hundreds. Therefore many men in the empire are alone, lacking wives, and many women are retained, lacking husbands. Men and women thus miss their opportunity [to unite], and the population has become small. If the lords truly desire a large population, then they must give up this practice.

13

MENCIUS

(Mengzi)

孟子

Mencius (Mengzi) (371–289 B.C.E.) is revered in East Asia as "the second sage," second only to Confucius himself in importance. He saw himself as defending Confucianism against the challenges of both egoism and an anti-familial commitment to the public good. In doing so, he developed the view that human nature is good. This went beyond anything that Confucius himself had said, but it became the basis of Confucian orthodoxy. For Mencius, the goodness of human nature amounts to the claim that humans have innate but incipient tendencies toward virtuous behavior, feeling, and perception that can and should be cultivated into full virtues. However, later Confucians (under the influence of Buddhist concepts) came to interpret Mencius as holding that humans share a transpersonal and fully formed virtuous nature, which is hidden in most of us by selfish desires.

   He seldom mentions women, but when he does, his comments on them are intriguing. He generally seems to share the dominant view in his culture that women are not capable of political and educational equality with men, but he also suggests that they sometimes show better ethical insight than men. This view is supported by the traditions about Mencius' mother.[1] She is said to have moved three times to find a good environment in which to raise the young Mencius, and she is also supposed to have rebuked the adult Mencius for his treatment of his wife.

Bryan Van Norden

3A4

Consider the way of common people: if they have a full stomach, warm garments, and comfortable surroundings but do not receive

---

Translated by Bryan Van Norden.
[1] For the story, see the selection in Biographies of Women (Lienü zhuan), pp. 151–155.

instruction, then they will practically become animals. Sage King Shun was concerned about this, so he directed Xie to be Master of Pupils and instruct people regarding human relationships: the relationship between father and children is love; between ruler and minister it is righteousness; between husband and wife it is distinction; between elder and younger it is precedence; and between friends it is faithfulness.[2]

3B2

Mencius said, "A daughter receives instructions from her mother when she gets married. When sending her off at the threshold, she warns her, 'When you join your new family, you must be respectful and circumspect. Do not disobey your husband.' The Way of a wife or concubine is to make obedience her standard."

3B3

When a man is born his parents hope he will find a wife; when a woman is born her parents hope she will find a husband. All parents feel like this. But those who do not wait for the command of their parents or the words of a matchmaker—and instead bore holes through walls to peep at one another, and jump over fences to go off together—are despised by parents and everyone else in their state.

4A5

Mencius said, "People have a common saying: 'The world, the state, the family.' The root of the world lies in the state; the root of the state lies in the family; the root of the family lies in oneself."

---

[2] These came to be known as the "five relations" (with "elder and younger brother" replacing "elder and younger" in some texts).

4B33

There once was a wife and a concubine who lived in the state of Qi. When their husband went out, he would always come back stuffed with wine and meat. When the wife asked whom he had been eating and drinking with, it was always the richest and most esteemed people. So the wife said to the concubine, "When our husband goes out, he always comes back stuffed with wine and meat. When I ask whom he has been eating and drinking with, it is always the richest and most esteemed people. However, nobody well known has ever come to visit us. I'm going to peak at where our husband goes."

Getting up early, she stealthily followed her husband. No one in all the city stopped to chat with him. He ended up among those performing sacrifices at the tombs beyond the eastern wall. He begged for their leftovers. If that was not enough, he would look around and go to another group. This was his way of stuffing himself!

His wife returned and told his concubine: "A husband is somebody you look up to for the rest of your life. And now he turns out to be like this!" So she and the concubine cursed their husband and broke down crying in the courtyard. But the husband returned, unaware of what had happened, strutting in from outside, walking proudly before his wife and concubine.

As a noble person sees it, it is seldom the case that the manner in which people seek wealth, rank, profit, and success would not shame their wives and concubines and make them break down in tears if they knew about it.[3]

5A1

When people are young, they have affection for their parents. When they come to understand taking pleasure in beauty, then they have affection for those who are young and beautiful. When they have a wives and children, then they have affection for their wives and children. When they take office, then they have affection for their

---

[3] Notice that Mencius regards a proper sense of "shame" as being one of the "sprouts" of human ethics (cf. *Mencius* 2A6, which is not in this volume). Consequently, this line suggests that women not only have an ethical sense, but sometimes have a better ethical sense than their husbands.

rulers, and if they do not get [the approval] of their rulers, then they burn within. But people of great filial piety, to the end of their lives, have affection for their parents.

5A2

Wan Zhang asked, "The Odes say how should one handle taking a bride, one must inform one's father and mother.[4]

"No one should be more faithful to this teaching than Sage King Shun. So why did Shun take a bride without informing his father and mother?"

Mencius responded, "He could not have taken a bride if he had informed them.[5] For a man and a woman to live together is the greatest of human relations.[6] If he had informed his parents, then he would have had to abandon the greatest of human relations, which would have led to tension with his father and mother. For this reason he did not inform them."

6B1

A person from the state of Ren asked Wuluzi, "Ritual or food—which is more important?" Wuluzi said, "Ritual is more important." He asked, "Sex or ritual—which is more important?" Wuluzi said, "Ritual is more important." He said, "Suppose that, if you try to eat in accordance with ritual, you will die of hunger. But if you do not eat in accordance with ritual, then you will get food. Must you then act in accordance with ritual? If you try to formally receive your bride at her parents' home, then you will not get a wife. But if you do not formally receive your bride, then you will get a wife. Must you then formally receive your bride?"

Wuluzi was unable to answer. The next day he went to the state of Zou to tell Mencius about this. Mencius said, "What difficulty is there in answering this? If one does not even up their bottoms but

---

[4] Ode 101. For more selections see *The Book of Odes*, pp. 6–24.

[5] Shun's parents were notoriously cruel to him, so they would have opposed the marriage.

[6] Compare the account of the "five relations" in *Mencius* 3A4.

Figure 3. Her beauty lies in her self-cultivation!" So said those who
Illustrations of the Biographies of Woman (Chou Hua Lienu Zhuan) by Chou Ying

remembered Zou's immersing herself in the study of the Classics. [From *Chou's* (1509–1552).]

lines up their tops, a square inch of wood can be made to be taller than the peak of a hill!

"Consider the statement, 'Metal is heavier than feathers.' Could that refer to a single metal buckle and a wagonload of feathers?! If you compare them, focusing on a case in which food is important and ritual is insignificant, why stop at food being merely important? If you compare them, focusing on a case in which sex is important and ritual is insignificant, why stop at sex being merely important? Go and respond to him, 'Suppose that if you twist your elder brother's arm to snatch his food, then you will get food. But if you do not twist it, you will not get food. Then will you twist it? If you climb over your neighbor's wall and seize his maiden daughter, you will get a wife. If you do not seize her, you will not get a wife. Then will you seize her?'"

6B6

Chunyu Kun[7] said, "... The wives of Hua Zhou and Qi Liang were skilled at singing, and thereby changed the customs of their states.[8] If one has something internally, it must take form externally."

7B9

Mencius said, "If one does not practice the Way oneself, one will not succeed in making one's wife practice it. If in directing others one is not in accordance with the Way, one cannot succeed in directing even one's own wife."

---

[7] Chunyu Kun is a philosophical opponent of Mencius' and is criticizing him in this passage. However, there is no reason to think that Mencius would reject this particular statement of Chunyu Kun's.

[8] Hua Zhou and Qi Liang were people who died in battle, and it is said that the mournful songs of their widows deeply affected their countrymen.

14

ZHUANGZI

莊子

The Zhuangzi is named for the philosopher Zhuang Zhou or Zhuangzi (ca. 369–286 B.C.E.), who was traditionally credited with authoring at least significant portions of this text. It is composed of thirty-three chapters that divided into three sections: seven inner chapters, fifteen outer chapters, and eleven miscellaneous chapters. Unlike many works of this period, the Zhuangzi is mainly concerned with the life of the individual as opposed to proper social and political order. It often employs anecdotes and allegories to expound on the ideas that it presents and explicitly criticizes the view that thinking and arguing allow one to attain full comprehension of the world. The text seeks to bring together the aspects of life that cannot be verbally elucidated with those that can be discussed and comprehended.

The Zhuangzi contains few explicit discussions about women. In those that we do find, women are evoked as metaphors that force us to rethink our conception of the world and what we should value in it.

Eirik Harris

Inner Chapters
(Neipian)

On the Equality of Things (Qiwulun)

Lady Li was the daughter of the border warden of Ai. When Qi first captured her, her weeping stained the collar of her dress. However, when she reached the King's palace and couch, and ate his grain and fodder-raised meat, she came to regret her tears.

Translated by Eirik Harris.

Main Symbols of Integrity Fulfilled (Dechonglun)

Duke Ai said to Confucius, "In the state of Wei there was an ugly man called Hunchback Ai. The men who lived with him were so fascinated with him that they could not leave. And there were tens of girls who, when they saw him, begged their parents saying, 'I would prefer to be this man's concubine than another man's wife,' and these girls have not yet stopped."

Responses for Emperors and Kings (Yingdi wang)

Liezi understood that he had not yet started to learn. He returned home and for three years did not leave. He cooked for his wife, fed the pigs as though he were feeding people, remained aloof in all his affairs, and went from a cut and polished gem to an unhewn log. Solitary and alone he took his stand. Within the disorderly he remained sealed off, united until the end.

Outer Chapters
(Waipian)

Heaven and Earth (Tiandipian)

The border warden of Hua said, "All men desire long life, wealth, and many sons. You alone do not desire them. Why is this?"

Yao replied, "If you have many sons, then you have many fears. If you have much wealth, then you have many troubles. If you have long life, then you have many disgraces. These three are of no use in cultivating virtue, and thus I decline them."

The Way of Heaven (Tiandaopian)

Long ago Wen asked Shun, "As the King appointed by heaven, how do you use your heart and mind?"

Shun replied, "I neither act haughtily towards those who lack anyone to whom to appeal, nor reject those who are poor. I grieve for those who have died, praise children, and sympathize with women. This is how I use my heart and mind."

Ultimate Joy (Zhiluepian)

Zhuangzi's wife died. When Huizi went to offer Zhuangzi his condolences, he found him sitting on the floor with his legs sprawled out, beating on a tub and singing.

Huizi said, "Your wife lived with you, raised your children, grew old with you, and died. Not crying for her is enough, but isn't beating on a tub and singing going too far?"

Zhuangzi replied, "It is not like this. When she first died, how could I alone lack sadness? But then I thought of her beginning and realized that she was originally unborn. Not only was she unborn, she originally lacked shape. Not only did she originally lack shape, she originally lacked vital breath. Then from within the disorder of vagueness and dimness there was a change and she had vital breath. Her vital breath changed and she had shape. Her shape changed and she was born. Now there has been another change and she is dead. This is just like the changes of the four seasons, spring to autumn, winter to summer. Now she sleeps happily in a large chamber. If I were to follow, crying for her, then it would be because I did not understand fate, and so I stopped."

Did you kill yourself because you had done an evil thing and were ashamed to disgrace your parents, your wife, and your children?

The Mountain Tree (Shanmupian)

Yangzi was going to Song and stopped for the night at an inn. The innkeeper had two concubines, one of them beautiful, the other one ugly. The innkeeper honored the ugly one but treated the beautiful one as worthless. Yangzi asked why this was so. A small boy at the inn replied, "The beautiful one considers herself to be so beautiful that we are unaware of her beauty. The ugly one considers herself to be so ugly that we are unaware of her ugliness.[1]

---

[1] Daoist conceptions of sex called for controlling appetites for beauty and sexual desires. The integration of perfect virtue (*quande*) and perfect form (*quanxing*) is the highest standard for female beauty. *Quande* is the Daoist spirit of purifying the mind and lessening desires. *Quanxing* is the perfection of natural form and entails refraining from artificial measures. Of the two, *quande* is the more important. Zhuangzi emphasizes long-lasting spiritual beauty rather than external beauty. This aesthetic judgment, the focus on a woman's spiritual beauty rather than on her physical beauty, has had a positive impact in later times.

Miscellaneous Chapters
(Zapian)

Wei Sheng made arrangements to meet a girl under a bridge. When the girl did not arrive but the waters started to rise, he would not leave. He held onto a bridge pillar and drowned.[2]

---

[2] This story was cited later by the well-known Yuan scholar, Xiu Mingkui, in his work: *Classic of Endurance (Renjing)*. It discussed one hundred ways to realize *ren* (endurance). This story is an illustration of the twenty-fourth way: "The Ren of Xing (Endurance of Loyalty, Trust, and Sincerity)."

15

XUNZI
荀子

Following Confucius and Mencius, Xunzi (fl. third century B.C.E.) is generally regarded as the third and final great Confucian thinker of the classical period of Chinese thought. As with many other intellectuals of pre-Qin times, there is little reliable information about Xunzi's life, nor is it even known for certain whether he wrote the book that bears his name. In contrast with the Analects and the Mencius, which are collections of sayings, the text of the Xunzi consists mostly of tightly constructed essays offering extended arguments on a variety of subjects. One of the most famous chapters claims that human nature is bad, in explicit opposition to Mencius. For Xunzi, since humans have no inborn guides to proper conduct, they must be restrained by external standards, especially the rituals of the sage kings. These rituals not only reform people so as to produce virtuous agents, but they also make social life possible in the first place by establishing a hierarchy in which authority, responsibility, and goods are distributed in such a way as to prevent contention among people. This emphasis on ritual and social hierarchy is perhaps the most prominent theme in the text.

What the following selections reveal is that to the extent that Xunzi takes an interest in the subject of women and the relations between the sexes, it is mainly in connection with this theme of ritual and social hierarchy. Specifically, Xunzi is very concerned that women be given distinct social roles and that the rituals governing male-female interactions be followed so that chaos can be averted. Note, though, that these passages stress the limitations imposed upon men as much or even more than those imposed upon on women (presumably because Xunzi considered men to be primarily responsible for the disorder of his age). Beyond this, Xunzi seems to pay very little attention to women, and although he might be faulted for such a lack of interest, it is worth noticing that in none of his remarks does Xunzi say that women are by nature inferior to men either intellectually or morally. Overall, then, his views on women are neither strongly positive nor strongly negative.

Eric L. Hutton

Translated by Eric Hutton. Excerpts from this selection were previously published in *Readings in Classical Chinese Philosophy*, edited by Philip J. Ivanhoe and Bryan W. Van Norden (New York: Seven Bridges Press, 2001), and appear here by permission of the publisher.

Chapter Five
Against Physiognomy

What is that by which humans are human? I say: It is because they have distinctions. Desiring food when hungry, desiring warmth when cold, desiring rest when tired, liking the beneficial and hating the harmful—these are things people have from birth. These one does not have to await, but are already so. These are what Yu[1] and Jie[2] both share. However, that by which humans are human is not that they are special in having two legs and no feathers, but rather that they have distinctions. Now the ape's form is such that it also has two feet and no feathers. However, the gentleman sips ape soup and eats ape meat. Thus, that by which humans are human is not that they are special in having two legs and no feathers, but rather that they have distinctions. The birds and beasts have fathers and sons but not the intimate relationship of father and son. They have the male sex and the female sex but no proper differentiation between male and female. And so among human ways, none is without distinctions. Of distinctions, none are greater than social divisions, and of social divisions, none are greater than rituals, and of rituals, none are greater than those of the sage kings.

Chapter Seven
On Confucius

Among the disciples of Confucius, even the young lads considered it shameful to speak in praise of the five hegemons.[3] How can that be?

---

[1] A legendary sage king who supposedly founded the Xia dynasty, which lasted from about the twenty-first to the sixteenth century B.C.E., according to traditional Chinese chronologies.

[2] Jie was the last ruler of the Xia dynasty. Because of his vice, he was overthrown by the sage king Tang, who supposedly founded the Shang dynasty (sixteenth to twelfth century B.C.E., according to traditional Chinese chronologies).

[3] There were different lists of the "five hegemons" circulating in ancient China, but Xunzi's own list seems to include: Duke Huan of Qi (seventh century B.C.E.), Duke Wen of Jin (seventh century B.C.E.), King Zhuang of Chu (seventh to sixth century B.C.E.), King Helü of Wu (sixth to fifth century B.C.E.), and King Goujian of Yue (fifth century B.C.E.).

I say: That was right. To praise them is truly worthy of shame. Duke Huan of Qi was the most successful of the five hegemons, but among his early deeds he killed his elder brother and seized the state. In conducting internal family matters, there were seven of his sisters and aunts whom he did not marry off. Within his private chambers he indulged in extravagant entertainments and music. He was presented with the whole state of Qi as his portion, but he did not consider it sufficient. In foreign affairs, he deceived Zhu and ambushed Ju,[4] and he annexed thirty-five states. Such was the impetuousness, corruption, perversion, and extravagance of his affairs and conduct. Simply how could he be worthy of praise in the school of the great gentleman!

Chapter Nine
The Regulations of a True King

Heaven and earth are the beginning of life. Ritual and the standards of righteousness are the beginning of order. The gentleman is the beginning of ritual and the standards of righteousness. Practicing them, habituating oneself in them, accumulating great regard for them, making oneself fond of them—these are the beginning of becoming a gentleman. Thus, Heaven and Earth give birth to the gentleman, and the gentleman brings order to Heaven and earth. The gentleman is a third partner to Heaven and earth, a key factor for the myriad things, and mother and father to the people. If there were no gentleman, then Heaven and earth would not be properly ordered, and ritual and the standards of righteousness would be without a unifying guide. Above, there would be no lords or teachers, and below, there would be no fathers and sons. Such a state is said to be in utmost chaos. Let the positions of lord, minister, father, son, older brother, younger brother, and husband and wife begin then end, end then begin; let them be part of the same order with Heaven and earth[5] and persist as long as the myriad generations—this is called the great root of things.[6]

---

[4] Zhu and Ju were small states located in what is now known as Shandong province.

[5] That is, the order that is imposed by the gentleman, as mentioned earlier in the passage.

[6] The "great root of things" here means the "root" of good government.

Chapter Ten
Enriching the State

People all desire the same things and all hate the same things. But although their desires are many, the things to satisfy them are few, and since they are few, people are sure to struggle over them. Thus, the products of the hundred crafts are means to nurture a person, but even the most capable cannot engage in every craft, nor can people each fill every official post. If they live apart and do not help each other, then they will be impoverished. If they live together but have no social divisions, then they will struggle with each other. Poverty is a catastrophe, and struggle is a disaster. If you wish to save the masses from disaster and eliminate calamity, then nothing is better than to make clear social divisions and so employ them. If the strong threaten the weak, if the wise terrorize the stupid, if the people below disregard their superiors, if the young bully their elders, if you do not govern by virtue—if it is like this, then the old and the weak will face the worry of losing their means of nurture, and those in their prime will face the disaster of divisive struggle. Work and labor are what people dislike, and merit and profit are what they are fond of. But if there is no division of occupations, then people will face the catastrophe of trying to complete their work by themselves and the calamity of struggling over merit. If the concord between male and female and the division between husband and wife are without rituals for introduction, betrothal, and marriage, then people will face the worry of losing concord and the disaster of struggling over mates. And so, the wise person makes divisions for these things.

■■

The gentleman relies on virtue. The petty man relies on strength.[7] Strength is the servant of virtue. The strength of the common people awaits [the gentleman], and only then does it have accomplishments. The community of the common people awaits him, and only then is it harmonious. The wealth of the common people awaits him, and only then does it pile up. The circumstances of the common people

---

[7] Given the lines that follow, "petty man" here seems best understood in its political sense, as the "lesser person," that is, the commoner.

await him, and only then are they comfortable. The life span of the common people awaits him, and only then is it long. Without him, relations between father and son will not be close. Without him, relations between brothers will not be smooth. Without him, relations between man and woman will not be happy.

Chapter Twelve
The Way of a Lord

[A student asks:] "May I inquire about the proper way to act as a person's wife?"

[Xunzi answers:] "If the husband follows the dictates of ritual, then compliantly obey him and wait upon him attentively. If the husband does not follow the dictates of ritual, then be apprehensive but keep oneself respectful."[8]

Chapter Twenty-Seven
The Grand Digest[9]

The *xian* hexagram of *The Classic of Changes* presents the relations for husband and wife.[10] The way of husband and wife must be correctly followed, for it is the root of relations between lord and minister,

---

[8] Instead of "but keep oneself respectful," the last part of this sentence might also be translated as "and keep oneself fearfully alert." It is unclear exactly which sense Xunzi intends.

[9] The contents of this chapter are a somewhat random collection of statements on various topics. Most scholars think it was compiled by Xunzi's students, and so it may not reflect his own thought.

[10] The hexagram *xian* ䷞, the name of which literally means "all," is composed of the trigram *dui* above and the trigram *gen* below. *Dui* is taken to represent a young female, and *gen* is taken to represent a young male, and hence the connection with marital relations. For more discussion see pp. 28–45 in the selections from *The Classic of Changes* (*Yijing*) included in this book.

father and son.[11] *Xian* is stimulus [and response]:[12] the lofty places
itself beneath the lowly, the male places himself beneath the female,
what is soft and yielding is above, and what is hard and firm is below.[13]

∎∎

The "descending frost"[14] is the time to welcome new brides [into the
home]. When the ice melts, then such receptions are to decrease.[15]
"Riding"[16] is to happen only once every ten days.

---

[11] An early commentary on the *Yijing* (the *Xuan Gua*) elaborates on this point in a helpful
way: "Only after there are Heaven and earth will there be the myriad things. Only after
there are the myriad things will there be man and woman. Only after there are man and
woman will there be husband and wife. Only after there are husband and wife will there
be father and son. Only after there are father and son will there be lord and minister."

[12] Here the text is playing with the fact that the name of the hexagram, when combined
with the word "heart," becomes the word *gan*, meaning "feeling" or "stimulus." See *Yijing*
selection in this book, pp. 28–45.

[13] Apart from describing the position of the trigrams, as well as possible sexual conno-
tations, the point of this claim seems to be that those occupying the stronger or higher
position must also be able to be humble and to that extent put themselves "beneath" the
other party.

[14] A traditional name for a specific period of time, around the end of October.

[15] Here the translation follows the reading of commentator Li Disheng.

[16] Most commentators regard this word, which literally means "driving [a chariot]," as
a euphemism for sexual intercourse.

16

HANFEIZI
韓非子

The book of Hanfeizi *is ascribed to the* Prince of Han *or* Hanfeizi *(279–233* B.C.E.*). It consists of fifty-five chapters arranged in twenty sections. It was regarded as the foundation of* Fajia, *the Legalist school in Chinese philosophy, which was influential in shaping the Qin dynasty (221–206* B.C.E.*) through its distinctive assumptions about the purpose and methods of Imperial government. Legalism is usually contrasted with Confucianism on virtually all significant teachings regarding the moral nature of human beings, the efficacy of moral education, and consequently, the use of coercive measures in order to govern well.*

*The following selection, "Precautions within the Palace" (Section 17), presents a view of family life in the Palace, in which the ruler is advised to be on guard against those closest to him, including his wives and their sons. Hanfeizi's warning against intrigues within the ruler's family, like Confucian exhortations to the ideal of family values taught, for example, in the five relationships (*wulun*), are based on a selective reading of earlier Chinese history. How different these perspectives are remains a matter of controversy: If Confucianism is regarded as a form of moral idealism, then Hanfeizi may be seen as moral cynicism. On the other hand, some regard Hanfeizi as a necessary correction, balancing the Confucian tendency toward idealism with a much-needed sense of political and social realism. In either case, Hanfeizi's remarks on family life, consistent with his moral skepticism about human nature in general, question the motives of wives and husbands, as well as children and parents, in their relationships with one another, and advise the ruler, like any male head of household, to be on the lookout for any signs of disloyalty.*

Robin R. Wang

Precautions within the Palace

It is hazardous for the ruler of men to trust others, for he who trusts others will be controlled by others. Ministers have no bonds of flesh and blood that tie them to their ruler; it is only the force of circumstance that compels them to serve him. Hence those who act as ministers never for a moment cease trying to spy into their sovereign's mind, and yet the ruler of men sits above them in indolence and pride. That is why there are rulers in the world who face intimidation and sovereigns who are murdered. If the ruler puts too much trust in his son, then evil ministers will find ways to utilize the son for the accomplishment of their private schemes. Thus Li Dui, acting as aid to the king of Zhao, starved the Father of the Ruler to death.[1] If the ruler puts too much trust in their consort, then evil ministers will find ways to utilize the consort for the accomplishment of their private schemes. Thus the actor Shi aided Lady Li to bring about the death of Shen-sheng and to set Xiqi on the throne.[2] Now if someone as close to the ruler as his own consort, and as dear to him as his own son, still cannot be trusted, then obviously no one else is to be trusted either.

Moreover, whether one is ruler of a state of ten thousand chariots or of a thousand only, it is quite likely that his consort, his concubines, or the son he has designated as heir to his throne will wish for his early death. How do I know this is so? A wife is not bound to her husband by any ties of blood. If he loves her, she remains close to him; if not, she becomes estranged. The saying goes, "If the mother is favored, the son will be embraced." But if this is so, then the opposite must be, "If the mother is despised, the son will be cast away." A man at fifty has not yet lost interest in sex, and yet at thirty a woman's beauty has already faded. If a woman whose beauty has already faded waits upon a man still occupied by thoughts of sex, then she will be spurned and disfavored, and her son will stand little chance

---

[1] "Father of the Ruler" was a title assumed by King Wuling of Zhao when he abdicated in 291 B.C.E. in favor of his son, King Huiwen. In 294 B.C.E. his palace was surrounded by soldiers headed by the high minister Li Dui, and after some three months of confinement he died of starvation. *Shi ji* 43.

[2] Lady Li, a later consort of Duke Xian of Jin, succeeded, with the aid of a court actor named Shi, in casting suspicion on the heir apparent, Shensheng, and forcing him to commit suicide in 656 B.C.E. Her own son by the duke, Xiqi, was then made heir apparent and succeeded to the throne in 651 B.C.E. *Guo yü, Jin yü* 2.

of succeeding to the throne. This is why consorts and concubines long for the early death of the ruler.

If the consort can become queen dowager and her son ascend the throne, then any law she issues will be carried out, any prohibition she decrees will be heeded. She may enjoy the delights of sex as often as she ever did while her late lord was alive and may rule a state of ten thousand chariots in any way she pleases without fear of suspicion. This is why we have secret poisonings, stranglings, and knifings. As the *Spring and Autumn Annals of Tao Zuo*[3] says, "Less than half of all rulers die from illness." If the ruler does not understand this, then he lays himself open to revolt on all sides. Thus it is said: When those who stand to profit by the ruler's death are many, he is in peril.

The charioteer Wang Liang was good to his horses, and Goujian, the king of Yue, was good to his men, the one so that they would run for him, the other so that they would fight for him. A physician will often suck men's wounds clean and hold the bad blood in his mouth, not because he is bound to them by any tie of kinship but because he knows that there is profit in it. The carriage maker making carriages hopes that men will grow rich and eminent; the carpenter fashioning coffins hopes that men will die prematurely. It is not that the carriage maker is kindhearted and the carpenter a knave. It is only that if men do not become rich and eminent, the carriages will never sell, and if men do not die, there will be no market for coffins. The carpenter has no feeling of hatred toward others; he merely stands to profit by their death. In the same way, when consorts, concubines, and heirs apparent have organized their cliques, they long for the ruler's death for, unless he dies, their position will never really be strong. They have no feeling of hatred toward the ruler; they merely stand to profit by his death. The ruler therefore must not fail to keep close watch on those who might profit by his death.

Though the sun and moon are surrounded by halos, the real danger to them comes from within.[4] Prepare as you may against those who hate you, calamity will come to you from those you love. Therefore the enlightened ruler does not rush into any undertaking that he has not properly studied beforehand, nor does he eat any unusual foods.

---

[3] This work is otherwise unknown and is different from *The Spring and Autumn Annals*.

[4] Hanfeizi is probably referring to the folk tale of the toad that lives in the moon and the three-legged crow that lives in the sun, which were said to cause the eclipses of these bodies. It is not certain how much the men of Hanfeizi's time understood the true nature of eclipses, but here he finds it convenient for his argument to regard them as internally caused.

He listens to reports from afar and scrutinizes the men close to him in order to ascertain the faults of those within and without the palace. He examines the agreements and disagreements in debate in order to determine how the various factions in the government shape up. He compares proposals and results to make certain that words are backed up by facts. He demands that what comes after shall match what went before, governs the masses according to the law, and carefully checks on the various motives of all. If he can make certain that men do not receive any unearned rewards not overstep their authority, that death penalties are justly handed out and no crime goes unpunished, then evil and malicious men will find no opening to carry out their private schemes.

17

THE YELLOW EMPEROR'S CLASSIC OF INTERNAL MEDICINE

(Huangdi neijing)

黃帝內經

The Yellow Emperor's Classic of Internal Medicine *is the work of various unknown authors who wrote during the Warring States Period (475–221* B.C.E.*) It is the oldest and greatest classic medical text in China. The foundation of this book is a philosophical understanding of* yin *and* yang. *The following selection is from the second chapter, where a conceptual explanation of* yin *and* yang *is systematically developed.*

The text presented here does not explicitly consider the traditional understanding of gender differences. It does, however, provide a basis for understanding how the different social roles and gender expectations for men and women—as explored in several other selections in this book—are rooted in a powerful cosmology whose power is manifest in its capacity to illuminate the complexities of human physiology, its spiritual presuppositions, and its moral consequences. In particular, the conceptual theory of yin *and* yang *can be deployed for the diagnosis of diseases and the prescription of remedies, including acupuncture, that doctors traditionally used to restore a person to health.*

As this text clearly indicates, the health of the human body, like all other forms of wholeness, depends upon reestablishing the proper harmony of yin *and* yang. *The physiological differences between men and women thus are not to be understood as some sort of essentialist dualism, but as a result of the complex interplay of two complementary and cosmic principles, with each individual exhibiting dominant characteristics of one or the other principle. This text, then, helps us to understand that traditional gender roles and expectations have not only a cosmic significance but also scientific validity. The proven success of traditional Chinese medicine thus has served to legitimate traditional understandings of what it means to be a man or a woman.*

Robin R. Wang

The Great Treatise on the Interaction of *Yin* and *Yang*

The Yellow Emperor (Huang di) said: The principle of *yin* and *yang* [the male and female elements in nature] is the basic principle of the entire universe. It is the principle of everything in creation. It brings about the transformation to parenthood; it is the root and source of life and death; and it is also found within the temples of the gods. In order to treat and cure diseases one must search into their origin.

Heaven was created by an accumulation of *yang*, the element of light; Earth was created by an accumulation of *yin*, the element of darkness. *Yang* stands for peace and serenity; *yin* stands for recklessness and turmoil. *Yang* stands for destruction, and *yin* stands for conservation. *Yang* causes evaporation, and *yin* gives shape to things.

Extreme cold brings forth intense heat (fever), and intense heat brings forth extreme cold (chills). Cold air generates mud and corruption; hot air generates clarity and honesty. If the air upon Earth is clear, then food is produced and eaten at leisure. If the air above is foul, it causes dropsical swellings.

Through these interactions of their functions, *yin* and *yang*, the negative and positive principles in nature, are responsible for diseases that befall those who are rebellious to the laws of nature as well as those who conform to them.

The pure and lucid element of light represents Heaven and the turbid elements of darkness represents Earth. When the vapors of the Earth ascend they create clouds, and when the vapors of Heaven descend they create rain. Thus rain appears to be the climate of the Earth and clouds appear to be the climate of Heaven. The pure and lucid element of light is manifest in the upper orifices,[1] and the turbid element of darkness is manifest in the lower orifices.[2]

Yang, the element of light, originates in the pores. *Yin*, the element

---

[1] The upper orifices are the mouth, ears, eyes, and nostrils.

[2] The two lower orifices correspond to *yin*; they are the rectum and the urethral opening.

of darkness, moves within the five viscera.[3] *Yang*, the lucid element of life, is truly represented by the four extremities; and *yin*, the turbid element of darkness, restores the power of the six treasuries of nature. Water represents *yin*, and fire represents *yang*. *Yang* creates the air, and *yin* creates the flavors. The flavors belong to the physical body. When the body dies the ethereal spirit is restored to the air, having thus undergone a complete metamorphosis (having thus become naturalized).

The ethereal spirit receives its nourishment from the air, and the body receives its nourishment from the flavors. The ethereal spirit is created through metamorphosis, and the physical shape assumes life through breath. Through transformation the ethereal spirit becomes air, and air is injurious to the perception of flavors. The flavors that are controlled by *yin* emanate from the lower orifices. The breath (air) that is controlled by *yang* emanates from the upper orifices. When the flavors are heavy, then *yin*, the female element, is weakened and allows *yang*, the male element, to enter into *yin*. When the air (breath) is thick and heavy, then *yang*, the male element, is reduced and allows *yin* to enter into *yang*. The heavy flavor (of the female element) then leaks out and extends itself and communicates with the aura (air) (of the male element). If this aura is thin, it tends to leak out; if it is thick, it becomes heated and inflamed. The pungent and the sweet flavors have a dispersing quality like *yang*, the male element. The sour and the salty flavors circulate and flow like *yin*, the female element.

If *yin* is healthy then *yang* is apt to be defective, if *yang* is healthy then *yin* is apt to be sick. If the male element is victorious then there will be heat, if the female element is victorious there will be cold. (Exposure to) repeated and severe cold will cause (a) hot fever (sensation). Exposure to repeated and severe heat will cause a cold sensation (chills). Cold injures the body while heat injures the spirit.

When the spirit is hurt severe pains ensue; when the body is hurt there will be swellings. Thus in those cases where severe pains are felt first and the swellings appear later, one can say that the spirit has injured the body. And in those cases where swellings appear first and severe pains are felt later, one can say that the body has injured the spirit.

When wind is victorious, everything moves and stirs. When heat overcomes the world then, in the end, swellings will ensue. When dryness overcomes the world, everything will be scorched. When cold overcomes the world, then everything becomes light and floating. When dampness overcomes the world, then moisture will be dispelled.

---

[3] The five viscera are the liver, heart, stomach, lungs, and kidneys.

Nature has four seasons and five elements.[4] In order to grant a long life, the four seasons and the five elements store up the power of creation within cold, heat, excessive dryness, moisture, and wind. Man has five viscera in which these five climates are transformed to create joy, anger, sympathy, grief, and fear.

The emotions of joy and anger are injurious to the spirit. Cold and heat are injurious to the body. Violent anger is hurtful to *yin*; violent joy is hurtful to *yang*. When rebellious emotions rise to Heaven, the pulse expires and leaves the body. When joy and anger are without moderation, then cold and heat exceed all measure and life is no longer secure. *Yin* and *yang* should be respected to an equal extent.

It is said: When people are injured through the severe cold of winter, the sickness will recur in spring. When people are hurt through the wind in spring, they will not be able to retain their food in summer. When people are hurt through the extreme heat of summer, they will get intermittent fever in fall. When people are hurt through the humidity of fall, they will get a cough in winter.

The Yellow Emperor said: It is said that in former times the ancient sages discoursed on the human body and that they enumerated separately each of the viscera and each of the bowels. They talked about the origin of the blood vessels and about the vascular system, and said that where the blood vessels and the arteries (veins) meet there are six junctions. Following the course of each of the arteries there are the (365) vital points for acupuncture. Each of these points has a place and a name, just as "hollow" refers to the bones, and they all have sections that set them apart from each other.

No matter whether people are rebellious or obedient there is method and regularity in the workings of the four seasons and *yin* and *yang*. Everything is subject to their invariable rules and regulations, which govern the relationship between external and internal influences.

Qi Bo said: Hence it is said: Heaven and Earth are the highest and lowest of all creation. *Yin* and *yang* [the two elements in nature] create desires and vigor in men and women. The ways of *yin* and *yang* are to the left and to the right. Water and fire are the evidences and symbols of *yin* and *yang*. *Yin* and *yang* are the source of power and the beginning of everything in creation. Hence it is said: *Yin* is active within and acts as guardian of *yang*; *yang* is active on the outside and acts as regulator of *yin*.

The Yellow Emperor asked: Is there any alternative to the laws of *yin* and *yang*?

Qi Bo answered: When *yang* is stronger the body is hot, the pores

---

[4] The five elements are metal, wood, water, fire, and earth.

are closed, and the people begin to pant; they become boisterous and coarse, and whether one looks up or down no perspiration appears. People become feverish (hot), their gums are dry and give trouble, the stomach is affected (oppressed), and they die of constipation. When *yang* is stronger, people can endure Winter but they cannot endure Summer.

When *yin* is stronger the body is cold and perspiration appears regularly all over the body. People see their fate clearly; they tremble with fear and get chilled. When they are chilled, their spirits become rebellious. Their full stomachs can no longer digest and they die. When *yin* is stronger people can endure Summer but they cannot endure Winter. Thus *yin* and *yang* alternate; their victories vary and so does the character of their diseases.

The Yellow Emperor asked: Can anything be done to blend and to adjust these two principles in nature?

Qi Bo answered: If one has the ability to know the seven injuries and the eight advantages, the two principles can be brought into harmony. If one does not know how to use this knowledge, then his span of life will be limited by early decay.

Yet it is said: Those who have the true wisdom remain strong, but those who have no knowledge and wisdom grow old and feeble. Therefore the people should share this wisdom and their names will become famous. Those who are wise inquire and search together, while those who are ignorant and stupid inquire and search apart from each other. Those who are stupid and ignorant do not exert themselves enough in the search for the Right Way, while those who are wise search beyond the natural limits.

Those who search beyond the natural limits will retain good hearing and clear vision, their bodies will remain light and strong, and although they grow old in years they will remain able-bodied and flourishing; and those who are able-bodied can govern to great advantage. For this reason the ancient sages practiced not to undertake any worldly affairs, and in their pleasures and joys they were dignified and tranquil. They followed their own desires, and they never directed their will and ambition toward the protection of a purpose that was empty of meaning. Thus their allotted span of life was without limit, like Heaven and Earth. This was the way the ancient sages controlled and conducted themselves.

Those who are experts in using the needle for acupuncture follow *yin*, the female principle, in order to draw out *yang*. And they follow *yang*, the male principle, in order to draw out *yin*. They use the right hand in order to treat illness of the left side, and they use the left hand in order to treat illness of the right side.

Those who are experts in examining patients judge their general appearance; they feel the pulse and distinguish whether it is *yin* or *yang* that causes the disease. If the appearance changes from clear to turbid, then the location of the disease is revealed. Coughing and short-windedness should be watched carefully; one should listen to the sounds and the notes, and then the location of the affliction will become apparent. One should examine irregularities that must be adjusted according to custom and usage, and then the location where the disease prevails will become known.

Treatise on the Parting and Meeting of *Yin* and *Yang*

The Yellow Emperor said: It is said that Heaven was created by *yang* (the male principle of light and life), and that the Earth was created by *yin* (the female principle of darkness and death). It is said that the sun represents *yang*, and that the moon represents *yin*. The large and the small months added together resulted in three hundred and sixty-five days and this made one year, and mankind always lived in accord with this system. Is it true that nowadays the three elements of *yang* no longer correspond with the system of *yin* and *yang* of old?

Qi Bo answered: *Yin* and *yang* may be added up to amount to the number ten; this can be extended and may mean one hundred; or the number may be estimated to be one thousand, and this can be extended and mean ten thousand, that is to say: it includes everything. Ten thousand is so large that it cannot be matched by any number, and the same is true of its importance.

Everything in creation is covered by Heaven and supported by the Earth; when nothing has as yet come forth (been grown, produced) the Earth is called: the place where *yin* dwells; it is also known as the *yin* within the *yin*. *Yang* supplies that which is upright, while *yin*, the Earth acts as a ruler of *yang*.

The Yellow Emperor said: I should like to hear more about the parting and meeting of *yin* and *yang*.

Qi Bo answered: The ancient sages faced the South and thus they established themselves. Whatever was before them was spoken of as shining space, and whatever was behind them was called the great thoroughfare or the Great *Yang*.

The Great *Yang* is located within the soil and in it is the lesser *yin*. When this lesser *yin* rises above the Earth, it comes under the influence of the Great *Yang*. The Great *Yang* is the foundation of existence from the beginning to the end. The Great *Yin* is the connecting link between life and the "Gate of Life,"[5] and thus it becomes evident that within the *yin* there is also a *yang*. It is within the body and above, and it is called shining space; but if this shining expanse sends its rays below, then it is spoken of as the Great *Yin*. The front of the Great *Yin* is known to be illuminated by the "sunlight."

The "sunlight" is the foundation of everything; it permeates everything, and it is therefore known as the *yang* within the *yin*. If *yin* becomes apparent externally, then it is known as the lesser *yang*. The lesser *yang* is the foundation of and brings to life the orifices of *yin*, and hence it is called the lesser *yang* within the *yin*.

This then is the parting and the meeting of the three *yang*. The Great *Yang* acts as the opening factor, the "sunlight" acts as the covering factor, and the lesser *yang* acts as the axis or central point. The three main arteries must not miss each other; they must be drawn together, and when their pulse does not sound superficial then its name is one *yang* (pulse).

The Yellow Emperor said: I should like to know more about the three *yin*.

Qi Bo answered: On the outside there is *yang*, but within it is *yin* that is active. *yin* is active in the interior and is effective below; there its name is the Great *Yin*. The Great *Yin* is the foundation of everything that is hidden, mysterious, and empty; and thus it is called the *yin* within the *yin*. The rear of the Great *Yin* is called the lesser *yin*.

The lesser *yin* is the origin of all that flows rapidly and of all the springs, and it is spoken of as the lesser *yin* within the *yin*. The front of the lesser *yin* is called the "absolute *yin*." This *yin* is the foundation of greatness and honesty. Where *yin* breaks off there is *yang*, and at that point it is called the *yin* within the absolute *yin*.

Here we have the parting and the meeting of the three *yin*. The Great *Yin* acts as the opening factor, the absolute *Yin* acts as the covering factor, and the lesser *yin* acts as the axis or central point. The three main arteries must not miss each other; they must be drawn together, and when their pulse does not sound deep then it is called one *yin* (pulse). The climate of *yin* and *yang* alternate, and their accumulated climates act as one complete unit. The internal spirit and the external physical shape perfect each other.

---

[5] The "Gate of Life," according to Chinese medicine, is located between the kidneys and is held to be the organ that transforms the blood into semen.

18

THE ANNALS OF LÜ BUWEI

呂不韋

(Lüshi Chunqiu)

呂氏春秋

Lüshi chunqiu *(literally* Springs and Autumns of Mr. Lü*) is an encyclope-dic text compiled under the direction of Lü Buwei (d. 235* B.C.E.*), a wealthy merchant who was so adept at peddling influence that he attained the post of Prime Minister in the state of Qin. His influence over the young king of Qin—the future First Emperor—is attributed in partisan sources to the fact that he may have been the boy's natural father. Their relationship soured as the King approached maturity (the same unsympathetic sources aver that Lü Buwei had a hand in a seditious plot that involved hiring a rogue to seduce the Queen Dowager); Lü Buwei was banished, and later required to commit suicide. It is thought that the bulk of the* Lüshi chunqiu *was completed in the last years of Lü Buwei's life, while he was living in exile. A postface to the first of three sections of the book is dated precisely, but according to a convention that is not transparent today; experts place this date around 240* B.C.E. *The other two sections may have been written later, but probably not after Lü Buwei's death.*

The meaning of the title is debated. The Spring and Autumn Annals *is the name of the classic chronicle of Lu, supposedly edited by Confucius himself, and Lü Buwei may have co-opted this title in order to suggest that new canons were needed for the dawning imperial age. But other explanations are possible. The text is orga-nized after the calendar, with a running account of the natural phenomena and agri-cultural tasks characterizing each month, interspersed with philosophical chapters on subjects ranging from self-cultivation to rulership. Thus the title* The Spring and Autumn Annals *may be intended to convey the idea that the work contains all the information necessary for the dexterous management of the yearly cycle. Finally,* The Spring and Autumn Annals *is a formula in ancient titles meaning something like "synoptic record"; perhaps it is not far-fetched, then, to render* Lüshi chunqiu *as* Mr. Lü's Alpha and Omega.

The selections below deal with sericulture and weaving, occupations traditionally associated with women. The passages are prescriptive and should not be taken as accu-

Translated by Paul R. Goldin.

rate reflections of daily life in the third century b.c.e. Nevertheless, they are useful as idealized depictions of women's labor. Moreover, the stipulated rituals contradict the stereotypical view that women were supposed to remain indoors at all times. The morality of the Lüshi chunqiu *is hardly liberal ("Women are enjoined not to frolic"), but it does not confine women within the household.*

Paul R. Goldin

In [the third month of spring], the Officer of Forestry is ordered not to fell the mulberry and *zhe*-trees.[1] The ringdoves flap their wings and the cuckoos descend onto the mulberries. One prepares the bamboo frames and round and square baskets [for raising silkworms]. The queen and royal consorts, after fasting, go to the eastern district and tend to the mulberries in person. Women are enjoined not to frolic. Women's assignments are reduced in order to encourage sericulture. When the tasks of sericulture are completed, the cocoons are divided, the silk weighed, and the women's handiwork verified, so that they may provide the vestments used in sacrifices to Heaven and to the ancestors. There are none who dare to loiter.

■■

It is said in the book of the Millet God: "Plowing and weaving are taken as duties because they constitute fundamental instructions." Thus the Son of Heaven himself leads the feudal lords in plowing the ancestral fields. The grand masters and men of service all have tasks and offices. Thus when it is time for their seasonal duties, farmers are not to be seen in the city; in this manner the people are instructed to honor the produce of the earth. The queen and royal consorts lead the nine concubines in tending to the silkworms in the suburbs and the mulberries in the common fields. Thus there are the tasks of hemp and silk in all four seasons, which promote the instruction of women. The husband does not weave, but has clothing; the wife does not plow, but has food. Males and females exchange their handiwork in order to survive: this is the regulation of the Sages. Therefore: revere the seasons and cherish the days; do not rest unless you are aged; do not stop unless you are ill; do not cease unless you are dead.

---

[1] The *zhe* is a tree that can be used, along with the mulberry, to cultivate silkworms.

19

NINE SONGS

(Jiu Ge)

九歌

Qü Yuan

屈原

The Nine Songs, or Jiu ge, were composed by Qü Yuan (ca. 340–278 B.C.E.), a patriotic poet of the Chu State in ancient China. Each of the Nine Songs depicted a mythic god who was popular in Southern China during Qü Yuan's times. Later, Liu Xiang (ca. 77–6 B.C.E.) of the Han dynasty compiled the Songs of the South, or Chuci, to include all Qü's poems as well as poems of later poets who followed Qü's style. The Chuci style of poetry used Chu literary expressions to portray the products, landscapes, customs, practices, folklore, and myths of the South. The following two poems describe an intense love between the god and goddess of the Xiang River. The god waits, worrying that his lover is either delayed or has had second thoughts about their love. The goddess mirrors his feelings, preferring like him to linger a little longer, hoping that soon they will be reunited. Though the poems offer many symmetries between the two lovers, their distinctive genders are observed, as the god proudly describes his swift moving dragon boat while the goddess tells of an underwater pleasure palace that she fancies her lover has prepared for her.

Ping Yao

The Prince of the Xiang[1]

You have not come; apprehensively waiting,
For whom do you linger on the islet?
Splendidly and perfectly dressed myself,
I ride a cassia boat going downstream.
May the Yuan and Xiang Rivers have no waves,
Let the Yangzi River flow calmly.
I look for you, but you have not come.

Translated by Ping Yao.

[1] The Prince of the Xiang was the god of the Xiang River. His name was Shun. This poem describes the Prince's longing for his wife, the Lady of the Xiang.

Whom do I miss as I blow a panpipe?
On this boat decorated with the flying-dragon I travel toward
  the North,
I circle around in the Lake of Dongting.
My awning is of fig leaves, fastened with basil,
My pole top is of sweet flag, and banners of orchids.
I gaze at the farthest shores of the Cenyang Sandbar,
Crossing the Yangzi River, I sail ahead.
I sail ahead, but I cannot find you,
My maid worries and sighs for me.
My tears flow in streams,
I miss you deeply and am in great sorrow.
My oar is of cassia and my rudder of orchid.
I accelerate my boat and the waves are stirred like drifting
  snow.
Can one pick fig leaves in the water?
Can one pluck lotus flowers from the tips of a tree?
When two hearts do not share the same passion,
The matchmaker labors in vain.
When affection is not deep, it is easily lost.
The rock shallows are difficult to pass,
But my flying-dragon boat moves swiftly.
When a relationship is not based on trust, grief extends.
You break your tryst, making excuses of being busy.
In the morning I gallop along the Yangzi River,
In the evening I stop my chariot at the Northern Sandbar.
The birds rest on the rooftop,
And the waters circle around the hall.

I offer my jade ring to the Yangzi River,
And yield my jade pendant to the bay of Li.
I gather the galingale on an islet of fragrant grasses,
Still hoping to present them to you.
If I leave, I might not have another chance,
So I'd rather stay here and linger a little longer.

The Lady of the Xiang[2]
The son of Heaven[3] descends down to the Northern Sandbar.

---

[2] The Lady of the Xiang was the goddess of the Xiang River and wife of Shun, the Prince of the Xiang. This poem describes the Lady's longing for her husband.

[3] "The son of Heaven" is Shun. The ancient Chinese considered rulers to be the sons of Heaven (tianzi). Shun was a ruler.

It saddens me that I cannot see him clear.
The autumn wind gently blows,
The Dongting Lake makes waves and the tree leaves drop.
Over the white nut-grass I gaze afar,
For a tryst with him was made at the evening time.
But why do birds gather in the middle of the duckweed?
And why are the fishnets hung on the trees?

The Yuan River has its angelica and the Li River its orchids.
I long for you but dare not speak.
I gaze at the distance in a trance,
Only to see the waters run by.

Why do the giant deer eat in the middle of the courtyard?
Why do the water-dragons come out to the riverbank?
In the morning I gallop my horses along the Yangzi River,
In the evening I cross to the western shore.
I can hear my beloved calling my name.
I shall hasten my chariot so I can ride beside him.

I fancy that you build a house underwater,
Thatching it with a roof of lotus leaves,
With walls of sweet-flag, the mid-courtyard of murex,
And plasters mixed with fragrant pepper adorning the hall,
Cassia for the beams, and tree-orchid the rafters,
Door-lintels of lily magnolia, and bowers of white angelica,
Weaving fig leaves for the curtains,
And split basil to make a screen.

Mat-weights are of white jade,
And the floor is scented with stone-orchids.
The lotus roof is thatched with angelica,
And the house is covered by assarum.
A hundred sweet plants are collected to fill the courtyard,
And delicious scents perfume the gate and corridor.
You send all the spirits of Jiuyi mountain to bring me,
They come together as numerous as clouds.

I drop my sleeves into the Yangzi River,
And present my thin dress to the bay of Li.
I gather the galingale on a flat island,
Hoping to offer them to you who are still far away.
If I leave, I might not have another chance,
So I'd rather stay here and linger a little longer.

PART THREE

HAN
漢

(202 B.C.E.–220 C.E.)

20

MASTER PRINCE OF HUAINAN
(Huainanzi)

淮南子

Liu An

劉安

Huainanzi, was compiled by Liu An, prince of Huainan, and his mentors, Su Fei, Li Shang, and Wu Bei, and was completed in 139 B.C.E. Compared to other major philosophical works of ancient China, Huainanzi has received much less attention among scholars of the past and present.

The main goal of Liu An's book is to provide a systematic interpretation of the universe and the position of human beings in and relation to the universe. Although the framework of the book is based on Daoist principles, concepts from Confucianism and Legalism, as well as the theories of yin and yang, the Five Phases (wuxing), and correspondences, are apparent as well. The two passages selected here, for example, define women's role and position in Confucian terms: one advocates a Confucian ideal of female chastity, and the other follows the Confucian tendency to blame women for political chaos.

The first passage is an excerpt from chapter one, "Principles of the Dao," which stresses the Daoist explanation of why the universe is the way it is. Here the Dao is used to persuade readers that, in the natural order of things, "a woman is faithful to only one man throughout her life." The second passage is an excerpt from chapter seven, "Principles of Mentality," in which Liu An discussed his understanding of human nature. Here his point is that any violation of the natural order of things, including disordered relations between the sexes, will only bring disaster.

Ping Yao

Translated by Ping Yao.

Master Prince Huaian (*Huainanzi*)

When a crow cries, it sounds like *ya-ya*; and when a magpie chirps, it sounds like *ji-ji*. These sounds will never change because of any change in atmosphere, whether winter or summer weather, whether dry or moist air. Thus, as long as one grasps and firmly believes the *Dao*, he will not change his understanding of the universe just because of vicissitudes no matter how sweeping or temporary. "Understanding the universe," as I mentioned above, means that the essence of life is placed in an appropriate position. Life and body are developed from the same origin. When body is formed, life is created, and when life is created, emotions, such as fondness and hatred, come along. Therefore, a gentleman keeps a steady view and a woman is faithful only to one man throughout her life. This will not be changed by any rules or restrained by any principles.

■■

If someone knew a certain object were useless, he would reject it even if he were a greedy person; however, if one did not know an object was useless, it would be very hard even for a decent person to walk away from it. Likewise, those rulers who ruined their states, abandoned their ancestors' shrines, died at the hand of their enemies, or became the laughingstock of the world, all had improper desires. The state of Qiu You was destroyed because of its ruler's craving for a huge bell.[1] The king of Yu was kidnapped because of his longing for Chui Ji's jade.[2] Duke Xian lusted after Li Ji's beauty and caused four

---

[1] The story of Qiu You was originally recorded in *Master Hanfei* (*Hanfeizi*). During the Spring and Autumn period (770–476 B.C.E.), the state of Jin persuaded the king of Qiu You to build a main road between the two states, claiming that the Jin intended to present a huge bronze bell to the king of Qiu You. When the construction was completed, the Jin instead used the road to conquer the state of Qiu You.

[2] Chui Ji, located in the state of Jin, was known for its fine jade. During the Spring and Autumn period, the state of Jin presented some Chuji jade to the king of Yu in exchange for using its roads to attack the state of Guo. Three years later, after conquering the Guo, Jin came back to conquer the Yu and took the king as prisoner.

generations of chaos.[3] Duke Huan loved Yi Ya's delicacy, and he did not get a decent burial.[4] The barbarian king indulged himself with female entertainers and thus lost his precious territory.[5]

---

[3] Duke Xian was the ruler of the Jin during 677–651 B.C.E. When Jin conquered the state of Lirong, Duke Xian took Li Ji and her sister, daughters of the Li Rong ruler, as his wives. Li Ji murdered and ousted Duke Xian's sons from a previous marriage and installed her son and later her sister's son as rulers.

[4] Duke Huan was the ruler of the Qi State and Yi Ya was his favorite subject. When Yi Ya heard that Duke Huan never tasted steamed baby, he cooked his own son and present the "dish" to the Duke. Duke Huan thus took political advice only from Yi Ya. When Duke Huan died, an internal turmoil erupted. He was not buried until sixty-seven days later when his body was badly decomposed.

[5] "The barbarian king" implies the king of Xirong who was presented with a group of female entertainers by the state of Qin. The Qin conquered Xirong soon after. Xirong is the collective name for the Rong people who lived in the northwest of China during the Pre-Qin and early imperial periods. The Xirong people were known for their nomadic life style.

21

STRATAGEMS OF THE WARRING STATES

(Zhanguoce)

戰國策

Stratagems of the Warring States (Zhanguoce) *is a Han dynasty miscellany comprised of anecdotes of variable authenticity, all set in the Warring States
period. The materials currently found in the* Stratagems *evidently derive from several
older sources, and, unlike such canonical works as the* Zuozhuan *or* The Canon
of Documents (Shujing), *the text as a whole is not characterized by a consistent ethic. Its value as a historical source is limited, because the author or authors of
these short pieces did not concern themselves with recording facts accurately. Rather,
the primary purpose of the stories seems to be entertainment. The basic theme of the
text is the employment of devious stratagems to fulfill one's worldly desires. Along the
way,* Stratagems of the Warring States *dismantles many cherished ideals of
the ancient Chinese world. Loyalty and fair dealing are shown to be eminently unprof-
itable. Many of the pieces, in their unabashed irreverence, are amusing even today.
Intrigue and machination are areas in which neither sex has an absolute advantage
over the other, and accordingly female characters are central to many of the anecdotes
in* Stratagems of the Warring States. *Like the* Discourses of the States,
the Stratagems *suggests that women can be as shrewd as men—and figures who
assume that women are naturally inferior usually live to regret their prejudice.*[1]

Paul R. Goldin

Translated by Paul R. Goldin.

[1] J. I. Crump, in *Legends of the Warring States: Persuasions, Romances, and Stories from the
Chan-kuo Ts'e*, Michigan Monographs in Chinese Studies 83 (Ann Arbor: University of
Michigan, 1999, pp. 103–121), has gathered and translated a broader selection of pieces
from the *Stratagems* pertaining to women than those selected here. Crump has also trans-
lated the entire text: *Chan-kuo ts'e*, revised edition, Michigan Monographs in Chinese
Studies 77 (Ann Arbor: University of Michigan, 1996).

Queen Dowager Xuan of Qin

Queen Dowager Xuan of Qin[2] loved Wei Choufu. When the queen
dowager was sick and about to die, she issued an edict: "When I die,
Master Wei[3] must be buried alive with me."

Master Wei was worried about this. Yong Rui persuaded the queen
dowager on behalf of Master Wei, saying: "Do you believe that the
dead have consciousness?"

The queen dowager said: "They have no consciousness."

"If the queen dowager, with her divine insight, knows that the dead
have no consciousness, why would you vainly take one whom you
loved in life and have him buried with a dead person who has no consciousness? And if the dead do have consciousness, then the former
king will have been accumulating his anger for a long time; your
Majesty, you will have no means by which to make amends for your
transgression.[4] What time will you have for private relations with Wei
Choufu?"

The queen dowager said: "Very well." Thus she desisted.

The King of Qi Sent an Ambassador to
Make Inquiries of Queen Wei of Zhao

The king of Qi[5] sent an ambassador to make inquiries of Queen Wei
of Zhao. Before the seal of the letter had been broken, Queen Wei
asked the ambassador: "Have there been no pests during the harvest?
Have the people also been without disease?"

The ambassador was displeased, and said: "I, your servant, am an
ambassador who has been sent to you, Queen Wei;[6] now you do not
ask about my king, but ask first about the harvest and the people. Is
this not putting the base first and the honorable last?"

---

2 The widow of King Huiwen of Qin (r. 337–311 B.C.E.).

3 Master Wei is otherwise unknown.

4 That is, the transgression of taking a new lover after her husband's death.

5 Commentators identify him as King Xiang of Qi (r. 282–265 B.C.E.).

6 "Wei" was a posthumous name, and commentators rightly point out that the ambassador could not have addressed her thus; this may be a sign that the text was corrupted
by later hands.

Queen Wei said: "Not so. If there were no harvest, how would there be people? If there were no people, how would there be a lord? In my questions, should I neglect the root and ask about the branches?"

Then she summoned him inside and asked him: "In Qi there is a hermit named Master Zhongli; is he well? His personality is like this: he feeds both those who do not have grain and those who do; he clothes both those who do not have clothes and those who do. This is to assist the king in supporting his people; why has he not, to this day, been assigned duties?

"Is Master Sheyang well? His personality is like this: he feels sorrow for the widowed; he feels compassion for the orphaned; he gives aid to the poor; he supplies those who do not have enough. This is to assist the king in succoring his people; why has he not, to this day, been assigned duties?

"Is Yingerzi, the daughter of the Beigong clan, well? She removed her bracelets and earrings, and refused into old age to marry, in order to care for her mother and father. These are all [actions] that guide the people to excel at feelings of filial piety; why has she not, to this day, been ennobled at court? These two gentlemen have not been assigned duties, this one woman has not been ennobled at court— how can [such a person] be the king of Qi and view his myriad subjects as his children?

"Is Zizhong of Wuling still alive? His personality is like this: above, he does not serve as a minister to his king; below, he does not keep his family in order; between [these spheres], he does not take pains to communicate with other feudal lords. This is one who guides the people to excel at uselessness. Why has he not, to this day, been executed?"

When King Min of Qi Was Killed

When King Min of Qi [r. 313–283 b.c.e.] was killed, his son, Fazhang, changed his clan name and given name and became a menial in the household of the Grand Historian of Ju. Grand Historian Jiao's daughter noticed that Fazhang's physiognomy was strange, and she considered him to be an extraordinary man. Pitying him, she secretly clothed and fed him, and had private relations with him.

The ruined ministers of Qi gathered in Ju and looked for King Min's son, desiring to raise him to the throne. Thus Fazhang spoke for himself in Ju.[7] Together, they anointed Fazhang as King Xiang.[8] When King Xiang came to the throne, he made the daughter of the Grand Historian his queen, and she gave birth to the child Jian. Grand Historian Jiao said: "A woman who marries without an intermediary is not of my seed; she has defiled my house." To the end of his life, he would not look on her. But the queen was virtuous and did not take his unwillingness to look on her as a reason to neglect the rituals between father and child.

When King Xiang died his son Jian was anointed as king of Qi.[9] The queen served Qin diligently and was trusted by the feudal lords; for these reasons, Jian reigned for more than forty years without being attacked. The first emperor of Qin once sent an ambassador to present the queen with linked rings, saying: "Qi knows many things; can you separate these rings?"

The queen showed [the rings] to her flock of ministers, but they did not know how to separate them. The queen grabbed a mallet and broke [the rings]; then she dismissed the Qin ambassador, saying: "I have diligently separated them."

When she was sick and about to die, she warned Jian, saying: "Those among your ministers who can be employed are so-and-so." Jian said: "Let me write this down."

The queen said: "Very well." He fetched a brush and board in order to receive her instructions. [When he returned], the queen said: "I am an old woman—I have already forgotten."

When the queen died, Hou Sheng became prime minister of Qi. He received much gold and jewelry from Qin; he sent his clients to Qin, where they all made treacherous speeches. He urged the king [of Qi] to yield to Qin and did not tend to preparations for war.

King Huai of Chu Arrested Zhang Yi

King Huai of Chu [r. 328–296 B.C.E.] arrested Zhang Yi and was about to put him to death. Jin Shang addressed the king of Chu on

---

[7] That is to say, he declared himself a pretender to the throne.

[8] Another historiographical absurdity: "Xiang" was also a posthumous name.

[9] King Jian reigned from 264 until 221 B.C.E., when he submitted to the first emperor of Qin.

behalf of Zhang Yi, saying: "If you keep Zhang Yi under arrest, the king of Qin will surely be enraged. When the world sees that Chu does not have [the support of] Qin, Chu will be surely taken lightly." He also addressed the king's main consort, Zheng Xiu, saying: "Indeed you know that you will soon be considered base by the king."

Zheng Xiu said: "Why?"

[Jin] Shang said: "Zhang Yi is a loyal, trusted, and meritorious minister of the king of Qin. Now that Chu has arrested him, the king of Qin wishes to have him set free. The king of Qin has a daughter who is lovely and fair; he has also decided to select [women] in his palace who are beautiful, playful, and skilled at music, and send them along to amuse [his daughter]. He will supply his daughter with gold, jade, and precious objects, and will grant her the six districts of Shangyong to serve as cities for her baths. His desire will be to rely on Zhang Yi to have her accepted into the king of Chu's harem.[10] The king of Chu will certainly fall in love with her. The lady from Qin will be considered important because of the might of Qin, and valuable because she bears treasures and territories. She will use her power as the king's wife to overawe the state of Chu. The king, besotted with entertainment and music, will surely honor and cherish his concubine richly; he will love her and forget about you. You will become ever baser and more distant [from him]."

Zheng Xiu said: "I shall entrust [this matter] to you, sir. What can be done?"

"Why not speak to the king urgently that he let Zhang Yi go free? When Master Zhang has attained his freedom, he will be kind to you to the end of time; the daughter of [the king of] Qin will not arrive, and Qin will surely value you. Within, you will monopolize the esteem of [the king of] Chu; without, you will be the knot binding relations with Qin. If you bridle[11] Master Zhang for your own uses, your sons and grandsons will surely be crown princes of Chu. This is no commoner's profit!"

Accordingly, Zheng Xiu persuaded the king of Chu to set Zhang Yi free.

---

[10] That is to say, he will rely on Zhang Yi to persuade the king of Chu to accept his daughter—along with her ladies-in-waiting—as a consort.

[11] Literally, "domesticate."

The King of Wei Sent a
Beautiful Woman to the King of Chu

The king of Wei sent a beautiful woman to the king of Chu; the king of Chu was pleased by her. His wife, Zheng Xiu, knew that the king was pleased by the new woman, and that he was very kind to her. Whatever clothing or baubles [the new woman] liked, [Zheng Xiu] gave her; whatever rooms and bed-furnishings she liked, [Zheng Xiu] gave her. She was kinder to her than the king was.

The king said: "A wife serves her husband with sex, but jealousy is her essence. Now you, Zheng Xiu, know that I am pleased by the new woman, and you are kinder to her than I am. This is how a filial son would serve his parents, how a loyal minister would serve his lord."

Relying on her knowledge that the king did not consider her jealous, Zheng Xiu addressed the new woman, saying: "The king loves your beauty! Though this is so, he dislikes your nose. When you see the king, you must cover your nose." So the new woman would cover her nose whenever she went to see the king.

The king addressed Zheng Xiu, saying: "Why does the new woman cover her nose when she sees me?"

Zheng Xiu said: "I, your concubine, know why."

The king said: "You must say it even if it is horrible."

Zheng Xiu said: "It seems she hates to smell your odor."[12]

The king said: "Shrew!" He ordered her nose cut off, and would not allow anyone to disobey the command.

King Kaolie of Chu Had No Sons

King Kaolie of Chu [r. 262–238 B.C.E.] had no sons. Lord Chunshen [d. 238 B.C.E.] was worried about this, so he sought out women who might bear children and presented a great multitude of them [to the king], but the king still had no son. A man of Zhao, Li Yuan, brought his younger sister to present her to the king of Chu, but when he heard that the [the king] could not father children, he feared that she would remain unfavored forever. Li Yuan sought employment with

---

[12] A commentator opines here that the king must have suffered from some illness that produced a foul odor.

Lord Chunshen as a retainer, and [immediately] asked for a leave of absence to return home. He deliberately overstayed his leave, and when he had finally come back to his employer, he was interrogated by Lord Chunshen about the situation.

[Li Yuan] replied: "The king of Qi sent an ambassador to request your servant's younger sister; because I was drinking with his ambassador, I overstayed my leave."

Lord Chunshen asked: "Has the bride-price been received?"

[Li Yuan] replied: "Not yet."

Lord Chunshen asked: "Could I see her?"

"Yes."

Thus Li Yuan presented his younger sister [to Lord Chunshen], and as soon as she was favored by him, she knew she was with child. [Li] Yuan then plotted with his younger sister.

Yuan's younger sister availed herself of an opportunity to persuade Lord Chunshen, saying: "The king of Chu esteems and favors you, my Lord, even more greatly than he does his brothers. Now, my Lord, you have been prime minister to the king for more than twenty years, and the king has no son. When he comes to the end of his life span, he will be succeeded by a brother. As the kings of Chu succeed to the throne, each will esteem those with whom he was once intimate. So, my Lord, how can you remain favored forever?

"Not only that, but you have been in charge of affairs for a long time and have often been impolite to the king's brothers; indeed, when his brothers come to the throne, disaster will reach you. How will you protect your ministerial seals and fief of Jiangdong? Now I, your concubine, know that I am with child, but no one else knows. Your concubine has not been favored very long; indeed, if you use your important [position] and present me to the king of Chu, the king will surely favor me. I shall rely on Heaven to make [my child] a boy. Thus your son will be king, and all the fiefs in Chu will be attainable; is this not better than to risk unfathomable punishments?"

Lord Chunshen fully agreed, so he moved Yuan's younger sister out of his [apartments], settled her cautiously in her own residence, and spoke of her to the king. The king of Chu took her in and favored her. Then she gave birth to a boy, who was raised as crown prince; Li Yuan's younger sister was raised to the rank of queen. The king of Chu esteemed Li Yuan, and Li Yuan was put in charge of affairs. Once he had installed his younger sister as queen and her son as crown prince, Li Yuan was afraid that Lord Chunshen would speak of the matter and grow more arrogant. He secretly supported thugs who would be willing to die for him, and wished to kill Lord Chunshen in order to do away with his mouth;[13] there were quite a few people in the city who knew of this.

When Lord Chunshen had been prime minister of Chu for twenty-five years, King Kaolie fell ill. A certain Zhu Ying addressed Lord Chunshen, saying: "In the world, there is unpredictable fortune and unpredictable disaster. My Lord, you live in an unpredictable generation and serve an unpredictable ruler; how can it be that you do not have an unpredictable person [on your side]?"

Lord Chunshen said: "What do you mean by unpredictable fortune?"

"My Lord, you have been prime minister of Chu for twenty-five years, and although your title is prime minister, in fact you are the king. Five of your sons are prime ministers among other feudal lords. Now the king is seriously ill and will die any morning or evening. The crown prince is young and weakly; when [the king] becomes so sick that he cannot stand up, my Lord, you will be the prime minister of an underage ruler. Thus you should succeed as regent, like Yi Yin and the duke of Zhou,[14] and return the government when the king reaches his majority. Or else you could face south,[15] call yourself the Orphan [i.e., the king], and possess the state of Chu. This is what I meant by unpredictable fortune."

Lord Chunshen said: "What do you mean by unpredictable disaster?"

"Li Yuan does not govern the state, but will be the uncle of the king; he is not a general of war, but has long been secretly supporting thugs who would die for him. When the king of Chu dies, Li Yuan will surely be the first to enter [the palace]; he will seize power, issue edicts, and determine your destiny, my Lord. He will wield authority and kill you in order to do away with your mouth. This is what I meant by unpredictable disaster."

Lord Chunshen said: "What do you mean by an unpredictable person?"

"My Lord, first make me an attendant in the palace. When the king dies, and Li Yuan is the first to enter [the palace], I beg permission to stab him in the breast and kill him for you. This is what I meant by an unpredictable person."

---

[13] "To kill someone in order to do away with his mouth" (*sharen miekou*) is still a common saying in Chinese.

[14] Yi Yin and the duke of Zhou were ancient ministers who had acted as regents in times of crisis.

[15] Facing south is the traditional position of the king.

Lord Chunshen said: "Sirrah, leave this be; do not speak of it again. Li Yuan is a soft and weak man, and yet I was good to him; how could all this come to pass?" Zhu Ying was afraid, and left.

Seventeen days later, King Kaolie of Chu died, and, as expected, Li Yuan was the first to enter [the palace]. He positioned his thugs within the barbican. Lord Chunshen arrived afterwards, and when he was stopped at the barbican, Yuan's thugs ambushed and stabbed him. They cut off his head and threw it down at the foot of the barbican. Then they sent agents to extinguish Lord Chunshen's entire family.

Thus Li Yuan's younger sister was first favored by Lord Chunshen and became pregnant by him, and the son that she bore after having been given to the king was eventually raised to the throne as King You of Chu. That year was the ninth year of the first emperor of Qin [i.e., 238 B.C.E.]. Lao Ai also fomented disorder in Qin; when he was discovered, his clan was extinguished to the third degree of relation, and Lü Buwei was forced to resign. [*The last line is a pointed reference to similar skullduggery in the state of Qin. Lü Buwei, the prime minister of Qin, is said to have been the natural father of the future first emperor, as a result of an affair comparable to the one presented here. Lao Ai was the secret lover of the queen dowager of Qin; he was plotting to place his own son on the throne.*]

Zhang Yi Fled to Wei

Zhang Yi fled to Wei, and Wei was about to welcome him. Zhang Chou expostulated with the king, desiring that he not take in [Zhang Yi], but did not obtain the king's [assent]. Zhang Chou retired, and then expostulated with the king again, saying: "Your Majesty, have you heard how an aged handmaid serves her mistress? When her sons have grown up and her allure has faded, she values her family and nothing more. Now I, your servant, serve your Majesty as an aged handmaid serves her mistress." Thus the king of Wei did not take in Zhang Yi.

Sima Xi Had Thrice Been
Prime Minister of Zhongshan

Sima Xi had thrice been prime minister of Zhongshan, but Yin Jian hated him.[16] Tian Jian addressed Sima Xi, saying: "When the ambassador from Zhao comes to negotiate, could you not speak of Yin Jian's beauty? Zhao will surely request her. If our lord gives her away, there will be no one left in the harem who hates you. If our lord does not give her away, you should urge him to raise her to the position of official wife; Yin Jian's kindness to you will then be boundless."

As expected, [the ruse] caused Zhao to request [Yin Jian]; the lord [of Zhongshan] did not give her away. Sima Xi said: "Lord, since you did not give her to Zhao, the king of Zhao is greatly enraged, and since he is greatly enraged, you are surely in danger. But if you raise her to the position of official wife—one cannot request someone else's wife and be enraged if one does not obtain her."

Tian Jian, through this affair, was able to act on behalf of Sima Xi, was able to act on behalf of Yin Jian, and was able to cause Zhao not to request her.

---

[16] Yin Jian was the favorite concubine of the king of Zhongshan, a tiny state in the north.

22

BIOGRAPHIES OF WOMEN

(Lienüzhuan)

列女傳

Liu Xiang

劉向

The Biographies of Women (Lienüzhuan) was compiled by the famous Confucian scholar Liu Xiang (79–8 B.C.E.) and is primarily composed of selections from earlier texts such as the Zuozhuan and the Guoyü. The work is the first extant book in China devoted solely to the subject of women. It consists of 125 biographies on virtuous and vicious women divided into seven categories: matronly deportment, sagacious clarity, benevolent wisdom, chaste obedience, pure righteousness, rhetorical competence, and depraved favoritism. This book was likely intended for the emperor, as a warning against employing vicious women, and for women, as a means to cultivate their virtues. The following selections present stories depicting women at various stages in their lives, as daughters, wives, and mothers.

Pauline C. Lee

Translated by Pauline C. Lee.

Chapter One
Biographies on the Deportment of Mothers

Number 11: The Mother of Meng Ke, of Zou[1]

The mother of Meng Ke of Zou[2] was known as Mother Meng. She lived near a cemetery when Mengzi was young. There, he played at imitating the tasks performed in a cemetery. With great enthusiasm, he built tombs and performed burials. Meng's mother said, "This is not the place for me to reside and bring up my son." Thereupon she departed and took up residence beside a marketplace. Mengzi pretended to perform the job of a peddler pushing goods. Meng's mother again said, "This is not the place for me to reside and bring up my son." Again they moved and lived next to a school. Mengzi then played by setting up sacrificial utensils, and performing the rituals of a guest bowing, giving way, entering, and departing. Meng's mother said, "Truly I can reside with my son here." And so they lived there.

When Mengzi had matured, he studied the six arts.[3] By the time of his death he had attained the fame of a great scholar. The gentleman[4] says, "Meng's mother possessed the gift for slowly transforming people." In The Book of Odes it says,

That admirable person,
What was he given?[5]

This saying describes this situation.

When Mengzi was young, one day he returned home as soon as he arrived at school. Meng's mother was spinning thread and asked, "How have your studies progressed?" Mengzi responded, "The same as before." Meng's mother took a knife and cut her weaving. Mengzi was

---

[1] For another translation of this story, see Albert Richard O'Hara's The Position of Woman in Early China (Washington, D.C.: The Catholic University of America Press, 1946), pp. 39–42.

[2] The famous Confucian lived from 391–308 B.C.E. For a selection of Mengzi's own comments on women, see the selections in "Mencius (Mengzi)," pp. 102–108.

[3] The six arts are those of propriety, music, archery, charioteering, writing, and mathematics.

[4] The voice of the "gentleman" is employed throughout the Biographies of Women as a mode for evaluating the vices and virtues of the characters.

[5] See The Book of Odes, part 1, book 4, ode 9, verse 2. For a selection of the odes that are particularly rich in images of Chinese women's lives and loves, see pp. 5–24.

frightened and asked her the reason for doing this. Meng's mother said, "My son has given up on his studies, much as I have cut this weaving. A gentleman studies in order to establish a name for himself. He inquires and so attains extensive knowledge. Because of his knowledge, in repose he is free from worry and when he takes action, he is able to avoid harm. Now that you are neglecting your studies, you will not be able to avoid working as a servant, and you will not be able to avoid disaster and misfortunes. In what way does what you are doing differ from spinning thread and weaving in order to provide food? If in mid-course one abandons one's work, how will one be able to clothe one's husband and continuously provide food? A woman who neglects the work that provides food is like a man who falls short in cultivating his virtue. If he does not become a thief, then he will become a servant!"

Mengzi became frightened. Morning and night he diligently studied without stopping. He took Zisi as his teacher.[6] Consequently he became known throughout the world as the famous scholar. The gentleman says, "Mother Meng knew the way of being a person's mother." *The Book of Odes* says,

That admirable person,
What was he told?[7]

This saying describes this situation.

After Mengzi had married, one day as he was about to enter the private chambers, he saw his wife half dressed in her room. Mengzi was displeased and left without entering. His wife went to bid farewell to Meng's mother and asked permission to leave saying, "I have heard that the relationship between a husband and wife does not include the sharing of their private chambers. Now, in a moment of laziness, I was in my room, half dressed and the master saw me. All at once he was displeased. This is treating me as a guest. The proper conduct of a wife does not permit her to stay as a guest overnight. I ask that I may return to my mother and father's."

Thereupon Meng's mother summoned Mengzi and said to him, "According to decorum, when one is about to enter through a door, ask who is there. In this way one practices proper respectfulness. When one is about to enter a hallway, you should raise your voice in order to warn others that you are coming. When you are about to enter a room, your gaze should be fixed downwards, as you fear seeing

---

[6] According to tradition, Zisi, the grandson of Confucius, was Mengzi's teacher.

[7] See *The Book of Odes*, part I, book 4, ode 9, verse 3.

Figure 4. Holding the cutter, the mother of Mengzi gives her unruly son an
becomes a Confucian sage. [From *Chou's Illustrations of the Biographies of Woman*

important lesson in life. Through her constant efforts, Mengzi eventually
(Chou Hua Lienü Zhuan) by Chou Ying (1509–1552).]

other's shortcomings. Now you have not examined your own practice of decorum, but instead censor the decorum of others. Are you not indeed far from practicing proper decorum?"

Mengzi confessed his faults, and then asked his wife to stay. The gentleman says, "Mother Meng understood proper decorum, and was insightful about the way of the mother-in-law."

Mengzi was residing in the state of Qi and had an air of sadness about him. Mother Meng saw him and said, "You seem to have an air of sadness about you. Why is that?" Mengzi said, "That is not the case." On a different day he was at leisure, leaning against a pillar, and sighed. Mother Meng saw him and said, "Earlier, I saw you had a look of sadness. You said 'That is not the case.' Now you are leaning against a pillar and sighing. Why is this?" Mengzi responded, "I have heard that a gentleman first cultivates himself, and then takes up an official position. He does not employ illicit means in order to receive rewards. He is not greedy for honors and emoluments. If the feudal lords do not listen to his words, he does not try to gain access to their superior. If they listen but do not implement his ideas, the gentleman does not set foot in their court. Now the Way is not practiced in Qi. I desire to leave but my mother is elderly. Because of this I am sad."

Meng's mother said, "The proper conduct of a woman is to prepare the five grains for food, ferment the wine, care for one's mother- and father-in-law, mend clothes, and that is all. Therefore, a woman is cultivated to care for affairs within the home, but does not have the ambition to care for affairs outside. *The Classic of Changes* says,

At home she provides sustenance,
She cannot be careless in her duties.[8]

The Book of Odes says,

No condemnation, no disputation,
Only thoughts are of wine and food.[9]

"That is to say, a woman should not determine affairs for herself but instead, should be guided by the three followings: When young, she follows her father and mother; when she enters into marriage, she follows her husband; when her husband passes away, she follows her son. This is proper decorum. Now my son has grown into a man, and

---

[8] For more selections from *The Classic of Changes* (*Yijing*), see pp. 25–45.

[9] See *The Book of Odes*, part 2, book 4, ode 6, verse 9. Also, see Arthur Waley, *The Book of Songs* (New York: Grove Press, 1960), p. 284.

I am elderly. My son should follow his duty. I shall follow my decorum."

The gentleman says, "Mother Meng understood the Way of a woman."

The Book of Odes says,

Looking pleasant and smiling,
Never impatient in her teaching.[10]

This saying describes this situation.

The eulogy says, "Mengzi's mother taught and transformed step by step. In finding a place for them to live, she considered the abilities he would be able to cultivate. And so, he cultivated an understanding of the human relations. When her son's studies did not progress, she cut the web of her loom in order to chastise him. Her son then fully developed his virtues, and became the most honored of his time."

Chapter Six
Biographies of Those Adept at Disputation

Number 15: The Woman of Taichang of the State of Qi[11]

The woman of Taichang of the state of Qi was the youngest daughter of Duke Shunyu, the magistrate of Taichang during the Han period. Her name was Tirong. Duke Shunyu had no sons, but he did have five daughters. During the period of the Emperor Han Wudi,[12] Duke Shunyu was guilty of committing a crime and had been sentenced to punishment. During this period, corporal punishment still existed, and the order was given to imprison the duke in Changan. As he was about to be seized, the duke cursed his daughters and said, "I have fathered children but have not fathered sons; in times of danger this is of no benefit."

Tirong sadly sobbed and followed her father to Changan. She submitted a letter to the emperor saying, "My father served as an offi-

---

[10] See *The Book of Odes*, part 2, book 4, ode 3, verse 2. For alternative English translations of these lines, see note 9, Waley, p. 267.

[11] For an alternative English translation of this story, see note 1, pp. 183–185.

[12] Han Wudi, also known as Xiao Wendi, was the eighth ruler of the Han period and ruled from 140–85 B.C.E.

cial. In the state of Qi, all called him honest and fair. Now he has
been tried by the laws of the land and sentenced to punishment. I
grieve that those who are dead cannot again be born. Those who are
punished cannot once again be rejoined with society. Although they
desire to change their wayward ways and start anew, there is no path
for them to do so. I desire to offer myself to be a palace servant in
order to redeem my father's crime and enable him to start anew." The
letter was presented to the emperor who sympathized with her views
and issued an imperial edict reading, "Now, I have heard that in the
time of Yu,[13] criminals were made to wear painted clothes and hats
and with strange insignia upon them. And so people did not commit
crimes. How did Yu arrive at such a perfect system of government?
These days we have five types of corporal punishments, and yet vil-
lainous behavior does not stop. Where rests the problem? Is it that
my kingly virtue is slight and my teachings are not clear? I am deeply
ashamed that the way is not well taught, and so the common people
have fallen into ruin. *The Book of Odes* says,

> A kindly gentleman
> Is a mother and father to the people.[14]

"These days, if someone has done wrong, punishments are already
piled on them before they are taught what is right and wrong. Some
people wish to correct their conduct and become virtuous, but they
lack a starting point. I deeply pity these people. When punishments
reach the extreme of cutting off one's limbs and tattooing one's skin,
for the rest of their lives they cannot redeem themselves. How cruel
and unvirtuous are such punishments! How can it be said that I am
father and mother of the people? Corporal punishment should be
abolished!"

From this time thereafter, those who would have had a hole
bored into their heads instead had their heads shaved. Those who
would have had the flesh pulled from their ribs instead were caned.
Those who would have had their feet cut off were instead manacled.
Duke Shunyu was then released from the sentence of corporal
punishment.

A gentleman says, "In one breath Tirong expressed the sage Kings'

---

[13] Yu, most commonly known as Shun, was a legendary ruler said to be infinitely benevolent and wise. He is traditionally believed to have ruled from 2255–2205 B.C.E.

[14] See *The Book of Odes*, part 3, book 2, ode 7, verse I. For an alternative English translation of the poem, see note 9, Waley, p. 182.

ideas. One can say that she achieved what was suitable for the situation."

The Book of Odes says,

If your words are pleasing,
The people will become peaceful.[15]

This saying describes this situation.

The eulogy says, "Tirong pleaded for justice on behalf of her father, and in this task she expressed great knowledge. In her letter submitted to the emperor she further elaborated truths that were known. The literary style of her letter was perfect. This young girl's words thus echoed the thoughts of sages. In the end corporal punishment was abolished, and in this way Tirong's father's affair was excused."

Chapter Six
Biographies of Those Adept at Disputation

Number 10: Zhongli Chun of Qi[16]

Zhongli Chun was a woman from the city of Wuyan in the state of Qi, and came to be King Xuan's[17] chief consort. She was a person without peer for her remarkable ugliness. She had a massive forehead and deeply sunken eyes, long fingers with large joints, a turned up nose, and a throat that sounded like it was made of knots. The nape of her neck was thick; she had little hair; she was bent at the waist and her bosom protruded; and her skin was like varnish. She was forty years old and at that time was not accepted in any position. She was unable to persuade anybody to take her hand in marriage; she wandered about on her own.

And so, she brushed and cleaned her short course clothing, and traveled by herself to see King Xuan. She told the palace receiver, "I, humbly, am the woman from Qi who cannot sell her hand in marriage. I have heard about the sovereign's sagely virtue. I wish to serve as a sweeper in the women's chambers of the palace. I will go *kowtow*

---

[15] See *The Book of Odes*, part 3, book 2, ode 10, verse 2.

[16] For a published translation of this story, see note I, pp. 171–174.

[17] King Xuan ruled in the state of Qi from 342–324 B.C.E.

outside of the palace's outer gate. Hopefully the King will grant me my desire."

The palace receiver passed on what he had heard. At that time King Xuan was throwing a feast on his Jian Terrace. Those around him heard this news and all covered their mouths and loudly laughed saying, "This shameless woman. She must be extraordinary!" Thereupon King Xuan summoned to see her and said, "In the past, the former Kings selected mates for me. All the positions have already been filled and there is a waiting list. Today you, woman, have not been selected for marriage by a common man in the countryside, and yet you desire to seek marriage with the King. What remarkable abilities do you have?"

Zhongli Chun responded, "I have none. I simply admire the great King's beautiful righteousness, and that is all!" The King said, "That is fine. But what are your strengths?" After a long period of time she said, "In the past I was good at making up riddles." King Xuan said, "Riddles are certainly something I desire to hear. Give me an example." Before she had finished speaking, everyone was utterly lost. King Xuan was greatly surprised and immediately consulted the *Book of Riddles*. He retreated and pondered the text and yet was not able to understand what he had heard.

The next day, he once again summoned the woman to come in order to question her. She did not respond by using her skills at making up riddles. She only raised her eyes, gritted her teeth, raised her hands, slapped her knees, and said, "Danger! Danger!" She did this four times. King Xuan said, "I desire fully to listen to what you are saying." Zhongli Chun responded, "Now the great King is ruling the country, but in the west, you must worry about the ruthless state of Qin. In the south is the enemy of the strong state of Chu. Abroad you have the difficulty of these two states. Inside one's state there are cliques of deceptive ministers, and the common people cannot rely on them. Although forty springs and autumns have passed under your rule, you have not chosen a primary heir. You do not focus on your multitude of sons, but rather on your multitude of wives. You respect what you are fond of, and overlook what you rely on. One day the King will pass away and the state will be unsettled. This is the first danger. Your Jian Terrace is constructed of five layers, each made of yellow gold and white and red jade as lattice work, with strings of emeralds and oval and precious pearls as decoration. The common people are made utterly weary. This is the second danger. Those who are talented hide in the mountains and forests while flatterers fight to be at your side. The wicked and the fakes have established themselves at the very foundation of your court. Those who admonish you cannot gain admittance to see you. This is the third danger. You imbibe wine and are steeped in drunkenness from dusk to dawn. Female musicians and theatrical performers are laughing all day. You have not established the rituals to be observed by nobles visiting from foreign states. Inside the state, you have not maintained the government. This is the fourth danger. Therefore I said, "Danger! Danger!" Thereupon King Xuan sighed, and sighing said, "Alas, it is only now that I hear the words of the Lady of Wuyan!"

Thereupon, the King ordered the dismantling of the Jian Terrace, stopped the performances of the female musicians, dismissed the flatterers, and sent away the artisans who carved and polished. He selected soldiers, fortified the state treasury, strengthened the borders of the state, and recruited those who spoke straightforwardly, extending his search to those of the humblest means. The court diviner selected an auspicious day whereupon the King established the heir apparent. He honored the mother of the heir and saluted the Lady of Wuyan as his empress. And so, the state of Qi's great peace was due to the power of an ugly woman.

The gentleman says, "Zhongli Chun was upright and eloquent." *The Book of Odes* says, "Since I have met a gentile person, my heart has been happy."[18] This could be said to refer to the Lady of Wuyan.

The eulogy says, "The woman from Wuyan sought to persuade King Xuan. She distinguished between four dangers and called the state chaotic and weary. King Xuan followed her advice. He strengthened the borders of the country, then established an heir apparent, and honored the Lady Wuyan."

Chapter Seven
Biographies of the Pernicious and Depraved

Number 3: Baosi of King You of Zhou[19]

Baosi was the daughter of a child concubine, and the chief consort of King You of Zhou.[20] When the Xia dynasty began to decline, the

---

[18] See *The Book of Odes*, part 2, book 3, ode 2, verse 3. For an alternative translation of this poem, see note 9, Waley, p. 105.

[19] For a published translation of this story, see note 1, pp. 189–192. For an earlier version of the story of Baosi, see the selections from the *Guoyu*, pp. 83–91.

[20] King You of Zhou is said to have ruled from 781–771 B.C.E.

spirits of two former rulers from the state of Bao were transformed
into two dragons. The two dragons met before the King's court and
said, "We are two lords of the state of Bao." The King of Xia sought
by divination whether to kill them or to chase them out of the
country. Neither option was deemed auspicious. The King inquired
whether it was auspicious to collect the dragons' spittle, and then to
hide it. This was deemed auspicious. When the King wrapped the
spittle in silk cloth, the dragons suddenly disappeared. The King then
hid the spittle in a case and placed it in a far away place. Up until the
Zhou period, nobody dared unveil the spittle. By the end of King Li
of Zhou's reign, the spittle was unveiled and examined. It flowed into
the court and could not be chased out. The King ordered the women
to disrobe themselves and make great noises to scare it off. The spittle
transformed into black turtles and entered the women's chambers.
One of the palace's child concubines, who had not yet cut her teeth,
encountered the two black turtles. By the time she became of marriageable age she was found pregnant. During the reign of King Xuan,
she gave birth to a fatherless child and nursed it. Soon she became
fearful and abandoned the child.

   In former times there existed a children's rhyme that went,

   A bow of mulberry wood and a basket quiver rounded like a
      basket
   These will be the end of the state of Zhou.

   King Xuan heard this rhyme and later on when a husband and wife
were found to be selling the bows of mulberry wood and basket
quivers, the King sent somebody to capture and kill them. The
husband and wife fled, running all night. They heard the howl of the
child concubine's abandoned baby girl. They pitied her, picked her up,
and fled to Bao. She grew up to be truly beautiful. When Xu of Bao[21]
was found to have committed a crime, he offered the abandoned child
in exchange for his redemption. King You accepted the child and
treated her as his favorite concubine. The King then released Bao's
prince, Xu. Therefore the castaway child was called Baosi.[22]

   After Baosi gave birth to a son named Bofu, King You dismissed
as empress the daughter of the Marquis Shen, and established Baosi
as the empress. He dismissed the heir-apparent Yijou and in his place
established Bofu. King You was dazed by Baosi. When he went out,

---

[21] Xu was at one time the prince of Bao.
[22] The suffix -si means elder sister, or the wife of a husband's elder brother.

he would ride in the same carriage as Baosi. He did not sympathize with the state's affairs. He often rode horses wildly and hunted out of season just to satisfy Baosi's desires. Together they would drink wine until flushed with drunkenness and watch singing girls perform from evening until the morning. Still, Baosi would not smile. King You simply desired that she smile. He tried ten thousand methods but still she would not smile. King You set afire the torches that were mounted upon large drums, the ones that were set afire when bandits were invading. Responding to this signal, the feudal lords all arrived to discover that there were no bandits. Baosi then laughed heartily. King You so desired to please Baosi that he lit the torches many times for her. After many incidents, the feudal lords did not trust the signal and no longer came when the torches were lit. Those who were loyal and pleaded with the king were executed. He only listened to the words of Baosi. Those above and below flattered him, and the common people left the state.

Marquis Shen then joined the state of Ceng and the barbarians from the western tribe of Quan Jong. Together they attacked King You. King You lit the torches to call his soldiers. Nobody came. After slaying King You at the foot of Li Mountain, they took Baosi as captive, plundered all of the treasures of Zhou, and departed. Thereupon the feudal lords turned to Marquis Shen and together reestablished Yijou as the heir apparent. Later he became King Ping. From this time on, the court of Zhou and the feudal lords were never at odds. In *The Book of Odes* it says,

> The Zhou was gloriously revered.
> Baosi destroyed it.[23]

This can be said to refer to Baosi.

The eulogy says, "The spirits of the former rulers of Bao transformed into dragons and gave birth to Baosi. When she grew up she became the mate of King You, who dismissed the empress and the heir apparent. He lit the torches and the soldiers arrived. Baosi laughed that no bandits had actually arrived. Marquis Shen attacked Zhou and truly destroyed its alters."

---

[23] See *The Book of Odes*, part 2, book 4, ode 8, verse 8.

23

LUXURIANT GEMS OF THE SPRING AND AUTUMN

(Chunqiu fanlu)

春秋繁露

Dong Zhongshu

董仲舒

In his time, Dong Zhongshu (c.195–115 B.C.E.) was most famous for his inter-pretation and transmission of the Gongyang commentary to the Chunqiu (The Spring and Autumn Annals) *attributed to Gongyang Gao (fl. c. 150 B.C.E.). Dong was the teacher of Humu Sheng who in turn taught the major Han exegetes, such as Gongsun Hong, about the Gongyang commentary. Dong's writings on these topics are contained in the Qing reconstruction called the* Chunqiu jueshi (Spring and Autumn Adjudications), *and some chapters of the composite* Chunqiu fanlu (Luxuriant Gems of the Spring and Autumn).*

Today, however, Dong is perhaps better known for the detailed development of what A. C. Graham called the "correlative cosmology" in the Chunqiu fanlu, *and for a set of memorials included in a biographical chapter contained in the* Hanshu (History of the Han). *He is also credited with making the "Five Classics" canonical, owing to his role in advising the emperor to issue a 136 B.C.E. edict making them the official curriculum for the imperial advisors, the Erudites (boshi), and for examinations at the Imperial Academy.*

Dong's views about women and men are most clearly articulated in the 123 chap-ters of the Chunqiu fanlu. *A primary focus of this text is the development of a detailed homology between Heaven and human beings, which divides the universe into several nested schemata——yin and yang, the four seasons, and the five elements being the most important. Zhou Guitian singles Dong out as the primary exponent of the doctrine that "Heaven and human beings resonate with one another" (tianren*

Translated by Mark Csikszentmihalyi.

ganying).[1] *As such, the* Chunqiu fanlu *is the locus classicus for the elaborate cosmology that developed along with a theory of portents and became extremely influential during the Han. Dong also became a focus of the condemnation of those later imperial and modern scholars who saw Han Confucianism as descending into "superstition" from its former levels of excellence.*

Dong believed that the natural and proper relationship between yin and yang is continually revealed to human beings through the behaviors and relationships between objects in the natural world. In the selections collected here, yin and yang are likened to the sun and moon (33) and Heaven and Earth. In turn, "the model of man and woman takes as its prototype yin and yang" (76). For Dong, yin and yang are neither equal and complementary, nor opposite and of radically different value. At times, yin is associated with what is clearly the negative pole of a contrast: the greedy part of human nature, as opposed to the benevolent yang side (35). In the same vein, it is the threat of yin overwhelming yang that is the subject of more discussion in the text. In this sense, it is clear that yang is more generally associated with positive characteristics. At the same time, yin and yang are associated with oppositions in which both parts are necessary. This is most clearly the case in nature: Heaven takes yin as the exception, and yang as the norm (43). Heaven also exhudes both yang qi and yin qi: "joyful qi is what nourishes life, and sad qi is for mourning death" (44). As a result, although yang receives precedence, the model of the natural world clearly dictates that both yang and yin have their own proper place and function.

This relationship of both hierarchy and interdependence between yang and yin is the explicit normative model for the relationship between husband and wife: "Yin is connected with yang as yang is connected with yin; a husband is connected with a wife as a wife is connected with a husband" (53). What this means is that although society needs the achievements that yang is responsible for, yang requires the presence of yin, so in a real sense any achievement is a result of the interdependence between the two: "At its beginning, neither is able to arise on its own, nor at its end is it able to achieve something separate, which is the meaning of having something to which it is connected" (53).

Dong's influence on later Han scholars was significant. According to the "Wuxing zhi" (Treatise on the Five Phases) in the Hanshu, *Dong Zhongshu placed yin/yang theory at the heart of Han Confucianism. In particular, the role of dependency or interconnectedness on the part of the three subordinate relations of subject, son, and wife, as well as the idea that this role was incipient in the patterns of Heaven, were influential for later writers who sought to structure claims to authority on natural patterns. Earlier writers had explored the natural categories of yin and*

---

[1] Zhou Guitian, *QinHan sixiang shi.* (Shijiazhuang: Hebei renmin, 1999), pp. 152–166.

yang, *but their systematic application to Confucian hierarchies is new in the work of Dong Zhongshu.*

                                              Mark Csikszentmihalyi

Thirty-Three

The heavens and the earth are the basis of the myriad beings, and also the source of the Great Ancestor. Large without measure, their virtue brilliant, they have existed for years upon years, forever and ever without limit.

The heavens produce the brightest light, so that the masses may understand their variety, so that everything that was hidden becomes apparent.

The earth produces the darkest obscurity, but when the stars and sun create light, it does not conceal things. The ways of ruler and subject, father and son, husband and wife, all derive from this.

Thirty-Four

Li (ritual) is what carries on the heavens and the earth, embodies *yin* and *yang*, and forms the careful attitude between the self and others. It orders the respected and despised, noble and base, high and low office, and sorts out their respective degrees of exterior and interior, distant and near, new and old, taking abundant virtue as its model.

Thirty-Five

As for the designations used for the body, they are taken from the heavens. The heavens send things down as either *yin* or *yang*, so the body has either a greedy or benevolent nature. The heavens have restrictions against either *yin* or *yang*; so too the body has restrictions against either desirous or covetous feelings and is consistent with the Way of the heavens.

This is the reason that *yin* actions cannot interfere in spring and summer, and that the dark portion of the moon cannot be seen in the brightness of the sun. Now whole, now injured—if the heavens restrict *yin* like this, how could the body fail to decrease desires and curb feelings so as to echo the heavens? What the heavens restrict, the body also restricts. That is why it is said that the body is like the heavens. Restricting the things that the heavens prohibit is not restricting the heavens.

It is necessary to understand that if the human nature one has inherited from the heavens is not uplifted through education, then in the end one will not be able to restrict things. The process of examining realities in order to make names—what basis did human nature have to do so in the age before education? That is why human nature may be compared to the rice plant and goodness may be compared to the rice kernel. The rice kernel comes out of the rice plant, but the rice plant may not be considered to be entirely the rice kernel. Goodness comes out of one's human nature, but nature may not be considered to be entirely constituted of goodness. Both goodness and the rice kernel are things that humans have inherited from the heavens and are completed through something that is external, rather than entirely being a matter internal to what the heavens have created. When heaven creates something, it stops when it reaches a certain point. Up to where it stops inside it is called heavenly nature, past where it stops outside it is called "human affairs." Affairs are external to nature, but if one's nature is not grasped then one cannot complete realize one's virtue.

The designation for "the people" (*min*) is taken from the term "asleep" (*mian*). If the nature of people is already good, then why is it that they are designated as being asleep? Without support, people will stumble and fall as if they were mad—so how could they be good? Human nature has something resembling eyes. When one lays down in the dark with the eyes closed, it is only when one awakens that one may see. When not yet awake, it is possible to say that one has the potential for seeing, but not yet possible to say that one can see. Now, the nature of the myriad people is that they have the potential but have not yet awakened, like a sleeper who has not yet awakened. It is only after educating the people that they will be good. When they have not yet awakened, they may be said to have the potential for goodness, but they cannot yet be called good. This idea may generally be compared to the eye when one is sleeping and then awake. One need only calm the mind and then carefully investigate into it, for the words to be understood. With one's nature still asleep and not yet awakened is how one is created by the heavens created. When a name was given to beings so created by the heavens, they were called "the people." The people are spoken of this way because they are as if "asleep." It is only once we have penetrated into the principle behind what they are called that we can grasp it.

Rectifying what things are called in this way with the heavens and the earth, what the heavens and earth give birth to may be called "human nature" and "feelings." The nature and feelings interact with each other and become one, and become one in being "asleep." Feelings are also a part of human nature, so to say that human nature is already good, what does this leave for feelings? Therefore the Sage never said human nature is good, and the reason was that he was troubled by these designations. The body's having a nature and feelings is like the heavens having *yin* and *yang*. Saying that a person has substance but no feelings is like saying that the heavens have *yang* and no *yin*——no matter how much one discussed it, it would never be accepted.

Forty-Three

This is the reason that the heavens take *yin* as the exception and *yang* as the norm. *Yang* emerges and flows south, while *yin* emerges and flows north. The norm is used when a thing is flourishing, while the exception is used when it is ending. Looking at things from this perspective, the heavens make norms obvious while hiding exceptions; virtue is first and only later comes punishment. This is why it is said:

> *Yang* is the virtue of the heavens, and *yin* is the punishment of the heavens.

Yang qi is warm while *yin qi* is cold; *yang qi* gives while *yin qi* takes away; *yang qi* is benevolent while *yin qi* is criminal; *yang qi* is lenient while *yin qi* is severe; *yang qi* is caring while *yin qi* is hateful; *yang qi* gives life while *yin qi* kills. That is why *yang qi* always dwells in meaningful positions and acts when a thing is flourishing, while *yin qi* dwells in empty positions and acts when a thing is ending.

Forty-Four

Now, when happiness, anger, sorrow, and joy come forth, they are really of a kind with coolness, warmth, cold, and heat. The *qi* of happiness belongs to warmth and matches spring; the *qi* of anger makes coolness and matches autumn; the *qi* of joy makes great *yang* and matches summer; the *qi* of sorrow makes great *yin* and matches winter. These four types of *qi* are something that both the heavens and human beings possess, and are not something that human beings can produce themselves. Therefore they can be regulated but cannot be stopped. If one regulates them then they will come in sequence, but if one stops them then they will be disordered. Human beings are born from the heavens and derive their changes from those of the heavens. The *qi* of happiness is taken from spring, the *qi* of joy is taken from summer, the *qi* of anger is taken from autumn, and the *qi* of sorrow is taken from winter. This is how the four types of *qi* enter the mind.

The four limbs each have their sphere of action, just like the four seasons. Hot and cold, like the limbs of the body, cannot be exchanged. To exchange the limbs and have them trade places, this is called "bringing on an early death." If cold and heat are exchanged and trade places, this is called a disastrous year. If happiness and anger are exchanged and trade places, this is called an age of chaos. The brilliant ruler governs with happiness in order to match the spring, governs with anger in order to match the autumn, governs with joy in order to match the summer, governs with sadness in order to match the winter. Those above and below model themselves on this in order to benefit from the Way of the heavens. The spring *qi* is caring, the autumn *qi* is severe, the summer *qi* is joyful, and the winter *qi* is sad. The fact that caring *qi* is what gives long life to creatures, severe *qi* is what allows accomplishment, joyful *qi* is what nourishes life, and sad *qi* is for mourning death, is all a matter of the intent of the heavens.

Therefore, in the spring the *qi* is warm, which is how the heavens care for and give birth to creatures. In the autumn the *qi* is cool, which is how the heavens are severe and bring things to completion. In the summer the *qi* is temperate, which is how the heavens are joyful and nourish them. In the winter the *qi* is cold, which is how the heavens are sad and store them. Spring signifies giving birth, summer signifies nurturing, autumn indicates collecting, and winter indicates storing. When alive, one takes pleasure in nourishing one's parents; when they have died one feels sadness at storing them away; this how to be a child. Therefore, it is the actions of the four seasons that form the Way of the parent and child; the intention of the heavens and the earth that make the obligations of the lord and ministers; the pattern of *yin* and *yang* that make the model of the sage.

Forty-Nine

What is constant about the heavens and the earth is that there is a
yin and then a *yang*. *Yang* is the heavens' virtue and *yin* is the heavens'
punishment.

Fifty-Three

In all cases, things necessarily are complementary. Complementary
means that there necessarily is a top and a bottom, a left and a right,
a front and a back, an exterior and an interior. If there is beauty there
must be ugliness; if there is agreement there must be opposition; if
there is happiness there must be anger; if there is cold then there must
be heat; if there is day then there must be night. They are all com-
plements. *Yin* is *yang*'s complement, a wife is a husband's complement,
a son is a father's complement, and a subject is a ruler's complement.
Everything in the world has a complement, and each instance of complementarity has *yin* and *yang*. *Yin* is connected with *yang* as *yang* is connected with *yin*; a husband is connected with a wife as a wife is
connected with a husband; a father is connected with a son as a son
is connected with a father; a ruler is connected with a subject as a
subject is connected with a ruler. The obligations of a ruler and
subject, father and son, husband and wife, all are taken from the Way
of *yin* and *yang*. The ruler is *yang* and the subject is *yin*; the father is
yang and the son is *yin*; the husband is *yang* and the wife is *yin*.

The Way of *yin* is devoid of anything that acts on its own. Neither
at its beginning is it able to arise on its own, nor at its end is it able
to achieve something separate——which is the meaning of being connected to something. This is why the minister's achievement is connected to the ruler, the son's achievement is connected to the father,
the wife's achievement is connected to the husband, and the earth's
achievement is connected to the heavens.

Fifty-Seven

When the heavens are about to let *yin* rains fall, human illnesses begin
to flare up ahead of these rains. This is because both have risen under
the mutual stimulus of *yin*. When the heavens are about to let *yin* rains

fall, it also causes people to want to go to sleep, which is also a matter of *yin qi*. When people are worried and so lie down, this is *yin* seeking them. When people are happy and so lie down, this is *yang* pursuing them.

Seventy

A father is a son's heavens, and the heavens are the father's heavens. There has never yet been a case of something being born independently of the heavens. The heavens are the ancestor of the myriad things, and if it were not for the heavens, the myriad creatures would not have been born. If they were only *yin* they would not have been born, and if they were only *yang* they would not have been born. *Yin* and *yang* interacted with the heavens and the earth, and only then were the myriad creatures born. Therefore it is said: "The son of the father should be respected, but the son of the mother should also be treated basely. Those that are respected take a respectful designation, whereas those that are base take a base designation."

Seventy-Six

The model of man and woman takes as its prototype *yin* and *yang*.

Seventy-Seven

The *yin* and *yang* of the heavens and the earth match with men and women, and human men and women match with *yin* and *yang*. *Yin* and *yang* also may be called man and woman, and man and woman may also be called *yin* and *yang*.

24

COMPREHENSIVE DISCUSSIONS IN THE WHITE TIGER HALL

(Baihu tong)

白虎通

Comprehensive Discussions in the White Tiger Hall (Baihu tong *or* Baihu tongyi) *is supposed to be the official transcript of an imperial conference on the Confucian classics convened in* 79 C.E. *The task of compiling this account of the conference is said to have fallen to Ban Gu (32–92* C.E.*), a leading scholar of the time and the main author of the* History of the Han. *The question of the authenticity of the received text has troubled scholars for centuries. The work is surprisingly sloppy, filled with erroneous quotations from the classics and dubious interpretations of canonical material. Some specialists also believe that the attitudes expressed in the* Comprehensive Discussions *are more characteristic of a later period— perhaps the third century—than the alleged date of* 79 C.E. *In view of its questionable pedigree and propensity for scholastic and ritualistic discourse, one might place the* Comprehensive Discussions in the White Tiger Hall *in the same category as* The Record of Rites (Liji), *another influential compendium that coalesced at the end of the Han dynasty (if not later) but pretends to be much older.*

The chapter of the Comprehensive Discussions *that deals most fully with the position of women is "Marriage," a long set of questions and answers about matrimonial ceremonies. Some of the explanations are fanciful and make use of cosmological and numerological principles that enclose the text within a particular doctrinal tradition. Only if one is prepared to follow certain elaborate operations involving even and odd numbers, for example, can one be impressed by the reasoning behind the injunction that men should be permitted to marry at thirty and women at twenty. Moreover, the ossified ritual precepts that dominate all aspects of social life seem to limit for both sexes the range of opportunities for personal development. In the world described in the* Comprehensive Discussions in the White Tiger Hall, *men and women occupy rigid and immutable places in the ritual system. All must learn*

Translated by Paul R. Goldin.

to conform to a set of universal regulations, and sometimes a great deal of casuistry is needed to make these prescriptions seem anything other than arbitrary and divorced from genuine experience.

Paul R. Goldin

Marriage [selections]

General Discussion of Marriage

Why is there marriage in the Way of humanity? It is because among the great natural urges, there are none as great as those between male and female. The intercourse between male and female is the beginning of human relations; there is nothing as [crucial] as [the bond between] husband and wife. It is said in the *Changes*:

> There is an intermingling of the genial influences of heaven and earth, and transformation in its various forms abundantly proceeds. There is an intercommunication of seed between male and female, and transformation in its living types proceeds.[1]

Man receives the task of Heaven and Earth in disseminating *yin* and *yang*; thus the ritual of marriage was established in order to emphasize human relations and broaden progeny. It is said in the "Record of the Protector and Tutor" in the *Rituals*:[2] "Be diligent in [arranging] marriages for your children; you must select a family that possesses humanity and righteousness."

Why is it that a male takes a woman in marriage and a female marries into a man's domicile? *Yin* is lowly, and thus cannot act on its own initiative; one brings it into contact with *yang* in order to perfect it. Thus the commentary says: "*Yang* takes the lead; *yin* acts in concert. The male acts; the female follows."[3]

---

[1] A quotation from "Appended Statements," an ancient commentary to *The Classic of Changes*. The translation is by James Legge. See more selections of *The Classic of Changes*, pp. 25–45.

[2] Currently found in *The Record of Rites of Dai the Elder* (*Da Dai Liji*).

[3] A quotation from an apocryphal commentary to the *The Classic of Changes*.

One Does Not Marry On One's Own Initiative

Why is it that males and females do not marry on their own initiative, but defer to their parents and wait for a go-between? This is to avoid shame and hinder licentiousness. It is said in the *Odes*: "How do we proceed in taking a wife? Announcement must first be made to our parents." It is also said: "How do we proceed in taking a wife? Without a go-between it cannot be done."[4]

The Time for Marriage

Why is it that males marry at the age of thirty and females at twenty? It is because *yang* numbers are odd and *yin* numbers are even. Why is it that the male should be older and the female younger? The Way of *yang* is slow; the Way of *yin* is fast. At the age of thirty, a male's sinews and bones are firm and strong; he can assume the responsibility of being a father. At twenty, a female's tissues and skin are engorged; she can assume the responsibility of being a mother. [Their ages] make fifty when combined; this corresponds to the number of Great Expansion, which engenders the myriad things.[5] Thus it is said in "The Pattern of the Family" in the *Rituals*:[6] "At thirty, a male becomes an adult and begins a household; at twenty, a female becomes an adult and is married."

Seven is the *yang* of the year; eight is the *yin* of the year. Seven and eight make fifteen, whereby *yin* and *yang* are fulfilled, and there is a desire to mate. Thus it is said in *The Record of Rites*: "At fifteen a female is permitted to marry; she receives her hairpin and her style-name."[7] The *Rituals* refer to the [hairpin and] style-name, as *yin* is bound to *yang*; hence the restriction that she be given exclusively to one man.[8] As *yang* is chief, there is nothing for it to be bound to. *Yang* is slow and *yin* is fast. Take ten three times: thirty is the fulfillment of being odd; it is the measure of *yang*. Take ten twice: twenty is the fulfillment

---

[4] Two quotations from Mao 101, "The Southern Mountain." The translations are by Legge.

[5] Numerology inspired by the *The Classic of Changes*.

[6] Currently found in *The Record of Rites* (*Liji*). The quotation is slightly inaccurate.

[7] Another slightly inaccurate quotation.

[8] An opaque passage in the original; the translation here represents a best guess. The point seems to be that the hairpin symbolizes the bond between male and female. The style-name (*zi*) is a name taken at the attainment of majority.

of being even; it is the measure of *yin*.[9] *Yang* attains Minor Perfection in *yin* and Major Perfection in *yang*; thus [a boy] is capped at twenty and married at thirty. *Yin* attains Minor Perfection in *yang* and Major Perfection in *yin*; thus [a girl] receives her hairpin at fifteen and is married at twenty.

According to another explanation, one is bound [to a woman] at twenty-five, because that is the node where [*yang*] comes into contact with *yin*.[10] It is said in the *Guliang Commentary to the Spring and Autumn Annals*: "At twenty-five, the hearts of males are bound. At fifteen, females are permitted to marry. They are stimulated by *yin* and *yang*."[11] The number of *yang* is seven, the number of *yin* eight. A male loses his milk-teeth at eight; a female loses her milk-teeth at seven.[12] *Yang* numbers are odd, so [the number] is tripled; thrice eight is twenty-four. Adding one makes twenty-five, and his heart is bound. *Yin* numbers are even, so [the number] is doubled; twice seven is fourteen. Adding one makes fifteen; thus, at fifteen, she is permitted to marry. One adds in each case because they have bound their hearts exclusively to one person.[13]

Why are their hearts bound? In order to hinder licentiousness. . . .

Sending Off One's Daughter and Admonishing Her

One sends off one's daughter at the ancestral temple in order to venerate the remains of one's forefathers. Not daring to act on one's own initiative, one announces [the impending marriage] to the ancestors.

Why do the father and mother personally admonish their daughter? It is the apex of treating one's family with intimacy.[14] The father says: "Let yourself be admonished by [your husband's family] and respect them; day and night, do not disobey their commands." The mother gives her a sash and kerchief, saying: "Be diligent and respect them; day and night, do not be disobedient in [carrying out] your

---

[9] More numerology based on the idea that *yang* is odd and *yin* even. Thirty is apparently considered "odd" for these purposes (even though it is obviously an even number), because it represents an odd number (three) taken ten times.

[10] That is, the midpoint between twenty and thirty.

[11] This quotation is not found in the *Guliang Commentary to the Spring and Autumn Annals*.

[12] Presumably the idea is that *yin* and *yang* complement each other; otherwise one would expect to read that the boy loses his teeth at the age of seven.

[13] Of course, this theory contradicts the earlier claim that *yang* is not bound because it is "chief"—and it also fails to explain why men are allowed to marry several concubines.

[14] Literally "treating with intimacy those with whom one ought to be intimate" (*qinqin*).

wifely duties." The father admonishes her by the eastern steps, the mother by the western steps. Her father's concubines accompany her to the edge of the gate; they give her a girdle and expound on her parents' commandments. They command her, saying: "Listen reverently to your parent's words; be without fault, day and night; remember your parents with this sash and girdle."[15]

When [the bride] leaves, she does not bid farewell or acknowledge these admonitions, because she is ashamed and is concerned with leaving. . . .

The Wife May Not Leave the Husband

Even if the husband's behavior is evil, the wife may not leave him, because there is no principle whereby Earth can leave Heaven. Even if the husband is evil, she cannot leave him. Thus it is said in "The Single Victim at the Border Sacrifices" in the *Rituals*: "Once mated with her husband, all her life she will not change [her feeling of duty to him]."[16]

Perverting human relations, killing the parents of one's wife, and abrogating the bonds [of kinship relations] are the greatest instances of disorder. Only when [a husband] violates [one of these] principles can [a wife] leave him.

The Son of Heaven Marries Nine Tribute-Brides
Along with the Main Bride[17]

Why is it that the Son of Heaven and the feudal lords marry nine women? It is in order to emphasize the state and broaden their progeny. Why are there nine tribute-brides? This is modeled after Earth, which has nine continents and receives Heaven's dissemination, so that there is nothing that fails to live. He marries nine women— they are indeed sufficient to receive his lordly dissemination. If he has no children with nine [wives], there would be no improvement with a hundred. It is said in the "Record of Royal Measures":[18] "The Son

---

[15] Much of this passage appears to be lifted from *Ceremonies and Rites* (*Yili*), one of the texts of the Confucian canon. The translation here relies on the commentary of Hu Peihui (1782–1849 C.E.) to that text. The phrase rendered as "Her father's concubines accompany her to the edge of the gate" is ambiguous and could also mean simply "her father's concubines and maids."

[16] Legge's translation.

[17] The Chinese term is *ying*, which denotes one or a group of women sent to the groom along with the main bride.

[18] A lost text.

of Heaven and the feudal lords marry nine women." It is said in the
Gongyang Commentary to the Spring and Autumn Annals: "If a feudal lord
marries [a woman] of one state, two other states send a tribute-bride,
along with [each tribute-bride's] niece and sister. What is meant by
'niece'? The child of one's older brother. What is meant by 'sister'?
One's younger sister."[19] Sometimes it is said that the Son of Heaven
marries twelve women; [this principle] is modeled after Heaven, which
has twelve months, during which the myriad creatures complete their
lives.

Why is it that he must marry but once?[20] It is to hinder licentiousness, the abandonment of virtue, and indulgence in sex. Thus he
marries no more than once. There is no principle whereby a lord of
men can marry a second time.

[The marriage] is fulfilled by [the bride's] niece and sister, in order
to prevent any mutual jealousy. If one of them has a child, all three
share it, as though they had borne it themselves.

Why does he not take two sisters? It is in order to broadcast different forms of *qi*.[21] Why does he marry women from three states? In
order to increase different kinds. One fears that the blood [of women]
of a single state may be similar, so they all may be without child.

Even if the niece and sister are young, they still follow the main
bride; this makes clear the principle that a lord of men cannot marry
a second time. They are returned in order to await their majority in
their parents' state, as they cannot yet assume the responsibility of
responding to the lord's [desires]. It is said in the *Odes*: "The virgins,
her companions, followed the lady, leisurely like a beautiful cloud. The
marquis of Han looked round at them, filling the gate with their
splendour."[22] It is said in the *Gongyang Commentary*: "Shuji was taken
home to Ji."[23] This makes clear that she awaited her majority.

When two states send tribute-brides, which of them is honored
more? The greater state is honored more. If the states are equal, [the
criterion] is their virtue; if their virtue is equal, [the criterion] is
the allure [of their women].

---

[19] This line is found under the nineteenth year of Lord Zhuang in the *Gongyang*.

[20] As we have seen, the Son of Heaven marries several women at one time, but he does
not marry again afterwards.

[21] In other words, it is better to marry women of different blood—we would say, so as
to widen the gene pool.

[22] Mao 261, "The Grandness of Han," translated by Legge.

[23] A line from the *The Spring and Autumn Annals (Chunqiu)* itself (Yin 7), not the *Gongyang
Commentary*. Shuji was a tribute-bride who went back to her parents' state to wait until
she was ready to be joined with her lord.

Families of substance act after Heaven and honor the left; families of refinement model themselves after Earth and honor the right.[24]

Why is it that concubines [as opposed to full wives] are not betrothed? When men have children and grandchildren, they wish to honor them; it is appropriate that one cannot ask another to treat [one's daughter] basely. It is said in the *Commentary to the Spring and Autumn Annals*: "Two states sent tribute-brides."[25] Why is it that one can ask another to become a man-of-service, but not to take [one's daughter] as a concubine? A man-of-service will gradually become honored, and, if he is talented, will not remain a man-of-service; but even if a concubine is talented, she will never become the main bride.

---

[24] This sentence is unclear. "Substance" and "refinement" appear to refer to ritual protocols observed by families.

[25] Presumably a reference to the *Gongyang Commentary* (Cheng 10), but the text there says "three states."

25

LESSONS FOR WOMEN
(Nüjie)
女誡
Ban Zhao
班昭

Lessons for Women (Nüjie) was written by Ban Zhao (45–114 C.E.), the first female historian and the greatest woman scholar in Chinese history. Ban Zhao came from a well-known family of scholars. Her father, Ban Biao started to collect materials for the Hanshu or Book of Han, which covers twelve emperors whose reigns span three hundred years of the Han dynasty. When it became impossible for Bao Biao to finish this ambitious work, Ban Gu, Ban Zhao's brother, continued it for another twenty years until his own death in prison. It was thus left to Ban Zhao to collect the remaining historical data and set them in order so that the Book of Han, the great work of her father and brother, might be completed. On her own she also wrote narrative poems, commemorative writings, inscriptions, eulogies, argumentations, commentaries, elegies, essays, and sixteen other works.

Ban Zhao was married at age fourteen to Cao Shishu. After his early death, Ban Zhao refused to remarry in observance of the tradition that widows must practice the virtue of chastity. Emperor He of the Eastern Han summoned her to his palace to give instructions in proper conduct to the empress and the imperial concubines. Here she became well respected for her literary talent as well as her moral integrity. People called her Cao Dajia (or Cao Dagu): Cao was the surname of her husband, and Dajia means a great master, in recognition of her achievements.

The Nüjie consists of seven short chapters, all of which are included here, and is the earliest text exclusively intended for the education of Chinese women. Ban Zhao addressed it to her daughters, that is, to all the younger women in her family, in order to provide them with guidance for achieving domestic harmony and for leading a better life. While her vision of the good life for women does not differ substantially from

From Pan Chao: Foremost Woman Scholar of China, by Nancy Lee Swann (New York: Russell & Russell, 1968, 1932). Reprinted by permission of the East Asian Library and the Gest Collection, Princeton University.

*the view of Chinese tradition previously advanced by male sages and scholars, she does
break new ground, based on her own experience, in using this same tradition to make
the case for women's education. She argues that an education in the Chinese Classics
is necessary so that both women and men can fulfill their familial roles more effectively. Just as the husband will never be able to guide his wife and family if he remains
ignorant about the teachings of the Chinese Classics, so, too, a wife will never be able
to serve her husband and family if she is kept from being instructed in the same texts.
As ought to be obvious from reading the* Nüjie, *Ban Zhao demonstrates the validity of her argument by citing the Classics as she makes her points about what women
should aspire to be and to do.*

*At a later time in Chinese history, Ban Zhao's insight helped inspire the opening
of higher education to women.* Lessons for Women *is commonly regarded as
having made a lasting contribution to Chinese tradition and women's education, and
thus was placed first among the* Four Books for Women (Nü sishu).[1]

Robin R. Wang

Introduction

I, the unworthy writer, am unsophisticated, unenlightened, and by
nature unintelligent, but I am fortunate both to have received not a
little favor from my scholarly father, and to have had a (cultured)
mother and instructresses upon whom to rely for a literary education
as well as for training in good manners. More than forty years have
passed since at the age of fourteen I took up the dustpan and broom[2]
in the Ts'ao family. During this time with trembling heart I feared
constantly that I might disgrace my parents, and that I might multiply difficulties for both the women and the men (of my husband's
family). Day and night I was distressed in heart, (but) I labored
without confessing weariness. Now and hereafter, however, I know
how to escape (from such fears).

Being careless, and by nature stupid, I taught and trained (my
children) without system. Consequently I fear that my son Ku may
bring disgrace upon the Imperial dynasty by whose Holy Grace he
has unprecedentedly received the extraordinary privilege of wearing
the Gold and the Purple, a privilege for the attainment of which (by
my son, I) a humble subject never even hoped. Nevertheless, now that
he is a man and able to plan his own life, I need not again have concern

---

[1] See footnote 1 in the Introduction pp. ix–x for the other three books of the *Four Books
for Women* (Nü *sishu*).

[2] An expression for the marriage of the young woman.

for him. But I do grieve that you, my daughters,[3] just now at the age for marriage, have not at this time had gradual training and advice; that you still have not learned the proper customs for married women. I fear that by failure in good manners in other families you will humiliate both your ancestors and your clan. I am now seriously ill; life is uncertain. As I have thought of you all in so untrained a state, I have been uneasy many a time for you. At hours of leisure I have composed these seven chapters of instructions under the title, "Lessons for Women." In order that you may have something wherewith to benefit your persons, I wish every one of you, my daughters, each to write out a copy for yourself.

From this time on, every one of you should strive to practice these (lessons).

Chapter One
Humility

On the third day after the birth of a girl the ancients[4] observed three customs: (first) to place the baby below[5] the bed; (second) to give her a potsherd with which to play;[6] and (third) to announce her birth to her ancestors by an offering. Now to lay the baby below the bed plainly indicated that she is lowly and weak, and should regard it as her primary duty to humble herself before others. To give her potsherds with which to play indubitably signified that she should practice labor and consider it primary duty to be industrious. To announce her birth before her ancestors clearly meant that she ought to esteem as her primary duty the continuation of the observance of worship[7] in the home.

These three ancient customs epitomize a woman's ordinary way of life and the teachings of the traditional ceremonial rites and regulations. Let a woman modestly yield to others; let her respect others; let her put others first, herself last. Should she do something good,

---

[3] Not necessarily only Ban Zhao's own daughters, but also the girls of her family.

[4] Ban Zhao does not indicate that any such custom existed in her time; it was the custom of ancients—people who were "ancient," or who lived more than eighteen hundred years ago.

[5] That is, on the floor, or the ground.

[6] The potsherd was an honorable symbol of domesticity; in ancient times it was used as a weight for the spindle.

[7] The worship and obedience due to parents and ancestors.

let her not mention it; should she do something bad, let her not deny it. Let her bear disgrace; let her even endure[8] when others speak or do evil to her. Always let her seem to tremble and fear. (When a woman follows such maxims as these,) then she may be said to humble herself before others.

Let a woman retire late to bed, but rise early to duties; let her not dread tasks by day or by night. Let her not refuse to perform domestic duties whether easy or difficult. That which must be done, let her finish completely, tidily, and systematically. (When a woman follows such rules as these,) then she may be said to be industrious.

Let a woman be correct in manner and upright in character in order to serve her husband. Let her live in purity and quietness (of spirit), and attend to her own affairs. Let her love not gossip and silly laughter. Let her cleanse and purify and arrange in order the wine and the food for the offerings to the ancestors.[9] (When a woman observes such principles as these,) then she may be said to continue ancestral worship.

No woman who observes these three (fundamentals of life) has ever had a bad reputation or has fallen into disgrace. If a woman fails to observe them, how can her name be honored; how can she but bring disgrace upon herself?

Chapter Two
Husband and Wife

The Way of husband and wife is intimately connected with *yin* and *yang*,[10] and relates the individual to gods and ancestors. Truly it is the great principle of Heaven and Earth, and the great basis of human relationships.[11] Therefore *The Record of Rites*[12] honor union of man and woman; and in *The Book of Odes* the First Ode[13] manifests the princi-

---

[8] Literally, "Let her hold filth in her mouth, let her swallow insult."

[9] The wife had special duties to perform in the periodical sacrifices. It was her duty to prepare the sacrificial cakes, the rice, the millet, and the fruits, and to see to it that they were served in the proper vessels.

[10] The fundamental basis of the Chinese conception of nature lies in the revolution of the seasons, in the alternation of heat and cold, of darkness and light. The two antithetic principles were later named *yin* and *yang*.

[11] The Chinese have always considered marriage to be the most solemn and important act of life.

[12] See pp. 48–60 for selections from *The Record of Rites* in this edition.

[13] See pp. 4–24 for selections from *The Book of Odes* in this edition.

ple of marriage. For these reasons the relationship cannot but be an important one.

If a husband be unworthy, then he possesses nothing by which to control his wife. If a wife be unworthy, then she possess nothing with which to serve her husband. If a husband does not control his wife, then the rules of conduct manifesting his authority are abandoned and broken. If a wife does not serve her husband, then the proper relationship (between men and women) and the natural order of things are neglected and destroyed. As a matter of fact the purpose of these two (the controlling of women by men, and the serving of men by women) is the same.

Now examine the gentlemen of the present age. They only know that wives must be controlled, and that the husband's rules of conduct manifesting his authority must be established. They therefore teach their boys to read books and (study) histories. But they do not in the least understand that husbands and masters must (also) be served, and that the proper relationship and the rites should be maintained.

Yet only to teach men and not to teach women—is that not ignoring the essential relation between them? According to *The Record of Rites*, it is the rule to begin to teach children to read at the age of eight years, and by the age of fifteen years they ought then to be ready for cultural training. Only why should it not be (that girls' education as well as boys' be) according to this principle?

Chapter Three
Respect and Caution

As *yin* and *yang* are not of the same nature, so man and woman have different characteristics. The distinctive quality of *yang* is rigidity; the function of *yin* is yielding. A man is honored for strength; a woman is beautiful on account of her gentleness. Hence there arose a common saying: "A man though born like a wolf may, it is feared, become a weak monstrosity; a woman though born like a mouse may, it is feared, become a tiger."

Now for self-culture[14] nothing equals respect for others. To counteract firmness nothing equals compliance. Consequently it can be said that the Way of respect and acquiescence is woman's most important principle of conduct. So respect may be defined as nothing other

---

[14] The self-cultivation of the person was of the utmost importance.

Figure 5. The demented and disheveled husband still is comforted by his
Chou's Illustrations of the Biographies of Woman (Chou Hua Lienu Zhuan) by Chou Ying

caring wife, who offers him herbal medicine while holding their son. [From (1509–1552).]

than holding on to that which is permanent; and acquiescence nothing other than being liberal and generous. Those who are steadfast in devotion know that they should stay in their proper places; those who are liberal and generous esteem others, and honor and serve (them).

If husband and wife have the habit of staying together, never leaving one another, and following each other around within the limited space of their own rooms, then they will lust after and take liberties with one another. From such action improper language will arise between the two. This kind of discussion may lead to licentiousness. Out of licentiousness will be born a heart of disrespect to the husband. Such a result comes from not knowing that one should stay in one's proper place.

Furthermore, affairs may be either crooked or straight; words may be either right or wrong. Straightforwardness cannot but lead to quarreling; crookedness cannot but lead to accusation. If there are really accusations and quarrels, then undoubtedly there will be angry affairs. Such a result comes from not esteeming others, and not honoring and serving (them).

(If wives) do not suppress contempt for husbands, then it follows (that such wives) rebuke and scold (their husbands). (If husbands) do not stop short of anger, then they are certain to beat (their wives). The correct relationship between husband and wife is based upon harmony and intimacy, and (conjugal) love is grounded in proper union. Should actual blows be dealt, how could matrimonial relationship be preserved? Should sharp words be spoken, how could (conjugal) love exist? If love and proper relationship both be destroyed, then husband and wife are divided.

Chapter Four
Womanly Qualifications

A woman (ought to) have four qualifications: (1) womanly virtue; (2) womanly words; (3) womanly bearing; and (4) womanly work. Now what is called womanly virtue need not be brilliant ability, exceptionally different from others. Womanly words need be neither clever in debate nor keen in conversation. Womanly appearance requires neither a pretty nor a perfect face and form. Womanly work need not be work done more skillfully than that of others.

To guard carefully her chastity; to control circumspectly her behavior; in every motion to exhibit modesty; and to model each act on the best usage, this is womanly virtue.

To choose her words with care; to avoid vulgar language; to speak at appropriate times; and not to weary others (with much conversation), may be called characteristics of womanly words.

To wash and scrub filth away; to keep clothes and ornaments fresh and clean; to wash the head and bathe the body regularly; and to keep the person free from disgraceful filth, may be called the characteristics of womanly bearing.

With whole-hearted devotion to sew and to weave; to love not gossip and silly laughter; in cleanliness and order (to prepare) the wine and food for serving guests, may be called the characteristics of womanly work.

These four qualifications characterize the greatest virtue of a woman. No woman can afford to be without them. In fact they are very easy to possess if a woman only treasure them in her heart. The ancients had a saying: "Is love afar? If I desire love, then love is at hand!" So can it be said of these qualifications.

Chapter Five
Whole-Hearted Devotion

Now in *The Record of Rites* is written the principle that a husband may marry again, but there is no Canon that authorizes a woman to be married the second time. Therefore it is said of husbands as of Heaven, that as certainly as people cannot run away from Heaven, so surely a wife cannot leave[15] (a husband's home).

If people in action or character disobey the spirits of Heaven and of Earth,[16] then Heaven punishes them. Likewise, if a woman errs in the rites and proper mode of conduct, then her husband esteems her lightly. The ancient book *A Pattern for Women (Nu Hsien)*[17] says: "To obtain the love of one man is the crown of a woman's life; to lose the love of one man is to miss the aim in woman's life."[18] For these reasons a woman cannot but seek to win her husband's heart. Nevertheless, the beseeching wife need not use flattery, coaxing words, and cheap methods to gain intimacy.

---

[15] Even following a husband's death, the worthy wife does not leave her husband's home.

[16] The belief in the personal intervention of the gods in human affairs was deeply implanted in Chinese faith.

[17] Thought to be the title of a long-lost book.

[18] The full translation is: "To become of like mind with one man may be said to be the final end; to fail to become of like mind with one man may be said to be the eternal end."

Decidedly nothing is better (to gain the heart of a husband) than whole-hearted devotion and correct manners. In accordance with the rites and the proper mode of conduct, (let a woman) live a pure life. Let her have ears that hear not licentiousness, and eyes that see not depravity. When she goes outside her own home, let her not be conspicuous in dress and manners. When at home let her not neglect her dress. Women should not assemble in groups, nor gather together (for gossip and silly laughter). They should not stand watching in the gateways. (If a woman follows) these rules, she may be said to have whole-hearted devotion and correct manners.

If, in all her actions, she is frivolous, she sees and hears (only) that which pleases herself. At home her hair is disheveled and her dress is slovenly. Outside the home she emphasizes her femininity to attract attention; she says what ought not to be said; and she looks at what ought not to be seen. (If a woman does such as) these, (she may be) said to be without whole-hearted devotion and correct manners.

Chapter Six
Implicit Obedience

Now "to win the love of one man is the crown of a woman's life; to lose the love of one man is her eternal disgrace." This saying advises a fixed will and a whole-hearted devotion for a woman. Ought she then to lose the hearts of her father- and mother-in-law?[19]

There are times when love may lead to differences of opinion (between individuals); there are times when duty may lead to disagreement. Even should the husband say that he loves something, when the parents-in-law say "no," this is called a case of duty leading to disagreement. This being so, then what about the hearts of the parents-in-law? Nothing is better than an obedience that sacrifices personal opinion.

Whenever the mother-in-law says, "Do not do that," and if what she says is right, unquestionably the daughter-in-law obeys. Whenever the mother-in-law says, "Do that," even if what she says is wrong, still the daughter-in-law submits unfailingly to the command.

---

[19] In the Chinese family system, children, even mature sons and their wives, were morally bound to dwell under the same parental roof. This often resulted in conflicts between the mother-in-law and the daughter-in-law, as well as between a wife and the wives of her husband's brothers, a wife and the unmarried daughters of the family, or the widows of deceased sons, or the young children of the family. There were many opportunities for friction.

Let a woman not act contrary to the wishes and the opinions of parents-in-law about right and wrong; let her not dispute with them what is straight[20] and what is crooked. Such (docility) may be called obedience that sacrifices personal opinion. Therefore the ancient book, *A Pattern for Women*, says: "If a daughter-in-law (who follows the wishes of her parents-in-law) is like an echo and a shadow, how could she not be praised?"

Chapter Seven
Harmony with the Younger Brothers- and Sisters-in-Law

In order for a wife to gain the love of her husband, she must win for herself the love of her parents-in-law. To win for herself the love of her parents-in-law, she must secure for herself the good will of her younger brothers- and sisters-in-law. For these reasons the right and the wrong, the praise and the blame of a woman alike depend upon the younger brothers- and sisters-in-law. Consequently it will not do for a woman to lose their affection.

They are stupid both who know not that they must not lose (the hearts of) younger brothers- and sisters-in-law, and who cannot be in harmony with them in order to be intimate with them. Excepting only the Holy Men, few are able to be faultless. Now Yanzi's[21] greatest virtue was that he was able to reform. Confucius praised him (for not committing a misdeed) the second time. (In comparison with him) a woman is more likely (to make mistakes).

Although a woman possess a worthy woman's qualifications, and is wise and discerning by nature, is she able to be perfect? Yet if a woman lives in harmony with her immediate family, unfavorable criticism will be silenced (within the home. But) if a man and woman disagree, then this evil will be noised abroad. Such consequence are inevitable. *The Classic of Changes*[22] says:

Should two hearts harmonize,
The united strength can cut gold.

---

20 Proper.

21 A favorite disciple of Confucius.

22 See pp. 25–45 for selections from *The Classic of Changes*.

Words from hearts which agree,
Give forth fragrance like the orchid.[23]

This saying may be applied to (harmony in the home).

Though a daughter-in-law and her younger sisters-in-law are equal in rank, nevertheless (they should) respect (each other); though love (between them may be) sparse, their proper relationship should be intimate. Only the virtuous, the beautiful, the modest, and the respectful (young women) can accordingly rely upon the sense of duty to make their affection sincere, and magnify love to bind their relationships firmly.

Then the excellence and the beauty of such a daughter-in-law becomes generally known. Moreover, any flaws and mistakes are hidden and unrevealed. Parents-in-law boast of her good deeds; her husband is satisfied with her.[24] Praise of her radiates, making her illustrious in district and in neighborhood; and her brightness reaches to her own father and mother.

But a stupid and foolish person as an elder sister-in-law uses her rank[25] to exalt herself; as a younger sister-in-law, because of parents' favor, she becomes filled with arrogance. If arrogant, how can a woman live in harmony with others? If love and proper relationships be perverted, how can praise be secured? In such instances the wife's good is hidden, and her faults are declared. The mother-in-law will be angry, and the husband will be indignant. Blame will reverberate and spread in and outside the home. Disgrace will gather upon the daughter-in-law's person, on the one hand to add humiliation to her own father and mother, and on the other to increase the difficulties of her husband.

Such then is the basis for both honor and disgrace, the foundation for reputation or for ill-repute. Can a woman be too cautious? Consequently, to seek the hearts of young brothers- and sisters-in-law decidedly nothing can be esteemed better than modesty and acquiescence.

Modesty is virtue's handle; acquiescence is the wife's (most refined) characteristic. All who possess these two have sufficient [virtues] for harmony with others. In *The Book of Odes* it is written that "here is no evil; there is no dart." So it may be said of (these two, modesty and acquiescence).

---

[23] In loving unity there is strength and beauty as the two (or the group) meet life's responsibilities.

[24] Literally, "praises the beauty of her character."

[25] The eldest daughter-in-law had control over the other sons' wives.

26

A GENERAL DISCUSSION OF CUSTOMS

(Fengsu tongyi)

風俗通議

Ying Shao

應劭

A General Discussion of Customs was compiled by Ying Shao of the Later Han dynasty (8–220 C.E.). It consists of thirty chapters, with topics ranging from rulership, rites, spirits, and music to naming practices, taboos, and penal laws. Because of its diverse topics and its discussions of unorthodox customs and practices, later scholars often categorized the book as a miscellany and rarely noted Ying's true intention in writing it: to restore Confucian tradition and ethics. The passage selected here is a typical example, in which Ying criticizes a husband's improper conduct towards the death of his wife, and reiterates the Confucian ideal regarding the woman's role in the husband-and-wife relationship.

Ping Yao

When Xue Gongzu of Runan, the governor of Shanyang,[1] lost his wife, he did not cry. When she was about to be buried, he stood next to the coffin and shouted: "It has been over forty years since we became a couple. She dressed and ate well and enjoyed high status; her sons and daughters are now all grown up. She was lucky that she did not die young. Her death is nothing to lament about! So be it."

Translated by Ping Yao.

[1] Both Runan and Shanyang are place names. Runan was Xue's hometown, while Shanyang was where Xue held an office. Gong Zu was Xue's courtesy name; his given name was Qin.

Here are my humble comments: *The Record of Rites* stipulates that a man holds the mourning cane for his principal wife during her funeral.[2] He cherishes the fact that she is a member of his clan. The term "wife" (*qi*) means "equal" (*qi*) to me (the husband).[3] She brews fine wines to serve the parents-in-law; diligently prepares meals for the household; manages sericulture and weaving; and honors the ancestors' heritage and passes it on to the younger generation. Her devotion is deep and her assiduity reaches the utmost. Even creatures as lowly as birds and animals have feelings of longing and sorrow, flying in a circle or twittering at the place where their companion has died. How could anyone have no grief to express when there is a death in the family and a person departs for good? If a man is woeful inside but swaggering in appearance, it is called self-styled superiority, and is regarded as hypocritical in the extreme. A proverb says, "A wife dies, and my stomach laments, but only my body knows about it." Another proverb says, "A wife is not one to whom a rite should be devoted." How elaborate a rite would that have to be? Isn't it ridiculous to use these proverbs to justify a husband's refusal to mourn his wife properly?

---

[2] In traditional China, holding a mourning cane symbolizes a high degree of mourning.

[3] Han scholars commonly defined "wife" as meaning equal or uniform, because the two characters have the same pronunciation. However, inscriptions on the oracle bones of the Shang dynasty suggest that the character of *qi* (wife) was an image of a woman with hair pins, indicating that a wife was a woman physically mature enough to be taken for one.

27

CLASSIC OF THE WHITE GIRL, OR THE ART OF THE BEDCHAMBER
(Sunüjing)
素女經

Sunüjing is considered to be one of the earliest Chinese books on sex and sexuality. Assumed to be compiled somewhere between the later Han and the Three Kingdom period (27–260 C.E.), it is a medical manual that teaches the principles of sex, or what the Chinese call "the art of the bedchamber (fangshu)." Traditionally, the book is said to be influenced by Daoist philosophy, particularly in its understanding of the cyclic movement of nature, yin/yang polarities, the five-element theory, and the connection of qi energy to the well-being of the human body in general.

The book is presented in a dialogue format in which Huangdi, the legendary Yellow Emperor, is receiving advice on sexual techniques from his chief female advisor, Sunü (whose name literally means the White Girl). According to an earlier mythological account, Sunü is an immortal being who lives in the land of immortality (xianjie) where she has obtained the secret knowledge of immortality that is based on absorbing the "vital energy" of "virgin men (tongnan)."

Three things need to be noted about the Sunüjing. First, the book connects the art of lovemaking to the principle of yin and yang represented by ancient Chinese cosmology. Second, the book follows the Chinese tradition that sees sexuality as part of the natural rhythms of life, and as such treats the issue of sexuality within the framework of the general physiological well-being of human beings. Third, the book emphasizes the role of women or feminine energy in the maintenance of health and balance of men or masculine energy. Although one can argue that the Sunüjing is a book intended to be read by men rather than women, the book implies a number of ideas about women that deserve attention.

Ellen Zhang

Translated by Ellen Zhang.

Huangdi asks Sunü: "I am feeling a lack of energy and a disharmony in my body. I am sad and apprehensive. What shall I do about
this?"

Sunü replies: "Men are likely to make a mistake during lovemaking. Women conquer men as water conquers fire. Those who know
the art of lovemaking are like those who know how to mix the five
flavors in a cooking pot to produce a good meal, and like those who
know the way of *yin* and *yang* and enjoy the five pleasures. Those who
are ignorant of this art die young, without enjoying the pleasure of
life. . . . A man must know how to control his emissions and also take
medicine. He cannot enjoy life if he is ignorant of the art of love.
Men and women are like Heaven and Earth, whose eternal nature lies
in their unity. . . . Those who understand the principle of *yin* and *yang*
will experience immortality."

Huangdi asks: "What will happen if one abstains from sex?"

Sunü replies: "That is absolutely out of the question. *Yin* and *yang*
have their alternations as does everything in nature. Human beings
should follow the rhythms of *yin* and *yang* just as they follows the
changes of the seasons. . . ."

Huangdi asks: "What are the essential elements that bring about
a harmonious union of *yin* and *yang*?"

Sunü replies: "For a man, the essential element is to avoid weak-
ening his strength; for a woman, what is important is orgasm. Those
who do not follow this method will decline into weakness. The function of female sexual sensibility is to keep the balance of one's energies, to calm one's heart, to strengthen one's will, and finally to clarify
one's mind.

"The person concerned should experience a deep sense of well-
being, without feeling heat and cold, hunger and satiety, thus the body
enjoys its pleasure in peace. The aim of this method is orgasm for the
woman, and preservation of energies for the man."

Huangdi asks: "Lately even when I have a strong desire for sex, my
'jade stalk' does not rise. I am so embarrassed that my face is covered
with shame and beads of sweat. Yet my desire is so strong, I have no
choice but to seek the assistance of my hand. How should I do it?"

Sunü replies: "Your question is a common one. When a man wishes
to have a sexual relationship, he must observe traditional preliminaries.
First, the breathing needs to be harmonized, and then the 'jade stalk'
is aroused according to the principle of 'five constancies' (*wuchang*),
while sensations flow through the nine parts. As for a woman, the five
colors are to be noted. Upon the change of color, the man collects saliva

from the woman's mouth, which in turn is transformed and fills the marrow of his bones as well the internal organs of his body. The man must obey the 'seven deficiencies,' follow the 'eight benefits,' and observe the 'five constancies.' In doing so, the disorder will be cured as energy strengthens the body. When his internal organs are harmonized, his face will shine. Should desire come, the 'jade stalk' that has been strengthened becomes erect. Where then is the shame?"

Huangdi asks: "How can one tell if a woman is experiencing orgasm?"

Sunü answers: "There are five signs, five desires, and ten movements. One can tell by observing the process of her transformation. The five signs include:

1. Her complexion becomes flushed. Now the man should caress her gently.
2. Her nipples harden and perspiration appears on her nose. Now the man should penetrate slowly.
3. Her throat becomes dry, and she swallows. Now the man should move gently.
4. Her vagina becomes slippery. Now penetration goes deeper.
5. Her secretions flow. Now the man should withdraw gently.

"The five desires that require responsiveness include:

1. Thought (*yi*): She is holding her breath.
2. Vagina (*yin*): Her nostrils and mouth are wide open.
3. Restlessness (*jing*): She is excited and hugs her partner.
4. Heart (*xin*): Her perspiration wets her garments.
5. Orgasm (*kuai*): Her body is stretched out and her eyes are closed.

"The ten movements include:

1. Embracing her partner in such a way that their genitals touch.
2. Stretching out her thighs so they rub against her partner.
3. Expanding her abdomen to increase excitement.
4. Moving her buttocks to stimulate stamina and pleasure.
5. Lifting her legs up to attain deep penetration.
6. Pressing her thighs together to prepare for orgasm.
7. Turning to one side for the deeper penetration while touching both sides.

8. Raising her body to show she is coming.
9. Stretching her body out to express her orgasmic satisfaction.
10. Finishing the act.

"If you see the above signs, you know the woman is experiencing orgasm."

PART FOUR

WEI, JIN, NAN-BEI CHAO
魏晉南北朝

(220–581 C.E.)

28

IN SEARCH OF THE SUPERNATURAL

(Soushenji)

搜神記

Gan Bao

干寶

No exact date of compilation is available for In Search of the Supernatural
(Soushenji). *The author, Gan Bao, a court official during the Eastern Jin period
(217–419* C.E.*), was well learned in the Confucian classics. As a court historian,
he compiled the* Records of Jin (Jinji). Soushenji *is a proof of his interests in
and curiosity about the strange and the supernatural, a popular trend among the
literati of his day. With the introduction of Hinayana Buddhism into China during
the Han period (202* B.C.E.–220 C.E.*), the persistence of shamanistic beliefs in the
Qin and the Daoist search for immortality, strange tales were flourishing in the Jin
period. It was said that Gan Bao was inspired to write the* Soushenji *because of
a preternatural incident that happened in his family. As the historian was also
intrigued by the Yin Yang School, he decided to try his hand at writing marvelous
and strange tales by gathering them from ancient texts and from oral traditions among
the older people. The result is a collection of over four hundred stories on the strange
and supernatural. To Gan Bao and his contemporaries, these stories carried as much
credence and significance as the official history itself, only they deal more with the
unknown and the mysterious. Though hardly Gan Bao's intent, his book on the supernatural marks the beginning of fictional writing for Chinese posterity. Some time later
in the Jin period (220–589* C.E.*), another scholar official, Tao Qian, continued the
tradition and came up with a collection of ten chapters called* A Sequel to the
Records on the Search for the Supernatural (Soushen Houji).*

From Kenneth de Woskin and J. J. Crump, *In Search of the Supernatural: The Written Record.*
Copyright © 1996 by the Board of Trustees of the Leland Stanford Junior University.
Reprinted with the permission of Stanford University Press, www.sup.org.

The eight stories chosen in this selection can be divided roughly into three categories: (1) female ghosts, found in "Wang Daoping's Wife Restored to Life," and "The Princess of Suiyang and Scholar Tan"; (2) female immortals in "Xuan Chao Visited by the Jade Lady," "Sun Jian's Consort Receives the Sun and the Moon," and "A Male Becomes a Female"; and (3) distinguished females in "Deng Yuanyi's Wife Remarries," "Origins of the Man Barbarians," and "Li Ji Slays the Great Serpent." In the ghost stories, the females are devoted to their lover or husband even in death. Similarly, the female immortals are there to comfort men and bring them extraordinary children and gifts. These immortals always cater to the man's needs, be it supporting him materially or bearing his children. The last category on distinguished females seems to be the most interesting and realistic. "Origins of the Man Barbarians" might be a myth to explain the origin of a certain minority group in China, yet the reader cannot fail to see the princess's insistence on chastity, accepting the "man" whatever he is; she helps her father to keep his promise to the man who kills his enemy. Li Ji, on the other hand, is an example of a brave young woman who solves a major problem for her parents. Both risk their lives in ridding the region of its enemy. Deng Yuanyi is probably one of the very few Chinese women who is still regarded as a heroine after she remarries. It is true that she loses her chastity by marrying another man and hence is looked down upon by her own son, but the story is memorable for its realistic portrayal of the conflicts between mothers and daughters-in-law caught in a Confucian context. In extricating herself from a hopeless situation with her first husband's family, Deng has the courage to rebuild her own life and change her destiny.

Fatima Wu

Xuan Chao Is Visited by the Jade Lady

Xuan Chao ("courtesy name" Yiqi) was an attendant in the Qibei commandery during the Wei dynasty. One night during the Jiapin era, he had a dream that a goddess came to accompany him in his lonesome bed.

"I am the Jade Lady from Heaven," she explained. "I was known as Chenggong Zhiqiong of Dongjun. Having lost both my parents at a tender age, the Heavenly Emperor, as an act of grace, sent down an order that I should become your consort."

During the dream Xuan was so deeply stirred by her unusual beauty, the transcendent loveliness of her face, that even awake he continued to yearn for her and remained uncertain whether she really existed.

He continued in this state for three or four days until one morning she came to him in person. Borne in a carriage with drawn curtains, she was attended by eight maidservants dressed in clothes of the finest embroidered silk. They were all so fair of face and form they rivaled fairies in flight.

She told him that she was actually seventy years old, though she had the appearance of a fifteen- or sixteen-year-old maiden. Her carriage was furnished with a wine ewer and five matching light green glass wine cups. Her food and drink were exotic and curious, and she set them all forth, each in its proper vessel to share the provisions with Chao.

"I am the Jade Lady of heaven," she said. "I was ordered to come to earth to be your wife not because of any special virtue, but because the time we spent together moved fate. We are now destined to be husband and wife. This will not be of any great benefit to you, nor will it bring you harm. However, when you travel you may share my weightless carriage, ride horses of the finest fettle, drink diverse wines of rare taste, and eat foods of strange savor. Nor will you ever lack fine silk for you garments. Being immortal, I cannot bear you children. However, I am by nature not jealous, so you may marry according to custom and live with another as husband and wife." Thereupon she gave him a poem that read:

> Leisurely I float or suddenly speed,
> A fairy plant nourished on cloud-damp stone,
> A flower which for nurture has no need.
> Great virtue ever finds its time;
> The gods are never moved for naught,
> But answer fate and then respond.
> Accept, and summon good for your kin,
> Reject, and summon misery in.

This was the general import of the verse, but since it ran to over two hundred words, we cannot quote it all here.

She also did annotations for the *Yijing* (*The Classic of Changes*) in seven chapters, directed to the hexagrams and the Images, and organized around the Judgments. Certainly these notes were cogent and could be as well used for divination as the *Taixuan* of Yang Xiong or Xue's *Zhongjing*. Chao was able to penetrate to the heart of the work and used it to divine with. She also composed the *Conjugal Classic*.

After some seven or eight years, when Chao's parents had secured him a wife, the Jade Lady would feast with him and spend the night with him occasionally. But she would come at night and leave by dawn as swiftly as though she had wings; Chao alone was able to see her. Although all their time was spent in private rooms, the sounds of voices could be heard, and though no one ever saw so much as a shadow, traces of her presence were evident. Eventually, the curious asked questions, and knowledge of the affair leaked out, so the Lady begged to take leave.

"I am an immortal," she said, "and do not wish others to know of our relationship. You have been careless enough to allow the story to come out, so I must end our liaison. Of course, to end a closeness of many years standing in one moment is painful. However, what must be will be. We must both look to our own needs."

She then called her attendants to bring wine and food, and opening other hampers, she brought forth two sets of silk robes for Chao and again gave him a verse. They embraced, weeping, and took leave of one another. She mounted her carriage and departed with the swiftness of flight.

Chao grieved for her for many a day until he was on the point of collapse. However, five years later when Chao was sent by his Commandery to Luoyang, he had gone as far as Mount Yu in Qibei when far off in the bend of his road he saw a carriage that greatly resembled Zhiqiong's. When he raced to overtake it, it did prove to be hers. They lifted their curtains and received one another with a mixture of joy and sadness.

He reined in by her left span-horse, seized its bridle,[1] and she rode with Chao in his carriage to Luoyang. There they established a household and lived in the same felicity as before. They were still there in the Taikang era of the Jin, but she did not come to him each and every day. She would descend on the third of the third month, the fifth of the fifth, the ninth of the ninth, as well as the first and the ides of all other months, to spend the night with him.

Zhang Hua (Rongxian) wrote his *fu*, *The Goddess*, about this.

A Male Becomes a Female

During the Jianping reign period of Aidi, a man became a woman in Yuzhang. She married and bore one child. Chen Feng of Chang'an said: "For the *yang* to change into *yin* will end the lineage: it is an omen of mutual self-destruction." One explanation said: "The person who became a wife and bore a child will skip one generation before the

---

[1] One reason this terse sentence is so difficult is that we can't know whether he saw her chariot in the distance going the same way he was or in the opposite direction.

lineage is brought to an end." For this reason, when Aidi died, Pingdi [succeeded]² and then Wang Mang usurped the throne.

Sun Jian's Consort Receives the Sun and the Moon

The wife of Sun Jian (née Wu), being pregnant, dreamed that the moon entered her bosom; thereafter she bore Sun Ce. When she was carrying Sun Quan, she dreamed the sun entered her breast. Then she said to Sun Jian, "What could it mean to have the moon entering me when I carried Ce and later to receive the sun?"

"The sun and the moon are the essences of *yin* and *yang* and are the most exalted of symbols. Our descendants are destined to flourish greatly!" replied Sun Jian.

Deng Yuanyi's Wife Remarries

During the Latter Han, the father of Deng Yuanyi from Nankang was one Deng Bokao, who served as Supervisor in the Imperial Secretariat. His son, Yuanyi, returned to the family's native district, leaving his wife behind in the capital to serve her mother-in-law, which she did with diligence.

The mother-in-law detested Yuanyi's wife, so she shut her up in a deserted part of the compound and limited her food and drink until she was so emaciated that her bones showed. Daily the young wife suffered more, though she never uttered a word of complaint.

Bokao became suspicious of all this and made inquiries. His grandson, Yuanyi's son Seng Lang, who was at the time only a few years old, told him, "Mother is not sick, she is suffering because she is being starved."

"Why should someone who has faithfully served her mother-in-law be treated in this fashion?" Bokao asked himself, weeping, and thereupon sent Yuanyi's wife back to her family.

Later she remarried and became the wife of [Yin] Hua Zhang—he was chief of Palace Builders at the time, so his wife could use an official carriage. Once she did so when Yuanyi stood on the verge, watching. To an onlooker he said, "That is my former wife. She was

---

² Pingdi was poisoned by Wang Mang in 5 C.E.

guilty of nothing, but our mother used her ill. She always had a noble physiognomy."

Her son [with Yuanyi], Deng Lang, was at the time a Gentleman Attendant, but when his mother wrote to him, he refused to respond. When she sent him gifts of clothing, he would immediately have them burned.

His mother was unable to understand why he acted thus, and wanting very much to see him, she went to the home of a relative— one of the Li clan—and had one of *them* request her son's presence.

When Lang arrived and saw his mother, he bowed low and wept. But then he left directly. His mother followed and called out to him: "I was almost starved to death. It was your family that abandoned me; I was not at fault, so why should you behave thus?" Thereafter she severed all relations with him.

Origins of the Man Barbarians

In the time of Gaoxin an elderly woman attached to the palace suffered from an earache for some time. The physician treated her and removed an insect the size of a silkworm cocoon. When the woman left, the physician placed the insect in a gourd pot (*hu*) and covered it with a dish (*pan*). In no time it turned into a dog, mottled with colorful patches. This is why the dog was called Panhu, and it was reared by the physician.

At the time the Wu barbarians had become numerous and strong and several time penetrated the borders. Generals were sent against them but could not gain victories. A declaration was sent throughout the kingdom: "Anyone bringing in the head of the Wu leader will be rewarded with a thousand catties of gold, an appanage of ten thousand households, and the hand of the emperor's youngest daughter."

Sometime later Panhu appeared carrying a head in its mouth and went straight to the palace. The king examined the head and concluded that it belonged to the Wu leader. What was he to do?

His officers all said, "Panhu is a domestic animal: he cannot be allowed to join the ranks of officials and certainly cannot be given your daughter to wed! Though he has achieved this merit, he cannot be given that reward."

When his youngest daughter heard this, she addressed the king: "Since Your Majesty promised me to anyone in the world and Panhu brought you the head, ridding your kingdom of danger, we have here the will of Heaven. This is not something Panhu's intelligence could have contrived. Kings must keep promises; rulers must be believed. You cannot repudiate your word, clearly given to the world, for the sake of my humble person; that would result in calamity for your kingdom."

The king feared she was right and ordered her sent to Panhu.

The dog took the girl into the southern hills where the undergrowth was so dense the feet of men never trod. There she discarded her court robes, donned those of a common freeman, and bound herself to Panhu as his servant. He then led her over mountains and through valleys until they reached a cave in the rocks.

Now, the king sorely missed his daughter, and he often sent men forth in search of her. However, the heavens would always rain, the mountain peaks would shake, and clouds would so darken the sky that his men could not reach her.

Nearly three years passed. The princess had given birth to six boys and six girls when Panhu died. Their offspring married one another. They wove cloth from the bark of trees dyed with the juices of berries and fruits—for they loved colorful garments—and they cut the cloth to fit their tails.

Later, their mother returned to the palace, and the king sent envoys to welcome the children—this time the heavens did not rain. But their clothes were outlandish, their speech barbaric;[3] they squatted on their haunches to eat and drink and preferred mountain wilds to cities. The king acceded to their wishes and gave them famed mountains and broad swamps for their home. They were called Man barbarians.

The Man barbarians appear stupid but are in fact crafty. They are contented in the lands they inhabit and set store by their old ways. They believe they were given strange capacities by the will of heaven, and therefore they act under laws not common to others. They farm and they trade, but they have no documents to show at borders, no identifications or tallies—nor do they have rents or taxes of any sort. They live in small villages where the headmen are given tallies and wear crowns of otter skin, for the Man secure their food from the waters.

Presently the Commanderies of Liang, Han, Ba, Shu, Wuling, Changsha, and Lujiang are all inhabited by Man. They eat rice gruel mixed with the flesh of various fish; they pound on containers and howl to honor Panhu with sacrifices. This custom has lasted until the present day. The above are the reasons for our saying:

---

[3] One annotator says the nonsense compound *zhuli* indicated how the barbarians' speech sounded to Han Chinese.

Bare buttocks, yellow trousers do
Reveal descendants of Panhu.

Wang Daoping's Wife Restored to Life

In the days of Qin Shihuang, Wang Daoping of Chang'an and Fuyu, the beautiful daughter of his fellow townsman Tang Shujie, vowed that they would be husband and wife, though they were still quite young.

Subsequently, however, Daoping was conscripted for the southern expeditionary forces and disappeared into the lands of the south. Nine years passed. Fuyu was full-grown, and her parents engaged her to Liu Xiang.

Now, the girl took her oath with Daoping very seriously and was completely unwilling to serve another. Her parents pressed her, however, until finally she left her home to become the wife of Liu Xiang. Three years passed, and in all that time Fuyu was miserable— yearning constantly for Daoping. Grief and resentment deepened until finally she died from anxiety and unrest.

Another three years passed, and Daoping returned home. He immediately inquired from his neighbors the whereabouts of Fuyu, and they told him: "The girl thought only of you, but her parents married her off to Liu Xiang, and now she is dead!"

"Then where is her grave?" he asked, and the neighbors led him to the tomb.

Daoping sobbed with grief; thrice he called out the girl's name as he walked around the tomb in bitter sadness, unable to contain himself.

"You and I swore an oath before heaven and earth that we would forever be true, each to the other," cried Daoping. "Who could have foreseen that official orders were to keep us apart for so long that your parents gave you to Liu Xiang? This done, we can never realize our original intention. The quick and the dead are parted forever; but if your spirit still resides here, grant me one more vision of your face as I knew it in life. If your spirit has vanished, then we must here and now take our leave forever."

Having spoken these words, Daoping continued weeping and pacing around her tomb. In but a short time, the girl's ghost came forth from the tomb and questioned Daoping: "Where have you been?" she asked. "We swore we would be with one another to the end of our days, but my parents forced me to go to Liu Xiang. For three years with him I longed for you day and night, until I finally died from the weight of anger and grief and went on my shadowy journey. But my thoughts of you and my longing for you in the past were never forgotten, and so strong was my wish to further comfort you that my body did not corrupt; it can again be brought back to life, and we can yet be husband and wife. Make haste, then. Uncover the tomb, break open my coffin, and restore me to life!"

Daoping took her words to heart, opened the doors of the tomb and the lid to her coffin, and she came back to life. Having done everything needed, she followed Daoping home.

Liu Xiang [the erstwhile widower] heard of the events and, finding them surpassing strange, put the case before the district magistrate. That official examined the circumstances and could find no law which applied. So he memorialized the king, who passed judgment that the woman should be given to Daoping to be his wife.

The couple lived to the age of one hundred and thirty years. In actuality, this was all brought about because of their deep commitment and sincerity of spirit (*jingcheng*), which penetrated both Heaven and Earth and brought forth this response from those entities.

The Princess of Suiyang and Scholar Tan

A certain scholar Tan of the Han dynasty was forty years old and still unmarried. He was deeply moved by reading *The Book of Odes*. Once, around midnight, a young woman of some fifteen or sixteen years, beautiful and elegantly attired—utterly without equal in the empire—came to him and offered to be his in marriage.

"However," said she, "I am unlike other humans, and you must never see me by lamplight or torchlight for three years. When that time is past, it will be possible to do so."

She became his wife and bore him a son. But after two years he could scarcely bear it longer. One night, when he had seen her to bed, he secretly brought a torch and shone it on her. Above the waist she was covered with flesh as an ordinary human; below her waist was only a skeleton.

His wife awoke and spoke: "You have betrayed me. I was going to become fully human—oh, why could you not have waited just one more year before exposing me to flame-light?"

Tan apologized, but she tearfully insisted she could stay no longer: "I know I must discontinue our marriage rituals forever, but I have great concern for my son and fear you two may not be able to sustain yourselves when I am gone. If you will follow me now, I will leave you a gift."

Tan followed her as she led him to a beautifully decorated mansions and a room that housed many unusual objects. From among them she chose a pearl-studded robe and gave it to him, saying: "This you may use to support yourselves." Then she tore a piece of material from Tan's garments and kept it when he left.

Tan took the robe to the marketplace, and the household of the Prince of Suiyang bought it for ten million coppers. The Prince recognized the robe: "This robe belonged to my daughter! What is it doing in the marketplace? Her tomb must have been violated!" Thereupon he had Tan arrested and beaten. Tan told the entire truth, but the Prince was inclined to disbelieve him. He inspected his daughter's tomb and all was complete as before. He had the coffin taken out and there, pinched under the lid, was a piece of cloth.

When the Prince called Tan's son to him, he saw that the lad did greatly resemble his daughter and finally believed the story. He summoned Tan and richly rewarded him, acknowledging him as his son-in-law. The boy he made a Gentleman-page in his court.

Li Ji Slays the Great Serpent

In the old country of Dongyue, in Minzhong Commandery, lies the Yong range. Its peaks tower over a score of li (a unit of distance) into the air. In a crevasse on its northwest face, there lived a giant serpent, seven or eight rods long and of a girth that ten men could not span. The locals went in terror of it, and the Commandant of Dongzhi [or -yeh] as well as a number of local officers had been killed by it. They sacrificed oxen and sheep to the serpent with no luck. Then the creature either caused someone to dream it, or told some medium to predict, that it required twelve- and thirteen-year-old virgins to eat.

The Commandant and village officials were all upset by this demand, but the creature's exactions became more severe, and they requisitioned children born to slaves of ordinary families—then later demanded daughters of criminals. The authorities would care for the victims until Eighth Month Morn when with proper ceremonies they delivered the girls to the mouth of the fissure, after which the serpent would come forth and eat them.

And so it went for some time—until they had sacrificed nine maidens. However, when they set out to recruit yet another victim, no one suitable was to be found.

The family of Li Dan of Jiangle District consisted of six daughters and not a single son. Dan's youngest child, named Ji, offered to go with the recruiters, but her parents would not allow it.

"My parents," she said to them, "you have been unfortunate; raising six daughters and lacking a single male child, you have no one to carry on the line, so it is as though you had no offspring at all. Your daughter is not the equal of Tiying,[4] who gained merit by saving her mother and father. Since, unlike a son, I cannot hope to support my parents later, the family resources to feed and clothe me are spent in vain," she explained. "Since there is no benefit to come from my living, it were better if I die soon. Sell me to the recruiters; then at least I will have contributed to the support of my mother and father. Is this not the better way?" Her parents were moved by pity and would not let her go, but Ji left home in secret so they could not prevent it.

Ji requested a snake-harrying dog and a good sword. Then on Eighth Month Morn she went to the shrine where the serpent ceremonies took place and seated herself, sword tucked in her bosom and dog by her side. She had provided herself with a number of sweet riceballs steeped in honey and rolled in fragrant roasted barley flour.

She placed these at the mouth of the cave and the serpent emerged—head as large as a storage bin, eyes blazing like two-foot mirrors. It scented the fragrant food and began to eat. Then did Ji loose the dog, which rushed into worry and snap at the serpent. Ji followed close behind the dog to strike and wounded the snake a number of times. In panic from the pain, it slithered from its lair, going as far as the shrine building where it died.

Ji walked into the cave and there found the bones of the other nine girls. She carried them out and sadly spoke: "It is truly a pity you were so timid and weak and therefore eaten by the serpent," said she, and leisurely made her way home.

The King of Dongyue heard of her deeds and chose young Ji to be his queen; he appointed her father Magistrate of Jiangle District and gave rich gifts to her mother and all her older sisters. From then on Dongzhi was untroubled by monsters or anomalies, and there to this day they sing of Li Ji slaying the serpent.

---

[4] Chunyu Tiying of the Han, offered herself for execution in her father's stead. The emperor was moved by the daughter's filial act and pardoned her father.

29

A NEW ACCOUNT OF TALES OF THE WORLD

(Shishuo xinyü)

世說新語

Liu Yiqing

劉義慶

The age immediately following the chaotic disintegration of the brilliant four centuries of Han rule (202 B.C.E–220 C.E.) might fairly be described as a reaction against the prescriptive morality of the then-dominant Confucian orthodoxy. A strong undercurrent of rebellion against collective social norms that were increasingly felt to be "unnatural," and a new sense of the importance of individual differences began to express itself. The movement has conventionally been labeled "Neo-Daoism," because of its rediscovery of latent principles found in the Laozi *and* Zhuangzi *texts, and its reinterpretation of Confucius himself as a Daoist "sage." The term used by Chinese intellectual historians for this movement is* Xuanxue *(literally, "dark learning"), with specific reference to the three "mysterious texts"—the* Laozi, *the* Zhuangzi, *and the* Yijing. *It would be misleading, however, to think of it merely in classical Daoist terms, for it involved a revolutionary change in how people involved in the movement viewed both government and society, to say nothing of personal behavior.*

One text produced in this period that illustrates through vivid interpersonal encounters how the old order was being reexamined is the Shishuo xinyü *(A New Account of Tales of the World), compiled by the Liu-Song Prince of Linchuan, Liu Yiqing (403–444 C.E.), with its commentary, incorporating a host of earlier sources now lost, by Liu Jun (462–521 C.E.). The work consists of a series of brief anecdotes and conversations involving over six hundred historical figures who*

From *A New Account of Tales of the World*, by Liu I-ch'ing with commentary by Liu Chün, translated by Richard B. Mather (Minneapolis: University of Minnesota Press, 1976). Reprinted by permission of Richard B. Mather.

*lived between 150–420 C.E. It is divided into thirty-six sections, each illustrating
a particular character trait, beginning with the four distinctively Confucian ideals:
"Virtuous Conduct" (Dexing), "[Brilliant] Conversation" (Yanyu), "[Correct
Conduct of] the Affairs of the State" (Zhengshi), and "Literary and Scholarly
[Prowess]" (Wenxue). From there it proceeds through a series of qualities, such as
"Cultivated Tolerance" (Yaliang), "Quick Perception" (Jiewu), and "Virility
and Boldness" (Haoshuang). There is a unique section on "Worthy Beauties"
(Xianyuan), which offers an exceptionally revealing glimpse of some very strong
female characters in the society of the time. Other sections follow, illustrating "Free
and Unrestrained [Behavior]" (Rendan), "Rudeness and Arrogance" (Jian'ao),
"Stinginess and Meanness" (Jianse), with its opposite, "Extravagance and Osten-
tation" (Taichi), and, finally, "Anger and Alienation" (Chouxi). Although this
series of personality traits, running the gamut of human emotions and behavior from
the sublime to the ridiculous and even depraved, appears to rest on a descending scale
of value judgments, all the traits are essentially treated nonjudgmentally as unique
characteristics distinguishing different individuals from each other. It is, in fact, a celebration of individuality in all its splendor and squalor.*

*The special significance for women in this book appears most prominently in Section
XIX, "Worthy Beauties," where they emerge from their traditional roles as obedient
and self-effacing daughters, wives, and mothers. The "beauties" described in these tales
set aside their customary spinning and weaving to become full equals of their male
counterparts. They are able at times, as in the case of Lady Ruan, the "extraordinarily homely" wife of Xu Yun (see section 6 in the selections here), to shatter the
smug hypocrisy of their husbands with withering scorn and prodigious cleverness.*

Richard Mather

Worthy Beauties

I

Chen Ying was a native of Dongyang Commandery (southern
Shandong). When he was young he cultivated virtuous conduct and
was known and praised in his home village. In the great disorders at
the end of the Qin (ca. 207 B.C.E.) the people of the Dongyang were
on the point of making Ying their chief (*zhu*), but his mother said
to him, "It won't do. Ever since I've been a wife in your family we've
rarely experienced anything but poverty and low station. To become
wealthy and honorable all at once is unlucky. It would be better to be
a man in the ranks under the command of somebody else. Then, if
his affairs are successful, in a modest way you'll share in his benefits.

And if they're unsuccessful, the calamity will have somebody else to fall on."[1]

2

Since the palace women of the Han emperor Yuan (Liu Shi, r. 48–33 B.C.E.) were numerous, he ordered an artist to make portraits of them, so that whenever he wanted to call one, he could always summon her according to her portrait. The ordinary ones among them all bribed the artist, but Wang Qiang, whose face and figure were very beautiful, was resolved not to seek favors by unfair means, and as a result the artist disfigured her appearance in her portrait.

Later the Xiongnu came on a peace mission, seeking a lovely lady from the Han emperor.[2] The emperor felt that Wang Qiang would fulfill the qualifications to go, but after having summoned her for an interview, was loathe to let her go. However, her name had already been sent on, and he did not wish to change in mid-course, so in the end she went.

When Wang Qiang was in her seventeenth year her manners and appearance were exceedingly beautiful, and she was known throughout the empire for her chastity. But her father, Wang Rang, would not promise her to any other important person who sought her hand, and in the end presented her to the Han emperor Yuan. The emperor was an impetuous and disorganized person who was unable to make distinctions between members of his harem, and Wang Qiang's resentment over this was of long standing. It happened that when the shanyu sent his emissary, the emperor ordered his palace ladies to adorn themselves and come out for the emissary to invite one of them. The emperor then announced throughout the palace, "Anyone who would like to go to the chanyu, rise!"

Sighing deeply, Qiang shifted from her mat and rose. When the emperor looked at her he was filled with surprise and remorse, but by this time the emissary had also seen her, and the emperor had no way of detaining her, so in the end he bestowed her upon the shanyu. The shanyu was greatly pleased and presented her with precious gifts.

---

[1] Chen followed this advice and offered his services to Xiang Liang.

[2] Comm.: In the first year of the Jingning era (33 B.C.E.), the chanyu Huhanxie came to court and said he wished to marry into the Han imperial family, so that he might become more intimately associated with it. Emperor Yuan bestowed on him the daughter of a good family from the rear palace named Wang Qiang. The shanyu was delighted and sent up a letter expressing his wish to protect the borders.

(The story is pure fiction, since the shanyu, Huhanxie, died in 31 B.C.E., only two years after his marriage to Wang Qiang, and was succeeded by the son of an earlier Xiongnu wife.)

Figure 6. Empress Chenxiao Zhang presides as a judge over the fate of a by Chou Ying (1509-1552).]

prisoner. [From *Chou's Illustrations of the Biographies of Woman (Chou Hua Lienu Zhuan)*

Wang Qiang had a son, named Shiwei. When the shanyu died Shiwei succeeded to the throne. The unusual custom with the Xiongnu is that when the father dies, the son takes his mother to wife. Wang Qiang asked Shiwei, "Are you a Chinese or a Xiongnu?"

Shiwei answered, "I just want to be a Xiongnu." At this Wang Qiang swallowed poison and took her own life.

3

The Han emperor Cheng (Liu Ao, r. 32–7 B.C.E.) doted upon Lady Flying Swallow, Zhao Feiyan. Feiyan slandered Ban Jieyu, claiming she was invoking imprecations (against Lady Zhao), whereupon they interrogated her. In her defense she said, "I've heard that 'life and death are appointed by Fate, and wealth and honor depend on Heaven.'[3] If even the cultivator of goodness doesn't find happiness, what can the doer of evil hope for? If ghosts and spirits have any understanding, they'll not accept the complaints of the evil and obsequious, and if they *haven't* any understanding, what advantage is there in complaining to them? Of course I didn't do it."[4]

4

When the Wei emperor Wu (Cao Cao) died (in 220 C.E.), his son, Emperor Wen (Cao Pi, r. 220–227 C.E.), took over all his father's palace women to serve as his own attendants. When Emperor Wen was ill and near death (in 227 C.E.), his mother, the Dowager Empress Bian,[5] came out of seclusion to visit the sick man. As the dowager empress entered the door she observed that the attendants were all

---

[3] *Analects of Confucius* XII, 5.

[4] Comm.: The emperor was going on an outing in the rear park and wished to have Lady Ban ride with him in the palanquin (*nian*). Jieyu declined his invitation. (The scene is illustrated, not without humor, in Gu Kaizhi's hand scroll, "Instructions of the Palace Preceptress," now in the British Museum, where the emperor is already accompanied by another woman.) When Zhao Feiyan slandered Empress Xu and Ban Jieyu, Jieyu countered with the defense (quoted in the anecdote above). The emperor took pity on her and presented her with one hundred catties of gold. Feiyan was arrogant and envious, and Jieyu, fearing her life would be endangered, requested to wait on the dowager empress Wang in the palace of Eternal Trust (Changxin gong). When the emperor died (7 B.C.E.), Jieyu was granted full rights of burial in the imperial mausoleum and placed there upon her death.

[5] Comm.: (When Empress Bian was born) there was a yellow vapor filling the room for several days, and her father, Marquis Jing, wondered at it and inquired of the fortune-teller Wang Yue, who said, "This is an auspicious omen." When she was in her twentieth year Lao Lao took her into his household in Jiao (Anhui). Her nature was simple and frugal, and she had no liking for flowery ornaments. She had the virtuous conduct befitting a mother.

the beloved favorites of the former days. She asked, "When did you come here?"

They replied, "We came over at the time of recalling the spirit (of the later Emperor Wu)."[6]

For this reason the dowager empress went no farther, but sighing, said, "Not even dogs and rats would eat your leftovers.[7] Death is certainly what you deserve!"

When she went to (his burial in) the imperial mausoleum, she did not even perform the ritual mourning.

5

Mother Zhao (Zhao Yi, d. 243 C.E.) once gave her daughter in marriage. When the daughter was about to depart for her husband's home, Mother Zhao admonished her, saying, "Be careful not to do any good."

The daughter said, "If I don't do good, then may I do evil?"

Her mother said, "If even good may not be done, how much less evil!"[8]

6

Xu Yun's wife was the daughter of Ruan Gong and the younger sister of Ruan Kan. She was extraordinarily homely. After the marriage ceremony was over, Yun had no intention of ever entering her apartment again. The members of her family were very upset over this. It happened once that Yun was having a guest come, and his wife had a female slave look to see who it was. She returned and reported, "It's Master Huan." Now "Master Huan" was Huan Fen.

The wife said, "Then there's nothing to worry about. Huan will surely urge him to come to my apartment."

---

[6] The departed spirit was recalled immediately after death by holding a garment formerly worn by the deceased.

[7] Comm.: The Marquis of Deng said, "(If I kill the Viscount of Chu,) people will not even eat my leftovers."

(When Wang Mang demanded the state seal from Empress Yuan in 9 C.E., she replied,) "Anyone who would take advantage of other people's misfortunes to seize their state, who no longer regards kindness or morality—not even dogs and pigs would eat his leftovers!"

[8] Comm.: There was once a man who was giving his daughter in marriage who instructed her, "If you do good, good people will resent it." She replied, "Then I suppose I ought to do evil?" He said, "If even good may not be done, how much less evil!"

Comm.: Empress Yang (consort of Sima Shi) said of this passage, "Although this advice is vulgar, it may be used to instruct people in the world."

As expected, Huan said to Xu, "Since the Ruan family gave you a homely daughter in marriage, he obviously did so with some purpose in mind. You would do well to look into it."

Accordingly, Xu had a change of heart and entered his wife's apartment. But the moment he saw her he immediately wanted to leave again. His wife foresaw that if he went out this time there would be no further chance of his returning, so she seized his robe in an effort to detain him. Xu took the occasion to say to his wife, "A wife should have four virtues.[9] How many of them do *you* have?"

His wife answered, "Where your bride is deficient is only in her appearance. But a *gentleman* should have a hundred deeds. How many have *you*?"

"I have them all."

"Of those hundred deeds, virtue is the first. If you love sensual beauty but don't love virtue,[10] how can you say you have them all?"

Yun looked ashamed, and thereafter held her in respect and honor.

7

While Xu Yun was serving as a clerk in the Board of Civil Office most of his appointments were from his own village. The Wei emperor Ming (Cao Rui, r. 227–239 C.E.) dispatched an officer of the Palace Guard to apprehend him. Yun's wife (Lady Ruan) came out and warned her husband, saying, "An enlightened ruler may be forced to yield through reason, but it is difficult to appeal to him through emotions."

After Yun arrived, the emperor closely interrogated him. Yun replied, "(Confucius said,) 'Recommend those who are known to you.'[11] Your servant's fellow villagers are the ones who are known to him. Your Majesty may investigate and see for yourself if they are suited to their offices or not. If they're not suited to their offices, your servant will bear the blame for it."

After investigation, it was found that for every office he had secured

---

[9] Comm.: The nine preceptresses have charge of the methods of womanly instruction in training the nine imperial concubines in womanly virtue, womanly speech, womanly appearance, and womanly work. (Zheng Yuan's comment interprets these to mean, respectively, chastity and obedience, graciousness and cultivation, complaisance and loveliness, and the weaving of silk and linen.)

[10] *Analects of Confucius* IX, 16: "I have not seen any who love virtue as they love sensual beauty."

[11] *Analects of Confucius* XIII, 2.

the right man, so that in the end the emperor released him. And since Yun's clothing was worn and tattered, the emperor issued an order to supply him with new clothes.

When Yun was first apprehended, his entire household was weeping and wailing, but his bride, Lady Ruan, said with complete self-composure, "Don't worry. After a while he'll return." Whereupon she cooked some millet gruel and waited for him. In a short time Yun arrived.[12]

8

When Xu Yun was punished (in 254 c.e.) by Prince Jing Sima Shi, his servants went in to tell his wife (Lady Ruan), who was just then at her weaving. Her spirit and facial expression showed no change. She only said, "I knew it was so, long ago."[13]

The servants wanted to hide Yun's songs, but his wife said, "Don't concern yourselves with the sons' affairs."

Later she moved to the neighborhood of Yun's tomb. Prince Jing dispatched Zhong Hui to visit the boys. If the level of their ability came up to that of their father, he was to apprehend them. The sons consulted with their mother about it, and she said, "Even though you two are fine boys, your ability and endowment are not excessive. If you speak out frankly with him whatever is in your hearts and

---

[12] Comm.: Earlier while Yun was serving in the Board of Civil Office, he selected and transferred the grand warden of a certain commandery. Emperor Ming suspected that the man he employed was not in the proper sequence and was about to punish him for it. Yun's wife, Lady Ruan, came out barefooted and said, "An enlightened ruler, etc." Yun nodded assent and went in. When the emperor angrily upbraided him, Yun replied, "Although the term for the warden of Such-and-such Commandery was full, and his documents had arrived first, nevertheless the year (of appointment) is secondary; the *day* is primary."

The emperor, coming forward, took up the case and examined it, and finally became reconciled. When he dismissed Yun, observing that his clothes were worn out, he said, "You're an honest official."

(It seems that the two wardens' terms of office were up simultaneously, and both were eligible for transfer. Yun had merely transferred the one whose documents indicated an early *day* of appointment, disregarding the fact that in terms of the *year* both were eligible.)

[13] Comm.: Earlier Xu Yun had been on intimate terms with Xiahou Xuan and Li Feng. There was a falsely fabricated edict making Xuan generalissimo and Yun grand marshal, both with noble rank and high authority. Without warning someone came riding before dawn and handed down the edict to Yun's gateman, announcing, "There's an edict!" and then galloped away. Yun threw the document in the fire and burned it without revealing its contents to Sima Shi.

thoughts, you'll have nothing to worry about. It's not necessary to show extreme grief, either; stop at whatever point Hui stops. Beyond that you might ask a few questions about affairs at court." The sons followed her advice. After Hui returned he reported the circumstances (to Prince Jing), and in the end they were spared.

9

Wang Guang took to wife the daughter of Zhuge Dan. When he entered her room and they exchanged words for the first time, Wang blurted out to his wife, "My bride's spirit and appearance are ignoble and low-class, totally unlike her father!"

His wife replied, "My great husband can't exactly compare with his father (Wang Ling), either, yet he's pitting a mere woman against a magnificent hero!"[14]

The following year (254 C.E.) Li Feng was arrested. Yun was about to go for an interview with the generalissimo Sima Shi and had already gone out the gate, but was vacillating and uncertain. When he was halfway there, he turned to go back to fetch his ceremonial trousers. When the generalissimo heard about it, he chided him, saying, "Certainly I have arrested Li Feng. What are all you gentlemen and great officers so nervous about?"

It happened that the General Governing the North, Liu Jing had just died, so Yun was appointed in his place. The generalissimo sent a letter to Yun in which he said, "Although General Governing the North is a post with few duties, you will be controlling an entire area. I will think of you beating the flowery drum, establishing your vermilion credentials, putting your local province in order. This is what might be called 'walking by day dressed in embroidered silks.'" (A parody of a celebrated remark by Xiang Yu.)

It happened that some official memorialized the throne to the effect that Yun had previously taken official food and monies and grain and distributed them without authorization to various riffraff and to his own underlings. His death sentence was commuted to banishment to the border. He died *en route*.

When Yun was appointed General Governing the North he was happy, and said to his wife, "Now I know I've escaped!" His wife replied, "Your ruin is obvious in this; what escape is there?"

Since Yun had correct (i.e., loyalist) feelings, and was on bad terms with "Emperor Wen" (Sima Zhao), the later had him killed in secret.

The Commentary also mentions a letter of Lady Ruan to her husband in which she describes the origins of his troubles in terms that are "exceedingly bitter and heartrending," but whose text it unfortunately finds "too long" to record.

[14] A later commentator, who refers to himself as "Your servant," writes: "Wang Guang was a famous gentleman; how could he have spoken lightly of his father-in-law? The story is untrue!"

10

When Wang Jing was young he lived in poverty and want, but after he became an official his salary reached two thousand piculs. His mother said to him, "You were originally the son of a poor family. Now that your salary has reached two thousand piculs, don't you think you might stop with this?"

Jin was unable to use her advice, and eventually became president of the Imperial Secretariat. But since he had assisted the Wei, he was deemed disloyal to the Jin, and was apprehended (in 260 C.E.). Weeping profusely, he apologized to his mother, saying, "Because I failed to follow your advice, we've now come to today's extremity!"

Without the slightest expression of reproach, his mother said to him, "As a son you were filial, and as a minister you were loyal. With both filial devotion and loyalty, in what way have you betrayed me?"[15]

11

The first time Shan Tao met Ji Kang and Ruan Ji he became united with them in friendship "stronger than metal and fragrant as

---

[15] Comm.: During the troubles of Cao Mao (in 260 C.E.), the palace attendants, Wang Chen and Wang Ye, hastened to inform Sima Zhao, but Wang Jing, because he was a proper and honest man, did not leave the palace with them. Through Chen and Ye he declared his intention, but later Zhao had Jing executed together with his mother.

Comm.: When Wang Chen and Wang Ye were about to leave (the palace), they called out to Jing, who did not follow them but said, "My dear friends, you go ahead."

Comm.: Earlier, when Cao Mao was about to punish Sima Zhao on his own, Jing had admonished him, saying, "Long ago when Duke Zhao of Lu (sixth century B.C.E.) couldn't endure the Ji family, he was defeated and fled and lost his state, becoming the laughingstock of the whole realm. Today the power has rested in the Sima family for a long time. It is not a matter of only one day's standing that everyone in court would give their lies for them, without any regard for principles either of rebellion or subservience. Moreover, the Palace Guard is an empty shell without an inch of armor. How could Your Majesty possibly make use of it? Yet, if suddenly you should do so, by attempting to rid yourself of evil, would you not only deepen it the more?"

Mao did not listen. Afterward, they killed both Jing and his mother. When he was about to die, he wept and apologized to his mother, but her facial expression did not change. Smiling, she said to him, "Who among men doesn't die? In the past the reason I restrained you was that I feared you wouldn't keep to your proper place. But now that we're both dying together, what is there to regret?"

Comm.: Wang Jing was a proper and honest man, but because he was disloyal to our dynasty (i.e., Jin) he was executed.

Comm.: According to what is recorded in other accounts, Jing was really loyal and blameless toward Wei. Yet the *Wei-Jin Shiyu* states on the one hand that he was "a proper and honest man," and on the other that "through Chen and Ye he declared his intention." What a contradiction! Therefore the words of the other accounts get closer to the truth.

orchids."[16] Shan's wife, Lady Han, realized that her husband's relationship with the two men was different from ordinary friendships,
and asked him about it. Shan replied, "It is only these two gentlemen
whom I may consider the friends of my mature years."

His wife said, "In antiquity Xi Fuji's wife also personally observed
Hu Yan and Zhao Cui. I'd like to peep at these friends of yours. Is it
all right?"

On another day the two men came, and his wife urged Shan to
detain them overnight. After preparing wine and meat, that night she
made a hole through the wall, and it was dawn before she remembered to return to her room.

When Shan came in he asked her, "What did you think of the
two men?" His wife replied, "Your own ability is in no way comparable to theirs. It's only on the basis of your knowledge of men and
your judgment that you should be their friend."

Shan said, "They, too, have always considered my judgment to be
superior."[17]

12

The daughter born to Wang Dun's wife, lady Zhong (Zhong Yan),
was beautiful and chaste. Her elder brother, Wang Ji, was looking
about for a good match for her, but had not yet found any. There was
a certain son of a military family who had outstanding ability, and
Wang, wishing to give his younger sister in marriage to him, consulted
his mother about it. Lady Zhong said, "If he really is someone with
ability, his background may be overlooked. However, you must be sure
to let me see him."

Wang Ji accordingly had the son of the military family mingle with
a crowd of commoners, and let his mother watch them from behind
the curtain. Afterward his mother said to Ji, "The one with such-and-
such clothes and physique—isn't he the one you had picked?"

---

[16] *The Classic of Changes*: When two men are of one mind, their keenness will cut metal;
the words of those who are of one mind are fragrant as orchids.

[17] Comm.: Shan Tao's cultivated tolerance was untrammeled and free, and his judgment
vast and far-reaching. His mind remained beyond the realm of worldly affairs, yet he
stooped and rose with the times. He once had a relationship with Ruan Ji and Ji Kang
that transcended words. But whereas all the other gentlemen encountered difficulties in
the world, Tao alone preserved his vast overflowing judgment.

Comm.: Lady Han possessed ability and understanding. Before Shan Tao became an
official he used to say to her in jest, "You can endure poverty, but when I reach one of
the Three Ducal Offices, I don't know whether you can stand being a lady or not, that's
all!"

Wang Ji replied, "He's the one."

His mother said, "This boy's ability is adequate to raise him above the crowd. However, his background is humble, and if he doesn't have a long life, he'll never get to exercise his ability or usefulness. As I observed his physiognomy and bony structure, it's evident he won't live to old age. You may not contract a marriage with him." Wang Ji followed her advice, and as it turned out, in a few years the son of the military family died.

13

Jia Chong's first wife, Li Wan, was the daughter of Li Feng. When Feng was executed (in 254 C.E.), she was divorced and exiled to the border (Lak-lang, Korea). Later, she was pardoned and allowed to return. But Chong had by then already been remarried to Guo Huai, the daughter of Guo Pei. Emperor Wu (Sima Yan, r. 265–290 C.E.) made a special dispensation, permitting Chong to have a left-hand and right-hand wife. But Lady Li, who was living apart outside the capital, was unwilling to return to Chong's house.[18] Lady Guo said to Chong, "I want to go over and have a look at this Li woman."

Chong said, "She's a firm, unbending person with ability and spirit. It would be better if you didn't go." In spite of this, Lady Guo decked herself out in her full regalia and went at the head of a large retinue of attendants and slaves. When she arrived and entered the door, Lady Li rose to greet her, and Guo unconsciously found her legs giving way of their own accord, and presently she was kneeling down, repeatedly making obeisance. After she had returned and related the incident to Chong, he said, "What did I tell you?"[19]

---

[18] Comm.: When Emperor Wu ascended the throne (265 C.E.), Lady Li was pardoned and returned to Luoyang, and her daughter, Jia Quan, the consort of Prince Xian of Qi (Sima You, d. 283 C.E.) wanted to have Chong send Lady Guo away and take back her mother. Chong would not agree to this, but built a villa for Lady Li outside Luoyang and had no communication with her.

When Chong's mother, Lady Liu, was about to die, Chong asked her what she wanted to say, and she replied, "I instructed you to welcome Lady Li back, and you still weren't willing. What point is there in asking about anything else?"

[19] Comm.: Emperor Wu, in view of the fact that Li Feng had offended the house of Jin, and moreover because Lady Guo was the mother of the consort of the crown prince, Sima Zhong (later Emperor Hui, r. 290–306 C.E.), and therefore had no reason to be divorced, accordingly sent down an edict requiring Jia to sever all relations (with Lady Li), and not permitting any communication with her.

Comm.: After Jia Chong had divorced Lady Li, he was remarried to Guo Huai, the daughter of Guo Pei, the grand warden of Cheng-yang. After the ban against Lady Li

14

Jia Chong's first wife, Lady Li, wrote a book called *Instructions for Daughters*, which gained currency in the world. Lady Li's daughter, Jia Quan, became the consort of Prince Xian of Qi (Sima You), and Jia Nanfeng, the daughter of Chong's second wife, Lady Guo (Guo Huai), became the empress of Emperor Hui (Sima Zhong, r. 291–306 c.e.). When Chong died (in 282 c.e.) the daughters of Ladies Li and Guo each wished to have her own mother buried with him. For years the matter remained undecided, until Empress Jia was deposed (300 c.e.). Lady Li was then duly buried with Chong and the matter was finally settled.

15

When Wang Zhan was young he had never been engaged to be married, and on his own behalf he sought the hand of the daughter of He Pu. Since his father, Wang Chang, considered him to be stupid, and there happened to be no marriageable person available, Chang let him let his son follow his fancy, and gave his consent.

After they were married, it turned out that the bride possessed both beautiful features and chaste virtue. After she gave birth to Wang Cheng, she became the maternal model of the Wang family. Someone asked Zhan, "How did you know what kind of person she was?"

---

had been lifted, and imperial rescript permitted Chong to have a left-hand and a right-hand wife, Chong's mother also admonished him to welcome Lady Li back. Guo Huai was furious. Baring her arms she scolded Chong, saying, "In your merit as codifier of the laws and aider in founding the dynasty, I have a part. Why does Li get to share it with me?"

Chong accordingly built a house in Yongnian Village (a suburb of Luoyang) to keep Lady Li safe. Guo Huai only learned of it later. Whenever Chong left the house, she always sent someone to keep an eye on him. So, although the imperial rescript permitted him to have a left-hand and a right-hand wife, Chong replied to it with humble protestations that he dared not fulfill this ritual obligation.

Comm.: Now the *Jin zhugongzan*, on the one hand, states that Emperor Wu sent down a rescript not permitting Lady Li to return, but the other sources, on the other hand, both state that the rescript permitted his having a left-hand and a right-hand wife, but that Chong, out of fear of Lady Guo, dared not welcome Li back. The accounts in these three sources are by no means unanimous, and it is not known which is correct.

However, there were other reasons for Lady Li's not returning, and the statement in the *Shishuo* that she herself was unwilling to return is mistaken. Moreover, Guo Huai was stubborn and wolfish, how could she have made obeisance when she approached Li? It's all nonsense!

He replied, "I once saw her at the well drawing water. In every movement and gesture she never departed from her normal manner, and never once did she cast an improper glance. It was by this that I knew."

16

Wang Hun's wife, Zhong Yan, a daughter of the Zhong family, was the great-granddaughter of the grand tutor, Zhong You, and in her own right possessed outstanding ability and womanly virtue.[20] Lady Zhong and Lady He, as the wives respectively of the elder and younger Wang brothers, Wang Hun and Wang Zhan, always treated each other with affectionate respect. Lady Zhong did not, because of her noble origin, act condescendingly toward Lady He, nor did Lady He, because of her lowly origin, act obsequiously toward lady Zhong. Within the household of Wang Zhan's son, Wang Cheng, they followed the rules of Lady He, and within the household of Wang Hun they took as their model the etiquette of Lady Zhong.

17

Li Zhong was the son of Li Bing and a famous gentleman of the central Xia (the area of Luoyang). At the time people compared him to Wang Yan. When Sun Xiu first wanted to establish his prestige and power (in 300 C.E.), everyone said, "Yue Guang is the people's[21] hope; he may not be killed. Someone less important than Li Zhong, on the other hand, isn't worth killing." So he compelled Zhong to take his own life.

Earlier, while Zhong was at home, someone ran in though the gate, and, taking a memorandum from inside his topknot, showed it to Zhong. As Zhong read it, his face paled. Entering the inner quarters, he showed it to his daughter, who immediately cried out, "It's all over!" Zhong, understanding her meaning, went out and proceeded to take his own life.[22]

---

[20] Comm.: Lady Zhong possessed literary ability, and her poems, poetic essays, hymns, and obituaries have become current in the world.

[21] Emending *shi*, "family," to the graphically similar *min*, "people."

[22] Comm.: The sources all state that Zhong, realizing that the Prince of Zhao, Sima Lun, was about to raise a revolt, became so sick over it that he eventually died. Yet this source claims that he committed suicide, which runs quite contrary to the facts. Moreover, Sima Lun and Sun Xiu were cruel and tyrannical men, who with every move inflicted death and execution. Since they wished to establish their authority and power, they would without question have killed Zhong openly. Why should they have forced him to commit suicide?

This daughter was extremely high-minded and intelligent, and Zhong always consulted her about every situation.

18

When Zhou Jun was serving as General Pacifying the East, he was once out hunting when a violent rainstorm came up, just as he was passing by the home of the Li family (Li Bozong) of Ju'nan Commandery (Henan). The Li family was wealthy and well provided for, but, as it happened, none of the men were at home. There was a daughter named Luoxiu, who, hearing that there was a noble person outside, with the help of one female slave slaughtered pigs and goats and prepared food and drink for several tens of men. Everything was carried out to perfection, and Zhou did not hear the sound of anyone. When he peeked in surreptitiously, all he saw was a lone girl, whose form and appearance were unusually beautiful. Jun took the occasion to seek her for a concubine, but her father and brothers would not give their consent.

Luoxiu said to them, "Since our household is 'ruined and in trouble'[23] why grudge a lone daughter? If we contract a marriage with a noble family, hereafter we might be greatly benefited."

Her father and brothers followed her advice, and subsequently she gave birth to Zhou Yi and his younger brothers, Zhou Song and Zhou Mo. When they were grown Luoxiu said to Yi and the others, "The only reason I compromised by integrity to become a concubine in your family was to provide for my own household. If you don't treat the members of my family as you would your own kin, I for my part don't care to live out my remaining years."

Zhou Yi and the others all obeyed her command, and from this time onward, as long as Lady Li lived, her family received openly equal treatment with members of the Zhou family.[24]

19

When Tao Kan was young he had great ambitions, but his family was desperately poor, and he lived with his mother, Lady Zhan. A native of the same commandery (Poyang, in Jiangsi), Fan Kui by name, had always been well known, and when he was recommended for the degree Filial and Incorrupt (in 303 C.E.), he stopped at Kan's house

---

[23] *The Book of Odes*, No. 264, stanza 5.

[24] Liu Jun notes in the Commentary that according to the Zhou Genealogy, Chou Jun "took to wife" the daughter of Li Bozong. She was not his "concubine."

for the night (on his way to the capital.) At the time, sleet and snow had been falling for days, and Kan's house was "bare as hanging stone chimes," yet Kui's horses and servants were extremely numerous. Kan's mother, Lady Zhan, said to Kan, "You just go and see to it that the guests stay. I'll think of something."

Since Lady Zhan's hair reached all the way to the floor, she cut it off and made it into two switches, which she sold for several *hu* of rice. She then chopped the pillars of the room, removing half of each for firewood, and ripped up the straw bed mats to make fodder for the horses. As the day drew toward evening, she served an exquisite meal, and no one in the company had any lack. Kui not only sighed in admiration over her ability and resourcefulness, but also thanked her profusely for her generous intentions.

The next morning, as Kui was leaving, Kan escorted him on his way, not stopping until he had traveled a hundred *li* or more. Kui said, "I think you'd better return, sir (*jun*)." But Kan still did not go back. Finally Kui said, "You (*qing*) may go now! When I get to Luoyang, I'll say a good word on your behalf." At this Kan finally turned back.

When Kui reached Luoyang, he proceeded to praise Kan to Yang Zhuo, Gu Rong, and the others, and thus he gained a great and excellent reputation.[25]

---

[25] Comm.: Tao Kan's father, Dan, took to wife the daughter of the Zhan family of Xin'gan (Jiangxi), who gave birth to Kan. Lady Zhan was modest and respectful and possessed wisdom and ingenuity. Because the Tao family was poor and low in status, she spun and reeled silk to provide for Kan, and had him make friendships with persons superior to himself. When Kan was young he served as a petty official in Xunyang Commandery (Jiangzi). The candidate for the degree Filial and Incorrupt, Fan Kui of Poyang Commandery, was once passing by and stopped overnight at Kan's house. Lady Zhan removed the straw mats on which they slept and ripped them up to provide for him. She secretly cut her hair and sold it to supply the needs of the guests. When Kui learned of it he sighed in admiration. As Kui was leaving, Kan accompanied him on his way. Kui asked, "Do you want to be an official?"

Kan replied, "I have an ambition to become grand warden of a commandery."

Kui said, "I'll talk with people and see if it can be done." When he passed by Lujiang Commandery (near Xunyang), he praised Kan to Zhang Kui, who summoned him to fill a vacancy on his staff, and recommended Kan for the degree Filial and Incorrupt. He was appointed secretary.

At the time, [the senior secretary of] Yuzhang [Principality] (Kiangsi), Yang Zhuo, was a fellow villager of Kan, and had been praised in the village evaluations. Kan went to visit him. Zhuo said, *The Book of Changes* states: 'The pure and steadfast is worthy to manage affairs' (Hex. I). Tao Kan is such a person." Riding with him in the same carriage, he went to see the clerk of the Central Secretariat, Gu Rong. [Rong admired him greatly.] Someone chided Zhao, saying, "What are you doing riding in the same carriage with a commoner?"

20

When Tao Kan was young he served as a minor official in charge of fish weirs (in Xunyang Commandery). He once sent a present of salted fish in an earthenware crock to his mother (Lady Zhan). His mother sealed the fish in the crock, and, handing it back to the messenger, sent back a letter upbraiding Kan as follows: "While you are serving as a minor official, if I receive official property as a present, it is not only of no benefit; it even adds to my unhappiness!"[26]

21

When Huan Wen subdued Shu (Sichuan, in 347 C.E.), he took Lady Li, the younger sister of the last ruler, Li Shi (r. 343–347 C.E.), as a concubine, and treated her with extreme favor, always keeping her in an apartment behind his study. Huan's wife, the Princess of Nan-Kang, knew nothing about it at first, but after she had heard,

---

Zhuo replied, "This is an impoverished man of ability."

(The garbled text has been restored by interpolations from *Jinshu* 66.7a [*History of Jin*], which appear in square brackets.)

Comm.: After Tao Kan's mother had cut off her hair to take care of her guest, someone hearing of it sighed and said, "Unless she were such a mother, she would never have borne such a son!" So saying, he recommended Kan to Zhang Kui. Yang Zhuo also recommended him. Later, when he became grader for ten commanderies, he recommended Kan for minor grader in Poyang Commandery, and after that he began to gain high rank.

[26] Comm.: Kan's mother, Lady Zhan, was worthy and intelligent and full of proper instructions. While Kan was in Wuchang (Hubei), he used to eat and drink at his ease with his underlings, but always observed a limit in his drinking. When someone urged him to take a little more, Kan was reflective for a long time, and finally said, "Long ago in my youth I was often under the influence of liquor, and as a consequence my two parents suffered want. It is for this reason I dare not overstep my limit."

When Kan was in mourning for his mother (d. ca. 307 C.E.) and was living beneath her tomb, two strangers arrived unannounced to offer condolences, and then withdrew without weeping. Their bearing and dress were unusual and strange, and Kan realized they were not ordinary men. He dispatched someone to follow and observe them, but the man saw only a pair of cranes flying away into the sky.

Comm.: Tao Kan caught a fish in a border area southwest of Xunyang, and personally gave the pool the name "Gate of Cranes" (Hemen).

(The inclusion of these seemingly unrelated events in the commentary seems to imply that two cranes—actually transcendent beings—were the fish that Lady Zhan refused to accept.)

Comm.: While Meng Zong (third century C.E.) director of works for the Wu Kingdom, was keeper of Thunder Lake (Leichi, in Anhui), he sent a present of salted fish to his mother, who refused to accept it. It was not Tao Kan who did so. I suspect some later person fabricated the story on the basis of Meng's experience.

she came with several tens of female attendants, brandishing a naked sword to attack her. It happened that just then Lady Li was combing her hair, and her tresses fell covering the floor, while the color of her skin was like the luster of jade. She made no movement of her facial expression, but said calmly, "My kingdom has been destroyed and my family ruined. I had no wish to come here. If I could be killed today it would only be what I have longed for from the beginning."

The princess withdrew in shame.[27]

22

Yu You was the younger brother of Yu Xi. When Xi was executed (in 272 C.E.), those who killed him, were on the point of killing You as well. Huan Nüyou, the wife of You's son, Yu Yuan, was the daughter of Huan Wen's younger brother, Huan Huo. Going to Huan Wen's home in her bare feet she sought to be let in, but the gatekeeper barred the way and would not admit her. In a shrill voice the girl cried out, "What kind of petty person are you who won't even let me enter my own uncle's gate!" So saying, she rushed in headlong. Amid wailing and tears she pleaded with Huan, saying, "Yu You has always been dependent on others. With one leg three inches short, how could he ever become a rebel?"

Huan replied, laughing, "Your husband (and his family) were really and truly in danger!" Whereupon he pardoned Yu You's entire family.[28]

23

Xie An's wife, Lady Liu, curtained off her female attendants and had them come out in front and perform music and dancing. She let Xie watch them momentarily and then lowered the curtains. When Xie

---

[27] Comm.: After Huan Wen had pacified Shu, he took the daughter of Li Shi as a concubine. The princess (Huan's wife), a ferocious and jealous woman, knew nothing about it at first, but after she knew she went with drawn sword to Lady Li's apartment, wishing to cut off her head then and there. When she saw Lady Li, the latter was at the window combing her hair. Staying her hand, she faced the princess, her spirit and expression calm and sedate. When she spoke, her words were extremely sad and poignant, whereupon the princess, throwing away her sword, came forward to embrace her, crying, "Dear child, even *I* feel affection for you as I see you; how much more must that old rascal!" And from that time on she befriended her.

[28] Comm.: Huan Wen killed Yu Xi's younger brother, Qian (in 371 C.E.). Xi, hearing of trouble, escaped (to Hailing, in Kiangsu). Xi's younger brother, You, was slated for execution, but his son's wife, a daughter of the Huan family, pleaded with Huan Wen, and You was pardoned.

sought to have them opened again, Lady Liu said, "I fear it might damage your abundant virtue."[29]

24

Huan Chong did not like to wear new clothes. Once after his bath his wife, Wan Nüzong, purposely sent some new clothes for his use. Chong was highly incensed and insisted on having them taken away. His wife had them taken back to him once more with the relayed message, "If your clothes never go through the stage of being new, by what process will they ever become old?" Lord Huan laughed aloud and put them on.

25

Wang Xizhi's wife, Lady Chi (Chixuan), said to her two younger brothers, Chi Yin and Chi Tan, "In the Wang household, whenever they see the two Xies, Xie An and Xie Wan, they overturn the baskets and put their clogs on backward (in their haste to meet them). But when they see you two coming, everything is calm and peaceful. You may as well not trouble yourselves to visit anymore."

26

Wan Ningzhi's wife, Lady Xie (Xie Daoyun), after going to lie in the Wang family, felt a great contempt for Ningzhi. On returning for a visit to the Xie household, her mood was most unhappy. Her uncle, Xie An, hoping to comfort and relieve her, said, "Master Wang is, after all, the son of Wang Xizhi, and as a person in his own right isn't at all bad. Why do you resent him so much?"

She replied, "In this one household, for uncles I have (you), Ada, and the central commander (Xie Wan or Xie Ju), and for cousins and

---

[29] Comm.: Lady Liu, the wife of the grand tutor, Xie An, would not permit him to have any favored concubines in separate quarters, but his lordship was very fond of music and female beauty, and, unable to maintain his chastity, wanted to set up female entertainers and concubines. His nephews on both sides of the family secretly understood his feelings, and together admonished lady Liu that she should make some accommodations, saying, "The songs Guanju ("Songs," No. I) and Zhongsi (No. 5), *The Book of Odes* display the virtue of not being jealous" Lady Liu, realizing they were criticizing her, asked, "And who wrote those songs?"

They replied, "The Duke of Zhou."

Lady Liu retorted, "The Duke of Zhou was a *man* and wrote them for himself, that's all. Now if it had been the *Duchess* of Zhou, the traditions wouldn't have contained these words!"

brothers I have Feng (Xie Shao), Hu (Xie Lang), E (Xie Xuan), and Mo (Xie Yuan). But who would have ever imagined that between heaven and earth there actually exists someone called Master Wang?"

27

The armrest (*ji*) on which Han Bo's mother, Lady Yin, used to lean was broken and falling apart. Her grandson on her daughter's side, Bian Fanzhi, seeing the armrest in such bad condition, was on the point of exchanging it, when Lady Yin replied, "If I didn't lean on this armrest, how would you ever get to see any antiques?"

28

Wan Ningzhi's wife, Xie Daoyun, said to her younger brother, Xie Xuan, "Why is it that [in your studies]³⁰ you make no progress whatsoever? Is it that you occupy your mind with worldly matters, or that there are limitations set by your heaven-appointed lot?"

29

When Chi Chao died (in 377 C.E.), the elder and younger brothers of his wife, Zhou Matou, wanted to welcome their sister back to the Zhou household, but to the very end she was unwilling to return home. She said, "Even though in life I can't share a common room with Master Chi, in death may I not 'share a common grave'?"³¹

30

Xie Xuan held his elder sister, Xie Daoyun, in very high regard, while Zhang Xuan constantly sang the praises of his younger sister and wanted to match her against the other. A certain Ji Ni went to visit both the Zhang and the Xie families. When people asked him which was superior and which inferior, he replied, "Lady Wang's (i.e., Xie Daoyun's) spirit and feelings are relaxed and sunny; she certainly has the manner and style of (the Seven Worthies) beneath the (Bamboo) Grove.³² As for the wife of the Gu family (i.e., Zhan Xuan's sister), her pure heart gleams like jade; without a doubt she's the full flowering of wifely virtue."

---

³⁰ The phrase in square brackets is interpolated from the *Jinshu* (*History of Jin*).

³¹ See *The Book of Odes* No. 73:

In life, though we have separate rooms,
In death we'll share a common grave.

³² Active in the third century.

31

Wang Hui once went to visit Wang Xizhi's widow, Chixuan and asked, "Haven't your eyes and ears suffered any impairment yet?"

She replied, "Hair turning white and teeth falling out belong in the category of the physical body. But when it comes to eyes and ears, they are related to the spirit and intelligence. How could I let myself be cut off from other people?"[33]

32

Han Bo's mother, Lady Yin, accompanied her grandson, Han Huizhi, to Hengyang Commandery (Hunan). In Helu Island they met Huan Xuan. Bian Fanzhi,[34] who was her grandson on his mother's side, also came at the time to pay his respects. She said to him, "To think that I haven't died before seeing these generations of upstarts (Huan Wen and Huan Xuan) both become rebels!"

After they had been in Hengyang several years, Huizhi met disaster (in 404 C.E.) at the hands of Xuan's nephew, Huan Liang. Stroking his dead body, Lady Yin wept and said, "When your father (Han Bo) quit his post long ago as grand warden of Yuzhang Commandery (Jiangxi), the letter summoning him to the capital arrived in the morning, and by evening he set out. You (have been meaning to) leave this commandery and town for several years, but because of (involvement with) certain persons, you've been unable to move, and now at last you've come upon disaster. What more is there to say?"

---

[33] Comm.: Citing Chi Xuan's "Memorial of Thanks" (Xiebiao): I, Chi Xuan, am ninety years old, and my solitary body survives alone. I desired to be favored with Your Majesty's pity, and You alone have vouchsafed to take care of me.

(Chi Xuan outlived her husband, Wang Xizhi [d. ca. 365 C.E.], by about forty years.)

[34] Bian Fanzhi was deeply involved in Huan Xuan's usurpation.

30

NEW SONGS FROM
A JADE TERRACE
(Yutai Xinyong)
玉台新詠
Xu Ling
徐陵

New Songs from a Jade Terrace (Yutai xinyong) *was edited by the South-ern dynasty's well-known writer,* Xu Ling (507–583 C.E.). *According to* The Historical Record of the South (Nanshi), *Xu Ling was well educated and was able to read at age eight and grasp the* Book of Laozi *and* Zhuangzi *at age twelve. He also served the Emperor in different posts open to the literati.* Yutai xinyong *is in fact one of the most important anthologies of poetry since* The Book of Odes (Shijing) *and the* Chuci. *It collected 769 poems organized in ten volumes, mostly from the Southern dynasty. Xu Ling employed a specific selection standard, that is, he favored poems expressing women's feelings* (guiqing), *and love poetry. Liang Qichao (1873–1929 C.E.), a modern reformer, highly praised Xu Ling for "evoking a new style of poetry." Among the many great values of the* Yutai xinyong *is the fact that the works of several female writers would not have been preserved apart from this collection.*

Selections here include a few anonymous poems, collected under the heading, "Old Folksongs"; a poignant lament, "The Deserted Wife," that may have been written by a woman; four of Lu Yun's "Four Letter-Poems Between a Husband and Wife"; and the anonymous "A Peacock Southeast Flew," a long poem—somewhat reminiscent of Shakespeare's Romeo and Juliet—*that laments the tragic suicide of a young husband and wife who had been forcibly separated from each other. These selections con-tribute to the range of images featured in this anthology, in that the poems suggest some variation in society's expectations regarding what is appropriate behavior for women,*

From *New Songs from a Jade Terrace: An Anthology of Early Chinese Love Poetry*, by Anne Birrell (London: George Allen & Unwin, 1982). Copyright © 1982 by Anne M. Birrell. Reprinted by permission of Anne Birrell.

possibly a reflection of the enduring cultural differences between southern and northern China, even to this day. The good wives depicted in the "Old Folk Songs," for example, are hardly confined to the inner quarters. One local beauty, Luofu, speaks directly when spoken to by the prefect, and brags of her handsome young husband proudly serving in the army. Another goes out to welcome her guests, and cheerfully drinks a cup with them after serving them wine for refreshment. "The Deserted Wife," on the other hand, expresses the anxieties of a wife not yet able to get pregnant. "Please, my lord, don't be impatient!" she pleads, having lamented earlier that "With child she [the wife] is the moon that sails the skies, / Childless she's like a falling star." Lu Yun's "Four Letter-Poems" models another perspective on how marital fidelity may be preserved. Here the wife elicits pledges of the husband's personal devotion to her, by suggesting that while he is away from home surely he will succumb to the allure of the brilliant city women whom he encounters in his travels. How could a man not protest his innocence with one so skillful in the rhetoric of love waiting for him at home?

The most memorable and challenging of these is the anonymous "A Peacock Southeast Flew." It dramatizes how the selfish exploitation of filial piety could lead to tragedy. Though the young couple clearly is in love, the mother-in-law wants to break up the marriage so that through her son she can enter into a socially advantageous relationship with another family in the neighborhood. The daughter-in-law is harassed to the point when she returns to her father's house. The son ineffectually protests his mother's actions, while trying to assure his wife of his good intentions. Now having returned home, she endures the reproaches of her parents, and faces increasing pressure from her brother especially to find another husband. Then, after the dutiful son seems to have acquiesced in his mother's plans for his new marriage, he has a chance encounter in the woods with his beloved first wife, and they unburden themselves of their mutual misfortune, renew their vows, and enter into a mutual suicide pact. The young wife is the first to go, and then her husband hangs himself on hearing the news. Awestruck by the depths of their children's faithfulness to each other, the families arrange a joint burial for them on Mount Hua. The final scene at their gravesite is filled with omens signifying their enduring love, as readers are urged to "Learn this lesson and never forget!" Parents who abuse their children using the pretext of filial piety may find themselves deprived of the very children on whom their small-minded schemes depended.

Robin R. Wang

Old Folk Songs

Mulberry Up the Lane
Sunrise at the southeast corner
Shines on our Qin clan house.

The Qin clan has a fair daughter,
She is called Luofu.

Luofu is good at silkworm mulberry,
She picks mulberry at the wall's south corner.
Green silk is her basket strap,
Cassia her basket and pole.

On her head a twisting-fall hairdo,
At her ears bright moon pearls.
Green silk is her lower skirt,
Purple silk is her upper shirt.

Passersby see Luofu,
Drop their load, stroke their beard.
Young men see Luofu,
Take off their caps, put on headbands.
The ploughman forgets his plough,
The hoer forgets his hoe.
They come home cross and happy—
All from seeing Luofu.

A prefect from the south is here,
His five horses stand pawing the ground.
The prefect sends his servant forward
To ask, "Whose is the pretty girl?"
"The Qin clan has a fair daughter,
Her name is Luofu."
"Luofu, how old is she?"
"Not yet quite twenty,
A bit more than fifteen."

The prefect invites Luofu,
"Wouldn't you like a ride with me?"
Luofu steps forward and refuses:
"You are so silly, Prefect!
You have your own wife, Prefect,
Luofu has her own husband!
In the east more than a thousand horsemen,
My husband is in the lead.
How would you recognize my husband?
His white horse follows black colts,
Green silk plaits his horse's tail,
Yellow Gold braids his horse's head.

At his waist a Lulu dagger—
Worth maybe more than ten million cash.

"At fifteen he was a county clerk,
At twenty a court official,
At thirty a chancellor,
At forty lord of his own city."

"As a man he has pure white complexion,
Bushy whiskers on both cheeks.
Majestic he steps into his office,
Dignified he strides to the courtroom,
Where several thousand in audience
All say my husband has no rival!"

The Perfect Wife

What's up there in the sky?
Twinkle, twinkle stands White Elm star,
Cassia trees starrily grow along the way,
Green dragons face across road corners,
Male and female phoenixes sing lullabies,
A hen leads her nine chicks.
And as I look back upon the world of men
There's a scene of joy quite unique.

A fair wife goes out to greet her guests,
Her face happy and cheerful.
Bending low, she kneels twice,
Asks the guests, "Was your journey pleasant?"
She invites the guests up the north hall,
Seats the guests on woolen cushions.
Of clear white wine each his own tankard,
Beaded bubbles full at the brim.
She pours wine, hands it to her guests,
The guests say, "Hostess, you have some!"
She declines, kneels down twice,
Then she accepts one cup.
Before talk and laughter are ended,
She looks back to the left, gives orders in the kitchen:
"Hurry up and make a fine meal,
Mind you don't dilly-dally!"

Cordially she shows her guests out,
Majestic they stride into the office.

In showing the guests out she doesn't go too far,
Her foot won't cross the gate-pivot!

Taking a wife might be like this,
But even Qi Jiang was not so good.
A hearty wife who keeps a good house and home
Is worth more than one fine husband.

A Peacock Southeast Flew

At the close of the Han dynasty, during the years 196–220 C.E., the wife of Jiao Zhougqing, the magistrate of Luchiang prefecture, whose maiden name was Liu, was dismissed from home by her husband's mother. She swore to herself that she would never remarry, but her own parents and family brought down a great deal of pressure to bear on her. So she committed suicide by downing herself. When her husband, Zhougqing, learned of this, he also committed suicide by hanging himself from a tree in the garden. A contemporary poet felt deep sympathy for these two and composed a poem about them. It goes as follows:

A peacock southeast flew,
After five leagues it faltered.

"At thirteen I could weave white silk,
At fourteen I learned to make clothes.
At fifteen I played the many-stringed lute,
At sixteen recited Songs and History.
At seventeen I became your wife
And my heart was full of constant pain and sorrow."

"You became a government clerk,
I kept chaste, my love never straying.
At cockcrow I went in to weave at the loom,
Night after night found no rest.
In three days I cut five lengths of cloth,
Mother-in-law still nagged at my sloth.
It wasn't my weaving that was too slow,
But it's hard to be a wife in your home.
I don't want to be driven out,
But there's no way I can stay on here.
So please speak with you mother
To let me be sent home in good time."

The clerk heard these words
And up in the hall spoke with his mother.
"As a boy my physiognomy chart was unlucky,
I was fortunate to get such a wife as she.
We bound our hair, shared pillow and mat,
Vowed to be lovers till Yellow Springs.
We both have served you two years of three,
From the start not so long a time,
Yet the girl's conduct is not remiss,
Why do you treat her so unkindly?"

His mother said to the clerk,
"How can you be so soft!
This wife has no sense of decorum.
Whatever she does she goes her own way.
I've borne my anger for a long time now,
You must not just suit yourself!
Our east neighbors have a good daughter,
Her name is Qin Luofu.
So pretty her body, beyond compare,
Your mother will seek her for your wife.
It's best to dismiss this one as soon as we can.
Dismiss her, we won't let her stay!"

The government clerk knelt down in reply:
"Now I only have this to say, Mother.
If you dismiss this wife today,
For the rest of my life I will not remarry!"
His mother heard these words,
Thumped her bed, then in a fierce rage:
"My son, have you no respect?
How dare you speak in your wife's defense!
I have lost all feeling for you,
On no account will I let you disobey me!"

The government clerk, silent, without a word,
Bowed twice and went back within their doors.
He started to speak to his new wife,
Stammered, unable to talk.
"I myself would not drive you away,
But there's my mother, scolding and nagging.
You just go home for a little while.
Today I must report to the office.

It won't be for long, I'll soon be coming home,
And when I come back I'll be sure to fetch you.
So let this put your mind at rest.
Please don't contradict me!"

His new wife said to the clerk:
"No more of this nonsense!
Long ago in early springtime
I left home to come to your gates.
Whatever I did I obeyed your mother,
In my behavior never dared do as I pleased.
Day and night I tried hard at my work.
Brought low I am caught in a vice of misery.
My words have been blameless,
I fulfilled my duties diligently.
Why then, as I'm being summarily dismissed,
Do you still talk of my coming back here?
I have embroidered tunics,
Gorgeous they shine with a light of their own;
Red silk funnel bed curtains,
At the four corners hang scent sachets;
Dressing cases sixty or seventy,
Green jasper, green silk cord;
Many, many things, each of them different,
All sorts of things in these boxes.
I am despised, and my things also worthless,
Not worth offering your next wife,
But I'll leave them here as gifts.
From now on we'll never meet again.
From time to time please bring me some comfort,
And never, never forget me!"

The cock crew, outside it was getting light.
The new wife got up and carefully dressed.
She puts on her broidered lined gown
And four or five different things.
On her feet she slips silk shoes;
On her head tortoiseshell combs gleam;
Round her waist she wears flowing silk white,
On her ears wears bright moon pendants.
Her hands are like pared onion stems,
Her mouth seems rich scarlet cinnabar.

Svelte, svelte she walks with tiny steps,
Perfect, matchless in all the world.

She went up the high hall, bowed to Mother.
The mother heard she was leaving, didn't stop her.
"Long ago when I was a child,
I grew up in the countryside.
I had no schooling from the start,
On both counts would shame the man of a great house.
I received from you, Mother, much money and silk.
I do not want to be summarily dismissed;
Today, though, I am going back home.
I am afraid I have brought trouble to your house."

She withdrew and took leave of her sister-in-law.
Tears fell, beads of pearl.
"When I first came as a bride
You were beginning to lean on the bed.
Now as I am being dismissed,
You are as tall as I, sister.
Care for Mother will all your heart,
Be nice and help all you can.
On the first seventh and last ninth of the month,
When you're enjoying yourself, don't forget me!"

She left the gates, climbed the coach, departed.
Tears fell in more than a hundred streams.
The clerk's horse was in front,
The new wife's coach behind.
Clatter-clatter, how it rumbled, rumbled!
They met at the mouth of the main road,
He dismounted, got into her coach.
With bowed head he whispered these words in her ear:
"I swear I won't be parted from you,
Just go home for a little while.
Today I am going to the office,
Not for long, I'll be back home.
I swear by Heaven I'll not betray you!"

His new wife said to the clerk:
"I feel you love me fondly,
And you seem to hold me in high esteem.
Before long I hope you will come for me.
You must be rock firm,
I must be a pliant reed.

The pliant reed is supple as silk,
The firm rock will not be rolled away.
I have my father and brothers,
Their temper is wild as thunder;
I fear they will not abide by my wishes,
But oppose me, destroy my hopes."
They raised their hands in a long, long farewell,
For both loves the same wistful longing.

She entered the gates, went up the family hall,
Approaching, withdrawing with expressionless face.
Her mother beat her fist loud:
"We didn't plan for you to return on your own!
At thirteen I taught you to weave,
At fourteen you could make clothes,
At fifteen you played the many-stringed lute,
At sixteen you knew ceremonial rites,
At seventeen I sent you off in marriage,
Telling you to swear not to give offense.
What have you done wrong now that
Uninvited you come home yourself!"
"I, Lanzhi, have brought shame on my mother,
But your child has truly done no wrong."
Her mother's heart was broken with deep sorrow.

She had been home more than ten days
When the district magistrate sent a matchmaker,
He said, "We have a third young master,
Charming beyond compare in all the world!
He is barely eighteen or nineteen,
Eloquent, very talented he is!"

Mother said to daughter:
"Go, you may answer yes."
Her daughter choked back the tears:
"When I, Lanzhi, first came home,
The clerk showed me great kindness,
Swore on oath he'd never desert me.
If I were now to betray our love,
I fear this act would be wrong.
Let's break off the betrothal talks.
In good time we'll discuss the matter again."

Her mother explained to the matchmaker:
"In all humility, I do have such a daughter.

She went away in marriage, but is returned to our gates.
She was reluctant to be an official's wife—
How would she please a fine gentlemen's son?

I hope you will be successful with other inquiries.
We cannot at present give permission."
The matchmaker was gone many days,
Then a deputy was sent for, asked to reconsider.
"They say they have a daughter, Lanzhi,
Whose forefathers for generations have held office.
Say, 'My master says he has a fifth son,
Elegant, refined, not yet married.
My deputy I've sent as matchmaker,
And a secretary to bring his message.'"

Immediately they put their case: "The prefect's family
Has such a fine son.
He wishes to take solemn vows of marriage,
And so we are sent to your house."

The mother refused the matchmaker:
"My daughter has already sworn an oath.
What dare a mother say?"
When her brother learned of this
He was disappointed and furious in his heart.
He broached the matter, telling his sister:
"In these arrangements, why are you so unreasonable?
First you married a government clerk,
Later you might marry a squire.
Fortune is like Heaven and Earth,
It can bring glory to your person.
Not to wed this lord now,
What will happen in the future?"

Lanzhi looked up and replied:
"In fact what my brother says is right.
I left home to serve my bridegroom.
Midway I returned to my brother's gates.
It's my place to follow my brother's wishes,
Why would I do as I please?
Though I made a vow with the government clerk,
I may never chance to meet him again.
Tell them straight away I agree to marry,
They may arrange a betrothal."

The matchmaker got down from the ritual couch:
"Yes, yes!" and "Quite, quite!"
He went back to the office and explained to the prefect:
"Your servant has carried out your command.
Our discussion has met with great success!"

When the prefect heard this
He rejoiced in his heart.
He scanned the calendar, opened the almanac:
"It will be auspicious this month,
The Six Cardinal Points are in conjunction.
The luckiest day is the thirtieth,
Today it's now the twenty-seventh,
You may go and conclude the nuptials."

Discussions on both sides hastened the wedding gifts,
In succession like floating clouds.
A green sparrow and white swan boat,
At the four corners were dragon banners
Softly curling in the wind.
A gold coach of jade its wheels,
Prancing piebald horses,
Colored silk threads and gold stitched saddles.
A wedding gift of three million cash,
All strung on green cord.
Assorted silks, three hundred bolts,
From Jiaoguang a purchase of fine fish.
A retinue of four or five hundred men
Densely massed set out to the palace.

Mother said to daughter:
"I have just received a letter from the prefect,
Tomorrow he will come to invite you in marriage.
Why aren't you making your clothes?
Don't fail to start now!"
Her daughter, silent, without a word,
Sobbed with her kerchief stifling her mouth.
Tears fell as if poured.
She moved her seat of lapis lazuli,
Set it near the window.
Her left hand held shears and rule,
Her right hand took the sheer silk.
By morning she finished an embroidered robe,

Later she finished an unlined dress of silk.
Dim, dim, the sun was about to darken,
With sad thoughts she left the gates and wept.

When the government clerk heard of this affair
He asked for furlough to go home a while.
Before he had come two or three leagues
His wearisome horse sadly whinnied.
His new wife recognized his horse's whinny,
Slipped on her shoes and met him.
Sadly from a distance they gazed at each other,
She knew it was her long lost one coming.
She raised her hand, patted his horse's saddle,
Her loud sighs tore his heart.
"Since you parted from me
Unimaginable things have happened!
Things have turned out not as we once wished,
Nor could I make you understand.
I have had my parents—father and mother,
Bringing pressure to bear joined by my brother,
To make me consent to marry another man.
You have come back, what do you hope for?"

The government clerk said to his new wife:
"Congratulations for winning such high promotion!
The firm rock square and strong
Could have endured a thousand years.
The pliant reed, once so supple,
Is reduced to this in the space of dawn to dusk!
You may reign supreme like the sun,
I will face Yellow Springs alone."

His new wife said to the government clerk:
"What do you mean by such words?
Together we have suffered this great crisis,
First you, and then your wife.
Down in Yellow Springs we will meet,
Don't betray our vow made this day!"
They held hands, then went their separate ways,
Each returning to their different gates.
For the living to make a parting unto death
Is more hateful than words can tell.
They think of their farewell from this world,
Never in a million years to be brought back to life.

The government clerk went back home,
Up in the hall he bowed to his mother:
"Today the great wind is cold,
Cold winds have crushed a tree,
Harsh frosts grip the garden orchid.
Your son today goes to darkness,
Leaving Mother to survive alone.
For I must carry out a most unhappy plan,
Torment our souls no more!
May your life be like South Mountain's rock,
Your four limbs healthy and strong!"

When his mother heard these words
Teardrops fell with each word:
"You are the son of a great family,
With official position at galleried courts.
Don't die for the sake of that wife!
About noble and base are you so naïve?
Our east neighbor has a good daughter,
Meek and mild, the loveliest in town.
Your mother will seek her for your wife,
All will be arranged between dawn and dusk."

The government clerk bowed twice and went back
Sighing long sighs in his empty rooms.
The plan he made was fixed as ever.
He turned his head toward the door,
Slowly he watched, grief's oppressive rage.

That day horses and cattle lowed,
His new wife goes into her green hut.
After dusk had fallen
A quiet hush, people start to settle down.
"My life will end today,
My soul will vanish, my corpse will linger a while."
She lifts her skirt, removes her silk shoes,
Stands up and goes toward the clear lake.

When the government clerk hears of this act,
His heart knows it is the long separation.
He hesitates under a garden tree,
Hangs himself from a southeast branch.

The two families asked for a joint burial,
A joint burial on the side of Mount Hua.

East and west were planted pine and cypress,
Left and right catalpa were set.
Branch with branch joins to form a canopy,
Leaf with leaf meets in wedlock.
Among them are a pair of flying birds,
Called mandarin ducks, drake and hen.
Lifting their heads they call to each other,
Night after night until the fifth watch.
Passersby stay their steps to listen,
Widows get out of bed and pace to and fro.
Be warned, men of the future,
Learn this lesson and never forget!

The Deserted Wife

A pomegranate planted in the forecourt,
Green leaves toss celadon tints,
Cinnabar blooms blaze with fiery flames,
Dazzling tones of bright glory,
Bright glory the sheen of rare turquoise
Where blessed spirits might flit.
These birds flock and fly,
Beat their wings in mournful choir.
In mournful choir, but why?
Cinnabar blooms have not borne fruit.

She strokes her heart, sighs long sighs,
The childless wife must be sent home.
With child she is the moon that sails the skies,
Childless she's like a falling star.
Skies and moon each wax and wane,
A falling star dies without a glimmer.
She lodged a while, failed in her duty,
Now she will fall among tiles and stones.

"Despair and longing surge within me,
My sighs go on till cockcrow.
I toss and turn unable to sleep,
Wander through the forecourt,
I pause in doubt, go back to my room,
Wistful bed curtains rustle.

I roll up the drapes, tidy my dress,
Stroke the strings and play my plain lute.
Anguish carries on echoing notes,
Haunting, sad, and clear.

"I hold back the tears, sighing long.
How did I offend the sacred Gods?
The Troubled Star waits for frost and dew.
Must spring and summer alone bring ripeness?
Late harvests make for fine fruits—
Please, my lord, don't be impatient!"

Lu Yun: Four Letter-Poems
Between Husband and Wife

1

I live in Three Rivers sunshine,
You live in Five Lakes shade.
Mountains, seas, a gulf so vast,
Like the gulf between fliers and divers.

My eyes imagine your clear kind face,
My ears hold echoes of your good sweet voice.
I sleep alone with many distant dreams,
Then waken, caressing your empty collar.
Oh beautiful heart of my heart!
My love is only for you.
(from the husband)

2

Far, far away you journey on,
Alone, all alone I stay still.
How to cross mountains and rivers?
Forever cut off, road of ten thousand leagues.

Mansions in the capital are full of pretty charms,
Brilliant, brilliant city of women.
Elegant footsteps, soft waists slender,
Bewitching smiles show white teeth.
Their loveliness is so enviable,
My ugliness hardly worth a mention.

I received your fond words from a distance,
I cherish the kind thought unexpected.
(from the wife)

3

Flurry, flurry windblown tumbleweed travels,
Lovely, lovely cold tree glorious.
Wandering, resting, to each his own nature.
To float, to sink, no two natures are alike.

Great love wed us in the past,
Vows of fidelity bound us to the Three Gods.
I keep my heart metal and rock firm—
How could I be lured by mere fashion?
Lovely eyes may pass, I don't look!
Slender waists are nubile in vain!
How shall I pledge my deep affection?
I look up and point at that pole-star!
(from the husband)

4

He who sails the ocean finds rivers dull.
He who roams forests finds other scenes pall.
Beauty at its peak more precious grows,
The flower of dawn mourns the passing day.

White, white those pretty girls,
Bright, bright kissed by springtime splendor.
The west side is skilled at courtly dance,
Concert halls resound with clear strumming.
Tuneful pipes ring out from cinnabar lips,
Scarlet strings vibrate beneath white wrists.
Light skirts quiver like lightning,
Twin sleeves streak like mist.
Flower faces suffuse spangled curtains,
Sad echoes pierce Cloudy Han.

Few in the world appreciate such music,
Except you, who could appraise them?
Forget your pole-star!
Solicit these Dark Dragon starlets.
Time grows late, no more words.
A wilting flower reason makes a reject.
(from the wife)

31

FAMILY INSTRUCTIONS TO THE YAN CLAN

(*Yanshi jiaxun*)

顏氏家訓

Yan Zhitui

顏之推

Family Instructions to the Yan Clan, or Yanshi jiaxun, *was written by Yan Zhitui (531–591* C.E.*), a literatus and ranking official who served several regimes during the division period and later the Sui dynasty. Yan's* Family Instructions *has been considered the first text of its kind, with its exclusive focus on family relations and household management, as well as its specifically targeted readers (clan members), and its staunch patronage of Confucian ideology. This genre became quite popular during later periods of Chinese history. In the following two passages, drawing on his observations of various regional practices, Yan cautions his readers on household disasters brought on by women and how to avoid them.*

The first selection warns widowers against remarriage. The widower's understandable desire for a spouse is subordinated to what Yan regards as the proper order of the household. Filial piety may be lost and the children will suffer the most because of the widower's unwise decision. The second selection reinforces the traditional Confucian teaching regarding women's roles within the household as daughter, wife, and mother. Despite its warnings about the calamities that may follow if women do not conform to these expectations, it also condemns female infanticide as contrary to the ordinances of Heaven itself. Both selections are memorable in that they teach family morality by comparing and contrasting folk customs from one province of China to another. The stories not only reinforce the ideal Confucian moral order, but also allow a revealing glimpse of the vast network of informal prejudices against women that could flourish within that order.

Ping Yao

Translated by Ping Yao.

Second Marriage and Stepmother

Jifu was a wise father and Boqi was a filial son. A wise father teach-
ing a filial son should have resulted in a natural perfection. However,
Jifu's second wife sowed discord between them and Boqi was consequently expelled.[1] When Zeng Can's wife died, Zeng said to his sons:
"I am not as wise as Jifu, and you are not as filial as Boqi."[2] When
Wang Jun lost his wife, he said to other people: "I am not as wise as
Zeng Can, and my sons are not as filial as Hua and Yuan."[3] Both Zeng
Can and Wang Jun never remarried. These tales should be enough
of a warning for later generations.[4] However, since their times, there
have been countless stepmothers who have abused stepchildren and
orphans, alienated family members, and caused severe emotional
harms. Beware! Beware!

   People of Jiangzuo do not shun a concubine's children. When a
wife died, a concubine would often be designated to take charge of
the household. Although small disputes are unavoidable, such families are bonded by principles and, therefore, scandals caused by violent
disturbances within the family are rare. People of Hebei, by contrast,
despise children borne to concubines, considering them illegitimate.
Therefore, once a wife died, the husband must take a new wife, in
some cases, up to three or four in his lifetime. As a result, a mother
would, sometimes, be younger than a son. And there are clear distinctions among the brothers who were borne to the first wives and
the second wives when it comes to clothing, food, marriage, official
career, and social status. People of Hebei consider it quite normal!
Thus, once the husband passed away, disputes would fill the court
and slanders were widespread. A son would accuse a mother of being
a concubine, and a younger brother would make an older brother his
servant. Very often people invoked the ancestors to uphold themselves:

---

[1] Jifu, whose last name was Yin, was a prominent official of the Western Zhou dynasty.
When Yin's second wife falsely accused Boqi, borne to Jifu's late wife, of making sexual
advances on her, Jifu banished Boqi. Later, when Jifu realized his mistake, he killed his
second wife.

[2] Zeng Can (505–436 B.C.E.) was a student of Confucius.

[3] Wang Jun (d.15 B.C.E.) was an eminent Han official. Hua and Yuan were Zeng Can's
sons.

[4] The remarks by Zeng Can and Wang Jun regarding Jifu and Boqi are obviously meant
to be ironic. Jifu's disastrous remarriage confirms Zeng Can's and Wang Jun's resolve to
follow Confucian tradition and never remarry, for the sake of the household itself.

either by broadcasting the ancestors' lives or by exposing their virtues and shortcomings. How sad! From time immemorial, so many cunning ministers and fawning wives have ruined people's lives just by talking. Because of this, the bond between husband and wife may change even in a day and servants and maids distort realities for their own convenience. If this continues for long, how can you ever find a filial son? This should be forever feared.

In terms of the general tendencies among the population, second husbands usually would pamper the children of the first husbands, and a second wife surely would abuse the children of the first wife. It is not only because women are jealous in nature and men have the bad habit of spoiling children, but also because the circumstances involved made it unavoidable. Children of a first husband naturally do not dare to compete with the children of the current husband for rights. On the contrary, the current husband would develop an emotional attachment after raising the children for some time, and thus tend to spoil them, while providing the children of the previous wife with schooling, an official career, and marriage before the children of the current wife. Thus, the current wife would be naturally very cautious about it and would tend to abuse the children. If the children are spoiled, then the parents are to blame for it; if the stepmother abuses her stepchildren, then the siblings will all become enemies. These are truly regarded as household disasters.

Marriage and Women's Position

Women are responsible for cooking in the household and observing only those rituals concerned with wine, food, and clothing. They should not be allowed to participate in the politics of the state, nor should they be allowed to interfere with the affairs of the household. If a woman possesses wisdom and abilities and is knowledgeable in history, then these merits should be used to help a gentleman, supplementing his insufficiency. A hen crowing at dawn should never happen, as it will cause disasters.

Women of Jiangdong do not socialize. Families of the married couple would sometimes never meet each other for years. Instead, they send letters and presents to each other to express courtesy. The custom of Yexia is rather different. Women are designated to run the household. They argue and dispute; pay visits and invite guests. Roads and small lanes are occupied by their chariots, government halls are filled with fine silk dresses. They request official positions for their sons, and pursue grievances for their husbands. Mustn't it be a foreign custom imposed during the Northern Wei period?

The South has long been a poor area. Therefore, the Southerners only pay attention to appearances. They keep their chariots and clothing nice and neat, but their wives and children at home are often hungry and cold. In Hebei, households are run by women, thus, fine silks and golden jewelry are necessities, while horses and servants in the households are weak and aged, barely enough to keep up appearances. Husbands and wives of this region impolitely address each other as "you."[5] Compared to the women of Jiangdong, however, the women of Hebei are much better in terms of their skills in weaving, knitting, sewing, and embroidery.

Taigong[6] said: "It is a great expenditure to have many daughters." Chen Fan[7] said: "Having a family with five daughters is worse than suffering a robbery." The burden caused by daughters is too much. Nonetheless, Heaven created human beings and ancestors passed down the body forms, so what can we do about this? People of this world do not appreciate girls and thus kill their own daughters. If they act like this, how could they expect blessings from Heaven? I have a remote relative who houses many concubines and courtesans. But whenever a woman was about to give birth, he would send servants to guard outside. Upon hearing the sounds of her labor, they would peep through windows and doors. If the child was a girl, they would immediately take her and toss her away. The mother would then cry out loud, and no one could bear listening to it.

Women are naturally inclined to pamper sons-in-law and abuse daughters-in-law. Pampering sons-in-law creates grudges among the sons, and abusing daughters-in-law yields slanders from the daughters. Whatever a daughter-in-law's actions are, they seem always to offend the family. This is all because of the mother-in-law. A proverb says: "Serving mothers-in-law a cold dish." This is what is called "retribution." Shouldn't we be aware of such common household problems?

---

[5] In Chinese tradition, spouses should address each other with "husband" and "wife"; addressing each other with "you" was considered rude.

[6] Taigong, whose last name was Jiang, was a legendary figure of the Western Zhou dynasty. He was known for his wisdom.

[7] Chen Fan (d.168 c.e.), a Han scholar and high-ranking official, was known for his courage and righteousness.

Matching family background is a marriage principle that was established by our ancestors. Nowadays marriage practices are quite different: some people sell their daughters by requesting a huge bride price, and some people buy wives by spending extravagantly. The fathers and grandfathers compete with each other and dispute with each other about assets. They demand more and give less, just like the merchants and mean people. As a consequence, sons-in-law from low families come in, and shrewish daughters-in-law are now in charge of the households. Coveting fame and profits leads to shame and embarrassment. Shouldn't we be careful about this?

32

THE BALLAD OF MULAN
(*Mulan ci*)
木蘭辭

*This is a work by an unknown author, written in northern China during the domi-
nation of the Wei Tartars (Northern Wei dynasty) during the fifth century* C.E. *It
became a popular story that inspired many literary works and plays for people of all
ages. Recently, in 1998, the story of Mulan also traveled to the West and was made
into a Hollywood movie of the same name.*

*The popularity of this Chinese tale of a Woman Warrior is somewhat akin to that
of the legend of St. Joan of Arc. But while both women are identified with the cause
of national resistance to foreign invaders, Mulan's decision to join the army is based
not on a religious vision but on her deep sense of filial piety. Her father is no longer
able to serve, and her brothers are still too young, so Mulan steps up, without her
parents' knowledge, to preserve the honor of her family. The memorable image of the
Woman Warrior, who knows how to read and whose exploits in battle made it impossible to tell her apart from any of her heroic male counterparts, thus reaffirms traditional Chinese family values. Once the war is over Mulan asks nothing more than
to be released from further service so that she can return home and resume the role
of a dutiful daughter. Nevertheless, the last lines of the poem hold out for something
different that could emerge in the relationship between women and men. Their loyal-
ties forged in the heat of battle, Mulan and her dumbfounded messmates have experienced the possibility of a new sense of gender equality and solidarity:*

> *For the male hare has a lilting, lolloping gait,*
> *And the female hare has a wild and roving eye;*
> *But set them both scampering side by side,*
> *And who so wise could tell you "This is he"?*

Robin R. Wang

From *The Temple and Other Poems*, translated by Arthur Waley (New York: Alfred A. Knopf,
1923).

Click, click, forever click, click;
Mulan sits at the door and weaves.
Listen, and you will not hear the shuttle's sound,
But only hear a girl's sobs and sighs.
"Oh tell me, lady, are you thinking of your love,
Oh tell me, lady, are you longing for your dear?"
"Oh no, oh no, I am not longing for my dear.
But last night I read the battle-roll;
The Kehan has ordered a great levy of men.
The battle-roll was written in twelve books,
And in each book stood my father's name.
My father's sons are not grown men,
And of all my brothers, none is older than I.
Oh let me go to the market to buy saddle and horse,
And ride with the soldiers to take my father's place."
In the eastern market she bought a gallant horse,
In the western market she bought saddle and cloth.
In the southern market she bought snaffle and reins,
In the northern market she bought a tall whip.
In the morning she stole from her father's and mother's
    house;
At night she was camping by the Yellow River's side.
She could not hear her father and mother calling to her by
    her name,
But only the song of the Yellow River as its hurrying
Waters hissed and swirled through the night.
At dawn they left the River and went their way;
At dusk they came to the Black Water's side.
She could not hear her father and mother calling to her by
    her name,
She could only hear the muffled voices of Scythian horsemen
    riding on the hills of Yen.
A thousand leagues she tramped on the errands of war,
Frontiers and hills she crossed like a bird in flight.
Through the northern air echoed the watchman's tap;
The wintry light gleamed on coats of mail.
The captain had fought a hundred fights, and died;
The warriors in ten years had won their rest.
They went home; they saw the Emperor's face;
The Son of Heaven was seated in the Hall of Light.
To the strong in battle lordships and lands he gave;
And of prize money a hundred thousand strings.

Figure 7. Already garbed in military uniform, Mulan says farewell to her *Hua Lienu Zhuan)* by Chou Ying (1509–1552).]

beloved mother and father. [From *Chou's Illustrations of the Biographies of Woman (Chou*

Then spoke the Kehan and asked her what she would take.
"Oh, Mulan asks not to be made
A Counselor at the Kehan's court;
She only begs for a camel that can march
A thousand leagues a day,
To take her back to her home."

When her father and mother heard that she had come,
They went out to the wall and led her back to the house.
When her little sister heard that she had come,
She went to the door and rouged her face afresh.
When her little brother heard that his sister had come,
He sharpened his knife and darted like a flash
Towards the pigs and sheep.

She opened the gate that leads to the eastern tower,
She sat on her bed that stood in the western tower,
She cast aside her heavy soldier's cloak,
And wore again her old-time dress.
She stood at the window and bound her cloudy hair;
She went to the mirror and fastened her yellow combs.
She left the hoe and met her messmates in the road;
Her messmates were startled out of their wits.
They had marched with her for twelve years of war
And never known that Mulan was a girl.
For the male hare has a lilting, lolloping gait,
And the female hare has a wild and roving eye;
But set them both scampering side by side,
And who so wise could tell you "This is he"?

33

WOMEN IN THE STANDARD HISTORIES

(Shishu)

魏晉南北史

Standard histories are the twenty-five government-sponsored official histories, covering over four thousand years of events. They were compiled in the annals-biographies style (jizhuanti), in which the annals of the dynastic emperors are followed by biographies of various people, with some having their own biographies and others represented in thematic collections. One of these collective biographies is called Biographies of Women (Lienüzhuan), *in which are gathered biographical sketches of women throughout the dynasty. An introduction (xu) and a eulogy (zan) are often placed at the beginning and at the end of the collection. The introduction usually contains the historian's view of what womanhood entails and what women were like in the historical period covered, and the eulogy is where the historian sings his praises to the women in the biographies. Thus, the introductions and eulogies provide us with a concrete sense of these historians' views about what womanhood meant; together, they reveal how these views have changed through time.*

The biography included here from The History of the Northern Dynasties (Beishi) *is one example of many biographies. Ms. Xian (c. 520–601 C.E.) was an ethnic regent of the Yue area (now Guangdong Province). Her family provided the local chieftain for generations, and her marriage to Feng Bao, the son of the regional inspector of Luozhou, enabled the Fengs to govern the region more smoothly. After Feng Bao died, she led the Fengs through three dynasties: the Liang, the Chen, and the Sui. In all, Ms. Xian was a strong emissary who mediated between the frontier tribal peoples and the Han regimes. Her prescience and sharp military sense enabled her to make shrewd political decisions. Each time the Han regime faced contenders, she aligned herself with the one that succeeded the previous regime. Her insightful mediation minimized the unnecessary devastations of war.*

Sherry J. Mou

Translated by Sherry J. Mou.

History of
The Later Han Dynasty (25–220 C.E.)
(Hou Hanshu)

Introduction (xu)

Both *The Book of Odes* and *The Canon of Documents* spoke of womanly virtues a long time ago. There are capable royal consorts who helped the rulers of the states in governing, able women who exalted the way of the families, worthy literati who spread wide their cleansing and edifying influence, and chaste women who illustrated the virtues of purity. Their excellence is no different from that of women recorded in *The Book of Odes* and *The Canon of Documents,* but more recent books have often omitted them. Thus, I gathered those incidents since the years of the Restoration and described them in this chapter of women.

The biographies of royal consorts such as Empresses Ma, Deng, and Liang can be found separately in the previous "basic annals" sections. Those of Liang Yi [VIII.20][1] and Li Ji are attached to their family biographies. People like these will not be written about here. As for the rest, those whose talents and behavior are particularly superior and distinguished whether in one way (or in many) are collected here.

Eulogy (zan)

To eulogize: Their upright virtue can be made visible, and their poised composure conforms with the standard of propriety. I have underscored their moral influence and the fortitude they left behind in order to illuminate what is recorded with the red brushes of the woman historians, namely, the history of women.

---

[1] The Roman and Arabic numbers within the brackets indicate that the woman features in Liu Xiang's *Biographies of Women* (*Lienüzhuan*; see above pp. 149–161 for selections of Liu Xiang's text). The Roman numeral indicates the chapter and the Arabic numeral the order of the biography. Hereafter, all brackets with Roman and Arabic numerals refer to Liu Xiang's collection. A set of brackets with a pound sign (#) followed by a number means that the woman or the event is found in the history of the dynasty from which the introduction comes. Brackets with names alone indicate alternative, often better known names.

History of
The Jin Dynasty (265–420 C.E.)
(*Jinshu*)

Introduction (xu)

Because the three elements in the great trinity have their separate positions, the way of the family can flourish; because two clans are acquainted with and like each other, the trend of fidelity and chastity becomes prominent. Because it arouses noble sentiments and outshines all the others, the history of Lu (*The Spring and Autumn Annals*) blossoms; because it sustains strict righteousness and stands high alone, the history of Zhou (*The Canon of Documents*) flourishes.

Looking through the dynasties, we see women with both beauty and exemplary righteousness, yet gentle and complacent beyond any fault; indeed they have not just one virtue. But Yu [Shun] rose from the bight of the River Gui; Xia [Yu] flourished because of help from the daughter of Tushan [I.4]; Yousong and Youxin promoted and expanded the career of the founder of the Shang dynasty [I.5]; Tairen and Taisi developed and increased the teaching of the Zhou house [I.6]; Empresses Ma [VIII.19] and Deng were respectful and frugal, and the Han dynasty could promote its virtues; Empresses Xuan and Zhao were good and virtuous, and thus the Wei dynasty could promulgate its fragrance. They all aggrandized the codes of *li* (propriety) in the palace and graced the court with distinguished righteousness. There are also others such as Gong Jiang, who took an oath to preserve her chastity; the mother of Mencius, who sought for humaneness [I.11]; the daughter of the Hua family, who managed the state of Qi, along with her governess [IV.6]; and Fan Ji who bestowed her stipulations and thus enabled the King of Chu to become the hegemon [II.5]. Wenbo was reprimanded by his mother for making his friend hold his sword [I.9]; Zifa was made by his mother to share his beans with the soldiers [I.10]; Shaojun obeyed the rite of frugality [Hou Hanshu, #1]; and Meng Guang matched her husband's will to withdraw from society [VIII.18]. These people not only illuminated the regulations of wives, but also were skillful in practicing the rectitude of mothers. Zizheng [Liu Xiang] assembled these first, and Yuankai [Du Yu, 222–284 C.E.] compiled them again later in order to praise women exemplars and to assist the teaching of females.

Thus, from the years of Taishi [265–274 C.E.] down to the emperors of Gong [419–420 C.E.] and An [397–418 C.E.], as long as there is one virtue worthy of compliment and one talent worthy of record, all are written, compiled, and made into biographies. Those who achieved the lofty position of empresses or royal consorts have their own biographies, and those whose importance dwelt in their husbands or sons are appended to the individual biographies of these men and are not being recorded here. As for those who resided in illegitimate states, and therefore temporarily avoided being included in the princely scheme, they could still be exemplars for the world and be used to admonish. Thus, their biographies were also collected and attached to the end of the chapter.

Eulogy (zan)

The historian states: When heavy frosts form, they underscore the upright mind as being the last to wither; when there are evil currents, they illustrate the belief in chastity with supreme virtue. Such people are not just gentlemen; some of them are women as well.

Since the decline of the Jin government, few moral principles have been established. People lacked etiquette and deviated from proper conduct; they followed each other and made such practices into customs. These were repeated by Liu [Yuan] and Shi [Le], and continued by Fu [Jian] and Yao [Chang]. After singing the barbarian songs for as short a time as three months, the women are seen only contending for fancier ornamentation; and when the women leave the Han after only a single day, they then have little nostalgic sentiment remaining. The customs of the nomads are loose; they drop the rites and rituals, and they are depraved and self-indulgent without limit. This is indeed very extreme!

As to the behavior of the following, they all trod the path of righteousness voluntarily, not owing to special teaching: Huifeng scolded Qiao Shu [#5], Daoyun taunted Sun En [#16]; the daughter of Xun did away with the danger of being besieged [#15]; the wife of Zhang avenged herself on the powerful bandits against whom she had nursed her grudge for killing her husband [#13]; the empress of the usurper [Fu] Deng would not turn back even in the face of death [#29]; the consort of the bogus ruler Zuan was not stingy in giving up her life [#32]; both Ms. Cong [#8] and Ms. Xin [#9] incurred untimely death, resisting others' desire for them; and Ms. Wang [#22] and Ms. Jin [#24] approached demise, guarding their virtues. Such virtues are like music that makes the leaves on tall trees quiver, resonating high into the sky, channeling virtuous sound; and they raise the spirits of drooping plants in the deepest ravines. With little shame they may even be compared to the most elegant melody. As for those who do not even wink when hanging themselves and those who confront suicide or killing swords as if going home, their efforts at rectification can indeed inspire for thousands of years to come.

To eulogize: Calmness and composure are women's etiquette; accommodating and complaisance are their obliging rules. They uphold and follow the six principles, and thus illuminate the four virtues. Their virtues are purer than the frost, and their fame spreads beyond their own states. There is nothing more cleansing and fragrant than lessons that are bequeathed through the red brushes, that is, these biographies.

History of
The Northern Dynasties (386–581 C.E.)
(Beishi)

Introduction (xu)

Although women's virtue is in their gentleness, establishing their virtue and making their names known depend on their sacrificing themselves for chastity. Gentleness is the root of humaneness, and sacrificing oneself for chastity is the epitome of righteousness. Without gentleness one cannot accomplish humaneness, and without sacrificing oneself for chastity one cannot manifest righteousness. That is why among those activities recorded in *The Book of Odes* and *The Canon of Documents*, formulated into social customs, depicted in paintings and pictures, and heard in the historical record, none transgressed the basic principles of locating the self in propriety and sacrificing life to fulfill humaneness.

People like the mothers of Wenbo [I.12] and Wang Ling [VIII.6], the wives of Baigong [IV.11] and Qi Zhi [IV.8], the righteous sister of the state of Lu [V.6], Gaoxing of the state of Liang [IV.14], the concubine of the head of the state of Wei, Lingzhu [IV.12], and the daughter of Xiahou Wenning, either embraced faithfulness to maintain chastity or practiced loyalty in order to exercise righteousness. They did not change their minds because of life and death, nor did they alter their virtues because of the rise and fall of the regimes. Their good names have illuminated the past, and their excellent reputation will live into immortality. Is this not wonderful?

Yet there were high officials' concubines and spouses who indulged in licentious and unusual customs. Though they dressed in embroidered clothes, ate exquisite food, lived in golden houses, and rode in jade carriages, they will not be entered into history or touched by the brushes of good historians. They will attend the withering of grass and plants and accompany the reindeer in their deaths. How can their numbers be minimized? Reflect upon these facts for a long while. It is indeed the shame of these women.

The Histories of Wei and Sui both include books on the biographies of women, but the Histories of Qi and Zhou do not. Now I also have the wife, Zhao, of Sun Daowen of Wugong and the wife, née Chen, of Sun Shen of Hebei. They are attached to the two biographies from the Histories of Wei and Sui to complete the present *Biographies of Women*.

Eulogy (zan)

To conclude: Women are primarily to take care of the affairs of weaving and cooking. Thus, always mentioning gentleness and obedience first is simply listing the norm, not the most outstanding virtues. As to the kind who have perspicacious knowledge and see far, who are loyal and extremely righteous, who have an unchangeable will to maintain widowhood, and who exalt only righteousness, if we examine histories, which dynasty does not have them?

There are all together thirty-four women described in the *Weishu* and *Suishu*. From the royal consorts and princesses down to the daughters and wives of common people, there are some whose personality is like that of pine trees in severe cold and some whose hearts' firmness surpasses that of stone. Some are loyal, splendid, and sincere, and others are very well learned. Although Zizheng [Liu Xiang] first assembled the biographies of women and Yuankai [Du Yu, 222–284 C.E.] compiled them afterwards, when we compare these beautiful virtues, what else can surpass them? Thus we know that their chastity, which is fragrant and pure like orchid and jade, is indeed their innate nature.

Biography of
Consort Qiaoguo Ms. Xian (ca. 520–601 C.E.)
From History of the Northern Dynasties
(Beishi)

The Consort of State Ms. Xian was from Gaoliang. For many generations, her family was the leader of Nanyue, and they commanded
over one hundred thousand households.

Ms. Xian was capable and virtuous from youth. Before marrying,
she often endeavored to placate her family's followers. She also commanded armies, subduing various Yue peoples and making peace with
them. She always advised her clan to do good. As a result, local people
were united owning to her family's truthfulness and righteousness.

The Yue peoples used to fight with one another. When Ms. Xian's
elder brother Ting was the regional inspector (*cishi*) of Nanliang district, he often used his military prowess and wealth to attack other
districts. Lingbiao was much in woe because of him. Ms. Xian repeatedly admonished him and thus deflected much bitterness. Over a
thousand households from Hainan and Zhan'er pledged their alle-
giance to him.

At the beginning of the Datong years (535–46 C.E.) of the Liang
dynasty (502–57 C.E.), the regional inspector of Luozhou, Feng Rong
heard that Ms. Xian was principled and purposeful. He offered to
marry her to his son Feng Bao, who was the grand protector (*taishou*)
of Gaoliang. Rong's ancestors belonged to the Miao people from the
Northern Yan (407–36 C.E.). At first, Feng Hong went south to attach
himself to Gaoli (now South Korea), and he sent Rong's uncle Ye and
three hundred subjects to go to the Song across the sea. From there on,
Ye stayed on at Xinhui. For three generations from Ye to Rong, the
Fengs were the probationary regional governors (*shoumu*). Because they
were not from local people, the locals often ignored their orders and
announcements. After Ms. Xian came, she admonished and made pacts
with her own clans to abide by the rites of the ordinary people. She
often accompanied her husband Bao to hear suits and requests. If local
chieftains infringed the laws, even if they were from her clan, she would
not relent in meting out punishment. From then on, government and
edicts became regulated, and people would not disobey the laws.

Later, during the rebellion of Hou Jing (d. 552 C.E.), the
commander-in-chief (*dudu*) of Guangzhou, Xiao Bo, tried to con-
script armies to aid the seat, so the regional inspector of Gaozhou,

Li Qianshi, occupied Dagaokou and sent for Feng Bao to assist him. Bao wanted to, but Ms. Xian stopped him from going, suspecting that Li was plotting a rebellion. A few days later, Li indeed rebelled, and he dispatched his chief commander, Du Pinglu, to Ganshi. When Feng Bao informed her of this, Ms. Xian said, "Pinglu led an army to Ganshi to fight the government troops, and they have not yet returned. Thus, Li Qianshi, who stayed back at the region (*zhou*), could not have done much. We ought to send delegates to trick him, just telling him: 'I dare not go public with your plot myself, so I want to send my wife to come and participate.' He would not be suspicious. I will lead over a thousand people to go on foot with me, carrying supplies and goods for our army and claiming those as miscellaneous presents for him. When we arrive at the barricade, we can then capture those bandits." Feng Bao followed her advice, and Li Qianshi was indeed pleased. He sent people to inspect the carriers and confirmed that they were indeed carrying gifts, so he took no further precautions. Ms. Xian attacked and won gloriously. She then gathered all the troops to rendezvous with the Duke of Changcheng, Chen Baxian (503–59 c.e.), at Ganshi. When Ms. Xian returned home, she told Feng Bao, "The grand protector Chen Baxian is very popular with people. He must be able to eliminate the bandits in the end. You should support him generously."

After Feng Bao died in 558 c.e., Lingbiao was in turmoil. Ms. Xian gathered her troops and made a coalition with all the other powers at Baiyue, bringing peace to nearby regions. In the second year of Yongding (557–59 c.e.) of the Chen dynasty (557–89 c.e.), she sent her son Feng Pu, who was nine years old, to lead all the chieftains to pay their respects to the then-Emperor Chen Baxian at Danyang. In return, Feng Pu was awarded the position of Grand Protector of Yangchun.

Later, the regional inspector of Guangzhou, Ouyang He, plotted to rebel. He summoned Feng Pu to Nanhai and connived to have Feng Pu join him. Feng Pu sent an emissary to report this to his mother, and Ms. Xian said, "I have been loyal and steadfast to the imperial court for two generations. I can't betray the State because of you." She refused to send troops to assist and defended the borders instead. As a result, Ouyang He's armies were defeated. Because of Ms. Xian's achievement, Feng Pu was titled Duke of Xindou, in addition to Leader of Court Gentleman Who Quelled the Yue (*Ping Yue zhonglang jiang*), and then was appointed Governor (*taishou*) of Shilong. The emperor also sent an emissary with an emblem from him conferring on Ms. Xian the title Grand Mistress of Gaoliang, a four-horse carriage with embroidery curtain and colorful braids, a military music band, an official banner, and a staff and a team of honorary guards appropriate in size for a regional inspector. In the middle of the Zhide years (583–86 C.E.), Feng Pu died.

Later, the Chen dynasty ended, and Lingnan was in turmoil, except for a few prefectures under Ms. Xian's control. Thus, the local people worshiped her as the "Holy Mother" who protected the area and its people. Meanwhile, Emperor Wen of the Sui dynasty (581–618 C.E.) dispatched the Area Commander-in-Chief (*zongguan*) Wei Guang to pacify the area beyond the Ling mountain ridge. The Chen dynasty general Xu Deng continued to resist in Nankang, and Wei Guang dared not advance.

Earlier on, Ms. Xian presented to the Chen throne a cane made of rhinoceros horn from Funan. Now, Prince Jin (ca. 569–618 C.E.) of the Sui dynasty demanded that the last emperor, Chen Shubao, notify Ms. Xian that the Chen dynasty had ended and that she should surrender. The letter was accompanied by a military tally and the rhinoceros horn cane from Funan as a token of recognition. Thus, when Ms. Xian received the letter, she was convinced that the dynasty was indeed over. So she summoned several thousand chieftains, cried for an entire day, and sent her grandson Feng Hun to welcome Wei Guang to Guangzhou. Lingnan became peaceful again, and the Sui dynasty conferred upon Feng Hun the title of "Unequaled in Honor" (*yitong sansi*) and upon Ms. Xian "Commandery Mistress of Songkang (*Songkang jun furen*)."

Not long afterwards, Wang Zhongxuan, a local chieftain of Fanyu (now Guangzhou), rebelled against the Sui dynasty. He encircled Wei Guang and moved his troops to encamp at Hengling. Ms. Xian dispatched her grandson Feng Xuan to help Wei Guang. But Feng Xuan was a good friend of one rebel, Chen Fozhi, so he dawdled. Ms. Xian was furious; she sent people to capture Feng Xuan and jailed him. Then, she sent another grandson, Feng Ang, to execute Chen Fozhi, and she sent troops to Nanhai to rendezvous with Lu Yuan to defeat Wang Zhongxuan. In order to protect and accompany the imperial emissary Pei Ju to inspect the nearby regions, Ms. Xian put on armor and rode a war horse, shielded under an embroidered umbrella, and led the cavalry with bow and arrows. All local chieftains, including Cangwu's Chen Tan, Gangzhou's Feng Cenwong, Lianghua's Deng Matou, Tengzhou's Li Guanglue, and Luozhou's Pang Jing, came to pay their respects to Pei Ju. Ms. Xian again was ordered to lead the tribes, and peace again was restored to the Lingnan area.

Amazed with the outcome, Emperor Wen installed Feng Ang as

Regional Inspector of Gaozhou, pardoned Feng Xuan and assigned him as the Regional Inspector of Luozhou, and made Feng Bao posthumously Area Commander-in-Chief and awarded him the title of Duke of Qiaoguo.

Ms. Xian established her own private secretariat (*mufu*), aides (*zhangshi*), and other subordinating officials. She was also given a seal and, with it, the power to dispatch troops of six prefectures in any emergency. Further, the emperor sent a decree praising her meritorious service and awarded her five thousand pieces of brocade; the empress also sent her jewelry and a formal banquet gown. Ms. Xian placed all these gifts in golden boxes and placed them in special storage, along with presents from the Liang and Chen courts. Every year during important festivals, she would take them out and display them in the courtyard to remind her children and grandchildren. She admonished them, saying, "You should all pay loyalty to the throne. I have served rulers of three dynasties, and it is all due to such a demeanor. Now all the awards from them are the evidence and token of loyalty and filial piety."

Some time later, many Li and Liao people rebelled or ran away because the Area Commander-in-Chief Zhao Na was greedy and atrocious. Ms. Xian dispatched her aide to the capital to submit suggestions to pacify local people and to point out Zhao Na's crimes. The throne sent an emissary to investigate him, discovered his graft, and had him executed. The emperor then appointed Ms. Xian to assuage those who had been offended and revolted earlier. She carried the imperial decree with her, declared herself an emissary, and made the rounds of over ten prefectures to proclaim the sentiments of the emperor and to comfort and reassure the many Li and Liao peoples. Wherever she went, the people surrendered themselves. Emperor Wen bestowed upon her the Fief of Linzhen (now Hainan Island) with its 1,500 families, and he installed Feng Pu posthumously as the Area Commander-in-Chief (*zongguan*) of Yazhou and Duke of Pingyuan. At the beginning of the Renshou years (601–604 C.E.), she died, and she received the posthumous title of Mistress of Sincerity and Respect (*Chengjing furen*).

PART FIVE

TANG AND SONG
唐宋

(618–1279 C.E.)

34

THE FORTY-TWO CHAPTERS SUTRA

(Sishierzhang jing)

四十二章經

The scripture that conveys the Buddha's teaching is called sutra *in Sanskrit. The Chinese translation of the Forty-Two Chapters Sutra (Sishierzhang jing) is attributed to Kashyapamatanga (Jiayemoteng) and Dharmaraksha (Zhufalan) during the Later Han dynasty, that is, in the first century* C.E. *at the White Horse Temple at Luoyang. Legend has it that this sutra is the first sutra translated from Sanskrit or Pali into Chinese. Some scholars today, however, believe that it was composed entirely in Chinese in China. As its name implies, this sutra contains forty-two items of ethical teachings for monks. These are translations of selected passages from Hinayana sutras such as the Zhengahan jing and the Zaahan jing, which were composed in Sanskrit or Pali in India and were translated into Chinese. Each item emphasizes the merits of renouncing the world to become a monk and the observance of the Buddhist precepts. They lay especially strong emphasis on eliminating carnal desire. In this sutra women are branded unilaterally as hindrances for male ascetics.*

Though some Buddhist commentators contend that the Buddha's original teachings did not disparage women or exclude them as such from achieving Supreme Enlightenment, this sutra clearly expresses the fears of the Buddha's first disciples who could neither overcome the cultural assumptions regarding sex and gender that were embedded in some forms of Hindu tradition nor understand fully the revolutionary potential of the Buddha's own teaching. This sutra not only disparages women as the occasion for "carnal desire" that is the greatest obstacle in the monk's path toward Supreme Enlightenment, it also conveys a deep ambivalence toward family life. On the one hand, Chapter 23 warns that family life, that is, living with a wife and children, "never free[s] a man from bondage." On the other hand, Chapter 29 advises that the proper way to deal with women, so as to minimize the confusion of carnal

---

Translated by Masatoshi Ueki and Makiko Ueki.

desire, is to treat all of them as if they were part of your family: "If she is an old woman, you should regard her as your mother; if an elder woman, think of her as your older sister; if a younger woman, look upon her as your younger sister; and if an infant girl, consider her your own daughter." Nevertheless, even proper familiarity remains suspicious, for a monk having contact with women is like "a lotus flower grow[ing] out of the mud without being defiled by the mud."

Despite the fear of women expressed in this sutra, it also clearly expresses the Buddhist "Middle Way" and thus is a deliberate repudiation of extreme forms of asceticism. Chapter 31, for example, warns monks against assuming that they can overcome "carnal desire" by performing extreme acts, like cutting off their penises: "Rather than cut off your penis, you had better eliminate from your mind that which gives rise to carnal desire. The mind is comparable to a public officer who has the power to appoint and dismiss, and reward and punish. If the officer restrains his subordinates, they will behave. Without eliminating your obscene mind, it is of no use cutting off your penis."

This sutra, then, presents a view of women strictly determined by the struggle against "carnal desire" that Buddhist monks undertake as part of their path toward Supreme Enlightenment. Just how representative this view is within the Buddhist tradition as a whole is a matter of some controversy. Scholars in the Mahayana Buddhist tradition, for example, regard this as part of the unfortunate legacy of Hinayana Buddhism and contend that their tradition has been purified of sexism and gender bias. However persuasive one may find such arguments, it is clear that this sutra represents a strand of monastic thinking that is fairly common in all religious traditions where spiritual perfection, however defined, is made contingent upon following a lifestyle based on renunciation of ordinary family life and a deliberate segregation of the sexes.

Masatoshi Ueki

Chapter Sixteen

The Buddha said: "For example, if the surface of the clear water is stirred with a hand, many people cannot see their faces reflected on the surface of the water. Likewise, if one bears carnal desire in one's mind, one cannot find the path of righteousness. Confused by carnal desire, one would often make one's mind impure. Therefore, one cannot find the path of righteousness. You, *shramana* (Buddhist monk), should put your carnal desire aside. If you wipe off the dirt of carnal desire, you can find the path of righteousness."

Chapter Twenty-Three

The Buddha said: "The restraint of a house in keeping a man chained onto his wife and children is stronger than that of a prison. Even though one is put in prison, he will be released someday. By contrast, a wife and children never free a man from bondage. A man of passion would often become attached to carnal desire without sparing expenses. Knowing enough to fear being bitten to death by a tiger, he would often submit himself to carnal desire. And he would often throw himself into the mud and cause himself to be drowned of his own accord. Such stupid persons are called unenlightened ordinary men. If he deepens his understanding of these teachings, he will reach the stage of *Arhat* where earthly desires are eliminated."

Chapter Twenty-Four

The Buddha said: "As for passion, nothing is stronger than the carnal desire, and the violence of carnal desire is not to be compared with others. Fortunately, however, there exists only one carnal desire. If two should exist, no one in the world would dare to practice the way of Buddhahood leading to Enlightenment."

Chapter Twenty-Five

The Buddha said: "A person seized with carnal desire is compared to a person who goes against the wind carrying a torch in his hand. The flame is blown to himself with the wind, and he will suffer a burn on his hand without fail."

Chapter Twenty-Six

Sending beautiful daughters to the Buddha, the King of Devils in the Sixth Heaven tried to tempt the Buddha and to defeat his mind. The Buddha said: "You are nothing but leather bags filled with dirt. Even though you come to see me, you can do nothing to me. Go away! I am unconcerned with you." Thereupon, the King of Devils in the Sixth Heaven began to respect the Buddha more and more, and at last he asked the Buddha about the significance of the way of Buddhahood. The Buddha explained, and instantly the King of Devils in the Sixth Heaven attained *Srotapatti-phala*, the stage of entering the stream of sanctification.

Chapter Twenty-Seven

The Buddha said: "Now, practicing the way of Buddhahood can be compared to a log floating down the running water. Not bumping against the banks, not being snatched by a person, not being blocked by a demon, and not being stopped by swirling pools, the log will be sure to reach the ocean. Like this log, a person who practices the way of Buddhahood—making every effort to attain the realm of eternity, not being tempted into carnal desire, and not being trifled by evils—will surely be protected by me. He will attain Buddhahood without fail."

Chapter Twenty-Eight

The Buddha said: "Be careful not to believe in your mind. Your mind is not enough to be believed in. Behave yourself prudently in order not to see a woman. Seeing a woman, you will fall into trouble. If you attain the *Arhat*-ship, at that stage you may well believe in your mind."

Chapter Twenty-Nine

The Buddha said: "[In practicing the way of Buddhahood,] be careful not to see a woman and not to talk with a woman. If you talk with a woman, you must think, keeping your mind right and correct, as follows: 'Becoming a *shramana*, I should stay in the corrupt world as a lotus flower grows out of the mud without being defiled by the mud.' If she is an old woman, you should regard her as your mother; if an elder woman, think of her as your older sister; if a younger woman, look upon her as your younger sister; and if an infant girl, consider her your own daughter. In this manner you should hold the mind resolved to attain Supreme Enlightenment and eliminate evil passions.

Chapter Thirty-One

The Buddha said: "There was a man who could not suppress his carnal desire. Worried about it, he made up his mind to cut off his penis." The Buddha told him, "Rather than cut off your penis, you had better eliminate from your mind that which gives rise to carnal desire. The mind is comparable to a public officer who has the power to appoint and dismiss, and reward and punish. If the officer restrains his subordinates, they will behave. Without eliminating your obscene mind, it is of no use cutting off your penis." The Buddha recited a verse for him:

> From the mind arises carnal desire.
> The mind gives rise to this thought and that.
> If the mind itself and mental functions become calm,
> Evil passions will never arise through the Five Aggregates.[1]

The Buddha said: "This verse was preached by Kashyapa Buddha, the sixth of the seven Buddhas in the past."

Chapter Thirty-Two

The Buddha said: "Being attached to carnal desire causes a man grief. This grief seizes him with fear. If he keeps away from attachment to carnal desire, however, he has no cause to grieve or fear."

Chapter Thirty-Six

The Buddha said: "It is difficult for one to be born as a human being escaping from the three evil worlds (hell, the world of hungry spirits, and the world of animals). Even though one could be born as a human being, it is difficult to be born as a man instead of a woman. Even though one could be born as a man, it is difficult to be born without any defect of six sense-organs (eyes, ears, nose, tongue, tactile body, and mind). Even though all of the six sense-organs are complete, it

---

[1] The five constituent elements of all existences, that is, form, perception, conception, volition, and consciousness. Also called the Five *Skandhas* in Sanskrit.

is difficult to be born in Central India (Madhyadesha). Even though one is born in Central India, it is difficult to be born in the time when the Buddha is living in the world. Even though one could be born in the time when the Buddha is alive, it is difficult to see an enlightened person. Even though one could see an enlightened person, it is difficult to be awakened to his faith. Even though one is awakened to his faith, it is difficult to resolve to attain Supreme Enlightenment. Even though one could resolve to attain Supreme Enlightenment, it is difficult to attain the ultimate stage where there is neither asceticism to be practiced nor Enlightenment to be attained."

Chapter Forty-One

The Buddha said: "A man practicing the way of Buddhahood is compared to a work ox carrying a heavy baggage on its back mired in the deep mud. However tired out the ox may be, it should go ahead without looking aside and should take a rest after getting out from the mud. A *shramana* should know that carnal desire is more difficult to get out from than the mud. If one fixes one's thought to practicing the way of Buddhahood single-mindedly, one will be freed from sufferings."

THE SUTRA OF THE TEACHING OF VIMALAKIRTI

(Weimojie jing)

維摩詰經

The Vimalakirti-nirdesha-sutra (Weimojie jing) *discusses the theme of men and women's ability to attain Enlightenment by means of a dialogue between* Shariputra[1] *and a divine maiden* (Devakanya). *It had been said that the Sanskrit original of this sutra was not found except as several fragments, but three Chinese translations and one Tibetan translation are extant, of which Kumarajiva's version, translated in the early years of the fifth century* C.E. *has been most generally used in China and Japan. An English translation of Kumarajiva's version is presented here. In December 2001, the Sanskrit original was found at Potala palace in Tibet.*

The hero's name, Vimalakirti, means "Honorable Person without Spots," and it was translated as Jingming *in Chinese. It was also transliterated as* Weimojie *in Chinese. It is said that he was a* Grihapati, *or a wealthy lay Buddhist community leader, and that he lived in the advanced commercial city of Vaishali in India. The* Vimalakirti-nirdesha-sutra *is one of the most important scriptures of early Mahayana Buddhism. This sutra is full of literary flavor and criticizes Hinayana Buddhist doctrines with bitter irony. Memorable for our purposes is a scene in which a divine maiden explodes Shariputra's prejudiced view of women by reasoning with him. This sutra compares and contrasts the Hinayana assumption that the difference between a man and a woman is an obstacle to Enlightenment with the Mahayana premise that the difference between a man and a woman is nonsubstantial* (Shunya). *There is no inherent and unchanging substance known as the "female body." It is nothing but an illusion. According to the logic of emptiness* (Shunyata), *which is described as "[Everything is] neither existence nor nonexistence," it follows that "all things of this world are neither male nor female." Thus, the divine maiden*

Translated by Masatoshi Ueki and Makiko Ueki.

[1] One of the ten major disciples of the Buddha. He was regarded as the most brilliant of the Buddha's disciples. In Mahayana Buddhist scriptures he played a role of the spokesman of Hinayana Buddhism.

exposes the frivolity of clinging to external appearances. Not being confined to the logic of Shunyata, Vimalakirti *makes it clear that the divine maiden herself has already attained the Stage of Non-Retrogression, characteristic of a Bodhisattva. Whenever she wanted, she could attain Buddhahood, but she refused to become a Buddha. She appeared in the form of a woman on her own volition and preached to living beings* (Sattvas). *That is to say,* Vimalakirti *explained that the divine maiden was born as a woman because of her own vow in a previous life. The* Vimalakirtinirdesha-sutra *thus signifies that the purpose of being born as a woman is to relieve living beings of their sufferings, especially those of other women.*[2]

As in the Forty-Two Chapters Sutra, *Hinayana Buddhism emphasized avoiding attachment to carnal desire. The* Vimalakirti-nirdesha-sutra, *however, boldly asserts the apparent paradox that no one can attain Enlightenment apart from carnal desire. This, some Mahayana Buddhist scholars assert, is the symbolic meaning of the flower petals discussed in the opening of the dialogue: although the flowers scattered by a divine maiden fell off from the bodies of the Bodhisattvas (i.e., Mahayana Buddhists), they never fell off from the bodies of the great disciples (i.e., Hinayana Buddhists) who thought that these flowers were not right for Buddhist monks. Although it may be true that this sutra held out the possibility for an improvement in women's social condition, it is doubtful whether Chinese Buddhists attached any particular importance to this possibility.*

Masatoshi Ueki

At that time there was a divine maiden (Devakanya) in Vimalakirti's room. Seeing many great men, and hearing the teaching of the truth (*Dharma*) expounded, she made her appearance and scattered red heavenly-flowers, *Mandarava*,[3] over the Bodhisattvas and the disciples. The flowers that reached the Bodhisattva's body fell off quickly. But, the flowers that reached the great disciples (*Shravakas*) [including Shariputra] adhered to their bodies and never fell off. All of the great disciples tried to remove the flowers through supernatural powers. However, they could not remove them.

---

2 Representative Mahayana Buddhist scriptures offering the same idea include: (1) the *Maha-ratna-kuta-sutra* (*Dabaojijing*, the *Sutra of Collection of Jewels*); (2) the *Maha-parinirvana-sutra* (*Dabanniepan jing*, the *Sutra on the Great Nirvana of the Buddha*); (3) the *Ratna-darika-paripriccha* (*Baonüsuowenjing*, the *Sutra on the Question of a Daughter Named Treasure*); (4) the *Maha-samnipata-sutra* (*Dajijing*, the *Sutra of the Great Collections*); (5) the *Strivivarta-vyakarana-sutra* (*Shunqüanfangbianjing*, the *Sutra of Application of Provisional Means*).

3 *Mandarava* was transated as *Mantuoluohua*.

Then the divine maiden asked Shariputra, "Why do you try to take off the flowers?"

Shariputra answered, "Because these flowers are not right for Buddhist monks. So, I am trying to take them off."

The divine maiden said, "You should not think these flowers are not right for Buddhist monks. These flowers have no ability to distinguish. It is only you that think with such distinctions. Even though one has renounced the world under the Buddha's Law (*Dharma*), if one insists on observing such distinctions, such a person is not fit as a Buddhist monk. If one does not distinguish matters, such a person is fit to be a Buddhist monk. The reason why the flowers do not adhere to the body of the Bodhisattvas is that they have already eliminated all delusory thoughts of distinction. For example, an evil demon can pounce upon a man who is filled with fears. In the same way, because you disciples are afraid of the cycle of birth and death, the five sense-objects—form, sound, smell, taste, and touch—all pounce upon you. All of the five desires for form, sound, smell, taste, and touch are quite powerless to delude a man who has already eliminated fears. It is because you have not eradicated the bonds of illusion that the flowers adhere to your body. When you have already eradicated the bonds of illusion, the flowers won't adhere to your body anymore."

Shariputra asked the divine maiden, "Have you been staying in this room for a long time?"

The divine maiden answered, "Venerable Shariputra, I have been staying in this room as long as you have been obtaining emancipation (*Vimukti*)."

Shariputra asked, "Well, have you been here for a long time?"

The divine maiden answered, "Venerable Shariputra, I wonder if you can say that a long time has passed since your obtaining emancipation."

Shariputra kept silence without answering.

The divine maiden asked, "Being endowed with great wisdom (*Maha-prajnya*), Venerable Shariputra, why do you keep your mouth shut?"

He answered, "Emancipation is indescribable in words, so I am at a loss as to what to say."

The divine maiden said, "All statements and words are marks of emancipation. Why? Because emancipation exists neither inside, nor outside, nor between them. Words also exist neither inside, nor outside, nor between them. Therefore, emancipation cannot be expounded apart from words. Why? Because all existing things have marks of emancipation."

Shariputra said, "Doesn't emancipation mean freedom from greed, anger, and stupidity?"

The divine maiden answered, "It is merely for the sake of the arrogant man who claims falsely to have realized the ultimate truth that the Buddha expounded, 'Emancipation is freedom from greed, anger, and stupidity.' If a man is free from arrogance, the Buddha expounded, 'The possession of greed, anger, and stupidity is emancipation itself.'"

Shariputra said, "Wonderful, wonderful! Divine maiden, you make an eloquent speech. What have you acquired, what have you realized?"

The divine maiden answered, "I have acquired nothing, realized nothing, and therefore I can speak eloquently like this. Why? A man who declares to have acquired something or to have realized something is regarded as arrogant according to the Buddha's teaching."

■■

Shariputra said, "Why don't you transform your female body into a male body?"

The divine maiden answered, "I have searched for the true character of femininity for twelve years, but I could not grasp it. Why on earth should I transform my female body into a male body? It is just like an illusory woman conjured up by a magician. If someone should ask an illusory woman why on earth she does not transform her female body into a male body, can I say that he asks a correct question?"

Shariputra answered, "It is not a correct question. An illusion has neither its own characteristics nor substantial nature. Why should it be transformed?"

The divine maiden replied, "All forms of existence in the world are also just like that. They don't have any substantial nature. Why, Shariputra, should you ask me, 'Why don't you transform your female body into a male body?'"

At once, through supernatural powers (*Abhijnya*), the divine maiden turned Shariputra's body into the body of a divine maiden and also changed herself into Shariputra's body. After that, the divine maiden asked Shariputra, "Why don't you transform your female body into a male body?"

Shariputra answered in the shape of the divine maiden, "I have received a female body. But, I cannot understand why it has occurred."

The divine maiden said, "Venerable Shariputra, if you could transform your own female body, all women would be able to transform their female bodies, too. Although you are not really a woman, you just took the shape of a woman. All women are the same as that. Although they take the shapes of women, in truth they are not women. That is why Gautama Buddha taught that all things of this world are neither male nor female."

Saying that, the divine maiden undid the supernatural spell. Thereupon, Shariputra's body changed into what it was before. The divine maiden asked Shariputra, "Where has your female body gone now?"

Shariputra answered, "The female body is neither in existence nor in nonexistence anymore."

The divine maiden said, "All things of this world are also like that. They are neither existence nor nonexistence. On the whole, it was the Buddha's teaching that '[Everything is] neither existence nor nonexistence.'"

Shariputra asked the divine maiden, "After ending your present life, where will you be reborn?"

The divine maiden answered, "I will be reborn where those whom the Buddha has made through his supernatural powers will be reborn."

Shariputra said, "Those whom the Buddha has made through his supernatural powers neither die nor are reborn."

The divine maiden answered, "In the same way, all living beings neither die nor are reborn."

Shariputra asked the divine maiden, "When will you attain the Unsurpassed Perfect Enlightenment (*Anuttara-samyak-sambodhi*)?"

The divine maiden answered, "When, Venerable Shariputra, you return to the state of unenlightened ordinary man, I will attain the Unsurpassed Perfect Enlightenment."

Shariputra said, "I will never become an ordinary man again."

The divine maiden answered, "Likewise, I will never attain the Unsurpassed Perfect Enlightenment. Why? Because Enlightenment has no place to be attained. Therefore no one can attain it."

Shariputra asked, "What is the meaning of such words as 'The Buddhas attain the Unsurpassed Perfect Enlightenment now,' 'The Buddhas attained it in the past,' 'The Buddhas will attain it in the future,' and 'The numbers of the Buddhas are as many as the sands of the Ganges (*Ganga*) River'?"

The divine maiden answered, "According to the common expression of numbers in everyday language, we merely suppose three periods (the past, present, and future). Enlightenment itself belongs to neither past, nor present, nor future."

The divine maiden asked in return, "Venerable Shariputra, have you attained the highest stage of *Arhat*?"

Shariputra answered, "There is nothing to be attained, and all phenomena are nonsubstantial (*Shunya*), so I have attained it."

The divine maiden said, "In the same way, the Buddhas and the Bodhisattvas have attained it, too, because there is nothing to be attained."

At that time Vimalakirti said to Shariputra, "This divine maiden has already finished holding religious services for nine billion two hundred million Buddhas. And she has already gained supernatural abilities to use as she pleases; she has achieved her wish, has gained *Anutpattika-dharma-kshanti* (*Wushengfaren*),[4] that is, the higher spiritual state in which one recognizes the immutable reality of all existence, and has attained the Stage of Non-Retrogression (*Avaivartika*) of Bodhisattva. Merely because of her own vow in her previous life, she took the shape of woman as she wished, and she is preaching to living beings."

---

[4] The stage attained by a Bodhisattva in which he or she perceives the *Dharmata* (the real nature of the phenomenal world), the higher spiritual state in which one recognizes the ultimate nature of things.

36

THE STORY OF THE DRAGON KING'S DAUGHTER

From the Devadatta Chapter of the Lotus Sutra
(Miaofalianhua jing)
妙法蓮華經

The representative Chinese versions of the Lotus Sutra[1] are Zhengfahua jing translated by Dharma-raksha (Zhufahu) in 286 C.E., and Miaofalian-hua jing translated by Kumarajiva (Jiumoluoshi) in 406 C.E. Of the two, Kumarajiva's version has prevailed most widely in China and Japan because of its flowing and refined style of translation.

Although Hinayana Buddhism denied lay believers, especially women, the ability to attain Buddhahood, the Lotus Sutra affirmed the ability of all living beings to do so, including women. This teaching seems to be the original intent motivating the creation of the Lotus Sutra. The Devadatta Chapter of the Lotus Sutra affirms women's ability to attain Buddhahood by telling the dramatic and symbolic story of the dragon king's daughter.

Mahayana Buddhists, as we have seen in the Sutra of the Teaching of Vimalakirti, based their distinctive teaching on the concept of Shunyata (voidness) and the compromise idea of "gender transformation from female to male." Above all, the Lotus Sutra sets forth the concept of One Buddha Vehicle (Ekam Buddha-yanam) as the basis of universal equality. There is, of course, controversy among modern-day feminists, some of whom reject "Gender Transformation" as merely a form of co-optation in which the female remains subordinated to the male. It is, however, a misunderstanding of this Devadatta Chapter of the Lotus Sutra. In order to deny

---

Translated by Masatoshi Ueki and Makiko Ueki.
[1] The Sanskrit original is called *Saddharma-pundarika-sutra*, which, according to the Sanskrit grammar of compounds, may be translated as the *Sutra of the Most Excellent Teaching Just Like the White Lotus*. It should not be translated as the *White Lotus of the True Teaching*.

Shariputra's preconception that the "Five Obstacles" would rule out Buddhahood for women, the Lotus Sutra *presents the idea of "Gender Transformation." It is intended as an antithesis, if you will, to the Hinayana Buddhist's prejudiced view of women.*

The key to understanding this point is that the dragon king's daughter, as we shall see, had already attained the Stage of Non-Retrogression (Avaivartika) of the Bodhisattvas before she transformed her female body into a male body. This is evident from the words of Bodhisattva Manjushri who declared that the dragon king's daughter had already attained the supreme state before she used her powers to transform her gendered appearance.

The text suggests that she would attain Buddhahood without fail in a matter of time. In other words, it is not a necessary and indispensable condition for women to transform themselves into male bodies in order to attain Buddhahood.

It should also be pointed out that the state of a Bodhisattva of Non-Retrogression was listed as one of the "Five Obstacles" for women. It can therefore be concluded that the Lotus Sutra *negated the idea of the "Five Obstacles" for women through the example of the dragon king's daughter.*

Although the dragon king's daughter herself and Bodhisattva Manjushri both said that she had attained Enlightenment, Shariputra never believed it. So her attaining Buddhahood was pointedly described by attributing to her the "Thirty-Two Marks" and "Eighty Minor Marks" of physical excellence that were considered by Hinayana Buddhists to be characteristics of the Buddha. These were important concepts for Hinayana Buddhism. Thus, in many ways, the Lotus Sutra, *using Hinayana Buddhism's own concepts, asserts that women could surely attain Buddhahood.*

Masatoshi Ueki

At that time Manjushri, seated on the thousand-petaled lotus flower as big as a wheel, flew out of the undersea palace of the dragon king Sagara and remained suspended in the air. He was attended by other Bodhisattvas seated on the jewel-made lotus flower. Approaching the Vulture Peak (*Gridhrakuta*), he got off the lotus flower. Coming near, in the presence of the Buddhas, he made obeisance to the two World-Honored Ones by putting their feet upon his head. After paying homage, he went to Bodhisattva Prajnyakuta (Accumulation of Wisdom), exchanged salutations with him, and stepped back and took a seat.

Bodhisattva Prajnyakuta asked Manjushri, "How many living beings have you converted at the dragon king's palace?"

Manjushri said, "The number is too immeasurable to count. Even a mouth cannot put it into words, and a mind cannot conjecture. Wait a moment, and you will see the evidence."

No sooner had he finished speaking than countless Bodhisattvas seated on the jewel-made lotus flowers rose up from the ocean and approached the Vulture Peak and stayed suspended in the air. These Bodhisattvas had all been converted by Manjushri. They have practiced the way of the Bodhisattva and all of them expounded the Six Kinds of Perfect Practice (Six *Paramitas*).[2] Those who were formerly Voice-Hearers (*Shravakas*) used to perform the Voice-Hearer's practice, but now all practiced the principle of voidness (*Shunyata*) as taught in the Great Vehicle (*Mahayana*).

Manjushri said to Prajnyakuta, "The teaching and converting that I accomplished in the ocean is as you have seen."

Then Bodhisattva Prajnyakuta recited a verse in praise of Manjushri:

A man of wisdom and virtue, you are brave and powerful,
have converted and saved countless living beings.
Now, all participants in this great assembly including myself
    have already seen
That expounding the teachings of the real state of all
    phenomena,
Opening and revealing the One [Buddha] Vehicle (*Eka-yana*),
You guided many living beings far and wide
Swiftly to accomplish Enlightenment.

Manjushri said, "In the ocean I merely expounded the *Lotus Sutra.*"

Prajnyakuta asked Manjushri, "This sutra is very profound and supreme, the highest and most precious treasure among all sutras. So we can rarely encounter it in the world. Among all living beings, are there any who could swiftly attain Buddhahood by practicing this *sutra* diligently and assiduously?"

Manjushri said, "There is the daughter of the dragon king Sagara who is eight years old. She has keen wisdom and knows well the workings of the sense organs (body, mouth, and mind) of all living beings. She has acquired the *Dharani* (the ability to hold firm to the teaching in her mind), decidedly accepted all the teachings of profound secrets expounded by the Buddhas, realized the real state of all phenomenal things by entering into deep meditation (*Samadhi*), and attained the stage of Non-Retrogression (*Avaivartika*) of the Bodhisattvas after aspiring to attain Supreme Enlightenment in an instant (*Kshana*).

---

[2] *Paramita* means "perfection of Buddhist practices." The Six *Paramitas* are *Dana-paramita* (donation), *Shila-paramita* (keeping precepts), *Kshanti-paramita* (forbearance), *Virya-paramita* (assiduity), *Dhyana-paramita* (meditation), and *Prajnya-paramita* (wisdom).

Fluent of speech, she keeps her mind on compassion for all living beings as if they were her own children. She is endowed with virtue (*Guna*). While concentrating in mind and expounding by mouth, she shows subtle and vast compassion and benevolence. She has a gentle and graceful mind, and has attained Enlightenment."

Prajnyakuta said, "According to my observation, Shakyamuni Thus-Come One (*Tathagata*) carried out hard and ascetic practices for immeasurable *Kalpas* (aeons).[3] Pursuing the Bodhisattva practices, he has not yet taken rest from accumulating virtuous deeds and continuing meritorious deeds. According to my observation of Triple-Thousand Great One-Thousand Worlds (*Tri-sahasra-maha-sahasro-lokadhatu*),[4] that is to say, one billion worlds, we cannot find any place as narrow as a mustard seed where Shakyamuni Thus-Come One has never thrown away his life while he was still a Bodhisattva. He has done so for all living beings. That was how he was able to complete the way to Enlightenment. Therefore, it is incredible that this girl could attain True Enlightenment in a moment."

No sooner had Prajnyakuta finished speaking than the daughter of the dragon king Sagara appeared before the Buddha all at once and made obeisance to the World-Honored One (*Bhagavat*) by putting his foot upon her head. Then she stepped back, took a seat, and recited a verse in praise of the Buddha:

> The Buddha has a profound insight into the characteristics of
> sin and good fortune, and illuminates all ten directions
> universally.
> His subtle and pure body is endowed
> with the Thirty-Two Marks of physical excellence.
> With the Eighty Minor Marks his body is adorned.
> Heavenly beings and human beings hold him in reverence,
> dragons and demons all pay homage to him.
> Among all living beings there is no one who fails to think
> much of him.

---

[3] *Kalpa* means an immeasurably long period of time. Its length is metaphorically explained, for example, as the period necessary for one to take away all the poppy seeds in a ten-mile square city by taking away one seed every three years. It was translated as *Qie bo* in Chinese.

[4] In Sanskrit *tri* means three, and *sahasra* means thousand. We should not, however, understand *Tri-sahasra* as "three thousand"; it means "one thousand cubed," or "one billion." It is said that "One World" (Skt. *Loka-dhatu*) corresponds to one solar system.

Only the Buddha is my witness that I have attained
Enlightenment after having heard his teachings.
I shall unfold the teachings of the Great Vehicle (*Mahayana*),
And relieve all living beings of sufferings.

Then Shariputra said to the dragon king's daughter: "You might
think that you have attained the Unsurpassed Enlightenment in an
instance. This, however, is incredible. Why? Because a woman's body
is defiled and cannot be a container of the Law (*Dharma*). How could
you ever attain the Unsurpassed Enlightenment? The way to Buddhahood is a great distance away. Therefore one can attain Enlightenment only after accumulating virtuous deeds with diligence and
practicing minutely all kinds of perfection (*Paramita*)—donation,
keeping precepts, forbearance, assiduity, meditation, and wisdom—
for immeasurable *Kalpas* (*aeons*). Furthermore, a woman is subject to
five kinds of obstacles. First off, she cannot become a Brahma
heavenly King. The other four kinds of status that she cannot attain
are Indra, Devil King, Wheel-Turning Sage King (*Cakravarti-raja*), and
the Buddha, to list in the order of increasing difficulty. How, then,
can a woman attain Buddhahood so quickly?"

The dragon king's daughter had a jewel of great worth comparable to the Triple-Thousand Great One-Thousand Worlds, that is to
say, one billion worlds. She presented it to the Buddha, who accepted
it immediately.

The dragon king's daughter said to Prajnyakuta and Shariputra, "I
presented a jewel, and the World-Honored One accepted. Was that
done quickly, or not?"

They answered, "It was done very quickly."

Thereupon the dragon king's daughter said, "Watch my attaining
Buddhahood through your supernatural powers. It will be quicker
than that."

Instantly all participants of the assembly saw the dragon king's
daughter transform her female body into a male body and carry out
the Bodhisattva practices. Going to the Spotless (*Vimala*) World
located to the south, and sitting on the jewel-made lotus flower, he
(she) completed the True and Perfect Enlightenment (*Samyak-
sambodhi*). They saw him (her), endowed with the Thirty-Two Marks
and Eighty Minor Marks of physical excellence, expounding extensively the Wonderful Teaching (*Saddharma*) for all living beings in the
ten directions.

There the Bodhisattva, Voice-Hearer (*Shravaka*), eight kinds of
heavenly beings and dragons, human beings, and non-human beings

in the *Saha* World[5] all witnessed this dragon king's daughter become a Buddha and preach extensively the *Dharma* to human beings and the heavenly beings in the assembly. Their minds filled with great joy, all paid homage reverently from a great distance. Hearing the *Dharma*, countless living beings comprehended it and attained the stage of Non-Retrogression of the Bodhisattva. Numerous living beings received a prediction (*Vyakarana*) that they would complete Enlightenment.

The Spotless World quaked in six ways. Three thousand living beings in the *Saha* World stood on the stage of Non-Retrogression. Three thousand living beings aspired to attain Supreme Enlightenment and received a prediction of Enlightenment.

Bodhisattva Prajnyakuta, Shariputra, and all the participants in the assembly believed and accepted [the fact that the dragon king's daughter attained Buddhahood].

---

[5] The Sanskrit word *Saha* means endurance.

37

GUANYIN CHAPTER OF THE LOTUS SUTRA

(Guanyin Pin)

觀音品

Although the so-called Guanyin sutra *is usually regarded as an independent* sutra, *it is actually the twenty-fifth chapter of the* Miaofalianhua jing *(the* Lotus Sutra*), entitled "The Chapter on the* Samantamukha *(Facing All Directions) of Guanyin." Guanyin, the name of a Bodhisattva, is the Chinese translation of Avalokitasvara,[1] which means Observer of the Sound [of the World], or the Lord who looks down with infinite compassion on all living beings.*

This work says that anyone uttering the name of Bodhisattva Avalokitasvara will be saved from all calamities such as shipwreck, fire, windstorm, or being killed, shackled, or robbed. This Bodhisattva appears wherever and whenever someone wants his help, manifesting himself in thirty-three forms of incarnation to save people in different states of existence, and delivers them from all troubles.

The concept of the Bodhisattva Avalokitasvara was brought into existence in Gandhara in northwestern India. It is also said that Avalokitasvara might have been formulated under the influence of an Iranian deity. Chronological examination of the Avalokitasvara statues excavated in Gandhara and Mathura reveals that Avalokitasvara statues had already come into existence in the second or third century C.E., and it is clear that people of the time worshipped this Bodhisattva.

From Gandhara, the Bodhisattva Avalokitasvara was brought to China and Eastern Asiatic countries by way of Central Asia and Dunhuang to be called

---

Translated by Masatoshi Ueki and Makiko Ueki.

[1] The Sanskrit word *Avalokitasvara* is a compound of *Avalokita* (to have looked down) and *Svara* (sound). *Avalokita* is also a compound of the prefix *Ava*, which means "down," and *lokita*, which is a past passive participle of the verb *Lok* (to look). *Avalokita* was translated into Chinese as *Guan*, and *Svara* as *Yin*. We should note that in later Sanskrit manuscripts of the *Lotus Sutra*, *Avalokiteshvara*, which is a compound of *Avalokita* and *Ishvara* (ruler, king, Lord, *Shiva*, and so on) is used. The name of the *Bodhisattva* must have been *Avalokitasvara* in the original text translated by Kumarajiva.

Guanyin. The Gandhara statues of the Bodhisattva Avalokitasvara wear a moustache, indicating that this Bodhisattva was originally a male. In China, however, this Bodhisattva was worshipped as a female deity. People in China have worshipped female deities, particularly in Daoist shrines, from time immemorial. Since Guanyin can manifest himself in thirty-three forms of incarnation, seven of which are in female shape, the Chinese may have felt special affinities to Guanyin among the many Buddhas and Bodhisattvas, and worshipped it as a female deity.

In China, the Guanyin cult came to be widespread after the Lotus Sutra (Skt. Saddharma-pundarika-sutra) was translated into Chinese, with the title Zhengfahua jing (286 C.E.) and Miaofalianhua jing (406 C.E.). Furthermore, the Chinese translations of Wuliangshou jing (Skt. Sukhavati-vyuha, 252 C.E.), Guanwuliangshou jing (Skt. Amitayur-buddha-dhyana-sutra, 424–442 C.E.), and the Huayan jing (Skt. Avatamsaka-sutra, 418–420 C.E.) gave an impetus to the surprisingly swift development of the Guanyin cult.

Many stories celebrating the miraculous virtues of Guanyin were recorded in the collections of Buddhist tales. From the fall of the Later Han dynasty in 220 C.E. to the unification of the Sui dynasty in 581 C.E., many miracles were attributed to the Guanyin cult in these stories. The Gaoseng zhuan (Biographies of Great Monks, 519 C.E.) also included many tales of Guanyin.

At the end of the fifth century C.E., the Mingxiangji was written, reflecting the actual state of Buddhist faith in those days. The Mingxiangji contains a tale about a man over fifty years old who was not blessed with children. Being taught by a monk of a neighborhood temple, he read and recited the Guanyin Sutra. Two or three days later, he had a revelation in his dream. Thereupon, his wife got pregnant and had a baby boy.

In the Tang dynasty (618–906 C.E.) also, the Guanyin cult flourished. The Fayüan zhulin was published in 668 C.E., containing still more tales of Guanyin's miracles. The greater part of these tales were meant to show that persons who were imprisoned, attacked by robbers, or held captive, could escape from death because they uttered the name of the Bodhisattva Guanyin. The contents of the prayers to Guanyin became rich in variety. One is a prayer for the recovery from illness. One is a prayer to hold position and money. One is a prayer to be blessed with good children. And one is a prayer to escape from disaster. Many people wanted Guanyin to favor them with this-worldly rewards.

Later in the Qing dynasty (1616–1912 C.E.), the Guanyin cilinji and the Guanyin jingchi yanji were compiled. The latter contains 116 Guanyin miracles. These compilations also suggest that the Guanyin cult was popular at that time primarily among people who wished to be blessed with baby boys.

Since seven kinds of female forms are included among the thirty-three forms of incarnation of Guanyin even while it was deemed a male deity in India, Guanyin has often been regarded mistakenly as an affirmation of femininity. Kumarajiva's translation does contain the seven female forms of incarnation. In the Sanskrit version,

*however, Guanyin manifests himself in sixteen forms, all of which are male.
Furthermore, the thirty-first verse in the Sanskrit version, which is neglected in
Kumarajiva's translation, says that no woman will be born in the Amitabha Buddha's
Pure Land where Guanyin is the leader of the World. There is a great difference
between the dragon king's daughter's "Gender Transformation from Female to Male"
and Guanyin's ability to manifest himself in both male and female bodies.*

*Certainly Guanyin can manifest himself in female forms, but in the author's view
this does not mean that all women are manifestations of Guanyin. Guanyin is merely
an object of prayers for help in times of distress. The author sees a striking contrast
between Guanyin's manifestations and the dragon king's daughter's attainment of
Buddhahood. Only the dragon king's daughter symbolically represents the ability of
all women to attain Buddhahood.*

*More attention must be paid to the difference in character between the Bodhisattva
Guanyin and other Bodhisattvas who appear in the* Dharmabhanaka *(Preachers
of the Law) Chapter, the* Sadaparibhuta *(Never Disparaging) Chapter, and so
on. The Guanyin Chapter tends to invite the reader to take up a passive position, so
as to be saved by Guanyin. When we read the* Miaofalianhua jing *(the Lotus
Sutra), from the tenth chapter on* Dharmabhanaka *to the twenty-second chapter
on* Anuparindana *(Entrustment), we are inspired to become Bodhisattvas and find
ourselves taking an active part as Dharmabhanakas (Preachers of the Law) dedicated
to saving others. This difference must arise from the fact that the chapters from the
twenty-third to the twenty-eighth of the* Lotus Sutra *were added later, when the
tendency toward a more this-worldly cult had increased. The* Lotus Sutra *is said
to have taken one hundred years in compilation, either from the first century to the
second century, or from the second to the third century. Its last six chapters, including the Guanyin Chapter, were added during the final stage. The Guanyin Chapter
is less promising as a source of Enlightenment for women than the concepts of voidness* (Shunyata) *and attaining Buddhahood of the dragan king's daughter, as presented in the Devadatta Chapter of the* Lotus Sutra.

Masatoshi Ueki

At that time Bodhisattva Akshayamati (Inexhaustible Wisdom) got
up from his seat and bared his right shoulder. Facing the Buddha
with his hands clasped, he said, "O World-Honored One, why is
Bodhisattva Guanyin (Skt. *Avalokitasvara*) called Guanyin (Observer of
the Sound [of the World])?"

The Buddha answered Akshayamati: "Young good man, suppose
that there are immeasurable hundreds, thousands, millions of living
beings distressed with sorrows and sufferings. When they learn the
name of this Bodhisattva Guanyin and call his name with single-

minded devotion, he will at once hear their voices and relieve them all from sufferings.

"Even if someone who holds fast to the name of Bodhisattva Guanyin is caught in a big fire, he will not be burned thanks to the supernatural powers of this Bodhisattva. When one is carried away by a great flood, if only he calls the name, he will at once get to a shallow place. Suppose that hundreds, thousands, millions of living beings sailed out on the ocean in search of treasures such as gold, silver, lapis lazuli, seashell, agate, coral, amber, pearls. And their ship was carried all the way to the land of *Rakshasa* by violent winds. If one of the living beings calls the name of Guanyin, all of them will be able to escape the danger of *Rakshasa*. This is the reason why he is called Guanyin, the Observer of the Sound.

"And if someone who is about to be killed calls the name of Guanyin, the sword or stick raised by his assailant will at once be broken into many pieces, and he will be able to escape from death.

"Even though *Yakshas* and *Rakshasas* filling the Triple-Thousand Great One-Thousand Worlds come and try to torment a person, if they hear him calling the name of Bodhisattva Guanyin, they will not be able even to cast their malignant looks upon him, much less cause injury to him.

"Suppose a person who may or may not be guilty is imprisoned in fetters, shackles, and chains. If he calls the name of Bodhisattva Guanyin, all of them will fall off, broken, and he will immediately be liberated.

"Suppose that the Triple-Thousand Great One-Thousand Worlds are filled with robbers, and that there is a merchant who leads a caravan carrying treasures of great value through a dangerous road. Then one of them declares, 'Young good men, you have nothing to be afraid of. I advise you to call on the name of Bodhisattva Guanyin with whole-hearted devotion. This Bodhisattva is able to bestow fearlessness to all living beings. If you call on his name, we can be saved from robbers.' After hearing this declaration, merchants will join their voices in chorus, saying, 'I sincerely believe in Bodhisattva Guanyin.' By invoking his name, they will immediately be liberated. You see, Akshayamati, the power of the Bodhisattva Guanyin is as great as this.

"Suppose that there are living beings who are seized with strong carnal desire. Whenever they invoke and pay homage to Bodhisattva Guanyin, they are immediately freed from carnal desire. Whenever living beings whose minds are filled with strong anger and hatred invoke and pay homage to Bodhisattva Guanyin, they will immediately be freed from anger and hatred. Whenever living beings who are very ignorant and stupid invoke and pay homage to Bodhisattva Guanyin, they will immediately be freed from stupidity. Bodhisattva Guanyin has such great supernatural powers and bestows benefits on numerous living beings. Therefore, all living beings should always invoke Bodhisattva Guanyin in their minds.

"Suppose that there is a woman who wants to bear a baby boy. If she pays homage and makes offerings to Bodhisattva Guanyin, she will bear a baby boy endowed with good fortune and wisdom. If she pays homage and makes offerings to Bodhisattva Guanyin wishing for a baby girl, she will bear a baby girl of great personal beauty who accumulated virtuous deeds in past lives, and who will be loved and respected by many people. Akshayamati, the power of Bodhisattva Guanyin is like this. If living beings pay homage and make offerings to Bodhisattva Guanyin, their good fortune will not be in vain. Therefore, all living beings should cherish the name of Bodhisattva Guanyin.

"Now, Akshayamati, suppose that there is a person who reveres the names of Bodhisattvas as many as the sands of the sixty-two million Ganges (Ganga) Rivers, and offers them food and drink, clothing, bedding, and medicine as long as he lives. What do you think? Will this young good man or young good woman obtain lots of benefits, or no?"

Akshayamati answered, "The benefits will be very many, O World-Honored One."

The Buddha said: "Suppose that there is another person who reveres Guanyin's name, and for a short time pays homage and makes offerings to him. The good fortune accorded to these two persons will be identical without any difference. It will never be exhausted even after the lapse of hundreds, thousands, millions of *Kalpas* (*aeons*). You see, Akshayamati, if one reveres the name of Bodhisattva Guanyin, one will obtain benefits of good fortune as immeasurable and limitless as this."

Bodhisattva Akshayamati said to the Buddha, "O World-Honored One, how does Bodhisattva Guanyin travel about in this *Saha* World? How does he expound the *Dharma* for the benefit of living beings? How does his power actually work?"

The Buddha said to Akshayamati: "Young good man, if living beings in the land expect to be saved by someone in the body of the Buddha, Bodhisattva Guanyin will manifest himself in the Buddha's body and will expound the *Dharma* for them. If they expect to be saved by someone in the body of the Self-Enlightened One (*Pratyeka-buddha*), he will appear in the Self-Enlightened One's body and expound the *Dharma* for them. If they expect to be saved by someone in the body of the Voice-Hearer (*Shravaka*), he will manifest in Voice-Hearer's body and expound the *Dharma* for them. If they expect to be saved by someone in the body of the Brahma heavenly King,[2] he will manifest in the Brahma heavenly king's body and expound the *Dharma* for them. If they expect to be saved king's by someone in the body of *Indra*, he will manifest himself in *Indra's*[3] body and expound the *Dharma* for them.

[The same format is repeated for *Ishvara*, *Maheshvara*, the Heavenly Great General, *Vaishravana*, the King of a small country, the rich man, the community leader (*Grihapati*), the minister, and the *Brahmana*.]

If they expect to be saved by someone in the body of the monk (*Bhikshu*), nun (*Bhikshuni*), layman believer (*Upasaka*), or laywoman believer (*Upasika*), he will manifest in a body of a monk, nun, layman believer, or laywoman believer and expound the *Dharma* for them. If they expect to be saved by someone in the body of the wife of a rich man, of a community leader, of a minister, or of a *Brahmana*, he will manifest in the body of such a wife and expound the *Dharma* for them. If they expect to be saved by someone in the body of a young boy or a young girl, he will manifest in the body of a young boy or a young girl and expound the *Dharma* for them.

[The same format is repeated for the heavenly being, dragon, *Yaksha*, *Gandharva*, *Asura*, *Garuda*, *Kimnara*, *Mahoraga* (big serpent), human being, or non-human being, and the Diamond-Holding God (*Vajra-pani*).]

"Now, Akshayamati, Bodhisattva Guanyin who has completed these virtuous deeds travels about many lands manifesting himself in various forms and saving living beings. Therefore you should make offerings to Bodhisattva Guanyin with single-minded devotion. This great Bodhisattva Guanyin can bestow fearlessness when one is seized with fear and in imminent danger. That is the reason why everyone in this *Saha* World calls him the Endower of Fearlessness."

Bodhisattva Akshayamati said to the Buddha, "O World-Honored One, I should make offerings to Bodhisattva Guanyin now."

He took off his necklace made of precious gems worth hundreds, thousands of taels of gold from his neck, and handed it [to the Bodhisattva Guanyin], saying, "Reverend, please accept this necklace made of precious gems as a gift of the *Dharma*."

---

[2] The highest god who created the universe according to Hindu. In Buddhism he was believed to protect Buddhism and its followers in cooperation with Indra.

[3] Originally a Hindu god but in Buddhism regarded as a god who protects Buddhism and its followers.

On that occasion Bodhisattva Guanyin declined to accept it. Akshayamati once more said, "Reverend, feel compassion for us, and please accept this necklace."

At that time the Buddha said to the Bodhisattva Guanyin, "Feeling compassion for Akshayamati, four kinds of Buddhists, the heavenly Kings, dragons, *Yakshas, Gandharvas, Asuras, Garudas, Kimnaras, Mahoragas,* human beings, and non-human beings, you should accept this necklace."

Immediately feeling compassion for the four kinds of Buddhists, the heavenly Kings, dragons, human beings, and non-human beings, the Bodhisattva Guanyin accepted the necklace. Dividing it into two parts, he presented one part to Shakyamuni Buddha and the other part to the Tower-of-Many-Treasures (*Prabhutaratna*) Buddha.

The Buddha said, "You see, Akshayamati, the Bodhisattva Guanyin has supernatural powers of perfect freedom like this, and travels about in the *Saha* World."

■■

At that time the Bodhisattva Earth-Holder (*Dharanimdhara*) got up from his seat, came near and said to the Buddha: "O World-Honored One, if living beings listen to this chapter on the Bodhisattva Guanyin who has freedom of action and supernatural powers to manifest himself facing all directions, we should know that the benefits for these living beings are not few."

When the Buddha expounded this chapter [of the Bodhisattva Guanyin] on Facing All Directions, eighty-four thousand living beings in the assembly were aroused to aspire toward the Unsurpassed True and Perfect Enlightenment (*Anuttara-samyak-sambodhi*) beyond compare.

38

THE BLOOD TRAY SUTRA

(Xuepen jing)

血盆經

The Blood Tray Sutra (Xuepen jing) *is thought to have been composed by a* Chinese *monk of the* Zen *sect around the tenth century* C.E. *Though some Buddhist scholars contest it, this sutra claims to be an authentic teaching of the Buddha, and was widely regarded as such in China during the Ming and Qing Dynasties. The translation provided here is probably the first in English to date. From the standpoint of women in the Chinese Zen sect, this sutra has had great significance. It puts forth the idea that women are very sinful, because they defile not only the earth and rivers but also gods and Buddhas with the blood of their childbirth and menstruation.[1] This sutra gave undeserved credence to the prevailing idea that women were impure.*

A careful reading of the Blood Tray Sutra *reveals that this text is meant to provide a way to overcome the impurity that it attributes to women. The monk Maudgalyayana, who discovers the sufferings of women inflicted because of their impurity, is moved by compassion to ask how the impurity might be removed, so that his mother—and all other women, presumably—might be liberated from the Blood Tray Lake and come to be reborn in heaven. He then is given instructions for a purification ritual that promises to liberate those in whose name it is performed. Thus, while the sutra clearly accuses all women of impurity, it is also consistent with the Mahayana Buddhist assumption that all beings eventually can achieve Enlightenment.*

Masatoshi Ueki

At that time the Venerable Maudgalyayana (chn. Mulian) came over to Zhuiyang prefecture in the State of Yü and saw the hell of the Blood Tray Lake. In the vast lake whose width was eighty-four thousand *Yojanas,*[2] one hundred twenty kinds of punishment were inflicted on

---

Translated by Masatoshi Ueki and Makiko Ueki.

[1] Such an idea is not found in Indian Buddhism.

[2] A unit of distance in Sanskrit. One *Yojana* is said to be 160 kilometers, 120 kilometers, or 64 kilometers. *Yojana* was translated as *youxun* in Chinese.

women. He saw a great many women with disheveled hair from the south continent of *Jambudvipa*.[3] Pilloried, handcuffed, and fastened to iron beams and iron poles with iron chains, they were punished in this hell. The warden, who was the king of demons in hell, made the sinners drink blood three times a day. The sinners resisted drinking it. As they were thrashed with an iron club by the warden, they moaned in pain.

Maudgalyayana felt compassion for the sinners and asked the warden, "I have never seen any men from the south continent of *Jambudvipa* being inflicted with pain, but I just saw a great many women being inflicted with pain. What is the reason?"

The warden answered the Venerable, "Here we do not punish men. It is only women that we punish. At the period of menstruation and delivery, they bleed and defile earthly deities with blood. Even if they wash the blood-stained clothes at a swamp far away from a river and a mountain stream, the flowing water is defiled by blood. The pious men and women ignorantly make tea with this water and offer it to gods and Buddhas. As a result, gods and Buddhas are defiled. The Heavenly Great General keeps people's names in the black book recording their good and evil deeds for one hundred years. In death, they will suffer the rewards of *karma*."

Feeling pity for them, Maudgalyayana could not help but ask the warden, "How can I repay my indebtedness to my mother who gave birth to me and liberate her from the hell of the Blood Tray Lake?"

The warden answered the Venerable Maudgalyayana: "Modest and dutiful sons and daughters should respect the Three Treasures of the Buddha, the *Dharma* (teachings), and the *Samgha* (priesthood) sincerely. Furthermore, they should observe the Purification of the Blood Tray for their mothers for three years by holding a superior Assembly of the Blood Tray and asking a monk to read and recite this sutra repeatedly. When the time is ripe and they repent their sins, a ship of *Prajnya* (wisdom) will leave the riverbank of hell and five lotus stalks will appear in the Blood Tray Lake. At that time, as soon as the sinners are overjoyed with this happening and overwhelmed with repentance, they will be born into the Buddha Land."

Coming back to the south continent of *Jambudvipa*, Maudgalyayana and many great Bodhisattvas said to people encouragingly: "Devout

---

[3] *Jambudvipa* (Skt.) was translated as *Yanfuti* in Chinese. It literally means the continent (Skt. *Dvipa*) where rose apple (Skt. *Jambu*) trees grow. According to the Buddhist cosmology, the continent situated to the south of Mount Sumeru (*Xunmushan*). In a narrow sense it means Indian subcontinent, in a broad sense the world in which we live.

men and women, you had better practice and awake to the Mahayana teachings soon. You ought to have the future in mind. Do not waste a myriad *Kalpas* (*aeons*) of time. The Buddha seldom reveals the *Blood Tray Sutra* to women. If you are firm in your faith, you should copy and embrace this sutra. And then you can let all mothers in the three periods (past, present, and future) be born in the heaven, let them get much pleasure there without lack of food and clothing, and let them live long to a great age and be wealthy and noble."

At that time all the heavenly beings, dragons, the eight kinds of gods and demi-gods, human beings, and non-human beings were all filled with joy. They believed him and put his teaching into practice. Then with a bow, they took their leave.

39

DUNHUANG PRAYERS

(*Dunhuang Yuanwen*)

敦煌愿文

Dunhuang Prayers, or yuanwen, *are Tang texts discovered in various caves in Dunhuang, China. The majority of the* Dunhuang yuanwen *are Buddhist prayers. They were to be recited before a statue of Buddha, asking for his protection and blessings. Buddhist prayers could be said during regular visits to a Buddhist temple, or on special occasions, such as natural disasters, long journeys, and especially sickness or the death of a family member, relative, friend, or even an animal. The rest of the* yuanwen *consist of Daoist prayers, Zoroastrian prayers, or prayers for special events such as weddings and housewarmings, as well as various festivals.*

The following prayers show how Buddhism, blended with traditional gender ideology and social values, came into play in the everyday life of Tang China. The first is a prayer for women preparing to give birth. It calls upon the Buddha and the Boddhisattvas, especially Guanyin, to show mercy to both mother and child during the birth labor. The second set consists of prayers uttered by the fathers of a bride and groom in a marriage ceremony uniting their deceased son and daughter in the afterlife. The ritual of an Afterlife Marriage is an unusual act of compassion based on the assumption that what goes on in the afterlife, and the needs and desires of the deceased, are not all that different from how things are in this world. The third set also concerns afterlife marriages, particularly, the proper etiquette for proposing such a marriage or accepting such a marriage proposal for one's deceased son or daughter. Here, too, what propriety demands of families arranging marriages for their children is carefully observed in the afterlife, just as it is in this world. The final set consists of formal messages of congratulations sent, respectively, to a groom and to a bride. The good wishes offered in the messages are a telling reflection of traditional Chinese family values, particularly as these relate to the distinctive gender roles and expectations for husbands and wives as they assume their own responsibilities for raising a family.

Ping Yao

Translated by Ping Yao.

Text of
The Difficult Month
(Sample Prayer for Women Entering the
Last Month of a Pregnancy)[1]

It is said that the true sages are abstruse and obscure; the Tathata[2] is near and yet distant; while divine power is unpredictable. If you sacrifice various treasures and still do not realize the true meaning of Buddhism, you should stop just listening to sermons and cultivate your heart by observing all the Buddhist practices. Then you will know that the Buddha is the highest almighty.

The purpose of my incense-burning is to make an offering for so and so's suffering. Because of the accumulation of past misfortunes, this sufferer received the body of a woman in this life, and thus cannot escape from the suffering of pregnancy. Now her pregnancy is near its completion and her term seems to be full. Her family worries nervously that some physical harms might occur, and they truly fear that chaotic disasters might strike. Therefore, with all my reverence and sincerity, I come to plead to the Buddha for protection. I sacrifice treasures and assets and respectfully bow at the Buddhist Temple.

I understand that the Buddha is the almighty who aids the endangered and eradicates their sufferings. I also understand that Bodhisattvas have great compassion and would never fail to answer or fulfill a prayer. I thereby recite the Buddha's name and the *sutras* by heart and by mouth so that good fortune and virtue shall embrace the sufferer. I pray that when the day is due and the term is full, a remarkable spirit will appear; the mother and the child will be fine, and the misfortune of distress and sorrow will not come to them. Bodhisattva Guanyin will pour water on her head and she will thus receive the divine medicine of averting death. Yaoshang[3] will touch

---

[1] "Text of the Difficult Month" is a type of prayer to be recited before a statue of Buddha when an expectant mother enters the last month of her pregnancy. A total of six such prayers were discovered in the Dunhuang caves.

[2] The indivisible, nondual "Suchness," or ground of all knowing. See Dale Wright, "Language and Truth in Hua-Yen Buddhism," *Journal of Chinese Philosophy* (Vol. 13, 1986), pp. 21–47

[3] Yaoshang here should be Yaowang (the king of medicine), the supreme Medicine Bodhisattva. He was also known as Bhaisajyaraja Bodhisattva.

her and charitably give her the delicacies of longevity. The mother will suffer no pain and agony, and she will be in peace all day and night. The newborn will be a divine baby, just like the one who wears lotus leaves.

Furthermore, this person and his whole family have prepared offerings at the temple and sincerely wish that our bodies will be as strong as the pines upon the hillside; our lives will be as long as mountains and rivers. Our fortune will be extended; our favor will be deepened; and our Buddha blessing days will increase. We will be spared from miseries for four lives and live peacefully for another three. We will observe the Buddha's laws together and eventually reach the stage of nirvana. Let us confess that the Buddha is mighty, fruitful, and victorious.

Letters on
The Occasion of an Afterlife Marriage

Sample Prayer to Be Recited By the Groom's Father During Wedding Ceremonies for Afterlife Couples

So and so, I hereby inform you: You died at a young age and thus did not fulfill the meaning of the husband and wife relationship. You sleep alone in the dark world and lack the intimacy of man with woman. Just as living people long for companionship, the dead fear loneliness as well. Unexpectedly, so and so's family had a daughter who also just passed away like an autumn leaf. We sent a betrothal for you so your souls might meet. We selected this auspicious day for the rite of your union. We also set out an offering next to your shrine tablet, furnished with all kinds of delicacies. Please send your spirit down to the banquet and eat the meal.

Sample Prayer to Be Recited By the Bride's Father During Wedding Ceremonies for Afterlife Couples

So and so, I hereby inform you: You died at a young age and did not have a husband. You sleep alone in the underworld and are kept away from the intimacy of man with woman. When you were not yet engaged, disaster struck our virtuous family and you left us suddenly. Two families have now agreed . . . to form an afterlife marriage. We selected this auspicious day to unite . . . now.[4]

---

4 ". . ." represents unreadable characters.

Letters on
The Occasion of an Afterlife Marriage

Sample Letter for Proposing an Afterlife Marriage

So and so kowtows once again: It is our honor to correspond with you. Fragrant like orchids, our families have been closely associated for a long, long time. When our son was alive, we considered finding a good match from your family. The accumulation of good deeds yielded no result and the sprout, alas, did not flower. Then there was your worthy daughter, who grew to the age of the hairpin. Word of her virtues spread far and wide, and her noble reputation was well known. But then Spring flowers were yet to blossom, autumn leaves already withered. What is worthy, what is not worthy? Looking back on the untimely deaths of both our offspring only intensifies our sentiments. Cao's family respectfully presents a proposal of Afterlife Marriage and wishes it be granted. We sincerely send this letter of intention. . . .

Sample Letter for Responding to an Afterlife Marriage Proposal

Although we haven't corresponded with you for a long time, we have admired your family sincerely. Our good deeds were not immense enough and thus our daughter was sacrificed. Your worthy son was an eminent person whose character embodied nobility. He was upright and virtuous at a young age. Though his great abilities were yet to be displayed, his family too soon had to grieve the enormous loss of his life. Since we undeservingly received your letter, we dare to accept it respectfully. Please take good care of yourselves. We sincerely send this letter of intention. . . .

Congratulatory Messages For
Wedding Occasions

Sample Congratulatory Message to a Groom

I wish the groom's body might be as strong as a calf, . . .[5] as a flying crow. His assets will heap up as high as the five great mountains, and the five great mountains will be just like so much sand to him. He will have longevity, wealth, and nobility for a thousand years, and his glory and prosperity will pass down for ten thousand generations. Attracted by the groom, immortals come to hit musical gongs and

---

[5] There are three unreadable characters in between.

jade ladies come to play Pipas.[6] His backyard will grow apple trees with flowers made of gems. His estate will reach to the East where one can see birds and to the West where one can find crows. His estate will cross to the north of the Han River where the sunshine is bright and lotus flowers grow on every leaf. All his sons will ride fine horses and all his daughters ride filigreed carriages. He will obtain a high official rank and serve at the court everyday. He will amass more than one thousand rare horses and more than ten thousand servants. White elephants will carry gold into his storage room and dark cattle will load wheat into his granary. Roads will be full of fine silks and halls full of treasures. He will have five sons and two daughters, all resembling phoenixes. The daughters will be betrothed by noble families and great clans, and the sons will become administrators of important prefectures. Their prosperity and nobility will be like a river, continuing generation after generation. They will always have over ten thousand camels and donkeys, and over ten thousand pairs of geese and ducks. They will all be born in golden houses and grow up in jade decorated beds. They will see such things everyday and enjoy their prosperity and honor. (This ends the congratulatory rite.)

Sample Congratulatory Message to a Bride

I hear that heaven and earth are in harmony, as *yin* and *yang* match each other. Opening a book to make a divination, we find that everything is in the right place. I wish that after entering the house, the bride will be very wealthy and worthy. The husband and wife will resemble mandarin ducks, which always live in pairs. She will be filial to her parents and delightful to her parents-in-law. She will be amicable to all her husband's relatives and especially to the members of his family. Silver will be used to build the south gate and gold will be used to build the north hall. Gems will be used to build the east room and agates will be used to build the west corridors. She will have piles and piles of bedding, all made of fine, embroidered silks. She will give birth to ten sons, and all of them will be able to compose a poem within seven steps.[7] She will give birth to four or five daughters, and all of them will be betrothed by nobles. She will be well-versed in sewing.

---

[6] Pipa is a four-stringed, pear-shaped lute. This music instrument was introduced to China from Central Asia during the Han dynasty. Since the Tang dynasty, the pipa has become one of the most popular Chinese instruments.

[7] "Composing a poem within the time required for taking seven steps" refers to Cao Zhi (192–232 C.E.), a literary genius.

40

TANG EPITAPHS FOR CONFUCIAN, DAOIST, AND BUDDHIST WOMEN

(Muzhiming)

墓誌銘

Epitaphs, or muzhiming, *are stone inscriptions for the dead, usually placed inside the tombs. Traditionally, Chinese epitaphs record a dead person's family background, life experience, merits, and immediate family members. The last part of a* muzhiming *is often a paragraph of eulogy, praising the deceased's personality and virtues. Epitaphs were usually written by officials, scholars, and literati, and thus only people with certain social status and wealth could afford having someone write an epitaph, inscribing the text on a stone, and providing a decent burial. Exaggeration was very common in epitaph writings in traditional China. However, the larger-than-life images created by the literary elite often reveal the social norms and perceptions about gender common during a certain historical period.*

The first two of these Epitaphs are in praise of deceased Furen,[1] *the wives of important Tang dynasty officials, Confucian women. The third and fourth Epitaphs celebrate the virtues of women who had died before they were married, in the one case after a long and debilitating illness, and in the other after a series of disasters that had afflicted her family and laid her low, apparently with stomach ulcer. The final Epitaph eulogizes an abbess, who dedicated her life to the Buddhist community. Each of the Epitaphs ritually mourns the passing of the deceased and praises her in conventional terms as an exemplar of the womanly virtues appropriate to her state of life—the Confucian triad of responsibilities as daughter, wife, and mother—or to her religious commitment as Daoist adept or Buddhist disciple, or both. Taken together, the Epitaphs are striking for both the similarities as well as the differences in the ideals of womanhood put forth by these three interrelated spiritual traditions. Beyond the*

Translated by Ping Yao.
[1] *Furen* was a term used only for the wives of officials.

obvious restrictions in women's lives that these Epitaphs indirectly suggest, one may appreciate the richness and complexity of the ways in which women made their own distinctive contributions to the civilization of the Tang dynasty.

Ping Yao

Selections of
Tang Epitaphs for Confucian Women

The Late Ms. Cui, Wife of Mr. Lu of the Tang Dynasty

Authored by Lu Jian, an Administrative Assistant to the Military Commissioner of Xichuan (Jiannan), Gentleman for Court Discussion, Acting Minister and Director of the Equipment Bureau, Concurrent Attendant Censor, Pillar of State, and Recipient of the Red Fish Sack.

My late Furen's ancestors were granted the fiefdom of Qinghe. The clan intermarried with eminent families, and Cui was the most prestigious last name in the realm. This was recorded in detail in the genealogy and the records of appointed officials. Furen's reputation has been widely praised for decades, thus, when it comes to narrating her life, how can we be negligent? Furen's great grandfather, named Chao, was the Prefect of Huai and Posthumous Director of the Palace Library; her grandfather, named Zhen, was the Acting Minister and Director of the Treasury Bureau, concurrent Attendant Censor, and Posthumous Defender-in-Chief. Her father, named Qun, was a Grand Councilor, Acting Vice-Director at Right for the Department of State Affairs, concurrent Minister of Personnel, a dynasty-founding Duke of the Qinghe Commandery, and the Posthumous Minister of Works. Qun's hereditary moral principles and noble character have long influenced our time. Ms. Cui's maternal grandfather was Mr. Li of Longxi, whose given name was Ba, the Defender of Dantu District of the Run Prefecture.

The glorious marriage of Cui and Li ensured a sound origin; and the Grand Councilor's loyal deeds were as luminous as blazing light. Ms. Li of Longxi gave birth to five children and Furen was the third child. At a young age, Furen was bright and virtuous. In addition, she was the middle child, thus the Grand Councilor and Ms. Li of Longxi doted on her particularly and regarded her as full of compassion and respect, and intuitive at an early age. Every time the Grand Councilor recorded her events, he would keep his own copy of it, stating that: "She will certainly be a worthy woman in the future."

When Ms. Cui reached the age for receiving the hairpin,[2] Ms. Li died. After the mourning period, it was time for her to find a home. Courting her as a future bride was the ambition of every young man in the world. At that time, Jian (myself) was a petty and obscure person and had no achievements. However, the Grand Councilor regarded his maternal clan highly and approved of my engagement to his daughter. Soon afterward, the Grand Councilor passed away, and Furen was still at home. Nonetheless, the uncles of the Cui clan were willing to sustain the prior engagement. Therefore, on New Year's Eve, in the Jiayin year (834 C.E.) of the Dahe reign (827–835 C.E.), I was able personally to receive Furen at her residence in the Changxing Lane of Changan. The next morning, on New Year's Day, the ceremony of Paying Respect to Parents-in-Law and Relatives was held.

At that time, Jian (myself) was preparing for the Civil Service Examinations and was stranded in the Capital. Furen dealt with poverty gracefully and encouraged me to complete my mission. A few years later, Jian passed the Literary Examination and was appointed to a series of offices. During military service, I was the Defense Commissioner of the Shang Prefecture, and then I was given the position of the District Defender of Jingyang and the Territory Inspector. Later I became the Supporting Official to the Record Keeper for Jinnan of Xuchang and the Assistant Case Reviewer for the Chief of Musicians. Furthermore I served in a few Censor positions: I was appointed directly by the throne to be the Palace Censor, and then promoted to Attendant Censor and Supernumerary Official for the Department of State Affairs.

During my service as a Capital official, I returned to Luoyang because of my brother's illness. The court thus suspended my official status. Time passed by and we were in straightened circumstances. The emotional support I owe to Furen was too tremendous to be recounted. The mundane world is full of uncertainty, and my only hope was simply to grow old together with her!

Since Furen lost her parents and came to my house, she diligently performed the ancestor worship and sacrifices and was amiable with her sisters-in-law. She was sincere and modest, never once violating the rites and principles. In the meantime, she missed her parents very

---

[2] The "age of hairpin" means the age when a young woman is eligible for marriage.

much and mourned for them throughout her life. On every death anniversary of the late Grand Councilor and Ms. Li, Furen could not help but grieve with wails and tears. When relatives came to pay condolences, some of them would turn away at the doorstep for they could not bear her sorrow. During the mid-Dahe Reign, Furen lost several of her sisters. She was so distressed and sorrowful that she was in a state of exhaustion. Later, when her sister who married into the Zheng clan died, Furen was in Shangyu. On the day she heard about the death, Furen grieved to the point of gasping for air. She cried to the point of bleeding and once locked herself up, refusing to eat and drink for seven days.

Next year, Jian (myself) left the Defense Commissioner position and returned to the Capital. When Furen heard of the move, she faced her hometown and cried. She was so sad and upset that she would keep to herself continuously from day to night, and often for days and months. Jian thus knew that this would be the root of Furen's future illness. In less than a half year, it surely happened. Since she had already caught the miasma, it took a heavy toll on her body. It became harder and harder for her to move, and gradually it became a chronic illness. It lingered for seven years. Last winter, however, Jian (myself) was upset and worried about the demotion. I thus left home for traveling. I was not able to be with Furen and spend time with her. Thus her illness was aggravated and eventually she caught the pestilence. She died on the fifth day of the second month in our home at the Qinren Lane. The evening before her death, she arranged her burial and expressed her feelings of love. All of these acts were well in accordance with moral principles. She also entrusted words to encourage Jian to realize his ambition.

Furen learned *The Record of Rites* and recited *The Book of Odes*. She was also versed in *The Analects*.[3] She believed in Buddhism and was very fond of Buddhist classics. She was excellent in reciting, reading, and analyzing all the sutras. She knew music well and mastered it without effort. Her skills in calligraphy and playing the zither both reached perfection. She was so knowledgeable, insightful, and so reasonable. Her female virtues and demeanor won her a good reputation among our relatives. Alas, she did not attain a long life; instead, she died in anguish. Is this the fate she was supposed to receive? Or maybe her

---

[3] *The Record of Rites, The Book of Odes,* and *The Analects* are all Confucian classics. See selections collected here on pp. 48–60, 4–24, and 62–67 respectively.

early death occurred because Jian (myself) lacked talent and acted recklessly, thus contributing to the breakdown of a virtuous and wise woman? Where is the answer?

Furen was born in the Renchen year (812 c.e.) of the Yuanhe reign (806–820 c.e.), died in the Dingchou year (857 c.e.) of the Dazhong reign (847–859 c.e.). She was married to Jian for twenty-four years. She gave birth to three sons, but only one survived. She also had a daughter. The son's name is Chu. Chu has already reached the age of capping, but has yet to serve in office. The daughter's name is Quan. She is engaged but yet to be married. Twenty days after Furen's death, Jian was appointed to serve at the office of the Minister of State, Mr. Wei of Julu, in Shuchuan. Twenty-two days later, on the seventeenth day of the third month, Jian led the children and other relatives to escort Furen's coffin back to Luoyang. On the day of Jiaowu, the twenty-seventh day of the fourth month of the year, she was temporarily buried at Duzai Plain, Pingle County, Henan District. She will be reburied at our clan cemetery at an auspicious time. When the coffin arrived, the family members, Furen's youngest brother, Hun, as well as relatives of both clans, all participated in her funeral with full grief and extended their farewell. Jian wiped away his tears in sorrow and wrote a summary of Furen's life to be put in the tomb. Furen had converted to Buddhism and placed her hope in the Buddhist doctrine of emptiness. When she was dying she obtained a Buddhist title-name called "Upper Vehicle," so she would have something to rely on in the dark world. It was for protection.

Eulogy: In this vast universe, the transit from past to present happens in a second. The ones who had just been united soon depart; the ones who were just delighted soon became sorrowful. Alas, Furen! She was from an eminent clan. A celebrated descendant of a brilliant family, she perseveringly obeyed the teachings. Her manners were amiable, her virtues were flourishing. She resembled an orchid that spreads fragrance and a fine jade that congeals high quality. Everything she did, such as making a harmonious family, admonishing children, worshipping ancestors, or providing hospitality to our guests, were all in conformity with the ancient teachings and compatible with the ancient sages. She was dutiful in arranging worship, and she cultivated herself with music. She was modest, ingenuous, peaceful, and pious. Heaven and earth are forever, but my joy and love ended. Her voice was still in my ears, but her trace vanished. Oh, Furen! Your virtues and good deeds yielded no result. And now you have gone like dew on the grass, forever leaving your relatives behind. Your beautiful face has disappeared, and you have no loved ones in the dark night.[4] You gaze at the ancient tombs alone, and you become a neighbor to the pines and shrubs. We are now waiting for an auspicious date, and then we will bury you at our clan's cemetery. Oh, Furen! I hope that you are content with this grave site and appreciate my earnestness.

Calligraphy done by her youngest brother, Hun, Gentleman for Managing Affairs, Acting Administrator of the Military Service of Henan Prefecture.

Epitaph for Ms. Zheng, the Late Wife of Mr. Yuan of Henan

On the sixteenth day of the ninth month of the first year (806 C.E.) of the Yuanhe Reign (806–820 C.E.), Ms. Zheng, the Grand Lady of Yingyang District, wife of the late Grand Master of Palace Leisure, the Director of the Bureau of Review, and the Administrator of Prince Shu's Establishment, Yuan Kuan, died. She was sixty. The next year, on the fifteenth of the second month, she was temporarily buried in Hongdouyuan Village, Fengxian Township, Xianyang District, beside her late mother-in-law's tomb.

Furen's great grandfather was Yuansi whose highest official titles were Prefect of Zhengzhou and Posthumous Chief Minister of the Court of Imperial Sacrifices. Her grandfather was Ai, a Grand Master for the Closing of the Court and the Assistant Prefect of Yizhou. Her father was Ji, the Prefect of Muzhou. Furen was Ji's second daughter. Ms. Zheng's mother was from the Lu clan of Fanyang, and her maternal grandfather, Lu Pingzi, was the Magistrate of Jingyang District of the Jingzhao Prefecture.

Furen had four sons and two daughters. The eldest son, Su, is the Defender of Ruyang District in the Caizhong Prefecture. Her second son, Ju, is the Defender of Wannian District of the Jingzhao Prefecture. The third son, Ji, is the Defender of Hancheng District of the Tongzhou Prefecture. And her fourth son, Zhen, is the Defender of Henan District of the Henan Prefecture. Her eldest daughter married Lu Han of Wuzhou. He is an Investigating Censor. Her second daughter became a Buddhist nun and took a Buddhist name, Zhenyi. Unfortunately, both daughters died before Furen.

When Mr. Yuan was appointed as the Director of the Bureau of Review, Furen was first granted the title of the Lady of Ying Yang. She attained this honor through her husband's promotion. When Zhen was appointed as a Reminder, Furen was further bestowed the

---

[4] In Chinese literary tradition, "dark night" means the world of the dead.

title of Grand Lady of Ying Yang. She gained this honor through her son.

There are five great clans in the realm, and the Zheng clan of Ying Yang is one of them. The meritorious achievements and nobility of the Zheng clan are recorded in the dynastic histories. The clan's origin, growth, and marriages were recorded in family genealogies. Mr. Yuan Kuan's official titles, achievements, literary ability, and moral conduct were recorded in his Epitaph written by Zheng Yunda, the Administrator of Jingzhao Prefecture. Therefore this epitaph will only narrate Furen's life.

When Furen was just a girl, she was well known for her filial piety to her parents. She was also well known for her friendliness toward her elder siblings and her sisterly love toward her younger siblings. These qualities were innate, not acquired through instruction. How virtuous a nature she had!

When Furen became a wife, the Yuan clan had been indigent for generations. Nonetheless, the clan maintained a tradition of worshipping the ancestors with fresh and abundant food. In every four-season-sacrifice conducted by the Yuan family, Furen would stay up all night, cooking and cleaning by herself. Although the sacrifices were often held during the hottest part of the summers and the coldest part of the winters, Furen always served her best and offered sacrifices in person. She never once showed a tired expression. How sincere and respectful she was!

Yuan and Zheng are two eminent clans that often intermarried with each other, therefore relatives by marriages multiplied. If people in the two clans had any uncertainty about weddings or funerals they would all consult with Furen. Furen always made the right decisions and never once contradicted the proper procedures of the rites. How intelligent and broadminded she was!

Ms. Zheng was a model mother as well. Mr. Yuan Kuan died early when Ji and Zhen were still young, and the family could not afford a teacher to educate their sons. Thus, Furen tirelessly taught the brothers literature and classics by herself. After four or five years, both Ji and Zhen became officials by being so well versed in the classics. Zhen not only passed the Classics examination, but also the Judgment Examination. He was soon appointed as the Editor of the Palace Library. After ascending to the throne, the Emperor held three special dissertation examinations to select the talented and the virtuous in the realm. Eighteen candidates passed and Zhen was at the top. He was then promoted from an Editor to the Reminder of the Left. However, a few months later, Zhen's outspoken remarks and straightforward criticisms agitated the court. He was subsequently demoted to the position of the Defender of Henan District.

Furen's eldest daughter married Mr. Lu. The couple lived with Lu's parents and many relatives. She treated the elders obediently and the youngsters graciously. Although she died two years later, her female virtue never left this world. All the relatives in the Lu and Yuan clans admired her as a role model. Were it not for Furen's faithful, diligent, and intelligent guidance, how could the sons be so successful in the government and the daughter make such a harmonious family? How excellent her teachings and admonitions were!

Nevertheless, though all of her sons were repeatedly assigned governmental positions, the official salaries were meager. Every month when Ms. Zheng distributed food and every season when she distributed clothes, she always started with the widows, the orphans, and the helpless. Next, it was the distant relatives and the humble. Therefore, the clothes often went to different people while everyone in the household shared the same meals. The close relatives were happy and the distant relatives increased their contact with the family. Even people such as maids, servants, and wet nurses did not want to leave Yuan's household when they suffered from cold and hunger or became old. Her generosity extended even to the slaves. How benevolent she was!

It has been twenty-five years since Furen became the mother of the family. She cast aside the method of corporal punishment. Instead, she only used exhortations and warnings to the younger generation. Furen often admonished the girls and wives by her stern and serious facial expression. Women in the household were always fearful and anxious as if they were walking on ice. She also cautioned the sons and grandsons by her righteous tone and words. All the male descendants always felt guilty and shameful as if they had been caned in public. Therefore the youngsters seldom made mistakes and the household enjoyed a great harmony. Maids and servants never bickered with each other and the children grew up not knowing what a paddle was for. The inner quarter was peaceful and harmonious as if it was occupied by a group of elderly people. How great a motherly teaching she gave!

Alas! Women such as Qi Shi[5] and Ti Ying[6] of olden days were famous as girls for their virtues, but they were unknown after they

---

[5] Qi Shi was a small town girl in the state of Lu in the Spring and Autumn period (770–453 B.C.E.). She worried about the state's crisis and howled in public. Her epitaph was narrated and written by her brother, Tu, a Prefecture Nominee for Literary Degree.

[6] Ti Ying was a bereaved daughter of the Han dynasty (206 B.C.E.–220 C.E.). When her father was sent to jail, Ti Ying asked to become an official slave to redeem her father.

became wives. Bo Zong and Liang Hong's wives[7] were famous for their wisdom, but they were unknown after they became mothers. Wenbo and Mencius's mothers were famous for their ways of being virtuous mothers, but they were unknown when they were daughters and wives. Now Furen was so perfect for her graceful manners as a daughter, her virtues as a wife, and later her motherly ways. She possessed all three virtues and was certainly the finest woman in history, from the past to the present. Alas! If Furen's virtues can be conveyed to other people and extended to other situations, everything will be perfectly functional. If her virtues propagate, the whole country would benefit. In this way, we will not be too far from the perfection of "The Chirping Bird" and "The Nest."[8] If her virtue is glorified, the whole realm could benefit. In this way, we will not be too far from the paragon of Jiang Yuan and Wenmu.[9] Her virtues truly were not limited to teaching her fours sons with her motherly morality and perfecting the family to benevolence and generosity.

Juyi (my humble self) was Ms. Zheng's young son Zhen's bosom friend. Therefore, I learned about her virtues most thoroughly. Zhen wept blood to mourn his mother; his grief moved many others. I was therefore asked to recount her life and inscribe it onto a tombstone. Tradition requires that a filial and pious child glorify his parents. Alas! My writing of this epitaph should not be just limited to the fulfillment of Zhen's request. I intended to let it pass on for a hundred generations, so people who hear of Furen's extraordinary example or pass by the tomb will be grateful. Let shrewish wives be harmonious, bossy mothers be benevolent, and impertinent daughters be obedient!

Eulogy: In the year of Yuanhe, the spring of Dinghai (806 c.e.). By the Road of Xianyang, the bank of the Wei River. Whose tomb is this? Furen Zheng.

---

[7] Bo Zong's wife was known for giving wise and prescient admonishment to Bo Zong. Liang Hong's wife was known for her respect for her husband. Every time she served him a meal she would hold the bowl up to her eyebrows.

[8] Both "The Chirping Bird" and "The Nest" come from *The Book of Odes* (see selections collected here, pp. 4–24). Bo Juyi used the titles to refer to the Zhou, a perfect society imagined by later Confucians.

[9] Jiang Yuan and Wenmu were two ancient virtuous mothers.

Selections of
Tang Epitaphs for Daoist Women

Epitaph for Miss Zhang of the Tang Dynasty

Alas! The supreme is not Heaven; the other world surely does not have gods. Otherwise, how could they prematurely transfer a sagacious girl into the other world?

In the Mid-Yuanhe Reign (806–820 C.E.), my father was a sub-official of Mr. Xi, the governor of Lu Prefecture. Chan was born then. Chan was her given name and she had a nickname, Yinnu. Father often told our servants: "My family never had long-lived daughters, thus for generation after generation daughters were cherished more than pearl and jade." Father personally picked a wet-nurse and several senior maids for Chan, instructing them to hold her regularly, play with her around the house, and do everything at her will. When she was barely old enough to be dolled up, all the rare and precious things were piled up in her sight.

In the middle of the Changqing Reign (821–825 C.E.), my father was promoted from a Real Director of the Bureau of Honor to the Governor of Hu Prefecture. Just when he was to pay his debt of gratitude to the Emperor and appease the people of all five districts in Hu Prefecture, Heaven imposed a disaster on our family. Chan was then just eight years old, but she wailed with sorrow day and night, making people who passed by all broken down in sympathy with her. Her filial piety, her gentleness and understanding, were all rooted in her natural deposition.

Unfortunately, from the year of hairpin up to now, for a period of ten years, not a single day could she step away from her bed. Even so, she still managed to be responsive to the facial expressions of relatives and elders and to be attentive to affairs inside and outside of the household. Thus, she was consulted on all household matters before decisions were made, and her responses were always appropriate. She also converted to Daoism, and was capable of finding pleasure in tranquillity. She even picked for herself a Daoist title-name, Immortal Recluse. Chan often said to me: "Your great-great-grandfather, great-grandfather, grandfather, and father were all court officials or governors of important prefectures. They often exonerated those who had been wronged and helped the poor. Should the nether world have sensibility, someone in that world will come to your salvation when it's necessary."

Who would expect that hurricanes would strike without warning, making a fine jade vanish without a trace. What a tragic loss! The Buddhist sutras always cautioned about one's *karma*. Although the prescribed medicine was taken carefully, still she could not avoid grave illness. Isn't that *karma*? Since then, our mother has wailed in extreme grief, lamenting that Chan was never married in spite of the fact that she was fully grown. Her brothers wailed in extreme grief as well, remembering that she was so bright and full of love. Everyone in the household, too, wailed in extreme grief, in appreciation of her kindness and constant compassion toward them.

All parents desire their sons and daughters to be eminent and live a long life. How come in her whole life Chan was never able to sit in a wedding hall, form a marital harmony, or enjoy music and dances to delight her sense and mind? Instead, she now rests her soul in the nether world. Is this fate? Is this destiny?

On the eleventh day of the second month, the fifth year (840 c.e.) of the Tang Kaicheng Reign (836–840 c.e.), Chan died at the Jinggong lane at Changan. She was twenty-five *sui*. Chan's great-grandfather, named Juzhan, was a Director in the Ministry of War; his son, named Xiang, was a Palace Censor and Posthumous Director of the Palace Library. Xiang's son was my father, his name was Shi Jie. He was the Prefect of the Hu Prefecture. They all possessed great virtues, and their writings have been distinguished in our family genealogy. Chan was my father's third daughter, and was in fact born to Ms. Li of Longxi.

Our Zhang clan gained its good reputation long ago. They originated in Anding. Later the clan continued and has never drained away. In the beginning of the Han Empire, to reward my ancestors' support, the throne granted my ancestors the fiefdom of Changshan. During the Jin period, again, the King of the Liang and Duke Xiping achieved great accomplishments.[10] The Zhang descendants perpetuated themselves generation after generation and never fell, and Heaven and the emperors have granted the Zhangs high status. Our ancestors' mourning cottage[11] is located in Jingu in Luoyang, therefore, my younger brother, Xun, will escort Chan's coffin from Changan to there. The burial will be held in the ninth day of the fifth month, this year. I,

---

[10] King of the Liang and Duke Xiping were titles of Zhang Gui, who was the Prefect of Liang Prefecture during the Jin dynasty (266–316 c.e.). Zhang Gui's descendants established the Liang Regime (317–399 c.e.) in Liang Prefecture during the Eastern Jin period (317–420 c.e.) and posthumously titled Zhang Gui a King.

[11] The mourning cottage was usually located next to a clan cemetery.

Tu, was instructed to write an epitaph on this stone, hoping that thus the writings will be preserved for the future.

Eulogy: Life and death are the course of nature, but my heart is not like the wise one, and I grieve deeply for my sister. How tragic it is that you were buried there. Next to ancestors, in the Mountain called Beimang, oh, soul, oh soul, please do not wander to other places.

Epitaph for Daoist Master Miss Zhi, the Eldest Daughter of Mr. Zhi of Langya, the Retired Chief Minister of the Court of State Ceremonial, Posthumous Minister of Work of the Tang Dynasty[12]

My sister was the thirty-second daughter of our clan in my generation, and had a Daoist name, Zhijian. Her nickname was Xiaoniangzi. Zhijian's great-grandfather was named Ping. He was a Vice Magistrate of Xunxiang District in Jiang Prefecture. Her grandfather, named Cheng, was a Vice Supervisor of the Household of the Heir Apparent and Posthumous Director of the Palace Administration. Her father, named ___,[13] was a retired Chief Minister of the Court of State Ceremonial and Posthumous Minister of Work. Zhijian's late mother was Ms. Tan of Runan, Posthumous Grand Lady of the Runan District. Her stepmother was Ms. Cui of Qinghe, who held a fiefdom as the Grand Mistress of the Lu State. Her eldest brother, Yu, died at a young age. Her second brother, Fang, was the Magistrate of Duanshi District in Ze Prefecture when he died. Her closest younger brother, Xiang, was the Manager of the Requisitioned Labor of E Prefecture. Among her younger brothers, Xun and Qian died early, while Na, Hui, Mo, Xiang,[14] Rang, Xin, and Yan all hold offices in the court.

My late sister had an inborn nature of virtuousness. Although she lost her parents at a young age, she was never a needy person. Instead, she was filial and kind, and possessed a stable personality. She had a miserable illness when she was still a toddler. Then at the age of nine *sui*, she converted to Buddhism. Although she did not live in a

---

[12] Written by her youngest brother, Mo, a Gentleman for Court Discussion, Acting Aide to the Court of the National Granaries, and Officer of the Special Reserves Vault in the Bureau of General Accounts.

[13] The epitaph left a space for the name. It is unclear why the name was not inscribed on the stone.

[14] Xiang, meaning "detailed," had a different Chinese character from Zhijian's eldest bother Xiang, which means "toward."

Buddhist monastery, she observed the Buddhist rules morning and night. If anyone in the family was sick, had an accident, or were separated from each other, she would always fast for a month and pray for them constantly. Her piety reached the level of the sages.

When my sister was eighteen years old, her mother, the Grand Lady of Runan, died. She observed the mourning rites more seriously than anyone. She was so sorrowful that she became as thin as wood sticks. Her grief even moved indifferent people. Although all the siblings lived in different places, her care and love never changed. She always admonished and encouraged the younger brothers, preventing them from failures. Loving the classics, she admired Lady Xie's achievements.[15] Selecting the neighbors, she followed Mencius' mother's rules.[16] Although she was not able to help her brothers in person, she devoted her heart and mind to them. In the midst of her life, Buddhism was persecuted and she had to convert to Daoism.

Since the seventh year (853 C.E.) of the Dazhong Reign (847–859 C.E.), she had been taking care of her brother's orphan in E Prefecture after the fall of his career. Since then that young girl and my sister have never separated from each other. In the second year (861 C.E.) of the Xiantong Reign (860–873 C.E.), brother Na was promoted to the Governorship of Teng Prefecture. It was said that the environment of Teng was as pleasant as Hui and Zhe, and the fine vegetables and sweet rice might be suitable for her diet. Na had hoped to extend his brotherly effort to take care of his sister. He thus accompanied them, via East Luo, to the southern region.

However, within a month after Na took the office, the local barbarians started their harassment. Na was thus transferred to Fuyang. He worked on collecting and sending grain supplies day and night, though meanwhile the local food was very simple and scarce. My sister then developed ulcers and soon died. During her last hours, she sat straight and sent off her wishes calmly without any uneasiness. At the age of fifty, on the twelfth day of the ninth month, the second year of the Xiantong Reign, she died in the official residence of the Fu Prefecture. Alas, the law of death is so uncertain: the person who accumulated good deeds does not live long; and the one who is the kindest cannot prosper!

---

[15] Lady Xie implies Xie Daoyun of the Jin dynasty. She was known for being a talented poet.

[16] Mencius' Mother of the Eastern Zhou Period (771–221 B.C.E.) was known for selecting a good neighborhood to ensure her son's success. (See the full story on pp. 150–155.)

Because of their official duties, Mo and Xiang could not join her journey back home. How regrettable that they could not repay their sister's love when she ascended to the Upper Pure Realm.[17] My sister's coffin was transported back from Fu to Yi.[18] On the eighth day of the tenth month, the third year of the Xiantong Reign, she was buried in the northwest part of the cemetery near Duzhai Village, Pingle Township, Henan District, Henan Prefecture. It was in accordance with the Rites. That time, Mo (myself) was on official duty at the Reserves Vault, but I requested a leave to return to the east.[19] The tomb site was selected after a divination, and the coffin was then interred. The rites were all conducted with our full devotion. I inscribe on this stone with a knife that cuts my heart and I moisturize the brush with my blood. Standing by the tomb I wail to the sky, the sorrowful voice sends my farewell. This epitaph is not enough to express our feelings; it only averts the disappearance of her life stories due to changes in worldly affairs.

Eulogy: the sky is bright and clear, but it is far and ambiguous. Life is short and mundane, who can interpret its turbulent course? It is said that Heaven aids the virtuous; who, then, would expect that it punishes the benevolent? She was as endurable as gold and as pure as jade, but now the crane has departed to rest among pine trees.[20] The unpredictable is fate; the unquestionable is Heaven. She was ill since her childhood, and the sickness lingered lifelong. She was a Buddhist believer, but Daoism nurtured her virtues. She recited Buddhist sutras and aspired to dwell in the Daoist spheres. Her nature was inflexible, but her form succumbed to changes. She lived just to middle age—surely that can't be called longevity. She disappeared to a noble destination, and her coffin now rests in the grave in Mang.[21] The clouds of the Song Mountain pass through her tomb from the east, the waves of the Lou River run in front of it. The tomb is there, but her soul has returned to a divine place. I hereby pierce my body and cut my hand to inscribe this epitaph for her.

---

[17] The Upper Pure is one of the three Pure Realms, the most divine places, in Daoism.

[18] Yi was another name for Henan where the clan's cemetery was located.

[19] Henan was located in the east of the Tang capital, Changan.

[20] In Chinese literary tradition, cranes were often identified with Daoists.

[21] Mang mountain was a cemetery site for Tang officials and their families.

Selections of
A Tang Epitaph for a Buddhist Woman

Epitaph for the Late Nun Wei, the Shangzuo[22] *of the Anguo Monastery in the Eastern Capital of the Tang Dynasty, Narrated by Yu Wenzong, a Henan Prefectural Nominee for the Literary Degree*

Honoring pedigree, the prominent clans should be the foremost. In revering the ladies, who can compete with the beautiful and the noble? If not for perpetual dispositions and natural insights, how could one have reached the stage of leaving the gate of the floating world, and realizing the realm of Tathātā? But our abbess (*Shangzuo*) had certainly achieved it.

The abbess' family name was Wei, and her Buddhist name was Yuanjing. She was from the southern Jingzhao Prefecture. Her foremost ancestor was Duke Nanpi. The pedigree of the Wei was distinguished among the eight great clans and the conferral of the title, Duke, was the highest among the five ranks. Her great-grandfather, named Zhiren, was a Vice Director of the Bureau of Provisions and Posthumous Director of the Weaving and Dyeing Office. Her grandfather, named Gun, was a Grand Master for the Closing of the Court and the Administrative Aide of the Danzhou Prefecture. Nothing in the world prospers forever, and so Gun experienced ups and downs in his official career. The abbess' father was Anshi, the Assistant Magistrate of Yongcheng District in the Bozhou Prefecture. He possessed high virtues, yet he was given a low position. His reputation, however, did reach far.

The abbess was the second daughter of a Yongcheng official. From this clan with an abundance of good deeds, a renowned saint was born. Her spirit symbolized ice and snow; her breadth embodied rivers and oceans. At an early age she aspired to a unique quality of mind and became even more resolute as she grew up. At the age of fourteen she left home and entered the religious order, becoming a novice nun under Abbess Li of the Anguo monastery. Abbess Li was the daughter of Prince Ji, and second cousin of Emperor Xuanzong's father. Since Li was from a noble clan and conducted herself estimably, learning from her must not have been easy. It is understandable, therefore, that Ms. Wei truly inherited a unique compre-

---

[22] *Shangzuo* is a Buddhist title for the head of a monastery, or abbess.

hension of the Buddha's teaching and the advantages of a nature already receptive to it. Whether as a novice or fully received into the community, once she had entered into this state of life, she always kept the whole faith.

Abbess Wei devoted her heart to the conduct of piety and disciplined her ambitions with the Buddhist sutras. When she reached middle age, her learning was refined and her attainments complete. She could forget about the fishing pole when she desired a fish;[23] she could abandon the boat after having crossed the river.[24] Abbess Wei had gone beyond the Hinayana theory of existence; and enjoyed the great principles of reaching *nirvana*. Her belief was reflected in her speeches, and her insights were firmly rooted in her heart. Her conduct was all in accordance with the Buddhist manner, and the root of her benevolence was cultivated in her mind. She was endorsed by everyone around her, and soon became the bhadanta of this monastery. On the twenty-eight day of the ninth month, the second year (782 C.E.) of the Jianzhong Reign (781–783 C.E.), she was further promoted to become the abbess. Abbess Wei has since satisfied her students' desire for learning and delighted everyone's mind in the monastery. Abbess Wei's good deeds were also respected by people of all classes in the region.

On the fourteenth day of the twelfth month, the first year (784 C.E.) of the Xingyuan Reign (784–785 C.E.), Abbess Wei abandoned this filthy world and returned to the Pure Land of the West. A deity forsakes this life and begins another; and a life span has its end. Abbess Wei was sixty years old. Her coffin was first placed in the East Hall of the monastery, a gathering place for people to pay respects. Everyone, both young and old, all grieved with tears for the loss. On the tenth day of the first month, the second year (785 C.E.) of the Xingyuan Reign, she was buried in the southwest area of Longmen Tianzhu monastery, in accordance with the Rites.

Qixu, Abbess Wei's disciple and niece, was orphaned at a young age and was raised by her. She (Qixu) followed her aunt's footsteps

---

[23] This phrase originated from *Zhuangzi*, meaning that one may forget about the tool once one has accomplished the goal.

[24] This phrase originated from the *Diamond Sutra* and means that the Buddhist canon may be compared to a boat. If the boat has already carried people to the other shore, then the canon is useless and should no longer be adhered to. Both "forgetting about the fishing pole" and "abandoning the boat" describe Ms. Wei's high achievements as a Buddhist.

and eventually became the bhadanta. Qixu's extreme mourning almost paralyzed her. She wailed from morning to night without stop. Disciple Mingcan, a cousin of the abbess, and disciple Chengzhao, fearing that worldly affairs are uncertain, thus entrusted this epitaph to fine stone.

Eulogy: The laws of the Buddha are profound yet abstruse, but our abbess comprehended them thoroughly. It was only from a prominent clan that such a sage would be born. She held high aspirations when she was young and never changed when she grew up. She gave up mundane superfluities and quested for the real meaning of life. She lived among the unenlightened but kept her wisdom and serenity. Her style of Weiyi[25] and her Buddhist practices became models for her time. The most esteemed position in this monastery surely only belongs to Abbess Wei. Her benevolence reached the others and her virtues benefited us. She inherited her teacher's position and superintended the monastery. She admonished the nuns in the monastery and disseminated the laws of the Buddha. Life and death are uncertain, and illusory baubles are frail. She now has disengaged from this mundane world and has fulfilled her mission in the Pure Land. Below the Buddhist classics and the monastery, and next to the Mahayana altar, a lamp[26] has guttered out. Who will light it again? Achieving *nirvana* might be a joy, but our mundane hearts are full of sorrow. We, filial disciples, respectfully carry her coffin to the mountain recesses. Our sorrowful wailing receives no answer, and looking around adds to our distress. We thus hope to inscribe these words to a fine stone and pass down Abbess Wei's virtues to the future.

---

[25] Weiyi is a set of rules in Buddhist practice. It defines a Buddhist way of eating, walking, residing, and sleeping.

[26] Lamp, or *deng*, has two meanings in Chinese. The other meaning is "Buddha dharma."

41

REFLECTIONS ON THINGS AT HAND
(Jinsi Lu)
近思錄

FURTHER REFLECTIONS ON THINGS AT HAND
(Xu Jinsi Lu)
續近思錄

Zhu Xi
朱熹

Commonly regarded as the greatest and most influential of the Neo-Confucian scholars, Zhu Xi (1130–1200 C.E.) is remembered for having provided an intellectual synthesis that restored Confucian thought in light of the challenges of the increasingly popular schools of Chinese Buddhism and Daoism. Zhu Xi himself believed that the line of Confucian sages that had effectively ended with Mencius (370–300 B.C.E.) had only recently been renewed through the efforts of his recent predecessors, Cheng Hao (1032–1085 C.E.) and his brother Cheng Yi (1033–1107 C.E.) as well as Zhou Dunyi (1017–1073 C.E.) and Zhang Zai (1020–1077 C.E.).

Along with his friend Lü Zuqian (1137–1181 C.E.), Zhu Xi compiled the teachings of these four in a practical demonstration of the enduring validity of Confucian teaching, the Reflections on Things at Hand (Jinsi lu), *published in 1175 C.E. This book was divided into fourteen volumes with 622 sections. The authors intended it for use as an introductory reader for understanding the teachings of these four Confucians.* Jinsi lu *has played an important role in developing and spreading the teachings of Neo-Confucianism ever since. Qing scholar Jiang Yong regarded it as "the best book since the* Analects *of Confucius and the* Mencius." *One of the selections presented here is Cheng Yi's biography of his mother, Hou, as it appears in* Jinsi lu's *chapter "The Way to Regulate the Family," interspersed with Zhu's supportive comments. The other selection, taken from a later work,* Further Reflections on Things at Hand (Xu Jinsi lu), *is a collection of Zhu Xi's sayings compiled by a later scholar. Here is presented Zhu's own teachings under the title "Family and Social Relationships."*

Though Zhu Xi's massive influence on Chinese intellectual history through the end of the Imperial period in 1911 C.E. is commonly recognized, the precise nature of his distinctive contribution remains controversial. More emphatically than other Neo-Confucians, Zhu saw scholarship itself as playing an indispensable role in Confucian self-cultivation. He thus committed himself to the investigation of how things work, with a diligence that approaches scientific objectivity, preferring disciplined scholarship to the passionate subjectivity that often emerged from introspective meditation. In seeking to understand how, in fact, things at hand actually work in the world, Zhu made an ontological distinction between the principle of heaven (tianli) and material forces (qi), and identified the latter as the source of all imperfection and disorder in the world because of their inevitable impurities. This distinction was also used to account for the vicissitudes observable in human affairs, notably the failure of most people to live consistently according to the best and noblest in human nature.

The selection from the Further Reflections on Things at Hand (Xu Jinsi lu) *illustrates how Zhu Xi's general perspective shaped his specific opinions about family and social relationships. In approaching these, Zhu affirms the bond between father and son as offering the highest natural coincidence of the principle of heaven and human desire, which would seem to give this relationship an edge over the traditional priority given to the relationship of husband and wife. In his actual remarks on marriage, however, Zhu observes that "To live as man and woman is the most intimate human affair, and the exercise of* Dao *is found therein. This is why the* Dao *of the gentleman is so widespread, and yet secret. . . ." Zhu's remarks seem to endorse the idea that the carnal knowledge shared in the intimacies of marriage itself is a manifestation of the* Dao, *and yet he withholds his enthusiasm, since marriage remains potentially contaminated because of the impurities of qi: "*Dao *exists in the matters of food and drink and man and woman, but anyone engulfed in its flow will not understand its essence." Further on he says: "The feelings between husband and wife are very intimate, but they can easily become overindulgent. Unless you are* *especially careful, personal desires will find you playing on the field of frivolity, and self-deceit will leave you in the arena of ignorance."*

Women, it seems, are somewhat marginal to Zhu's philosophical concern with the challenge of disciplining human, or perhaps better, men's, desires. Though he extols the example of the Cheng brothers' mother, and thus shares in their praise of her virtues and her impressive success in disciplining her children, the passage may also have strategic significance, for its Chinese readers would have heard an echo of the praises heaped upon Mencius' mother. The passage therefore may have been intended less in order to praise the virtues of motherhood and more to establish the Cheng brothers as the true inheritors of Mencius' sagely legacy. In his Further Reflections on Things at Hand, Zhu clearly teaches a subordination of women that is so severe as to call into question any unstinting praise of their virtues: "Master Zhu said: To do wrong is unbecoming to a wife, and to do good is also unbecoming to a wife. A woman is merely to be obedient to what is proper. . . . Therefore, a woman should bear the refinement of the inner chambers and desist from any ulterior motives." Zhu's point suggests that women, more so than men, must hew very closely to the expectations already set out in their roles as daughters, wives, and mothers. They must embrace the restrictions of living in the inner quarters, and aspire to nothing more and no less.

Robin R. Wang

Selections From
Reflections on Things at Hand
(Jinsi lu)

The Way to Regulate the Family

My late father[1] was a chief officer of the first rank.[2] His private name was Xiang and his courtesy name was Bowen [1006–1090 c.e.]. Over the years he obtained five hereditary positions due an official's son and gave them to descendants of his brothers. When he gave orphaned girls in the community in marriage, he always did his best. He gave away his official remuneration to support poor relatives. His brother's wife, whose maiden name was Liu, became a widow, and he supported

---

[1] In this biography Cheng Yi called his father "sir" or "the gentleman" and his mother "madame." I have used "father" and "mother" instead.

[2] During the Song dynasty, this was an honorary position with a salary but no official duties. Previously the duty of a chief officer had been to deliberate on state matters.

and took care of her wholeheartedly. When her son-in-law died, he welcomed my cousin, supported and provided her son with an education, and treated him like his own son and nephew. Later, when my cousin's own daughter also became a widow, fearing that my cousin was deeply grieved, he took the widowed daughter home and gave her in marriage. At that time his official position was minor and his remuneration slight. He denied himself in order to be charitable to others. People felt that he did what was difficult for others to do.

Someone asked, "Taking the widowed grandniece home and giving her in marriage seems to contradict the teaching that a widow should not remarry. How about it?"

Zhu Xi answered, "Generally speaking, that should be the case. But people cannot follow that absolutely." (Zhu Xi, *Zhuzi yulei*, 96:13a)

Father was kindhearted and altruistic but at the same time firm and decisive. In his daily associations with the young and the lowly, he was always careful lest he hurt them. But if they violated any moral principle, he would not give in. Not a day passed when he did not inquire whether those who served him were adequately fed and clothed.

He married Miss Hou.[3] My mother was known for filial piety and respectfulness in serving her parents-in-law. She and father treated each other will full respect, as guests are treated. Grateful for her help at home, father treated her with even greater reverence. But mother conducted herself with humility and obedience. Even in small matters, she never made decisions alone but always asked my father before she did anything. She was humane, altruistic, liberal, and earnest. She cared for and loved the children of my father's concubines just as she did her own. My father's cousin's son became an orphan when very young, and she regarded him as her own.

She was skillful in ruling the family. She was not stern, but correct. She did not like to beat servants but, instead, looked upon little servants as her own children. If we children should scold them, she would always admonish us, saying, "Although people differ in noble and humble stations, they are people just the same. When you grow up, can you do the same thing?"[4] Whenever father got angry, she always gently explained the matter to him. But if we children were wrong, she would not cover up. She often said, "Children become unworthy if a mother covers up their wrongdoings so the father is unaware of them."

---

[3] Daughter of Hou Daoji, a magistrate and a native of Taiyuan Prefecture in modern Shanxi.

[4] Which the little sons presumably had accused the servants of failing to do.

Mother had six sons. Only two are still living.[5] Her love and affection for us were of the highest degree. But in teaching us she would not give in a bit. When we were only several years old, sometimes we stumbled when we walked. People in the family would rush forward to hold us, for fear we might cry. Mother would always scold us with a loud voice and say, "If you had walked gently, would you have stumbled?" Food was always served us by her side. If we swallowed the sauces, as we often did, she would immediately shout and stop us, saying, "If you seek to satisfy your desires when you are young, what will you do when you grow up?" Even when we gave orders to others, we were not allowed to scold in harsh language. Consequently my brother and I are not particular in our food and clothing, and do not scold people in harsh language. It is not that we are this way by nature but that we were taught to be like this. When we quarreled with others, even though we were right, she would not take sides with us. She said, "The trouble is that one cannot bend and not that one cannot stretch out." When we were somewhat older, we were always told to keep company with good teachers and friends. Although we were poor, whenever someone wanted to invite a guest, she would gladly make preparations for it.

When mother was seven or eight, she read an ancient poem, which says,

Women do not go out off doors at night.
If they do, they carry a lighted candle.[6]

From then on, she never went outside the gate of her living quarters after dark. As she grew up, she loved literature but did not engage in flowery compositions. She considered it vastly wrong for present-day women to pass around literary compositions, notes, and letters.

In all collections of Cheng Yi's literary works, this biography comes first, but here it is placed at the end of the quotations from him. The reason is that it deals with the regulation of the family in a summary way. All the principles of serving superiors, caring for inferiors, harmony with relatives, and charity toward the lonely are present.

---

[5] Cheng Hao and Cheng Yi. The other four died young.
[6] This is a paraphrase of *The Record of Rites*, "Regulations for Domestic Life."

Selections From
Further Reflections on Things at Hand
(Xu Jinsi lu)

Family and Social Relationships

This section discusses regulation of the family, which originates with oneself and extends to others. Nothing comes before the family. The daily practice of proper social relations must not for a moment be lost. When you have sincerely achieved self-discipline, you can apply this to the family and the family can be so regulated.

1. Master Zhu said: The *Dao* which pervades the world truly originates with the nature of heaven's endowment, and is carried out in the relations between ruler and subject, father and son, brother and brother, husband and wife, friend and friend.

2. Master Zhu said: Relations between father and son, and brother and brother are universal relationships, and serve as cornerstones in the triadic relations of the union of individuals. The relation between spouses is the source from which universal relationships depend on for completion. Relations between friends are what universal characteristics depend on for being upright. These, then, comprise the social network in the *Dao* of humanity, and establish humankind's highest moral standard, and cannot even for a day be neglected.

3. Master Zhu said: The reason why a person has this body is to receive the outer appearance from the mother while the inner disposition comes from the father. Although someone may be extremely violent, he will see a child and feel compassion. On the other hand, a baby infant will see its father and laugh. How can it be otherwise?

4. Master Zhu answered Chen Fuzhong: It is worrying that domestic affairs and various and sundry matters interfere with one's learning. There certainly does not seem to be anything that can be done except to be very diligent, and to recognize that in all things there is the principle of *Dao*. Don't let it easily get away from you. Even more, if you see some everyday illness, you really have to root it out, and then you will be on the proper way to learning. But what more can we do? If an uncaring mind develops, or disinterest arises, then affairs and principles will be split in two. Studying books will certainly be of no use.

5. Someone said: Fathers and sons hope for there to be familial love between them. Ruler and subject hope for there to be rectitude and justice between them.

Master Zhu said: It isn't that they hope for it to be like this. It is just that of itself there is familial love between father and son, and of itself there is rectitude and justice between ruler and subject.

6. Master Zhu said: Admonish frequently, but be gradual and cautious. Do not be rash and violent; rather exercise composure.[7]

7. Master Zhu said: The intimacy between a father and son is the acme of the principle of nature and human feelings.

8. Someone asked: The feelings that parents have for a child are of inexhaustible tenderness and love, and a desire that they be intelligent and firmly established. Is this what is called a sincere heart?

Master Zhu said: For parents to love their children is only proper. But loving them without limit and expecting them to be of some account is wrong. This difference between the principle of heaven and human desire should be carefully determined.

9. Ye Chengzhi asked a question concerning the unfortunate situation wherein a stepmother and half brothers are unable to get along.

Master Zhu said: From old it has been this way. You can look at the case of Shun for that.[8] And later on such situations were even more numerous. All we can do is hope that children will be filial.

10. Yu Yin had this to say: Zhongzi's brother was not unkind. Why avoid him? Zhongzi's mother was without compassion. Why set her apart?[9]

Master Zhu said: Even if it is a case of lacking compassion or being unkind, still there is no reason for avoidance. Just look at the way Shun conducted himself and you will understand him.

11. Master Zhu said: The kindness between brothers may be different in form but is the same in spirit. Whether in matters of life

---

[7] Zhang Boxing comments that this passage refers to a child admonishing his parents.

[8] For one account of Shun's treatment of his parents and half brother see *Mencius*, 5A.1–7; also, 4B.26, 28.

[9] Yu Yin is likely a reference to the alleged usurper of the throne from his half brother, Guang (Duke Zhuang). The Marquis of Qi, being childless, declared Guang, his niece's eldest son, as successor. Later, however, Rongzi, his favorite concubine, bore him a child, Zhongzi (probably the one in question in this passage) whom the marquis favored over Guang. The Marquis of Qi unsuccessfully tried to prevent the successions of Guang in favor of Zhongzi. Rongzi eventually was executed and Zhongzi arrested. See *Zuozhuan*, Dune Xiang, year 19.

and death, or misery and joy, there is no occasion when they are not mutually dependent.

12. Master Zhu said: Brothers may have the misfortune of being contentious and quarrelsome at home, but when there is outside insult only in common accord can they guard against it. Even if you have a very good friend, how can you help him? Fu Chen said: "Though brothers may have minor squabbles, this is no cause to throw away fraternal affection."[10]

13. Someone asked: Loyalty is simply an honest heart. In the day-to-day exercise of human relations everyone should go by this. Why is it that the word "loyalty" is used only in connection with service to a superior?

Master Zhu said: Fathers and sons, brothers and brothers, husbands and wives—all these relations are natural principles. There is no one who does not himself understand love and reverence. Even though the ruler-subject relationship is also based on the principle of Heaven, and thus one of justice and harmony, still the average person easily becomes morally lax. Therefore, it is necessary to speak of "loyalty," but even this does not sufficiently explain it.

14. Master Zhu answered Hu Bofeng: To live as man and woman is the most intimate human affair, and the exercise of *Dao* is found therein. This is why the *Dao* of the gentlemen is so widespread,[11] and yet secret. It lies within darkness and obscurity where it cannot be seen atop the sleeping mat [where passions may be aroused],[12] and people may look on it with contempt. But this is not the way of our natural endowment. The *Dao* of the gentleman begins its rise in the confidential moments between husband and wife,[13] but in its furthest extent it reaches from the heights of heaven to the depths of the earth.

---

[10] Zhu's comparison of friends and brothers is probably a reference to the ode noting the affection between brothers.

Brothers may quarrel within the walls,
But will guard against insult from without.
There always are good friends,
But numerous though they be, are of no help.

[11] For Zhu's exclamation that the *Dao* of the gentleman is widespread, see the *Doctrine of the Mean*, 12.

[12] The parenthetical remarks concerning "darkness and obscurity" and the "conjugal mat" follow the comments of Zhang Boxing.

[13] For the "confidential moments between husband and wife," see the *Doctrine of the Mean*, 12.

If we fail to understand the personal caution of the gentleman,[14] then how can we ever realize it? *The Classic of Changes* begins with [the hexagrams] Qian and Kun, and ends with [the hexagrams] Xian and Heng.[15] *The Record of Rites* counsels the "Da Hun."[16] *The Classic of Odes* takes the "Two Souths"[17] as the correct beginning of *Dao*. For this reason, the Understanding Words says: "*Dao* exists in the matters of food and drink and man and woman, but anyone engulfed in its flow will not understand its essence." It also says: "Through contact [husbands and wives] will know propriety; through intercourse they will know *Dao*. Only through concentration can we protect it without losing it." This is the meaning.

15. Master Zhu said: [The relationship between] husbands and wives is the most intimate and the most private of all human relations. We may not want to tell something to a father or brother, but it can all be told to one's wife. These are the most intimate of human affairs, and *Dao* is exercised therein.

16. Master Zhu said: The feelings between husband and wife are very intimate, but they can easily become overindulgent. Unless you are especially careful, personal desires will find you playing on the field of frivolity, and self-deceit will leave you in the arena of ignorance. If you understand the importance of the beginning of things, and the moment of secret subtlety, exercise caution and be in awe. Then moral cultivation will come from within—use it to serve fathers and brothers, and to deal with companions and friends. In all of this your efforts will easily be effective.

17. Master Zhu said: The beneficial rain that falls from the mixing of *yin* and is like the *Dao* of the home that comes from the harmony between husband and wife. Therefore, those who are husband and wife should endeavor to be united in mind for it is not fit to reach the point of anger.

---

[14] The "personal caution of the gentleman" refers to Confucius' dictum that part of the make-up of such a person is to be watchful over himself even when he is alone, that is, to guard against self-deception (*shendu*). See both the *Great Learning*, 6 and 10; and the *Doctrine of the Mean*, 1 and 20.

[15] Hexagrams Xian and Heng are actually found at the beginning of the second section of *The Classic of Changes*, hexagrams 31 and 32.

[16] For the "Great Rites," *Dahun*, see chapter 27, Aigong Wen. Cf. Legge, *Li Ki*, II, 261.

[17] The "Two Souths," *Zhounan* and *Shaonan*, are books 1 and 2 of the *The Book of Odes*.

18. Someone asked: A wife is subject to seven grounds for divorce.[18] Nevertheless, is this the proper principle of *Dao* and not a measure of expediency?

Master Zhu said: It is.

19. Master Zhu said: To do wrong is unbecoming to a wife, and to do good is also unbecoming to a wife. A woman is merely to be obedient to what is proper. If a daughter does nothing wrong, that is enough. If she does good, then likewise, that is neither a favorable nor a desirable thing. Only spirits and food are her concern, and not to occasion sorrow to her parents is all that is called for.[19] *The Classic of Changes* says, "Do not give in to presents and gifts; only through firm correctness will there be auspicious things." And Mencius' mother said, "All a wife needs to do to fulfill her proper station in life is to prepare the five dishes, cover the wine, take care of her in-laws, and mend the clothes."[20] Therefore, a woman should bear the refinement of the inner chambers and desist from any ulterior motives.

20. Master Zhu said: Of all the human relationships, those between friends are the most important.

21. Master Zhu then talked about poverty: If friends can manage their money with mutual benefit and without violating the principle of *Dao*, it is all right to have money. Clearly, if their relationship is in accordance with *Dao*, and meets with propriety, even Confucius would accept this. If you do not mutually entrust in the right way, but simply benefit each other with money, that is definitely out of the question.

22. Master Zhu said: When friends are at odds the problem should be cleared up, but cleared up gradually. If there is no outstanding reason, then it isn't necessary to break relations. When there is intimacy, do not lose that which makes it intimate; when there is something important, do not lose that which makes it important.

---

[18] The seven grounds for divorce (*qi chu*) stipulated that in ancient China there were seven reasons for which a man could divorce his wife: (1) failure to produce a male heir (*wuzi*); (2) adultery (*yinyi*); (3) disrespect to parents-in-law (*bu shi xiugu*); (4) being contentious or quarrelsome (*koushe*); (5) stealing (*daojie*); (6) jealousy (*duji*); and (7) incurable disease (*eji*). The theory was that any of these would result in a ruined household, and to prevent this the wife would be forced to leave (*chu*) the home on any one of the seven (*qi*) grounds.

[19] For the basis of the view concerning women, see *The Book of Odes*, Xiao Ya, 5.9, "Si gan."

23. Master Zhu said: When a gentleman is going to build a residence he should first set up the ancestral shrine in the east corner of the main hall, and use the four niches[21] for presenting the tablets in rectitude of one's departed ancestors.[22] If there are no descendents in the collateral line, then use it to respect those extended ancestors. Lay out the sacrificial fields, prepare the sacrificial implements, and the headman will hold audience at daybreak within the main gate. All those who enter and depart must be announced. Adhere precisely to the proper dates,[23] pay respect to the local customs, and observe the seasonal offerings. Announce all affairs.

24. It was asked: If someone wishes to carry out a marriage or a capping ceremony, is a thorough knowledge of the phrasing beneficial, such as the terminology of the three caps[24] or the vow outside the gate? If only the ancient phraseology is used to call the ceremony, what will it be called?

(Master Zhu) answered: If they only use the modern vernacular to announce it, and thereby enable the people to understand it thoroughly, this is certainly to the good.

25. Master Zhu said: When the groom goes to receive his bride at her home without seeing her parents, this is because she has not yet met her in-laws. If [the bride] enters his home without meeting the in-laws, this is because her proper role as a wife has not yet been completed.

26. Someone asked: If the ancient practice of sending precious gifts to the family of the bride was to present five double rolls [of silk], I fear that only five single bolts is too little.

Master Zhu said: Trying to reckon between too much and too little is why there is all this talk about profit. As for my generation, there is no hope in restoring the ancient practice. Alas, how can the present customs be changed by anyone?

---

[20] I have not been able to locate the quotations.

[21] The "four niches" (si gan) are where the idols are placed.

[22] The tablets of departed ancestors (shenzhu) are long and narrow, usually of wood or bamboo, and painted or inscribed with the deceased individual's name (hao, zi, etc.).

[23] The "proper dates" (shuowang) are the first and the fifteenth of the lunar month.

[24] The "terminology of the three caps" (san jia zhi ci) refers to the different caps, in increasing importance, bestowed on the subject. See the The Record of the Rites (Liji), 43, "Kuan Yi."

42

THE ANALECTS FOR WOMEN
(Nü lunyü)
女論語
Song Ruoxin and Song Ruozhao
宋若新，宋若照

The Analects for Women (Nü lunyü)[1] *was written by the Tang dynasty scholar, Song Ruoxin, and her sister, Song Ruozhao. Song Ruoxin was one of the best-known female scholars of the Tang dynasty and the oldest of five daughters of a well-known Confucian scholar, Song Tingfen. All five daughters were well read and recognized for their knowledge and literary talents. Thus the Emperor De Zong (780–805 C.E.) summoned the five Song sisters to the palace to test their knowledge of the Classics, history, and poetry, and was very much impressed by their abilities and talents. As a result, the emperor invited all five sisters to attend his literary events as scholars or masters, and placed the oldest sister, Ruoxin, in charge of administering the women's routines at the palace. The second-oldest sister was appointed as an instructor for the prince and princess. These two sisters then vowed never to marry.*

The Analects for Women (Nü lunyü) expanded the basic view of female virtues presented in Ban Zhao's Lesson's for Women (Nüjie).[2] *The Nü lunyü thus consists of twelve chapters set in rhyming verses, each composed of four Chinese characters. The work is memorable, not only because it is the second of the* Four Books for Women (Nü sishu), *which were actually composed by women for women, but also because it extends the construction of female virtues to everyday behavior in women's lives. Each chapter not only commends certain attitudes and*

From Heying Jenny Zhan and Robert Bradshaw, "The Book of Analects for Women," *Journal of Historical Sociology* 9 (1996): 261–268. Copyright © 1996 Blackwell Publishers Ltd. Reprinted by permission of Blackwell Science Ltd.

[1] This version of *Nü lunyü* [*The Analects for Women*] is from *Gujin tushu jichen* Vol. 395, p. 10a and 10b., Zhonghua Shuju [China Books], 1934. All Chinese names are given in pinyin except for those taken from quotations using other systems.

[2] See the full text on pp. 177–188.

behaviors as models for women's virtue, but also warns against learning from women whose specific attitudes and behaviors contradict the exemplary models. The most frequently invoked reason for following the advice of the Nü lunyü is the fear of shame and disgrace (see Book 3). People will talk. One's extended family, one's neighbors, even the whole village will soon know who is sincerely seeking to cultivate virtue and who is not. The fear that one's actions might result in a loss of face, not only for oneself but especially for one's parents, one's husband, and one's family, appears to be sufficient reason for any normal filial woman to be ever diligent in practicing virtue.

Due to its simple and easy writing style, the Nü lunyü exerted a much deeper influence upon the common people than did its predecessors. In its detailed advice on what to do and what not to do, it provides a fascinating perspective on the social conditions that shaped ordinary women's lives during the Tang dynasty. But these very details, taken narrowly as a recipe to be strictly followed in training women for their responsibilities in a properly managed household, may also have been the pretext for imposing even greater restrictions on Chinese women's lives than were apparent in earlier periods.

Robin R. Wang

Cao Dagu[3] said: I[4] am the wife of a virtuous man, the daughter of an eminent family. I observe all the four proprieties and am well-read in history. As I pause[5] from women's work and read, (I find that) there have been many[6] heroines praiseworthy and some virtuous women admirable. I feel sorry that posterity has not followed their model. I thus write this work entitled *The Analects for Women* in the hope of teaching women to inherit the good and guard against the evil. Those who follow these teaching will be regarded as virtuous women, whose names will rank among those of their predecessors and be passed down to future generations.

---

[3] Cao Dagu, also know as Ban Zhao. See pp. 177–178.

[4] Literally, "A humble woman such as I," often a modest way a woman used to refer to herself in conversation in Pre-Qin times.

[5] *Chuo*: to rest, pause, stop, or cease. It is quite likely that a palace woman like Song Ruoxin had ceased to do women's work, which in this context means sewing, weaving, cleaning, etc.

[6] *Jiulie sanzhen*: *jiu* means nine; *lie*, virtuous women who are ready to die to preserve chastity; *san*, three; and *zhen*, chaste and faithful.

Book One
On Deportment

The first thing for any woman to learn is the principle of deportment: that of purity and chastity.[7] If you are pure, then chastity will follow; if you are chaste, then you will be honored.

Don't turn your head and look while walking. Don't show your teeth while speaking. Don't move your knees while sitting. Don't sway your dress while standing. Don't laugh out loud when happy. Don't shout when angry.

Indoors or out, men and women should be in separate groups. Don't peep beyond the outer wall, and don't go beyond the courtyard. Hide your face when watching something. When going outside you must cover yourself.

Don't give your name to a man who is not your relative. Don't become friendly with a woman who is not from a good family.[8] Only by being decorous and proper will you be a [proper] person.

Book Two
On Learning to Work

A woman should learn women's work. In plaiting hemp and weaving ramie, one is rough and coarse, the other is fine, do not hasten on the loom or spinning wheel. In watching the silkworms and in boiling the cocoon, you should be cautious from dawn to dusk. In picking red or yellow mulberry leaves, you should watch for wind or rain: adding new leaves for the silkworms immediately when they get wet and cold, and drying them over a fire when it is cold. Always choose proper ones to feed silkworms. Choose silk threads for the warp and the woof to turn into bolts of silk cloth. Keep yarn on spools and thread on bobbins. With fine silk, ramie, hemp, and coarse fiber you will have a lot to weave. These you can either sell or keep for you own use—making shoes or socks, using the thread for embroidering, mending, and basting; you should be able to do everything. If you can follow these teachings, you will have no worry about coldness; when the cold

---

[7] *Qingzhen*: purity and chastity.

[8] This sentence may also be understood as "don't become friendly with a woman who is not considered good." I find the former more suitable in this context.

comes you will be leisurely and dignified, worrying neither about clothes being torn, nor about your family being poor.

Don't learn from those lazy women, who are petty and foolish and not eager to do women's work, who don't plan for spring or autumn, and who sew brusquely and are attacked by others. When they marry, they bring shame to the new family. When clothes become torn, they rob Peter to pay Paul,[9] are pointed at, and scornfully laughed at in the village. I venture to exhort all women to heed the words above.

Book Three
On Learning Rites

All women should know women's affairs. If any female guest comes, you should arrange a place for her to sit. Tidy yourself up, walk slowly and tread lightly, withdrawing your hands while speaking softly, and invite her to the vestibule. Greet her according to her title[10] and tell her the time.[11] Answer questions attentively, and speak softly in a low voice. Make her tea and bring it directly to her, and take away [the empty cups]. Don't learn from those who neglect their guests, behaving stiffly toward them in a cool manner, and treating them in an insulting way.

When you visit someone, you should behave according to rites and etiquette. Help serve tea and then immediately get to the point. As soon as you finish, stand up and thank your hostess repeatedly, then leave. If the hostess invites you to stay for a meal, you should behave politely. Drink slightly, just moistening the lips, and eat slowly and politely.[12] Push away your cup and refuse further offers.

Don't learn from those women who order soup or vinegar,[13] and become wild and crazy when they get drunk. Whoever meets them

---

[9] *Qiandong zhexi*: literally, "tear down the east [wall] to cover the west," a popularly used idiom.

[10] *Congtuo chengxu*: to greet according to one's title. *Tou* here means title or official title for a woman; it is derived from her husband or family.

[11] In pre-modern times, burning incense was a way of marking time. Telling the time to a guest or any traveler during the day was understandably important and a common practice.

[12] *Shiwu youzhu*: finish what you have [in your mouth or in your bowl] before you get some more.

[13] The verb *jia*, to drink or to swallow, is used before vinegar.

feels disgusted, and their bad name will have defiled them before they reach home. Stay at home and don't roam about. When you encounter someone, you should lower your head and look askance.

Don't learn from those who, day and night, idle about the village, gossiping here and there, provoking nasty comments and causing abuse and anger, defiling the reputation of the family and involving the parents, destroying themselves, and becoming the laughingstock of others. People such as those are like dogs and rats. Don't learn fear, shame, and disgrace from them.

Book Four
On Rising Early

All women should make this a customary practice. When the rooster crows at the fifth watch,[14] get up and dress, wash up and rinse your mouth, and comb your hair in good time. Gather firewood for the fire and go to the kitchen early. Brush out the wok and wash the cauldron, boil water and cook soup, and steam and boil food in accordance with the means of the family. Arrange vegetables, cook beans, pound the ginger, and have foodstuff, sweet, plain, and fragrant, ready. Place bowls and plates in order, arranging them properly. Prepare three meals at proper times from morning to evening, and you will have no difficulties with anything.

Don't imitate those lazy women who don't know how to think things over. They go to sleep right at dusk, sleeping all the way through till daylight. When the sun has risen high they are still not out of bed, and when they finally get up, the meal time is already over. Feeling nervous and ashamed, they rush abruptly into the kitchen after washing up and combing their hair. Looking disheveled and behaving peevishly, they hurriedly make tea and cook food, but are still later than normal.

There is another type of woman, eager to sneak some food or drink before it is even laid out on the table. Her disgraceful manners become known all over the village, humiliating her parents. Is it not shameful to be talked about by people?

---

14 *Wugeng*: the fifth watch or just before dawn. The night is divided into five watches, the third being at midnight.

Book Five
On Serving the Parents

While still at home, every woman should revere her parents. Every morning get up early and ask after their health. When it's cold, start a fire. Use a fan to cool them when it is hot. Serve food when they are hungry, and bring tea when they are thirsty. If your parents rebuke you, don't become flustered; listen attentively and think about what they have said day and night. If there is anything that is not done accordingly, correct it as you were told. Don't take what they have said as commonplace, but obey their instructions, and never argue with them. If there is something you don't understand, don't hesitate to ask them.

When parents get old, be concerned for them morning and evening, making shoes, darning socks, and sewing clothes for them. For four seasons and eight festivals, you should show your filial piety and care for them. When parents suffer from any illness, don't leave their bedside, and don't loosen your clothes.[15] Steep the medicine and try it yourself. Pray for the help of the spirits and Buddha, and hope for recovery. In case misfortune should occur or death take them, let pain penetrate to the marrow of your bones, wail and lament,[16] never forgetting the three years of suckling. Clothe the dead and don mourning clothes. Prepare for burial and arrange the sacrifices. Do obeisance and burn joss sticks. Continue to cultivate dignity so that your parents can rise to Heaven.

Don't learn from those obstinate and unfilial women who are clamorous. When someone utters just one word, they have a thousand in reply, saying this or that to suit themselves, and hurting others the minute they open their mouths. Women such as these will only be bad examples of a village.

Book Six
On Serving Parents-in-Law

Parents-in-law are masters of the husband's family. When you enter their gate, you become his bride, and you should behave towards your

---

[15] Because women's clothes were tied at the waist, the expression "not to untie the clothes" means being prepared to work at any time, even at night.

[16] *Kuduang ganchang*: literally, "cry until your liver and intestines burst."

husband's parents as you would towards your own. Serve your father-in-law with respect. Don't look directly, and certainly do not walk with him or converse with him. If given an order, do as you are told. If your mother-in-law is sitting, then stand, and if given an order, do as you are told immediately. Don't startle or frighten her when you open the door in the morning. Prepare warm water and bring it to her room. Take clean towels, dentifrice, and soap, change water outside her room, and go out and wait until she has bathed. Greet her [with ten thousand happinesses], and withdraw immediately. Prepare tea and soup and arrange spoons and chopsticks. The rice should be cooked soft and the meat tender, because as is known, old people's teeth may be loose or decayed. Never let them lack tea, soup, or porridge. When it is late and time for bed, you should get things ready and bid them good night, then go to your bedroom. Day in and day out, if you remain the same, your deeds will be spread among women's quarters and people will call you a virtuous woman.

Don't learn from those who jump at[17] disgusting opportunities, screaming and shouting at venerable old folks. They complain about hardships and difficulties, don't come when called, and don't give a whit about people's hunger and coldness. These kinds of people are called evil women, whom Heaven and Earth cannot bear, and who provoke the rage of thunder. So much rebuke will fall upon them that there will be no way to repent or regret.

Book Seven
On Serving One's Husband

When a woman is married, her husband will be her master among relatives. The affinity[18] to the former life becomes the marriage of the present life. To compare one's husband to Heaven is not meaningless. The husband [should be] firm and the wife yielding. An affectionate couple rely on each other. At home, treat your husband as respectfully as you would a guest. When he speaks to you, listen attentively. If your husband has some evil ways, remonstrate repeatedly. Don't learn from those ignorant women who bring evil on themselves.

---

[17] *Tiaoliang kewu*: literally, (*tiaoliang*) jumping up to the beams (rafters), and (*kewu*) loathsome, disgusting, or hateful.

[18] *Yuanfen*: the idiomatic expression means "the fate by which persons are brought together."

When your husband goes out, ask politely where he is going. If he is not back at dusk, long for him and anticipate his return. With lights off, keep the food warm and wait for the knock at the door. Don't learn from the lazy woman who goes to bed before dark. When your husband is sick, wait on him wholeheartedly, search everywhere for medicine and pray to the gods. Try every means possible to find medicine for the sake of a long life. Don't learn from those doltish women who don't worry at all. When your husband gets angry, don't be annoyed, but withdraw and beg him [to calm down]. Restrain your anger and remain silent.[19] Don't learn from those foolish women who are incessantly quarrelsome.

Be vigorous in mending and washing, whether it is rough silk or fine fiber. Don't let cold harm your husband. Prepare and serve all food diligently. Don't let hunger and thirst cause him to become thin and miserable. Share happiness and misery, prosperity and poverty. Share the same bed while living, and the same coffin when dead. Don't learn from those shrews who are only good at sweet words and wheedling. If you can follow these instructions you will be as harmonious as [the music of] a zither, and the name of such a woman will be spread by hundreds of mouths [i.e., far and wide].

Book Eight
On Instructing Girls and Boys

In general, there are boys and girls in a family. As they grow old there is a sequence in teaching them. The right to instruct belongs, in fact, to the mother. Boys should be sent to school, or a teacher [should be] engaged. They should study the Rites and Ceremonies and how to recite poetry and compose verse. You should respect teachers and scholars, [and pay] a teaching fee, [serving] wine and dried meat [on] five plates and three cups; don't let them be empty. Once every ten days according to etiquette, arrange a feast or banquet, offering goblets of wine. On moonlit nights or fragrant mornings, [let them] stroll in the garden casually, offer them pots of tea or jugs of wine. When you meet the guest, greet him [with ten thousand happinesses] and return immediately.

Keep your daughter in the women's chambers and seldom let her

---

[19] *Renqui tunsheng*: literally, hold your anger, swallow your voice. It is often used to mean "swallowing an insult quietly."

go out. She should come immediately when called and go immediately when told to do so. If she shows any inclination to disobey, scold her and make her feel ashamed. In the household, instruct her to be diligent in everything: sweeping floors, burning incense, weaving hemp, and sewing ramie. For visiting someone, you should teach her etiquette: how to give a greeting of happiness in a humble voice, and how to pass the tea and withdraw. Don't indulge her childish foolishness, lest she howls with rage. Don't let her jump about,[20] lest she becomes frivolous and ridiculous. Don't let her recite poetry or sing songs, lest she picks up evil ways. It is indeed laughable that nowadays people do not take responsibility.[21] Men do not read but allow each other to talk idly, wrangling with each other and drinking. They listen to singing, enjoy dancing, and don't worry about officialdom or think about their native place. Women don't read, but use overbearing language and cannot distinguish between respect and humility. They don't sew or weave, and they bring shame to respectable relatives, but the complaints come to the parents. This foul language falls on all sides. This [raising children such as these] is [like] raising pigs and rats.

Book Nine
On Ministering to the Family[22]

A woman who administers a family should be thrifty and diligent. If she is diligent, then a family's fortunes rise; if lazy, then a family collapses; if thrifty, then a family prospers; if extravagant, then it is impoverished. A woman should not procrastinate. The key to life is found only in diligence, just as spring to the year and dawn to the day. Take up the dustpan and broom, and wipe up the dust and dirt and carry it away. The usefulness of these things is not insignificant. In your eyes, the house sparkles, and is clean and tidy.

Don't let dirt and filth appear in your house. Don't complain about the hardships of ploughing and planting. Learn in detail the preparation of food. Don't delay bringing tea and food while people are ploughing in the field. People are hungry. Gather the chaff and collect

---

[20] Again, *tiaoliang* (or jumping up to the beams) is used to describe ill-mannered behavior.

[21] *Buneng weizhu*: cannot do what they are supposed to; or are irresponsible for their behavior.

[22] *Yingjia*: ministering to or managing the family.

the hogwash to feed the animals; let them out and gather them in; always count them and search for them. Don't let them run astray and disturb the neighbors on each side.

When your husband has money and rice, you should put them away and manage them. When your husband has wine or foodstuff, you should store them and keep them well. When guests or visitors come, don't pilfer or appropriate. While great riches may be decided by fate, small wealth comes from diligence. Cereal grains, hemp, millet, and wheat [should be put] in storehouses and bins. Oil, salt, pepper, and beans [should be] in pots and containers. Pigs, chickens, ducks, and geese are in flocks and herds. During all four seasons and at the eight festivals [do this] so as not to run back and forth, and to have a surplus of wine and food. [In this way] a couple will enjoy riches and delightful happiness.

Book Ten
On Treating Guests

Generally speaking, there are guests and a host in every family. In anticipation of guests, you should gather up hot water and bottles and wipe them bright and clean. [When a guest comes,] prepare hot water and bring it forward, and then withdraw to the front of the hall, waiting for your husband's call. When needed, pass cups, doing it immediately. If you want to invite the guest to stay, wait for your husband to come to you. Carefully deliberate [with your husband] about whether you should kill a chicken for food. If the flavors blend and the vegetables are plentiful, and there is plenty of wine to drink, if will bring glory to your family. At sunset, invite the guest to stay. Light candles or hold a lamp; arrange places to sit. [Arrange] mat and pillow, covers and bedding; treat him with respect so that he is neither too hot nor too cold. The following morning, if the guest expresses thanks and is about to depart, pay special attention and be diligent about serving a farewell drink. [In this way your] husband will be happy with your ability in family care, and family members will praise you for your efficiency and mindfulness.

Don't learn from those women who don't do any housework and, when guests arrive, have no hot water and, being flustered, don't know what to do. When the husband invites a guest, the wife harbors anger, and has chopsticks, but no spoon; salt, but no vinegar. She quarrels about sipping and chewing, and flirts with the men and curses the women.[23] Her husband will feel ashamed and embarrassed and guests will be chagrined.

If a guest comes to your door when there is no one [male] at home, you must send your boy servant to enquire where he is from. If the guest is earnest, he will give his official and courtesy name. Then tidy up your appearance and go to the vestibule to receive him. Provide tea and hot water, and never behave in a way lacking in etiquette. Ask of his surname and enquire his reason for visiting. When your husband returns, remember to tell him this immediately. When the guest descends the steps to leave, go back in immediately. I venture to advise you for the sake of posterity, earnestly and sincerely, to learn all these.

Book Eleven
On Conciliation and Yielding

The rules for managing a household for a wife are to prize harmony and filial piety above all else.[24] When your mother-in-law rebukes you, don't feel hurt. When your father-in-law has any criticism, listen to it quietly. In the upper rooms and in the lower chambers, with nephews and nieces, you should behave harmoniously. Whether [disagreements are] right or wrong, don't get involved. [Whether an issue involves] good or bad, don't argue. Shameful family matters should never be exposed to the public. Be as good as you can in etiquette to neighbors both to the east and west. Greet them as they come and go, and behave cordially to them; [offer] a cup of tea or water, exchange pleasantries joyfully; say only what needs to be said; do whatever needs to be done. Idle talk of right or wrong should not enter your door. Don't learn from those stupid women who gossip in vile language without knowing the truth of the matter, thus offending and insulting the venerable elders. I venture to advise women to look to the past and to think ahead.

---

[23] *Danan manu:* literally, "beating the man and scolding the woman"; but often it is interchangeable with the idiomatic phrase *daqing maqiao,* meaning "flirting with the men and cursing/scolding the women."

[24] Literally, even when the wife is capable, harmony should be prized and filial piety is intrinsic.

Figure 8. Despite her son's disapproval, the widow Liang is disfiguring her face
[From *Chou's Illustrations of the Biographies of Woman (Chou Hua Lienu Zhuan)* by Chou

in order to discourage her many male suitors and thus preserve her chastity. Ying (1509–1552).]

Book Twelve
On Preserving Chastity

Women of old, both chaste and virtuous,[25] have had their names recorded in the annals of history and passed down to the present day. Women nowadays who have not learned from them should not consider it too difficult to begin. The first [principle] is that of preserving chastity;[26] the second, that of purity and virtuousness. If there is a daughter in a family, don't [let her] leave the inner chambers. When there are guests, don't go beyond the main hall. Don't spread gossip, or speak in vile language. When dusk falls, hold a candle or lamp when going in or out of dark places to avoid uncleanliness. If one step is wrong, then a hundred spells failure. The bonds of the first marriage weigh more than a thousand pieces of gold. If there occurs the misfortune of the husband dying at a young age, wear mourning clothes for three years, and remain firm in your will to preserve your chastity. Protect your family and manage your property. Clean and sweep your husband's tomb. In life or in death, it is one life shared.

This essay *The Analects for Women* discusses all topics exhaustively. Women from now on should follow this, day after day and month after month, remembering it always, taking unquestioned guidance from it. If you persist in this, you will enjoy boundless happiness.

---

[25] Again, *jiulie sanzhen* is used to describe many virtuous and chaste women.
[26] *Shoujie*: preserving or guarding chastity.

43

EXAMINATION ESSAYS

(Panbacui)

判拔萃

Bo Juyi[1]

白居易

The civil service examination system was used by the Chinese imperial dynasties to recruit officials. This method was adopted first by the Sui dynasty (581–618 C.E.) and became increasingly important after the Tang dynasty (618–907 C.E.). It was not abolished until 1905, when Western curricula and school systems were introduced. Although the categories and subjects of the examinations varied throughout Chinese history, the principle of the examinations remained the same: the candidates were tested on their knowledge of the Confucian classics and their abilities to make arguments based on the Confucian ideology.

The following are five sample essays written by one of the Tang literati, Bo Juyi (772–846 C.E.), during his preparation for an examination called Panbacui, or Judgment Essays. Only those who passed the Literary Examination (jinshi), the highest degree, were allowed to take the Panbacui examination. Therefore, sample essays written by Panbancui candidates were widely distributed and served both as literary masterpieces and as test preparation models.

In the first four of these five essays, a case is presented in which a woman has been put in the wrong and is subject to condemnation according to a superficial reading of traditional Confucian moral codes. Each of these four essays, however, exonerates

---

Translated by Ping Yao.

[1] Bo Juyi (772–846 C.E.) was one of the most celebrated literati in Chinese history. Born to a low-ranking official family, Bo Juyi ascended quickly to become an influential literati and a top official of the Tang court. His rise was largely due to his various successes in the civil service examinations. Bo Juyi was known for his adoration of beautiful women, liaisons with courtesans, an intimate relationship with his wife, and extensive contact with women of lower classes. Bo left a total of 3,840 pieces of writing, more than any other literati in the entire Tang period, providing us with a great resource in understanding Tang society and Tang culture.

the woman by appealing to certain higher-order Confucian principles, like compassion and filial piety. Taken together these four essays suggest that for all their embeddedness in a patriarchal family structure, Confucian values could be invoked to defend women as well as accuse them. The fifth case, by contrast, goes the other way, siding with the people who regard a widow as unchaste because of the way she seeks to avenge her husband's murder. The woman is criticized for promising marriage in order to gain an assassin's cooperation in her plan. The ideal of only one marriage in a woman's lifetime, apparently, is more sacred than her understandable desire for vengeance.

Ping Yao

Tang Civil Service Examination Sample Questions and Answers

(1) When C's wife was observing the rituals of mourning, C played musical instruments by her side. The wife criticized his action, but C disagreed. If there is mourning, there should be grief. Whoever sees mourning should act respectfully. Music meant to enhance happiness should be used appropriately. The most valuable thing between a husband and a wife is empathy, not to mention that mourning and celebration are two separate matters. C's wife is in grief, but C did not remove musical instruments from his house. He continually indulged in the sonorous sound of the music and thus impaired the marital harmony. He not only neglected a husband's duty but also violated the proper mourning rules. If one is still wearing the mourning garments, it is a great grief. How could you feel comfortable playing instruments to satisfy your ears under such circumstances? C's behavior very much contradicted the proper respect between a husband and wife, and truly violated the mourning decorum of human beings. He thus caused disharmony in the marriage by creating a conflict of pleasure and sorrow. It is said that one should change one's attitude at once when seeing a person wearing a mourning garment, and that people should stop playing music if their neighbor is having a funeral. C indeed does not have a heart of compassion and should be punished as an ignoramus.

(2) B was working in the fields while waiting for his wife to bring him his meal. However, the wife never brought the meal to him. On the way to the fields, she met her father who told her that he was hungry. The wife thus fed her father the meal. B was very angry and dismissed the wife. The wife complained. A wife resembles the earth while a husband resembles the heaven; there-

fore, it is her duty to be obedient to her husband. However, when it comes to the general principles of human nature, it is the father to whom we owe all our debt. It is appropriate to present food to the elders first, while meals to those in the field can always wait. The husband anxiously waited for the wife to bring the meal to the field. He was expecting the proper respect between a couple. On the other hand, the father was truly hungry, and he knew that a filial child would feed her parents. Although the wife disobeyed the rules of marriage, her filial action reflected her love for her parents. Why would the husband not praise the wife's devotion toward her father, instead of expressing anger over the fact that she failed to bring a meal? Whom did she worry about the most? Apparently she chose not to ignore her father's feeling. It is desirable to have a perfect situation, but when things are not ideal, one should always act like a gentleman. If even animals take care of their parents, how could B react in such an ignorant manner? It is unacceptable to me that the harmonious relationship between a husband and wife should be disrupted by such an action.

(3) *A's wife yelled at a dog in front of her mother-in-law. A was agitated and thus expelled her. A's wife appealed, claiming that the divorce did not fall on the "Seven Grounds for Dismissing a Wife."*[2] *A cited "being disrespectful to parents-in-law."* The wife's conduct was flawed and certainly contradicted a wife's duties. However, if a man cannot tolerate a small mistake, how can he fulfill a husband's duty of being congenial to his wife? Although A fulfilled his obligation of filial piety and respect, he surely neglected his duty of marital harmony. Cooking meals for the parents-in-law is how a daughter-in-law shows her obedience, and we did not hear that A's wife failed in that respect. Yelling at a dog may be less than appropriate, but why can't A be more forgiving toward small grudges? If a woman is soft-spoken but otherwise quite senseless, I would be worried. If a man cannot forgive a slip of the tongue, then can he find anyone who has not made a mistake in his entire life? Since A has been respectful to his mother, it will be appropriate for him to make up with his wife as well.

---

2 "Seven Grounds for Dismissing a Wife" are rules for filing a divorce. They were set by Confucian scholars during the first century B.C.E. in *The Record of Rites*. The seven grounds are: bearing no male heir, adultery, being disrespectful to parents-in-law, being talkative, stealing, jealousy, and terminal illness.

(4) After A dismissed his wife, she committed a crime. She asked to be excused from punishment on the ground of Offspring Protection.[3] *A angrily rejected her plea.* Marriage is meant to associate two families, but disharmony will happen from time to time. Nonetheless, a mother's years of devotion in rearing a child should never be disregarded. Although the male phoenix (the husband) may have been deprived of a harmonious marriage, how could its offspring (the child) forget his mother's caring? In this case, the husband only remembered the couple's distressful past and thus failed to comply with the plain meaning of the Tang Code.

When Wang Ji dismissed his wife, he did not marry again. When Mr. Kong ousted his mother, he still took care of her.[4] A mother's effort in raising her children should always be taken into consideration, especially in rescuing her when she is in an unfortunate situation. Furthermore, although the marriage was not a harmonious one, appeasing a mother would reflect the virtue of filial piety. Although a small piece of property may have to be sacrificed in order to do this, it is the husband's obligation to redeem his ex-wife based on Offspring Protection. Even though the husband still held grudges against the ex-wife, how could he disregard the bond between a mother and her children? One hears the happiness of having children whenever he recalls the song of "The Plantain";[5] how can anyone not protect his lineage when he contemplates the meaning of the song of "The Climbing Plant."[6]

The husband's rejection is unreasonable, while the wife's request is sincere and appropriate.

(5) H's husband died of a robbery; H thus sought for an assassin to kill the robber and promised to be his wife if he succeeded. People accused H of lacking chastity. H objected to it. Marital love comes from devotion, so how can one bestow it merely to satisfy a grudge? If a woman marries again, the love between her and her husband is severed. What is the purpose, then, of carrying out this revenge? H planned on wiping out her

---

[3] Article 15 of the *Tang Code* stipulates that if a woman offends her husband or maliciously harms him or his relatives, she can avoid any penalty on the ground that she had given birth to his child. This protection extends to divorcees.

[4] Both Wang and Kong were figures of ancient tales.

[5] "The Plantain" is found in *The Book of Odes*. It expresses sympathy towards people with grave illness. In Chinese literary tradition, the plantain also symbolizes fertility.

[6] "The Climbing Plant" is also a piece from *The Book of Odes*. It describes the miseries of the Zhou people. A climbing plant was often used by literati to symbolize the protection of one's lineage.

grievances and thus neglected propriety. Although H wanted the robber dead so she would have no regrets, her promise of a marriage contradicted the ideal of female chastity. Moreover, she was still in the mourning period, when a remarriage certainly was not justifiable. If a woman lost the dignity of a "not yet dead,"[7] what would she have even had she succeeded in revenge? It is not an offense if a woman does not carry out revenge for her husband. On the other hand, she should feel terribly ashamed of herself if she does not live up to the expectations of female virtue. *The Book of Odes* stresses the vow of faithfulness. This has been known for a hundred generations. *The Record of Rites* stipulates that a woman should not remarry. That says it all. H should not imitate Lady Zhu who lacked chastity; instead, she should follow the good example of Gongjiang.[8]

---

[7] In Chinese society, the widow is often referred as "not yet dead," in order to honor her bond to the deceased husband. It implies that the purpose of the widow's remaining life is to wait to join the spouse in the afterlife.

[8] Both Lady Zhu and Gongjiang are recorded in Liu Xiang's *Lienüzhuan* (*Biographies of Women*).

THE DAOIST GODDESS, QUEEN MOTHER OF THE WEST

(*Xiwangmu*)

西王母

From Assembled Transcendents of the Fortified Walled City

(*Yongcheng jixian lu*)

墉城集仙錄

Du Guangting

杜光庭

The Queen Mother of the West (Xiwangmu) was the highest goddess of Daoism, the native major religion of China from medieval through early modern times. As her name suggests, she was a ruler and royal ancestress. In addition, she governed the West, the region of death and eternal life. The West is the direction associated with yin, the dark female force. The Queen Mother had the authority to grant or withhold individual immortality, the goal of Daoist believers. She also governed relations between gods and humans. Finally, she was the patron of women in Daoism, especially women outside the family such as nuns and courtesans.

The text translated here comes from the Assembled Transcendents of the Fortified Walled City (Yongcheng jixian lu). This collection of lives of goddesses and female saints, compiled by the Tang dynasty Daoist master and courtier Du Guangting (850–933 C.E.), is the only work in the Daoist canon devoted exclusively to accounts of female figures. In his entry on the goddess, Du Guangting

Translated by Suzanne Cahill.

uses her formal title: Jinmu yuanjun *("Primordial Ruler, Metal Mother"). Du's hagiographical account of the Queen Mother takes the form of a biography such as those found in the official dynastic histories. Like the official biographer of an important person, Du includes his subject's name, rank, lineage, place of origin, and significant deeds. Like an official historian, Du also makes editorial comments intended to edify his readers. This form of writing had legitimacy and familiarity among his literati audience, lending credibility to accounts of often mysterious and otherworldly events. Du Guangting's intentions in writing his account are to preserve information about the acts of the goddess among humans, give the faithful an accurate picture of her appearance for their visualization exercises, and encourage the religious practices of his own tradition, the Supreme Pure Realm school of Daoism. Submitting it to the emperor, he also hoped to promote Daoism as an effective means of salvation in times of peril and inspire the court to support the Daoist church.*

In keeping with her eminence, the Queen Mother's biography is unusually long. It contains material from several earlier sources, both literary and canonical. Du begins by listing several titles by which she is known, identifying them as diverse expressions of a single being who represents the ultimate yin. *Next we read of her origin and that of her consort, the Eastern King, Wood Sire, from the primordial* Dao *at the beginning of creation. Her birth and her mandate to nourish living beings and protect all women assert her primacy as a deity. Du then turns to a description of her paradise on Mount Kunlun, a mythical mountain far to the west in the exotic occident. He names other places linked to her cult. He describes her appearance as a beautiful, mature, elite woman of the upper classes. She wears a headdress shaped like the brake wheel of a celestial loom with which she weaves the universe into being. Du must delineate her precisely so adepts can visualize her correctly. Reconciling contradictory images, Du claims that portrayals of the goddess as part tiger are mistaken references to her feline messenger. Her teacher, the Celestial King of the Primordial Commencement, is one of a triad of primal Daoist deities; her position in the lineage of such an important teacher underscores her legitimacy and power. With such introductory matters covered, Du Guangting moves to his real interest: her encounters with human heroes.*

The first human the Queen Mother meets is the Yellow Emperor (Huangdi), legendary first Chinese emperor and first Daoist immortal, founder of the Chinese imperial system and traditional Chinese medicine. The Queen Mother grants Huangdi a magical talisman that assures him victory in the battle between chaos and order that results in the founding of China. Her later gifts verify his legitimacy and teach him the means to become an immortal.

Next Du Guangting narrates two short tales in which the Queen Mother bestows seminal gifts upon early sages of Confucianism and Daoism. When she encounters the legendary emperor and paragon of Confucian virtue, Shun, she gives him tokens that attest to his political legitimacy and cosmic power. Later she teaches Laozi, the attributive founder of Daoism and one of its highest deities, the contents of a major text associated with him. Also present at that time is the gatekeeper Yin Xi, who according to legend forced Laozi to transcribe a foundational text of Daoism, the Daodejing *("Scripture of the Way and its Power").*[1]

After mythological persons, Du turns his attention to actual historical figures. The Queen Mother of the West meets King Mu of the Zhou dynasty (r. 1001–946 B.C.E.) by the Turquoise Pond on Mount Kunlun. As the story goes, he traveled with his eight exquisite steeds to paradise, where they toasted each other, exchanged sad poems, and parted. He wanted to learn her secrets of immortality, but duty to his people called him home. He returned to his capital and subsequently died. After relating King Mu's story, Du Guangting takes the opportunity to give his readers a lesson on the various classes of immortals.

About a thousand years later (as long as some accounts say it takes the peaches of immortality on her tree to ripen), the Queen Mother descends from the heavens with an elaborate entourage to visit Chang'an. She sweeps into the court of the Martial Thearch of the Han (Han Wudi, r. 140–87 B.C.E.). The year is 110 B.C.E. The emperor, a devout Daoist, receives her with great ceremony and requests her teaching. She provides him with a feast including peaches of immortality, a performance of divine music and dance, and a long lecture on the benefits of asceticism. She encourages him to fast and meditate rather than ingest elixir drugs, of which she then recites a long list. He vows to become her disciple. In the end, unable to stop making war and behaving licentiously, the emperor dies and his precious texts go up in flames. Emperor Wu, like King Mu, was a flawed but admirable human hero who held immortality in his grasp and then lost it. The two rulers' stories, favorites of later Chinese writers and artists, have both tragic and erotic resonance.

The last encounter of the goddess and a human recorded by Du Guangting takes place in 1 B.C.E. The Queen Mother successfully passes on her teachings along with a divine wife to Mao Ying, god of Mount Mao and a patron deity of the Supreme Pure Realm school of Daoism. The divine wife is Lady Wei Huacun, herself a major deity of the same Daoist school. After investing Mao Ying and his two younger brothers, the Queen Mother of the West returns with her attendants to her holy mountain.

The final part of Du Guangting's account recapitulates the main functions of the goddess as a teacher, transmitter of sacred scriptures, and keeper of the keys to immortality. He leaves the door open for further visits from the Queen Mother to our world by closing with the statement: "This is not a complete account." And, in fact, the goddess has continued to appear throughout Chinese history, most recently to groups of women in Taiwan today who write down and publish texts they say she transmits to them while possessing their spirits.

Suzanne Cahill

---

[1] See pp. 67–72 for some selections from the *Daodejing*.

Names and Titles

The Primordial Ruler, Metal Mother, is the same as Metal Mother of Tortoise Mountain, She of the Nine Numens and the Grand Marvel. One source calls her Metal Mother of Tortoise Terrace, She of the Grand Numina and the Nine Radiances. Another source calls her Queen Mother of the West. She is, in fact, the Perfected Marvel of the Western Florescence and the Ultimate Worthy of the Grotto Yin.

Origin of the Goddess and Her Consort

At the time of the Former Way, the breaths were congealed and quiescent, deeply imbued with and embodying non-action. About to disclose and lead to the mysterious accomplishment of creation, and to produce by transformation the myriad phenomena, first the Way produced [the Queen Mother's consort] Wood Sire by transformations from the breath of the perfected realization of the eastern florescence. Wood Sire was born beside the Cyan Sea, in the Barrens of the Gray-Green Numen, where he governs the breaths of *yang* harmonies, and arranges the internal structure of the eastern quadrant. He is also called King Sire.

Then the Way produced Metal Mother by transformation from the breath of the perfected marvel of the western florescence. The Queen Mother was born at the Yi River in Divine Island. Jue is her surname and Kou her clan. As soon as she was born, she soared up in flight. She governs the breaths of the *yin* numina and arranges the internal structure of the western quadrant. She is also called the Queen Mother.

In all respects, she derives her substance from the great nonexistent; she nurtures her spirit with the mysterious enigma. In the midst of impenetrable clouds in the western quadrant, the unmixed seminal breaths of the great Way were divided, and the breaths were bound together to make her shape. Together with the Eastern King, Wood Sire, through structuring of the two primal breaths, she nourishes and raises heaven and earth, firing and casting the myriad phenomena. She embodies the basis of the pliant and yielding, functioning as the origin of the ultimate *yin*. Her position corresponds to the western quadrant. She mothers and nourishes [all] classes and categories of beings. In Heaven, beneath Heaven, in the

three worlds and the ten directions, all women who ascend to transcendence and attain the Way are her dependents.

Her Home in the Daoist Western Paradise

The palaces and watchtowers where she lives are located in the capital
city of the Western Nuo at Pestle Peak in the Tortoise Mountain
range, and in the hunting parks of Mysterious Orchard and Vacant
Wind peaks at Mount Kunlun. There are metal city walls of a thousand layers, surrounding twelve jade-storied buildings, with watchtowers of rose-gem florescence, halls of radiant cyan, nine-storied
mysterious terraces, and purple kingfisher cinnabar chambers. On the
left, the palace compound is girded by the Turquoise Pond; on the
right, it is ringed by Kingfisher River. Beneath the mountains, Weak
River, in nine layers of swells and rolling waves, rushes along for one
hundred thousand feet. Unless one has a whirlwind cart with feathered wheels, he can never reach this place. The jade watchtowers mentioned above stick up into the heavens; green terraces receive the
empyrean. Under azure blue-gem eaves, inside vermilion purple chambers joined blue-gems make variegated curtains, and the bright moon
shines distinctly on all four sides.

Her Appearance

She wears a flowered *sheng* headdress [a crown in the shape of a celestial loom with which she weaves the universe]. She carries at her belt
numinous emblems.

   Her attendants on the left are transcendent girls; her attendants on
the right are feathered lads. Precious canopies match reflections, while
feathered banners shade the courtyard. Beneath the balustrade and
steps of her shaded courtyard, the grounds are planted with white
bracelet trees and a cinnabar diamond forest. There are myriad stalks
of "hollow blue" mineral, and a thousand lengths of turquoise tree
trunks. Even when there is no wind, divine reeds spontaneously harmonize sounds, clinking like jade belt pendants. In all cases, they
perform the timbers of the eight unions.

   Her divine isle-land is southwest of Mount Kunlun. As the *Erya*[2]

---

[2] A Han dynasty glossary for reading the classics.

[a Han dynasty glossary for reading the classics] says, "This is the Queen Mother's land beneath the sun."[3] It also says, "The Queen Mother has disheveled hair and wears a *sheng* headdress. She has tiger's teeth and is good at whistling."[4] Now this is actually the Queen Mother's envoy, the spirit of the white tiger from the metal quadrant. It is not the Queen Mother's veritable shape.

Her Teacher

The Celestial King of the Primordial Commencement bestowed upon her the Register of the Ninefold Radiance from Tortoise Mountain, from the Primordial Unification of the Myriad Heavens. With it he commissioned her to control and summon the myriad numina, to unify and gather the realized ones and the paragons, to oversee oaths, and to verify faith. At all formal observances of feathered beings of the various heavens, at meetings during court appearances or feasts of celestial worthies and supreme paragons, at the places for examining and editing texts, the Queen Mother in all cases presides, reflecting divine light on the proceedings. Precious Scriptures from the Realm of Supreme Clarity, Jade Writs of the Three Grottos, and in general whatever is bestowed at ordination: all these are either obstructed or given by her.

Meeting with the Legendary Yellow Emperor

Formerly the Yellow Thearch punished Chiyou[5] for his violence and aggression. Before he was checked, Chiyou performed illusionistic transformations using many methods. He raised the wind and summoned the rain; he blew smoke and spat mist. The leaders and masses of the Yellow Thearch's army grew greatly confused. The thearch returned home to rest in a fold of Mount Tai. Bewildered, he went to bed depressed.

The Queen Mother sent an envoy wearing a dark fox cloak to bestow a talisman upon the thearch, saying, "Grand Unity is located on its front, Heavenly Unity on its back. Whoever obtains it will

---

[3] Subcelestial home.

[4] This description is from *The Classic of Mountains and Seas.* See selections, pp. 93–94.

[5] Later a war god.

conquer; when he attacks, he will overcome." The talisman was three inches wide and a foot long, with a blue luster like jade. Cinnabar-colored drops of blood formed the text upon it. The thearch hung it at his waist.

Once he had done this, the Queen Mother commanded a woman with a human head and bird's body to come to him. She told the thearch, "I am the Mysterious Woman of the Nine Heavens," and bestowed [sacred scriptures] upon the thearch. [These included] plans of *Yin* and *Yang* for Five Intentions from the Three Palaces, Techniques from the Grand Unity for Concealing the *Jia* Cyclicals, Calculating the Six *Ren* Cyclicals,[6] and Pacing the Dipper, in addition to the Mechanism of the Yin Talisman, Five Talismans of Numinous Treasure, and the Text of Fivefold Victory. Consequently, he subdued Chiyou at Zhongji. After he had exterminated this descendent of Shen Nong and executed the rebel Yu Wang at Banquan, the empire was greatly settled. Then he built his capital at Zhuolu on the Upper Valley.

After a number of years, the Queen Mother sent her envoy, the white tiger spirit. Then, riding a white tiger, she perched in the thearch's courtyard and bestowed upon him some territorial maps.

In later years, she further bestowed upon the thearch the [scripture known as the] *Rectified and Realized Way of Pure Quietude and Non-Action*. The words to it went:

> If drinking and pecking [eating grains] do not cease, your body will not become light. If thinking and worrying do not cease, your spirits will not become pure. If sounds and forms do not cease, your heart will not become tranquil. If your heart is not tranquil, then your spirits will not become numinous. If your spirits are not numinous, then the Way cannot accomplish its requisite marvels. It does not depend on paying homage to the stars and treating the Dipper with ceremony, causing yourself bitter suffering and exhausting your frame and wealth. It depends on not "building" anything and yet building the Way of the divine transcendents deep within your heart. Then you can extend your life.

Meeting with Legendary Emperor Shun

After that, Yu Shun took the throne. The Queen Mother sent an envoy to bestow a white jade bracelet upon Shun. She also bestowed some

---

[6] *Jia* and *ren* are units in the traditional Chinese system for measuring time.

territorial maps on his advisor, Yi. Consequently, Shun extended the Yellow Thearch's territory of nine isle-lands to twelve isle-lands. The Queen Mother also sent her envoy to bestow an illustrious tube upon Shun, which he blew to harmonize the eight winds.

Meeting with Laozi

In the twenty-fifth year of King Zhao of the Zhou dynasty (1028 B.C.E.), when the planet Jupiter was in B-hare (*yiqiu*),[7] Lord Lao and the realized person Yin Xi went traveling to look around the eight cords.[8] They wandered west to the Tortoise Terrace. On their behalf, the Queen Mother explicated the Scripture of Constant Purity and Quiet. Thus the Transcendent Sire Ge Xuan[9] of the Left Palace of the Grand Bourne, in his preface to that scripture, states:

> Formerly I received it from the Thearchic Lord of the Eastern Flores-
> cence. The Thearchic Lord of the Eastern Florescence received it from
> the Thearchic Lord of the Golden Watchtowers. The Thearchic Lord of
> the Golden Watchtowers received it from the Queen Mother of the West.
> In every case it was transmitted orally from one to the next, without
> recording worlds or graphs. At this time, I am writing it down and making
> a record for the generations.

Meeting with the Zhou Dynasty Ruler, King Mu (r. 1001–946 B.C.E.)

A long time later, King Mu gave the command to harness his eight fine steeds in two teams of four. In the team drawing the imperial chariot, the inside pair of horses consisted of Flowery Bay on the right and Green Ears on the left. The outside pair of horses was Red Thoroughbred on the right and White Sacrifice on the left. In the main chariot, Father Cao was holding the reins and Shang was to the right. In the team of the next vehicle, the inside horses were Big Yellow on the right and Faster-Than-Wheels on the left, while the outside

---

[7] *Yiqiu* is a unit the same system as *jia* and *ren* for measuring time.

[8] Eight longitudinal markers of the night sky.

[9] Daoist Patriarch of the third C.E.

horses were Robber Black on the left and Son of the Mountain on the right. Bo Yao was in charge of the chariot, Can Bai acted as rein-holder, and Pai Wu was to the right.

Riding full speed ahead for a thousand li,[10] they reached the nation of the Great Sou Clan. The head of the Great Sou Clan head then offered as tribute the blood of white swans for the king to drink; he set out ox and horse milk to use for washing the king's feet. After the men from the two vehicles drank, they proceeded along the road. They spent the night in a fold of Mount Kunlun on the sunny side of the Red Water River. Another day, they ascended Kunlun Hill in order to inspect the palace of the Yellow Thearch. They heaped up dirt to make a mound on it, in order to hand down knowledge of it to later generations.

Subsequently, King Mu was a guest of the Queen Mother of the West. As they toasted each other with drinks at the side of the Turquoise Pond, the Queen Mother of the West composed poems for the king. The king matched them. Their lyrics were sad. Then he observed where the sun set: in a single day, it had gone ten thousand li. The king sighed and said, "I, the Unique Person, am not over-abounding with virtue. Later generations will certainly trace back and count my excesses!" It is also said that the king grasped a white jade tablet and heavy, multicolored tabby weave silk, offering them in order to acquire the secrets of the Queen Mother's longevity. She sang the "Poem of the White Clouds." On top of Cover Mountain, he carved stone to record his traces, then returned home.

Interlude: Lecture on Classes of Transcendents

As for the transcendents in the world who have ascended to heaven, in general they fall into nine classes. The first supreme transcendents are called Realized Rulers of the Nine Heavens. The next transcendents are the Realized Illustrious of the Three Heavens. The third are called Grand Supreme Realized People. The fourth are called Realized People Who Fly Through the Heavens. The fifth are called Numinous Transcendents. The sixth are called Realized People. The seventh are called Numinous People. The eighth are called Flying Transcendents. The ninth are called Transcendent People. All these class ranks may not be skipped or superceded.

---

[10] A Chinese "mile"; a measurement of distance now used to refer to a kilometer.

So it is that at the time one ascends to heaven, first one must salute the Wood Sire, and afterwards pay a ceremonial visit to the Metal Mother. Only when the business of receiving transmissions and ordinations is finished can one ascend to the Nine Heavens. One enters the Three Clear Realms, salutes the Grand Supreme, and receives an audience with the Celestial Worthy of the Primordial Commencement.

Thus it is that at the beginning of the Han dynasty there were four or five children playing in the road. One child sang: "Wearing a blue apron, I enter gate; I bow to Metal Mother and salute Wood Sire." Among the people of the time, no one recognized him. Only Zhang Zifang[11] recognized him. Zhang went over to salute him, saying: "This is none other than a jade lad of the King and Sire of the East. A transcendent person who attains the Way and ascends to heaven must bow to the Metal Mother and salute the Wood Sire. Anyone who is not himself a master who skims the void and climbs to realization cannot recognize the ferrying over."[12]

Meeting with Han Wudi, the Martial Emperor of the Han Dynasty, in 110 B.C.E.

The Filial and Martial Illustrious Thearch of the Han, Liu Che, was fond of the Way of extending life. During the original year of the Primordial Enfeoffment reign period (110 B.C.E.), he climbed the heights of Marchmount Song[13] and there built a terrace for seeking realized ones. He fasted, observed abstinence, and made his thoughts seminal. On an E-dragon (*wuchen*) day in the fourth month, the Queen Mother sent Wang Zideng, the Jade Girl from the Fortified Walled City, to come and talk with the thearch for her. She said: "I have heard that you are willing to slight the emoluments of the four seas and keep at a distance the noble rank of a myriad vehicles in order to seek the veritable Way of extended life. How diligent! On the seventh day of the seventh month, I will certainly come for a little while."

The thearch inquired of Dongfang Shuo[14] to find the proper

---

[11] An early hero of the cult of immortality who departed in 187 B.C.E.

[12] Liberation of a transcendent.

[13] The holy mountain of the center.

[14] A courtier of Han Wudi who was considered an immortal in disguise.

response to this divinity. Then he purified himself and fasted for one hundred days, burning incense in the palace.

On the night in question, after the second watch,[15] a white cloud arose in the southwest. Dense and thick, it arrived and crossed over the courtyard of the palace. It gradually drew near; then came clouds and evening mists of nine colors. Pipes and drums shook empty space. There were semblances of dragons, phoenixes, men, and horses, with a guard mounted on *qilin*[16] and harnessing deer. There were ranks of chariots and heavenly horses. With rainbow banners and feathered streamers, the radiance from a thousand vehicles and myriad outriders illuminated the palace watchtowers. Celestial transcendents, both followers and officials, arranged in ranks, numbered one hundred thousand multitudes. All were ten feet or more tall. Once they had arrived, the followers and officials disappeared.

The Queen Mother rode an imperial carriage of purple clouds, harnessed with nine-colored, dappled *qilin*. Tied around her waist, she wore the whip of the celestial realized ones; as a pendant she had a diamond numinous seal. In her clothing of multicolored tabby weave silk with a yellow background, the patterns and variegated colors were bright and fresh. The radiance of metal made a shimmering gleam. At her waist was a double-bladed sword for dividing phosphors. Knotted flying clouds made a great cord. On top of her head was a great floriate topknot. She wore the crown of the realized ones with hanging beaded strings of daybreak. She stepped forth on shoes with squared, phoenix-patterned soles of rose-gem. Her age might have been about twenty. Her celestial appearance eclipsed and put in the shade all others. She was a realized numinous being.

She ascended the dais and sat down facing east. The thearch saluted her, kneeled, and inquired how she fared. Then he stood in attendance. After a good long while, she called the thearch and allowed him to be seated. She laid out a celestial feast consisting of fragrant flowers, a hundred fruits, purple mushrooms, and magic mushrooms —as variegated as prismatic shellfish. Their seminal essences were rare and odd; they were not what regularly exists in this world. The thearch could not even name them.

She also ordered a serving girl to fetch peaches. A jade basin was filled with seven of the fruits. They were as large as bustards' eggs. She took four and gave them to the thearch. Mother herself ate three of them. When the thearch had eaten his peaches, he hastily put away the pits. Mother asked him why he was doing this. He said, "I just want

---

[15] 9:00–11:00 P.M.

[16] The *qilin* is a mythical auspicious beast.

to plant them." Mother told him, "These peaches only bear fruit once in three thousand years. The land in the Middle Kingdom is poor; even if you plant them, they will not grow. So what is the point?"

Thereupon the Queen Mother commanded her serving girls: Wang Zideng to play the eight-orbed chimes, Dong Shuangcheng to blow the Cloud Harmony Mount Organ, Sh Gongzi to strike the jade sounding stones from the courtyard of Mount Kunlun, Xu Feiqiung to sound the Thunder Numen Flute, Wan Linghua to hit the musical stone of Wuling, Fan Chengqun to strike the Lithophone of the Grotto Yin, Duan Anxiang to play the "Harmony of the Nine Heavens," and An Faying to sing the "Tune of the Mysterious Numen." The whole ensemble of sounds was exciting and distinct; their numinous timbers startled empty space.

When the song was finished, the thearch got down from his mat, kowtowed, and asked about the Way of extending life. The Queen Mother told him: "If you can consider glory cheap and delight in humble living quarters, if you can become addicted to the void and acquire a taste for the Way, then you will naturally revert to excellence. But if your passions are licentious and your body desirous, if your lewd behavior is unbalanced and your excesses extreme, if you kill and attack in battle without the right to do so, then you will waste and squander your vital energies. Excessive licentiousness becomes a means to rip open your body, and lust becomes an ax to smash your body. Killing produces an echo in response; profligacy wastes the heart. If you store up desire, then your spirits will fail. If you accumulate all these pollutions, then your life span will be cut short. With your own unworthy body, you provide lodging for thieves who will annihilate your frame. It is just as if you took a piece of wood a little over a foot long, and attacked it with a hundred knives. If you want in this fashion to sever and cast off the three corpses and to make your body whole and permanently enduring, it cannot be done. It would be the same as a wingless quail wanting to drum its wings on the Heavenly Pond, or a mushroom born in the morning wanting to enjoy whole springs and autumns.

"Cleanse yourself of this whole multitude of disorders; reject annihilation and change your intentions. Protect your spirits and vital energies in the scarlet archives; lock up the palace of debauchery and do not open it. Still your profligacy and extravagance in a quiet room. Cherish all living beings and do not endanger them. Observe compassion, devote yourself to clarity, refine your vital energies, and hoard your seminal essence. If you behave in this fashion, you will be close to ideal. If you do not act like this [seeking the Way of extending life] would be like trying to cross the Long River carrying rocks."

The thearch received the Queen Mother's admonitions on his knees, then said: "I, She, the untalented one, am plunged into a capricious mode of life. Having inherited the work of my predecessors, I am impeded by earthly ties. In my punishments and government, I rely upon error and falsehood. My sins pile up, making hills and mountains. After today, please allow me to practice your words of instruction."

The Queen Mother said: "As for the Way of nourishing your nature and the essential requirements of regulating the internal order of your body, by now you already have a solid understanding of these. But you must practice diligently without being remiss. Formerly, on the Lofty Empyrean Terrace, my master, the Celestial Worthy of the Primordial Commencement, bestowed on me his essential words: 'Whoever wants to extend his life must first grasp it within his own body before going outside his body.' Make firm and preserve the three ones. Protect the numinous root [tongue]. Take the floriate vintage of the mysterious vale [saliva] and force it into the deep treasure passage. Irrigate and extend the pure seminal essence; have it enter the celestial gate [mouth]. At the golden apartment, have it turn and go inside the central barrier [nose]. Then divide the bright light into blue and white, and have it reach the mud ball [in the center of your brain].[17]

"Nourish the fluids and lock up the seminal essence and you will make the body and spirits whole. Keep the spirits of the three palaces in good order and well defended; then you will preserve the scarlet palace. The unflowing source of the E-snake (*wusi*)[18] organ from the yellow courtyard [spleen] will penetrate and pass through the five viscera and twelve threads. It will be exhaled from and inhaled into the six archives [lesser viscera]. Then the cloud-souls and earth-souls will be delighted. You can drop the hundred afflictions of the present place and block extremes of heat and cold. You will protect your seminal essence, retain your life span, and permanently extend and preserve your life.

"This is what is called the Veritable and Requisite Way of Exhaling and Inhaling the Grand Harmonies to Preserve and Protect the Spontaneous. Even when ordinary people do it, all of them automatically extend their lives. They can also control and make messengers of ghosts and divinities, and can wander and play on the Five Marchmounts. All they cannot do is fly through empty space or ascend into the void. If you can practice this, it will be adequate to

---

17 This describes the practice of internal alchemy.

18 *Wusi* is a unit in the traditional measurement of time and in this case, of space.

allow you to escape this world. Of those who have studied transcendence, there has never been one who did not start with this.

"Now when we reach things like numinous drugs of the Grand Supreme, rare phenomena of the Supreme Thearch [drugs] produced in concealment beneath the earth, and marvelous grasses from the multilayered clouds: these are all drugs of the divine transcendents. One who obtains drugs of the supreme class will not grow old until the age of Latter Heaven. These are what beings of the Grand Supreme ingest. They are not treasured by middle transcendents.

"Some drugs of the middle category, if obtained and ingested, will allow one not to pass away until the age of Latter Heaven. These are in fact what celestial realized beings ingest. They are not pursued by lower transcendents. Among this next class of drugs are: ninefold cinnabar elixir and gold fluid, purple floriate rainbow blossoms, nine times recycled elixir of the Grand Clear Realm, liqueur of five clouds, mysterious frost and scarlet snow, three ascending and prancing yellows, white incense from Ying Isle-Land in the east [drugs] born in flight from the Mysterious Isle-Land, eight minerals and a thousand fungi, *weixi* plant and ninefold radiance, stone gall from Western Flow, blue-green cash from Watchet-Wave River, leftover grain rations from High Hill [produce of] Piled Stone Mountain and Rose-Gem Field, recycled cinnabar elixir from the Grand Barrens, golden orchids from Chengzi, scarlet grasses with extended radiance, and cloud lads' flying bucklers.

"If one obtains and ingests these, he will ascend to heaven in broad daylight. They are what flying transcendents ingest. They are not anything heard of by earthly transcendents.

Among the lowest class of drugs are: pine and cedar resins, mountain ginger and sinking seeds, chrysanthemum flowers and water plantain, boxthorn and pachyma fungus, acorus rush and gate-winter [asparagus], great victory and yellow seeds [Solomon's seal], numinous flyer and red arrow, peach gum, wood, and blossoms, climbing hemp and connector-of-the-broken [teasel], *weirui* and golden thread.[19]

"Such are the lesser drugs. I have only enumerated a fraction of them. The botanicals are exceedingly numerous, their names numbering in the thousands. If you obtain and ingest them, you can thereby prolong your years. Although you cannot extend your enjoyment without any limits or ascend on high to the blue heavens, still they

---

[19] These are all elixir drugs. Some may be identified with certainty, but probably the author does not intend for us to understand all as this is esoteric knowledge.

may be used to make your body radiant and glossy and return a youth's complexion to you. They allow you to control flocks of ghosts and use them as messengers, and to become an earthly transcendent.

"Those who seek the Way must first follow these steps, then gradually they can reach distant victories. If you can inhale and exhale, and rein in the seminal essence, you will protect and make firm the spirits and breaths. When the seminal essence is not cast off, then you will permanently endure. If the breaths are extended and preserved, then you will not die. This method does not require expenditures for drugs and minerals, or the hard work of scheming to lay hands on them. Just grasp it in your own body. The common folk of a hundred surnames use this method daily, without recognizing it. This is therefore the Way of the supreme class, the requisite essential of naturalness.

"Furthermore, as for a person's single body: heaven stores it with spirits, the earth stores it with a shape, and the Way stores it with breaths. If the breaths are preserved, you live. If the breaths depart, you die. The myriad creatures as well as woody and herbaceous plants are all also like this. The body takes the Way as its basis. So how could you not nourish its spirits and make firm its breaths in order to complete your frame? For a person's corporeal frame and spirits together to be whole: that is what the supreme paragons valued. If the frame is annihilated, the spirits are cut off. How could this not be painful? Once you lose your present body, for myriad *kalpas*[20] it will not return. Don't you think you should treasure it? What I have been saying is in fact the words bestowed upon me by my master, the Celestial King of the Primordial Commencement. Afterward I will command the jade girl, Li Qingsun, to write it out and grant it to you. You are to put it skillfully into practice."

The Queen Mother, having commanded that her vehicles be harnessed, was on the point of departing, when the thearch got down from his mat, kowtowed, and requested that she stay. The Queen Mother then commanded her serving girl to summon the Lady of the Supreme Primordial to descend and join them at the thearch's palace. After a good long while, the Lady of the Supreme Primordial arrived. Again they sat. She provided a celestial feast. After a long time, the Queen Mother of the West ordered the Lady to bring out the Writ of the Eight Unions, the Veritable Shape of the Five Marchmounts, the Talismans of the Six Cyclicals of the Five Thearchs, and the [Talisman of the] Numinous Flying Beings: altogether twelve items.

---

[20] World ages (from Sanskrit).

She said: "The texts may be transmitted from above the heavens only once in four myriad kalpas. Once they are among humans, every forty years they may be bestowed upon a gentleman who possesses the Way."

The Queen Mother then commanded the serving girl Song Lingbin to open the cloud-patterned multicolored tabby weave silk bag and take out a fascicle to bestow on the thearch. The Queen Mother stood up holding the text. With her own hands, she granted it to the thearch. As she did so, the Queen Mother recited an incantation:

Heaven is high and Earth low;
The Five Marchmounts fix their configurations.
Spurting breaths of the Primordial Ford,
Mysterious seminal essences of the Great Conduits,
Nine paths encircling the heavens;
Extended peace of the six harmonies,
Eight Unions of the Grand Supreme,
Accomplishments of the flying celestials:
All are credentials of realized transcendents.
On the basis of these you communicate with numinous
    beings.
Leak them and you will fall into annihilation and putrescence;
Treasure them and you will return home to long-toothed old
    age.
You, Che, be careful of them!
I'm telling you, disciple Liu!

When the incantation was finished the thearch saluted and bowed to receive the Queen Mother's words: "Now that you are beginning to study the Way and have received talismans, it would be appropriate for you to perform special sacrifices to various veritable numina of the rivers and marchmounts and to purify yourself and fast before hanging the talismans on your belt. After forty years, if you are going to transmit and hand down what you possess, then Dong Zhongshu[21] and Li Shaojun[22] may be bestowed with it. You should be all the more diligent since you are the thearchic King. Sacrifice to the rivers and marchmounts in order to pacify the state and households. Cast tallies to the veritable numina to pray for the black-haired masses."

Her words finished, she commanded the chariots, giving the word to depart, together with the Lady of the Supreme Primordial. Their

---

[21] A Confucian thinker of the second century B.C.E. See selection, pp. 162–169.
[22] A Daoist magician of the same era.

followers and officials collected in the dark. When they were about
to ascend to heaven, she laughed, and pointed at Dongfang Shuo,
saying: "This is a little boy from my neighbor's household. His nature
is very mischievous. Three times he has come and stolen my peaches.
Formerly he was a transcendent official of the Grand Supreme, but
because he sank into drunkenness on jade wine and caused a loss of
harmony among the bureaucrats, he was banished to serve you. He is
not of the common run of men."

After that the Martial Thearch could not make use of the Queen
Mother's admonitions. He abandoned himself to strong drink and
good looks.[23] He killed and attacked without respite. He invaded the
Liao Peninsula to strike Korea, and opened communications with the
southwestern barbarians. He constructed terraces and kiosks, raising
them out of earth and wood. Inside the realm bounded by the four
seas, the people were depressed and angry. From this time on, he lost
the Way. He made an imperial visit to Xizhong in the northwest and
then presided over the three shrines at the Eastern Sea. The Queen
Mother did not come again. The texts he had received he arranged
on the Cedar Beam Terrace, where they were burned by a celestial fire.
Li Shaojun discarded his form and departed. Dongfang Shuo soared
up in flight and did not return. The affair of the shamans and their
dangerous potions arose. The thearch grew more and more regretful
and resentful.

In the second year of the Primordial Commencement reign period
(87 B.C.E.), the thearch died at Five Oaks Palace and was buried at the
Fertile Tumulus. Later the Daoist texts that had been deposited in the
Fertile Tumulus—fifty or more scrolls filling a golden box—came out
one day at Mount Baodu. There was also a jade casket and jade staff
that emerged in Fufeng market town. When [officials] examined the
Fertile Tumulus, they found it undisturbed as of old, and yet his casket
and staff had come out among people. This might be evidence of liberation of the corpse by entrusting it to shapes.[24]

Meeting with Lord Mao, God of Mount Mao and Patron of Supreme Pure Realm Daoism

Again there was the Great Lord Mao Ying who ruled over Bucklebent
Mountain in the south. In the second year of the Primordial

---

[23] Women, sexuality.

[24] Things, forms.

Longevity reign period (1 B.C.E.), in the eighth month, on the F-Cock (*chiyu*) day, the Realized Person of the Southern Marchmount, Lord Chi, and Wang Junfeng of the Western Walled City, along with various blue lads[25] followed the Queen Mother and descended together to Mao Ying's chambers. In an instant, the Celestial Illustrious Great Thearch sent his messenger in embroidered clothing, Ling Guangzi Qi, to present Ying with a divine seal and jade emblem. The Lord Thearch of Grand Tenuity sent the Autocrat's Notary of the Left Palace of the Three Heavens, Guan Xiutiao, to present Ying with an eight-dragon multicolored tabby weave silk carriage and purple-feathered floriate clothing. The Grand Supreme Lord of the Way sent the Dawn Assisting Grandee, Shi Shumen, to present Ying with the Veritable Talisman of the Metal Tiger and a folly bell of flowing metal. The Incomparable Lord of the Golden Watchtower commanded the Realized Person of the Grand Bourne to send the Jade Squires of Rectified Unity and Supreme Mystery: Wang Zhong, Bao Qiu, and others, to present Ying with swallow wombs of the four junctions and divine fungi of flowing brightness.

When the messengers from the four deities had finished their bestowals, they had Ying eat the fungi, hang the seal at his belt, don the clothing, straighten his cap, tie the talismans at his waist, grip the folly bell, and stand up. The messengers from the four told Ying: "He who eats concealed fungi from the four junctures will take up the position of Steward of the Realized Ones. He who eats jade fungi of the Golden Watchtowers will take up the position of Director of Destiny. He who eats metal blossoms of flowing brightness will take up the position of Director of Transcendent Registers. And he who eats the paired flying plants of extended luminosity will take up the position of Realized Sire. He who eats the grotto grasses of night radiance will always have the responsibility of governing the autocrat's notaries of the left and right. You have eaten all of these. Your longevity will be coequal with Heaven and Earth. Your place will be situated as the Supreme Realized Person who is Director of Destiny and Supreme Steward of the Eastern Marchmount [Mount Tai]. You will control all divine transcendents of the former Kingdoms of Wu and Yue, and all the mountains and water sources left of the Yangtze River."

Their words finished, all the messengers departed together. [Next] the Five Thearchic Lords[26] each in a square-faced chariot, descended in submission to [Mao Ying's] courtyard. They carried out the com-

---

25 Minor Daoist deities.

26 Deities of the four directions and the center.

mands of the Grand Thearch, presenting to Ying a purple jade plaque, writs carved in yellow gold, and patterns in nine pewters. They saluted Ying as Supreme Steward of the Eastern Marchmount, Realized Lord Who Is Director of Destiny, and Realized Person of the Grand Primordial. Their business finished, they all departed.

The Queen Mother and Ying's master, Lord Wang of the Western City, set forth drinks and a feast from the celestial kitchen for Ying. They sang the "Song of the Mysterious Numen." When the feast was over, the Queen Mother took Lord Wang and Ying to examine and inspect Ying's two younger brothers. Each had bestowed upon him the requisite essentials of the Way. The Queen Mother commanded the Lady of the Supreme Primordial to bestow on Mao Gu and Mao Zhong the Hidden Writs of the Supreme Empyrean, the Seminal Essence of the Way of Cinnabar Elixir and the Phosphors, and the like, comprising the precious scriptures of the Daoist Canon in Four Sections. The Queen Mother held the Hidden Writs of the Grand Empyrean and commanded her serving girl Zhang Lingzi to hold the oath of exchanging faith, while she bestowed [the texts] on Ying, Gu, and Zhong. The affair concluded, the Queen Mother of the West departed by ascending to heaven.

After this, the Primordial Ruler of the Purple Heavens, Lady Wei Huacun, purified herself and fasted on the Hidden Primordial Terrace at Yangluo Mountain. The Queen Mother of the West and the Incomparable Lord of the Golden Watchtower descended to the terrace. They were riding an eight-phosphor carriage. Together they had visited the Supreme Palace of the Pure Void and had received by transmission the Hidden Writs of the Realm of Jade Clarity in four scrolls in order to bestow them upon Huacun. At this time the Lady of the Three Primordials, Fengshuang Lizhu, along with the Left Transcendent Sire of the Purple Yang, Shi Luzheng, the Lofty Transcendent Sire of the Grand Bourne, Yan Kai Gongzi, the Realized Person of the Western City, Wang Fangping, the Realized Person of the Grand Void, Chi Songzi of the Southern Marchmount, and the Realized Person of Paulownia-Cedar Mountain, Wang Ziqiao—over thirty realized beings in all—each sang the "Tune of the Yang Song and Yin Song of the Grand Bourne."

Then the Queen Mother sang a song for them:

I harness my eight-phosphor carriage;
Like thunder! I enter the Realm of Jade Clarity.
Dragon pennants brush the top of the empyrean;
Tiger banners lead vermilion-clad men-at-arms!

Footloose and fancy-free: the Mysterious Ford separates me
   from the human world;
Among myriad flows, I have no temporary resting place.
Grievous—this alternate departing and lingering of unions;
When a kalpa is exhausted, heaven and earth are overturned.
She must seek a phosphor with no center,
Not dying and also not born,
Embodying the spontaneous Way,
Quietly contemplating and harmonizing the great stygian
   realm.
At Southern Marchmount she displays her veritable trunk,
Jade reflections shining on her accumulated essences.
Having the responsibility of office is not your affair;
Empty your heart and you will naturally receive numina.
This "Scarlet River Tune" [narrates] your auspicious meeting;
The joy you give each other is neverending.

The Queen Mother had finished her song, and the answering song
from the Lady of the Three Primordials also reached an end. Then
the Queen Mother, along with the Lady of the Three Primordials,
the Left Transcendent Sire of the Purple Yang, and the Transcendent
Sire of the Grand Bourne, as well as Lord Wang of the pure Void,
departed together with Wei Huacun. They went to the southeast and
all visited Mount Huo in the Heavenly Terrace Mountains. When
they passed the Golden Altar on Bucklebent Mountain, they gave a
feast for the Grand Primordial Realized Person Mao at the Grotto-
Heaven of the Floriate Yang. Leaving Huacun behind, beneath the
jade eaves of the grotto palace at Mount Huo, the whole flock of
realized beings ascended following the Queen Mother of the West
and returned to Tortoise Terrace.

The Grand Realized Metal Mother is master and maker of the
myriad classes of beings, teacher and leader of the whole flock of realized ones and paragons. Her position is honored and lofty; she holds
central control of the registration of both the secluded and the
revealed. Now, in the matter of approaching the grotto-mystery, one
must come in person to her court to receive the Way. And as for thank-
ing the spontaneous: effulgent ones attend her and then climb to transcendence. Therefore transmissions of grotto-mysteries and the
spontaneous are said to come from Master Metal Mother. This is in
fact the Queen Mother. In affairs for which evidence is given in the
mysterious scriptures, her traces are certainly numerous. This is not a
complete account.

45

THE DAOIST SAINT
XUE XUANTONG

薛玄同

From Assembled Transcendents of the
Fortified Walled City
(*Yongcheng jixian lu*)

墉城集仙錄

Du Guangting

杜光庭

Xue Xuantong was a female Daoist saint of the Tang dynasty. The biographical account of her life translated here is found in a work by Du Guangting (850–933 C.E.) called Assembled Transcendents of the Fortified Walled City (Yongcheng jixian lu), *the only text in the Daoist canon devoted exclusively to the lives of female subjects. Du's hagiography resembles in form both official biographies found in the dynastic histories and accounts of heroic women found in the* Lienüzhuan *tradition. Du Guangting was a late Tang courtier and Daoist master of the Supreme Pure Realm school, the tradition favored by the Tang royal family. In addition to telling Xue Xuantong's life story, Du Guangting also wants to convince the reader of her sanctity and promote the Daoist religion.*

To verify Xue Xuantong's sainthood, Du recounts her religious practices, her rewards, and the manner of her death. Her religious practices follow a progression from charitable good works and asceticism (fasting and celibacy), through ritual and chanting, to visualization and meditation. The Scripture of the Yellow Courtyard (Huangting jing) *that she recites is a classic account of gods and practices still found in the Daoist canon today.[1] In reward, Xue is visited by deities, includ-*

Translated by Suzanne Cahill.

[1] Weng Tu-chien, *Daozang Zimu Yinde: Combined Indices to the Authors and Titles of Books in Two Collections of Taoist Literature.* (Peking: Harvard-Yenjing Institute, 1935), HY#8.

ing a great goddess of Supreme Pure Realm Daoism, Lady Wei Huacun (d. c. 340 C.E.). Lady Wei encourages her efforts, gives her the elixir of immortality, and promises to take her back to heaven in eight years. Later Xue is approached on the banks of the Zhi River by heavenly hosts who summon her to paradise. At the moment of death, the saint is transformed, growing lustrous dark hair, appearing youthful, and emitting purple vapor. Cloud cranes, favored mounts of the divine transcendents, attend her passing. The next day, accompanied by heavenly commotion, her coffin flies open to reveal that her corpse is gone. Only light (overcoming the darkness of the tomb) and exotic fragrances (overcoming the stench of decay) remain. She has conquered death and escaped to heaven, gaining "liberation by means of the corpse" (shijie), a form of transcendence achieved by the holiest Daoist saints—proof of her sainthood.

    Xue Xuantong's exemplary life story shows how one Daoist woman faced conflicts between religious practice and loyalties to family and state. Unlike other female saints who were often unmarried nuns or hermits, Xue practiced Daoism within her marriage. She lived separately from her husband, the official Feng Hui. There is no record of her bearing children. When her choices caused friction, she endured Feng Hui's criticism and remained in his household without weakening in her resolve. Such gentle but successful defiance of the dominant patriarchal institutions must have been rare. During the Huang Chao rebellion (878–884 C.E.), Xue accompanied her husband and household into exile, first to Szechwan and then to Zhejiang, where she finally departed for the heavens.

    On the very day that Xue Xuantong's body disappeared, the local military governor Zhou Bao sent a hastily composed memorial to Emperor Xizong in Chengdu, Sichuan, where the emperor and his court had fled during the Huang Chao rebellion. The literati official Zhou Bao requested that Xue Xuantong's presence during his majesty's reign be interpreted as an auspicious omen, portending hope for the failing Tang dynasty, and that Xue be honored as a saint. Zhou's wishes were granted the following year.

Suzanne Cahill

Ms. Xue was the wife of Feng Hui, the Lesser Governor of Hezhong Province [in the southern part of modern Shansi]. Her Daoist name was Xuantong ("Dark Unity"). After being sent in marriage to Feng Hui at the age of twenty, she told him she wanted to live chastely and used illness as her pretext for dwelling alone. Having vowed to burn incense and chant Daoist scriptures, she consistently chanted the *Scripture of the Yellow Courtyard* two or three times a day.

    Thirteen years later, two blue-clad jade girls[2] descended to her room one night. Just before they arrived, radiance like that of the

---

[2] Minor Daoist deities.

moon illuminated her courtyard, and a fragrant wind breezed through. The season must have been early autumn. Although the scattering heat was intense just then, the clean cool void[3] acted as her parasol, while the wind breezed through as if the place were a grotto. The two girls announced: "The Primal Ruler of the Purple Barrens Who Governs the Southern Quadrant [the Daoist goddess, Lady Wei Huacun] sends down this register of instruction:

> I command all the various realized ones and great transcendents from outside the four seas and inside the six directions, from famous mountains and great rivers, [along with all those adepts] who seek and desire long life, profundity of mind, and the veritable Way, to descend and instruct her. Xuantong's good works put her in the category of deities who govern the earth; her memorial tablets are in the archives of the Purple Barrens. In addition, I hear that my daughter has set her mind [on immortality]. The Primal Ruler is especially delighted with her devotion. After a few days I will personally descend here.

It went on like this for five nights in all. Xuantong burned incense and increased the strictness of her practice as she waited for the Primal Ruler. And then, in the fifteenth year of the Universally Penetrating reign period (of Emperor Xicong, 874 C.E.), on an A-horse (*jiawu*)[4] day, the Primal Ruler descended to Xuantong's room together with a flock of serving girls and twenty-seven realized ones. [Xuantong] bowed to welcome them at the gate. The Primal Ruler sat down and rested. After a good long while, she showed Xuantong the [esoteric] orders from the Yellow Courtyard for enrolling deities, visualizing, and doing religious practice. She gave her one grain of the ninefold floriate elixir, ordering: "Swallow it after eight years. Then I will certainly send jade girls and a whirlwind chariot to welcome you to Marchmount Song."[5] Saying their farewells, [the visitors] scattered and departed.

From this time on, Xuantong [engaged in Daoist practice to] deepen her mind and still her spirits. She never ate. Although realized transcendents descended to invite her with presents, although radiant phosphors lit up empty space while numinous winds [carried] strange fragrances and the harmonious music of cloud harps was per-

---

[3] The sky.
[4] A day in 60 day cycle, counting in the traditional way.
[5] The holy mountain of the center.

formed in her room, Feng Hui was not aware of any of this. Because Xuantong had a separate room to practice the Way, Feng Hui was distant and could not be intimate with her. Harboring ignorant and jealous feelings, he regularly slandered and ridiculed her. This was just like the suspicions [of an earlier angry husband that led local officials] to seize the Incomparable Mother of the Eastern Tumulus.[6]

During the G-rat (*kangzi*) year of the Broad Greatness reign period (of Xicong, 880 C.E.), great thieves[7] penetrated the [capital] city watchtowers. Those wearing the cap strings of office fled and escaped. Those who remained made an illegitimate peace [with the rebel leaders]. Feng and Xuantong sojourned at Jinling in Chang Province.[8] She was now visualizing deities ceaselessly, and growing in her practice of reverence and respect.

In the tenth month of the primal year of the Central Harmony reign period (of Xicong, 881 C.E.), [Feng and Xuantong] traveled by boat to the mouth of the Zhi watercourse.[9] Riding on the current with numerous family members, neighbors, and female companions, they were approaching their country villa. Suddenly they saw vermilion- and purple-clad official envoys along with armed and armored military officers, all standing on the riverbank in orderly array as if waiting for Xuantong's boat to row over to them. Now this was a region of many villains from all four borders, a place of marauders and thieves. When the people on the boat saw [the assembly on the riverbank], they were startled and alarmed, unwilling to draw closer. Xuantong said, "Don't be afraid," then moved her boat right up to them. The officers and envoys all saluted her. Xuantong commanded them, saying: "Not yet! I will only depart next spring from my private residence. Don't rush me." Officers and envoys thereupon scattered and departed. The people sharing the boat with her all witnessed this event, but none understood its meaning.

The next year (882 C.E.), in the second month, Xuantong washed her hair and face, then took out the tidbit of elixir that the Primal Ruler of the Purple Barrens had given her. Two transcendent girls descended in secret to her room, urging her to proceed to the heights

---

[6] The Incomparable Mother was a fourth-century C.E. Daoist saint who flew out a prison window after her husband had her jailed for neglecting her domestic duties in favor of religious practice.

[7] Leaders of the Huang Chao rebellion, 878–884 C.E.

[8] In modern Sichuan.

[9] In modern Zhejiang.

of Marchmount Song. On the fourteenth day of that month she presented symptoms; and in a single evening it was finished. At her private
residence, thirty-six wingspans of transcendent cranes gathered atop
her room. Xuantong's form and substance were light and warm, her
appearance like that of a living person. The centers of her cheeks
looked misty, with a spot of white radiance that transformed after a
good long time into purple vapor. [Earlier], when she had washed her
hair and face, her dark hair had increased in thickness and grown
several feet in length.

On the night of the fifteenth day, clouds of variegated colors filled
her room, and suddenly people heard sounds of thunder and lightning shaking and crashing. Her coffin lid flew up inside the courtyard. Her corpse had disappeared, leaving behind just her empty burial
garments and quilt. Strange fragrances arose. The cloud cranes stayed
ten days before departing.

The Regulating and Ordering Notary from Zhexi Province,[10]
Minister Zhou Bao[11] memorialized:

> This humble one has heard that on the day Lady Chao[12] ascended to
> distant regions, her jade appearance was like that of a living person. And
> at the time when Prior-Born Tao[13] tired of the world, strange fragrances
> were ceaseless. These instances of feathered transformation[14] are both
> recorded in the transcendent classics. Might we say that in these brilliant
> times we are once again seeing such events? This humble one takes Feng
> Hui's wife, Ms. Xue, as someone who rejected dirt and vulgarity from
> early on. For a long time she practiced at the mysterious gate, according
> to texts containing the esoteric secrets of the divine transcendents. She
> was able to gather women's [elixir of] florescence of lead, in accord with
> the impenetrable decree. If she had not annoyed and clashed with her
> scholar-official husband, then she would not have abstained from grains
> [fasted], eaten magic mushrooms, preserved the genuine [Way], seen the
> unbleached white [pure Way], and walked with generations of paragons.
> The transformations of non-action exhaust the regulations of the
> Mysterious Prime for preserving the one [Way]. As for those who are not
> so, how can they obtain [elixir] recipes or meditate?

---

[10] Southeast of the Yangtze River.

[11] A military governor from an elite family serving under Emperor Xicong during the
Huang Chao rebellion.

[12] A second century C.E. saint from an eminent Daoist family.

[13] The great editor and Daoist master Tao Hongjing, 456–536 C.E.

[14] Ascents to immortality.

Drums and bronze *lei* ritual vessels decorated with numinous birds descended to her. Right in the mirror with its image of a grieving simurgh,[15] her hair doubled and grew. Thunder and lightning together with auspicious clouds and auroral haze manifested her difference. When she returned to heaven, stringed and wind instruments were heard in broad daylight. Her coffin was empty; only her clothes and quilt were there. She came in exile to dwell temporarily among humans. Becoming a transcendent, she returned to her home above the heavens. Her story transmits a thousand old and beautiful praises up to this singular time. Although she belongs among the blessings and auspicious omens of this commandery, her story is also a bountiful event for the nation and the dynasty. Your servant respectfully divides the abundance, sending along this hastily completed memorial. Having heard with surpassing delight the news of our government's rushing heaven and extending our territory without the responsibility of combat, I offer my utmost congratulations. Memorialized this year on the fifteenth day of the second month in Chengdu [Sichuan].

[Zhou Bao's] wishes were carried out by an imperial order that read:

[Xue Xuantong's] was in fact the Way of the teachings of heaven as manifested in the transcendent classics. Those of the highest virtue diligently practice hidden good works. This order is meant to cause people viewing it to extend Zhou Bao's memorial and incline towards harmonizing different auspicious signs. Like Ms. Wei [Huacun's] ascent to transcendence or Hua Gu's[16] descent into our world, she adds comparable radiance to her commandery and county in addition to illuminating our nation and dynasty. It would be appropriate to pay history officials to compile [her story] on tablets and fascicles. And I charge officials from the circuit level on up to donate money to the places where she dwelt for the purpose of repairing Daoist altars with their golden ordination registers. Thereby we respond to the highest mysteries and extend reverent feelings. Written during the third year of residence at the imperial halting place in Chengdu (883 C.E.).

---

15 Term for an auspicious bird in Persian mythology.
16 An early Tang female Daoist saint.

46

THE BOOK OF FILIAL PIETY
(Xiaojing)

孝經

THE BOOK OF FILIAL PIETY FOR WOMEN
(Nü xiaojing)

女孝經

By Song times, several didactic texts considered useful for the education of girls were in circulation. The two most famous had been written approximately a thousand years earlier and required a relatively high degree of literacy—these were the two classics of the Han Period, Liu Xiang's Biographies of Women (Lienüzhuan) and Ban Zhao's Lessons for Women (Nüjie). Many women's biographies state that their subjects had studied these texts, and leading Neo-Confucian scholars urged that parents instruct their daughters in them. In addition, however, there were at least two short works written in later centuries and composed in a style simple enough to be used as primers: The Book of Filial Piety for Women (Nü xiaojing) and The Analects for Women (Nü lunyü). These texts were not mentioned very often in the writings of leading Song scholars, perhaps because they were considered too elementary. That The Book of Filial Piety for Women circulated in Song time, however, can be seen in the paintings made to illustrate it, some of which have survived. Moreover, along with The Analects for Women, it was copied into the fourteenth-century C.E. compendium, the Shuofu, and in subsequent centuries into other collectanea, the last in the late nineteenth century.

From "The Book of Filial Piety for Women," translated by Patricia Buckley Ebrey, in *Under Confucian Eyes: Writings on Gender in Chinese History*, edited by Susan Mann and Yu-Yin Cheng. Copyright © 2001 The Regents of the University of California. Reprinted by permission of the University of California Press.

Evidence for the dating of the Book of Filial Piety for Women *is scanty. The preface is signed by a Miss Zheng, the wife of an official named Chen Miao. She says that she wrote the text for her niece, who was about to marry Prince Yong. The Tang histories mention a Prince Yong who was the sixteenth son of Emperor Xuanzong, which would date this text to around 730* C.E.

In terms of its moral message, The Book of Filial Piety for Women *could have been written at almost any period after the Han.[1] Its primary goal is to expand the message of* The Book of Filial Piety *to apply to girls and women. Like its prototype,* The Book of Filial Piety for Women *presents filial piety as the supreme virtue required of everyone in society. The moral vision presented is one in which seemingly small acts can have major consequences as one person's virtue transforms those he or she comes into contact with, who can in turn transform others, in ever-widening circles. Thus, even women who do not leave their home can exert a moral influence that extends outward to people they never meet. For instance, a daughter-in-law, through her influence within the household, can by degrees transform others, beginning with her relatives and working outward; and the wife of the Son of Heaven (the Emperor), through her influence on her husband, can have an impact that reaches everywhere in the realm. Such a theory of moral influence is well attested in early Confucian texts, such as the* Analects *and the* Great Learning. *Moreover,* Biographies of Women *supplies many concrete examples of women who transformed the men around them and thus indirectly had an impact on larger political realms. Still, Miss Zheng may be the first author to be so direct in implying that women's moral power is comparable to men's.*

Differentiation by station is also central to this text, as it is to the original Book of Filial Piety. *Miss Zheng aims not merely to convince girls that filial piety applies to them, but also to convey to them the ways in which the station of a woman determines how she expresses her filial piety. Positive evaluation is placed on wives who admonish their husbands, mothers who educate their children, and widows who refuse to remarry. Condemned as immoral and unfilial are wives who become jealous of*

---

[1] Some scholars have tried to assign a date to *The Book of Filial Piety for Women* on the basis of its message, but they have not agreed on its message. Some say it celebrates women's moral influence and thus deserves a mid-Tang date; others argue that it reinforces constraints on women and thus deserves a late-Tang or early-Song date. For my part, I find most such arguments flawed: in neither period was only one set of ideas expressed, and the ideas expressed in texts never correspond to behavior in a simple way. Just because Empress Wu did not define herself in terms of the Triple Obedience does not mean that people in the seventh century no longer admired the mother of Mencius or read the *Biographies of Women.* So also, the fact that Emperor Taizong did not define himself in terms of submission to his father and elder brother does not mean that no one read *The Book of Filial Piety* or admired the *Twenty-Four Filial Sons* anymore. However, I do consider it worth noting that due largely to the spread of printing, *The Book of Filial Piety for Women* seems to have circulated more widely in Ming and Qing times than in Tang or Song.

their husband's concubines, and concubines who use their sexual allure to lead men astray. Miss Zheng's debt to Liu Xiang's Biographies of Women *is particularly noticeable in her selection of examples. By contrast, even though Miss Zheng casts Ban Zhao as the female equivalent of Confucius in this text, she borrows relatively little from the* Lessons for Women *other than to use the language of yin and yang. Ban Zhao's work focuses on the relationship between a woman and her husband, and Ban quotes the saying, "To obtain the love of one man is the crown of a woman's life; to lose the love of one man is to miss the aim of a woman." By contrast,* The Book of Filial Piety for Women *gives no more attention to a woman's relationship with her husband than to her relationship with her parents-in-law or children.*

The translations that follow are not full translations of either text (about a quarter of each has been omitted to save space), but include enough to give the flavor of each.[2]

Patricia B. Ebrey

The Book of Filial Piety

Opening the Discussion and Explaining the Principles

Confucius was at home and Zengzi was attending him. Confucius said: "The former kings had the highest virtue and the essential Way. By recourse to them they kept the world ordered and the people in harmony, and neither superiors nor inferiors resented each other. Is this something you know about?"

Zengzi rose from his mat and replied, "Since I am not clever, how can I know about this?"

Confucius said: "Filial piety is the root of virtue and the source of civilization. Sit down again and I will explain it to you. Since we receive our body, hair, and skin from our parents, we do not dare let them be injured in any way. This is the beginning of filial piety. We establish ourselves and practice the Way, thereby perpetuating our name for future generations and bringing glory to our parents. This is the fulfillment of filial piety. Thus filial piety begins with serving our parents, continues with serving the ruler, and is completed by establishing one's character."

---

[2] In the translation, the honorific title "Dagu" is translated "Lady Ban," and the title "Zi," meaning "the Master," is translated "Confucius." An alternative would have been to use "the Instructress" and "the Master."

In the *Daya* it says: "Think of your ancestors and maintain the practice of their virtues."

The Feudal Lords

"Although in superior positions, they are not arrogant and thus can hold lofty positions without peril. By exercising restraint and caution they can have plenty without going to excess. Holding a lofty position without peril is the way to preserve high rank for a long time. Having plenty without going overboard is the way to preserve wealth for a long time. If they retain their wealth and rank they will later be able to protect their heritage and keep their people in peace. This is the filial piety of the feudal lords."

In *The Book of Odes*, it says: "Be as cautious as if you were standing on the edge of a chasm or treading on thin ice."

The Ministers and High Officers

"They dare not wear garments not prescribed by the former kings; they dare not use words not approved by the former kings; they dare not behave in ways outside the virtuous ways of the former kings. Thus, they will not speak improper words and will not follow anything against the Way. Their words are not arbitrary, nor their actions capricious; their words reach all in the world, yet offend no one; their actions fill the world, yet give no one cause for complaint. Those who fulfill these three conditions are able to preserve their ancestral altars. This is the filial piety of the ministers and high officers."

The Book of Odes says: "Never negligent morning or night in the service of the One Man."

The Common People

"They follow the laws of nature to utilize the earth to the best advantage. They take care of themselves and are cautious in expenditures in order to support their parents. This is the filial piety of the common people. Thus, from the Son of Heaven to the common people, unless filial piety is pursued from beginning to end, calamities will surely result."

The Three Powers

Zengzi said, "How exceedingly great is filial piety!"

Confucius responded: "Filial piety is the pattern of heaven, the standard of the earth, the norm of the conduct for the people. When people follow the pattern of heaven and earth, they model themselves on the brilliance of heaven and make use of the resources of the earth and through these means comply with all under heaven. Thus, [a ruler's] instruction succeeds without being stringent, and his policies are effective without being severe. The former kings, realizing that their instruction could transform the people, showed them an example of universal love. As a consequence, men did not neglect their parents. These kings set an example of rectitude and virtue, and as a consequence the people enthusiastically copied them. The kings showed an example of respectful yielding, and the people did not contend with each other. They taught through ritual and music, and the people lived in concord. They made clear to them the difference between good and evil, and as a consequence the people knew restraint."

The Book of Odes says: "How dignified is Master Yin! The common people all look on him with reverence."

Bringing Order through Filial Piety

Confucius said: "Formerly the illustrious kings brought order to the world through filial piety. They did not dare neglect the ministers of small states—not to mention their own dukes, marquises, earls, counts, and barons. Thereupon they gained the support of all the states, making them better able to serve the former kings. The rulers did not dare insult the widows and widowers—not to mention the upper class of the common people. Therefore they gained the support of all the people, making them better able to serve their former rulers. The heads of families did not dare mistreat their servants and concubines—not to mention their wives and children. Therefore they gained their support, making them better able to serve their parents. Accordingly, while living, parents were well taken care of; after their deaths, their ghosts received sacrifices. In this way the world was kept in peace and harmony. Calamities did not occur nor was disorder created. Such was the way the former illustrious kings brought order to the world through filial piety."

The Book of Odes says: "The states in the four directions will follow the one whose conduct is truly virtuous."

The Rule of the Sages

Zengzi said, "May I ask if there isn't anything in the virtue of the sages that surpasses filial piety?"

Confucius replied: "Of all the creatures in heaven and earth, man is the most important. Of all man's acts, none is greater than filial piety. In the practice of filial piety, nothing is greater than respecting one's father. For respecting one's father, nothing is greater than placing him on the level with heaven.

"The person who did all this was the Duke of Zhou. In former times the Duke of Zhou sacrificed to the Spirit of Agriculture, placing him on a level with heaven. He sacrificed to his father, King Wen, in the Bright Hall, placing him on a level with the Supreme Lord. Therefore, within the four seas all of the lords, according to their stations, came to sacrifice. Thus, how can there be anything in the virtue of the sages that surpasses filial piety? From infancy a child's desire to care for his parents grows daily more respectful. The sages used this natural reverence for parents to teach respect and used this natural affection to teach love. Thus, the teachings of the sages were effective though not severe, and their rule was orderly though not harsh. This was because they relied on what was basic to human nature.

"The proper relation between father and son is a part of nature and forms the principles that regulate the conduct of rulers and ministers. Parents give life—no tie is stronger that this. Rulers personally watch over the people—no care is greater than this. Therefore to love others without first loving one's parents is to reject virtue. To reverence other men without first reverencing one's parents is to reject the rules of ritual. If one copies such perversity, the people will have no model to follow. Although a person who does not do good but only evil may gain a high position, a man of honor will not esteem him. The practice of a man of honor is different: his speech is praiseworthy, his behavior is pleasing, his standards are respected, his management of affairs can be taken as a model, his deportment is pleasant to observe, his movements are deliberate. When a man of honor deals with his people, they look on him with awe and affection; they imitate and seek to resemble him. Thus he can carry out his moral instruction and put into effect his political directives."

The Book of Odes says: "The good man, the true gentleman, his deportment is impeccable."

Filial Conduct

Confucius said: "Let me comment on the way a filial son serves his parents. While at home he renders the utmost reverence to them. In supporting them he maximizes their pleasure. When they are sick he takes every care. At their death he expresses all his grief. Then he sacrifices to them with full solemnity.

"Only a son who has fulfilled these five requirements is truly able to serve his parents. He who really loves his parents will not be proud in a high position. He will not be insubordinate in an inferior position. And among equals he will not be quarrelsome. If he were proud in a high station, he might be ruined. If he were insubordinate in an inferior position, he might incur punishment. If he were quarrelsome among his equals he might end up fighting. Thus, unless these three evils are eliminated, a son cannot be called filial—even if every day he supplies his parents with the three choice meats.

The Five Punishments

Confucius said: "There are three thousand offenses subject to the five punishments, but of these the most heinous is lack of filial piety. To use force against the ruler is to defy authority. To deny the sages is to be unprincipled. And to decry filial piety is to renounce kinship ties. These are the roads to chaos."

Elaborating on the Idea of Highest Virtue

Confucius said: "A man of honor in teaching the duties of filial piety need not go daily to the people's homes to observe them. He merely teaches the principles of filial piety, and all the fathers in the world receive the filial respect due to them. He teaches the principles of fraternal love, and all the elder brothers receive the respect due to them. He teaches the duties of subjects, and all the rulers of the world receive the reverence due to them."

The Book of Odes says: "Affectionate the man of honor, a father and mother to the people." Unless he possessed the highest virtue, who could educate the people to such an extent?

Elaborating on the Idea of Perpetuating One's Name

Confucius said: "The man of honor's service to his parents is filial; the fidelity involved in it can be transferred to his ruler. His service to his elder brothers is deferential; the obedience involved in it can be transferred to his superiors. Self-disciplined at home, he can transfer his good management to official life. When his conduct is perfected at home through these means, his name will be perpetuated to later generations."

Admonishing

Zengzi remarked, "I understand your teachings concerned kind affection, loving respect, comforting one's parents, and bringing glory to one's name. May I ask if a son who obeys all of his father's commands can be called filial?"

Confucius replied: "What kind of talk is this? What kind of talk is this? In ancient times if the Son of Heaven had seven ministers to point out his errors, he would not lose his empire, even if he were imperfect. If a feudal lord had five good ministers to point out his errors, he would not lose his state, even if he were imperfect. If a high officer had three officials to point out his errors, he would not lose his patrimony, even if he were imperfect. If a gentleman had a friend to point out his errors, he would not lose his good name. And if a father had a son to point out his errors, he would not fall into doing wrong. Thus, when he might do something wrong, a son must not fail to warn his father against it, nor a minister fail to warn his ruler. In short, when it is a question of doing wrong, one must admonish. How can following a father's orders be considered fulfilling filial piety?"

Mutual Interaction

Confucius said: "In ancient times, because the illustrious kings were filial to their fathers, they were able to serve heaven intelligently. Because they were filial to their mothers, they were able to serve earth with circumspection. Superiors could govern inferiors because the young obeyed their elders. Thus, because heaven and earth were served with intelligence and care, the spirits manifested themselves brilliantly. Even the Son of Heaven had someone he paid reverence to, that is to say, his father. He had someone he deferred to, that is to say, his elder brothers. At the ancestral temple he was reverential, not forgetting his parents. He cultivated his character and acted prudently, for fear of disgracing his ancestors. When he paid reverence at the ancestral temple, the ghosts of spirits sent blessings. When his filial piety and fraternity were perfected, his influence reached the spirits. He illuminated the four seas; there was no place his virtue did not penetrate."

The Book of Odes says: "West, east, south, north, no one fails to submit to him."

Serving the Ruler

Confucius said: "In serving his superior the man of honor makes every effort to be faithful when he is in office. In retirement he tries to make up for his shortcomings. He encourages his superior in his good inclinations and tries to keep him from doing wrong. In this way, the relations between superiors and inferiors can be cordial."

The Book of Odes says: "In his heart is love. Why not admit it? He stores it in his heart. When could he forget it?"

Mourning for Parents

Confucius said: "When mourning a parent a filial son weeps without wailing loudly; he performs the rites without attention to his appearance; he speaks without attention to the beauty of his words; he feels uncomfortable in elegant clothes; he gets no joy from hearing music; he does not relish good food—all of this is the emotion of grief. After three days he eats again to show men that the dead should not hurt the living and that the suffering should not lead to the destruction of life. This was the regulation of the sages. The period of mourning is not allowed to exceed three years, thus showing the people that everything ends. [The filial son] prepares a double coffin and grave clothes. When he sets out the sacrificial vessels, he grieves. Beating his breast, jumping up and down, and crying, he bids a last sad farewell. He divines to choose the burial place where the body can be placed to rest. He prepares an ancestral altar, so that the ghost can receive sacrifices. Spring and autumn he offers sacrifices, thus thinking of the dead one every season. When his parents were alive he served them with love and reverence; in death he grieves.

"With the man's fundamental duty fulfilled, relations between the living and the dead are complete, and the filial son's service to his parents is finished."

The Book of Filial Piety for Women

Opening the Discussion and Explaining the Principles

Lady Ban was at home at leisure and the women were sitting in attendance. Lady Ban said, "In antiquity, the two daughters of the Sage Emperor [Yao] had the filial way and went to the bend of the Gui River [to marry Shun]. They were humble, yielding, respectful, and frugal; they concentrated their thoughts on the way to be a wife. Wise and well-informed, they avoided problems with others. Have you heard about this?"

The women rose from their seats and apologized, "We women are ignorant and have not yet received all of your teachings. Could you tell us about it?"

Lady Ban said: "Study involves gathering information, questioning and evaluating it, and discarding the doubtful. In this way one can become a model for others. If you are willing to listen to my words and put them into practice, I will explain the principles to you.

"Filial piety expands heaven and earth, deepens human relationships, stimulates the ghosts and spirits, and moves the birds and beasts. It involves being respectful and conforming to ritual, acting only after repeated thought, making no effort to broadcast one's accomplishments or good deeds, being agreeable, gentle, pure, obedient, kind, intelligent, filial, and compassionate. When such virtuous conduct is perfected, no one will reproach you."

This is what is meant by the passage in the *The Canon of Documents*, "Filial piety is simply being filial and friendly to one's brothers."

The Noble Ladies

"Although occupying honored positions, they are able to show restraint, and thus they can hold their positions without relying on partiality. They observe the diligent toil [of others] and understand their viewpoints. They can recite the *Odes* and *Documents*; they can perform the *Rituals* and *Music*. As a consequence, they consider it a misfortune to be well-known but unworthy, and a calamity to be great in status but little in virtue, and in fact take a warning from such cases. By first ensuring that their persons conform to propriety whether at rest or in motion, they are able to get along well with their children and grandchildren and preserve the ancestral temple. This is the filial piety of the noble ladies."

The Classic of Changes says: "He wards off depravity and preserves his integrity," and "His virtue spreads far and transforms others."

The Wives of Officials

"They dare not wear garments not prescribed by the ritual codes; they dare not use words not modeled on the *Odes* and *Documents*. They dare not behave in any way outside the virtuous ways based on honesty and moral principle. There is nothing better than not saying what one wishes others would not hear, not doing what one wishes others would not know, and not performing what one wishes others would not pass on. Those who fulfill these three conditions are able to preserve their ancestral altars. This is the filial piety of the wives of officials."

The Book of Odes says: "She picks the artemisia by the pond on the islands for use in service to the lords."

The Common People

"They follow the way of the wife and utilize moral principle to the best advantage. They put others first and themselves last in order to serve their parents-in-law. They spin and weave and sew clothes; they prepare the sacrificial foods. This is the filial piety of the wife of a common person."

The Book of Odes says: "Women do not have public affairs, [for if they did] they would stop their weaving."

Serving Parents-in-Law

"With regard to a woman's service to her parents-in-law, she is as reverent as to her own father, as loving as to her own mother. Maintaining this attitude is a matter of duty, and adhering to it is a matter of ritual. When the cock first crows, she washes her hands, rinses her mouth, and gets dressed to make her morning call. In the winter she checks that [her parents-in-law] are warm enough, in the summer cool enough. In the evening she checks that they are settled, in the morning that they are getting up. She is reverent in correcting inside matters, principled in her dealings with the outside. She establishes herself as a person of principle and decorum and then acts on them."

The Book of Odes says: "When a woman departs, she distances herself from her parents and brothers."

The Three Powers

The women said, "How exceedingly great is the husband!"

Lady Ban responded: "The husband is heaven. Can one not be devoted to him? In antiquity, when a woman went to be married, she was said to be going home. She transfers her heaven to serve her husband. The principle in this is vast. It is the pattern of heaven, that standard of the earth, the norm of conduct for the people. When women follow the nature of heaven and earth, model themselves on the brilliance of heaven, make use of the resources of the earth, guard against idleness, and adhere to ritual, then they can bring success to their families. On this basis, a wife acts first to extend her love broadly, then her husband will not forget to be filial to his parents. She sets an example of rectitude and virtue, and her husband enthusiastically copies it. She takes the initiative in being reverent and yielding, and her husband is not competitive. If she follows the path of ritual and music, her husband will join in harmoniously. If she indicates the difference between good and evil, her husband will know restraint."

The Book of Odes says: "Intelligent and wise in order to protect her person."

Bringing Order through Filial Piety

Lady Ban said: "In ancient times, virtuous women brought order to their nine relations through filial piety. They did not dare neglect the lowest ranking concubine, not to mention their sisters-in-law. There-fore they gained the support of their six relations, making them better able to serve their parents-in-law. Those placed in charge of family business did not dare insult the chickens and dogs—not to mention the lower-ranking family members. Therefore they gained the support of their superiors and inferiors, making them better able to serve their husbands. Those in charge of the women's quarters did not dare mistreat the servants—not to mention the master. Therefore they gained the support of the people, making them better able to serve their parents. Accordingly, while living, parents were well taken care of; after their deaths, their ghosts received sacrifices. In this way the nine relations were kept in peace and harmony. Pettiness did not occur, nor disorder arise. Such was the way virtuous women brought order to superiors and inferiors through filial piety."

The *Book of Odes* says: "Not erring, not forgetting, conforming in all matters to the old rules."

Wisdom

The women said, "May we ask if there isn't anything in the virtue of a wife that surpasses wisdom?"

Lady Ban replied: "Humankind is patterned on heaven and earth; *yin* and *yang* are interdependent. Making use of one's intelligence is always beneficial, especially when done in a purposeful manner.

"In former times, King Zhuang of Chu was holding court in the evening. Lady Fan entered and said, 'Why don't you end this court session? It is so late. Aren't you tired?' The king said, 'Today I have been talking with a wise person and have been so happy, I have not noticed the time.' When Lady Fan asked the identity of the wise person, the king said Yu Qiuzi. Lady Fan covered her mouth and laughed. The king, perplexed, asked her what made her laugh. She answered, 'Yu Qiuzi may be wise, but he is not loyal. For eleven years I have had the favor of occupying a place in your rear chambers, where I still attend to you with wash basin, towel, and comb and clean up. During this time I have introduced nine other women. Today two of them are wiser than I am, and the other seven are my peers. Even though I know how to safeguard your love for me and snatch your favor, I would not dare keep you in the dark [about other women] for selfish reasons. Rather, I wish that you be broadly informed. Now, Yu Qiuzi has been prime minister for ten years, but the only people he has recommended are his descendants or his collateral relatives. I have never heard of him recommending someone wise or demoting someone unworthy. Can he be called wise?'

Figure 9. Filled with such courage that she is oblivious to the tiger's attack,
Woman (Chou Hua Lienu Zhuan) by Chou Ying (1509–1552).]

the filial daughter is saving her father. [From *Chou's Illustrations of the Biographies of*

"When the king repeated this to him, Yu Qiuzi, in his confusion, abandoned his home and slept outside. The king sent someone to invite Sun Shuao, and on his arrival made him prime minister. Thus, because of the wisdom of a single person's advice, the feudal lords did not dare attack, and in the end King Zhuang became the paramount leader of the states. All this was due to the effort of Lady Fan."

A poem says: "Those who obtain the right men prosper; those who lose them are defeated." *The Book of Odes* says, "When language is harmonious, the people will be united."

Virtuous Conduct

Lady Ban said: "Let me comment on the way a woman serves her husband. From the time her hair is arranged and she meets him [during the wedding ceremony], she maintains the formality appropriate between an official and the ruler. When helping him wash or serving him food, she maintains the reverence appropriate between father and child. When reporting her comings and goings, she preserves the manner appropriate between siblings. She always keeps agreements, thus maintaining the trust appropriate among friends. Her words and actions are unblemished, giving her the capacity to manage the family.

"Only a woman who has fulfilled these five requirements is truly able to serve her husband. Such a woman will not be proud in a high position. She will not be insubordinate in an inferior position. And among equals she will not be quarrelsome. If she were proud in a high station, she might be ruined. If she were insubordinate in an inferior position, she might incur punishment. If she were quarrelsome among her equals, she might end up fighting. Thus, unless these three evils are eliminated, a woman cannot be called wifely—even if she harmonizes with her husband as well as the lute with the zither."

The Five Punishments

Lady Ban said: "There are three thousand offenses subject to the five punishments, but of these the most heinous is jealousy. It is the first among the seven grounds for divorce. The teachings of the sages are encompassed in purity, obedience, rectitude, straightforwardness, gentleness, absence of jealousy, orderliness in the inner quarters, absence of contact with the outside, and the ability to not be so stimulated by sight and sounds that desires are pursued recklessly. You women should put this into practice."

The Book of Odes says: "Fine his deportment and appearance! He models himself on the ancient rules and applies himself to attaining dignity."

Elaborating on the Idea of Preserving Trust

"The way of establishing heaven is called *yin* and *yang*; the way of establishing earth is called gentle and firm. *Yin* and *yang*, gentle and firm, these are the beginnings of heaven and earth. Men and women, husbands and wives, these are the beginnings of human relationships. *Qian* and *kun* are interconnected and pervasive, with no space between them. The wife is earth, the husband is heaven; neither can be dispensed with. But the husband has a hundred actions; the wife has a single purpose. For men there is the principle of successive marriages, but there is no text authorizing women to marry more than once.

"Formerly, King Zhao of Chu took a trip and left [his wife] Miss Jiang at Qian pavilion. The river flooded and the king sent someone to get the lady, but the messenger should have carried a tally; she would not go with him. Miss Jiang said, 'I have heard a chaste woman, as a matter of principle, does not break an agreement, just as a brave soldier does not fear dying. Now I know that I will surely die if I do not leave. But without a tally I dare not break the agreement. Although if I leave I will surely live, to lie without faith is not as good as dying to preserve principle.' It happened that when the messenger returned to get the tally, the water rose above the pavilion and she drowned. Such was the way she preserved trust. You should strive to emulate her example."

The Book of Changes says: "The crying crane resides in *yin*; its child joins it in harmony."

Elaborating on the Idea of Perpetuating One's Name

Lady Ban said: "A daughter's service to her parents is filial; the fidelity involved in it can be transferred to her parents-in-law. Her service to her sisters is deferential; the obedience involved in it can be transferred to sisters-in-law. Self-disciplined at home, her reputation for discipline will reach the six relations. When her conduct is perfected at home through these means, her name will be perpetuated to later generations."

Admonishing

The women said, "We now understand your teachings concerning modest purity, filial principles, serving one's mother-in-law, respecting one's husband, and bringing glory to one's name. May we ask if a wife who obeys her husband's orders can be called worthy?"

Lady Ban replied: "What kind of talk is this? What kind of talk is this? In ancient times when King Xuan of Zhou [stayed in bed so long he] was late for court, Queen Jiang [accused herself of leading him astray and] took off her hairpin and earrings to wait for her punishment at the end of the alley. This brought King Xuan to his senses. When Emperor Cheng of the Han dynasty ordered Consort Ban to board the carriage he was in, she declined, saying, 'I have heard that in the three dynasties enlightened kings all had wise officials at their side. I have never heard of one who rode with a favored woman,' which caused Emperor Cheng to change color. Because King Zhuang of Chu was fond of hunting, Lady Fan would eat nothing from the wilds, which moved the king and led to his giving up hunting.

"Viewed in this way, if the Son of Heaven had ministers to point out his errors to him, he would not lose his empire, even if he were imperfect. If a feudal lord had ministers to point out his errors to him, he would not lose his state, even if he were imperfect. If a high officer had officials to point out his errors to him, he would not lose his patrimony, even if he were imperfect. If a gentleman had a friend to point out his errors to him, he would not lose his good name. If a father had a son to point out his errors to him, he would not fall into doing wrong. And if a husband had a wife to point out his errors to him, then he would not slip into incorrect ways. For instance, Lady Wei reformed Duke Huan of Qi so that he no longer listened to lewd music, and it was because Qi Jiang sent Duke Wen of Jin that he become hegemon. Thus, when a husband might do something wrong, a wife warns against it. How can following a husband's orders be considered wise?"

The Book of Odes says: "When his plans are not farsighted, it is time to admonish strongly."[38]

Prenatal Education

Lady Ban said: "With regard to the way people receive the five constant virtues, at birth they have an intrinsic nature, but much is also learned. If they are exposed to good, then they will be good; if exposed to evil, they will be evil. Even while they are in the womb, how can they not be given education! In ancient times, when women were with child, they did not lie on their side while sleeping, nor sit to one side, nor stand on one foot, nor eat anything with a strange taste, nor walk on the left side of the road, nor eat anything not cut straight, nor sit on a mat that was not laid straight, nor look at or listen to any evil sights or sounds, nor utter any wild words, nor touch any deviant objects. At night they would recite the classical texts; in the morning they would discuss ritual and music. When these women gave birth, their children's form was correct and their talent and virtue surpassed that of others. Such was their prenatal education."

Maternal Proprieties

Lady Ban said: "Anyone who is a mother needs to understand the ritual proprieties. Get along with your child through kindness and love. Offer a model to your child by being stern and correct. Your movements should conform to ritual forms; your words must have principles behind them.

"When your sons reach six, teach them the names of numbers and directions; at seven see that they do not sit on the same mat or eat together with the girls; at eight have them study elementary learning; at ten have them study with a teacher. They must report when they are going out and come to see you in person on their return. Their amusements must have some regularity to them; their studies must have some substance to them. When at home, they should not occupy the innermost place; they should not sit in the middle of a mat, nor walk in the middle of the road, nor stand in the middle of the doorway. They should not climb high places or stand on the edge of deep chasms. They should not make unwise oaths or laugh foolishly. They should keep no private property. When standing they should be straight and square. Their ears should not be swayed by what they hear. They should maintain the separation between males and females to avoid cause for suspicion and should share neither towel nor comb.

"As for your daughters, at seven you should teach them the four virtues.

"Such is the way of maternal proprieties. The aunt of Huangfu Shi'an once said, 'The mother of Mencius moved three times to help form his character and bought meat to teach him to preserve trust. By not properly selecting the neighborhood we live in, I am responsible for making you so obtuse.'"

The Book of Odes says: "Instruct and advise your children so that they come to resemble you."

Removing Evils

The women said, "We have reverently heard your instructions on the way of the wife. Even though we, your pupils, are not clever, we wish to devote our lives to putting your teachings into practice.

"May we ask, were there also any bad women in antiquity?"

Lady Ban responded: "The rise of the Xia dynasty was because of [the wife of the founder], Tushan. Its fall was due to [the concubine of the last king], Moxi. The rise of the Yin dynasty was because of [the wife of the founder], Youxin; its fall was due to [the concubine of its last king], Danji. The rise of the [Western] Zhou dynasty was because of [the mother of the founder], Tairen; its demise was due to [the concubine of the last king], Baosi. It was because of women that the kings of these three dynasties lost the realm, their lives, and their states. This is even more true at the level of feudal lords, greater officers, and common people. Thus the calamity that befell Shensheng [the crown prince of Jin] resulted from [the slander of his father's concubine], Linu. The demise of [the last heir of the Liang dynasty], Minhuai, began with [the Jin empress], Nanfeng.

"When viewed in this way, there are women who deserve credit for founding their families and others who destroyed their families. Then there is the case of Miss Xia, the wife of Chen Yushu, who brought about the deaths of three husbands, a son, and a ruler, chased away two ministers, and brought on the destruction of a state—this must be the most extreme case of evil. It is appalling to think that a single woman could destroy the patrimony of six families.

"If, however, you practice the way of goodness, you will never reach such extremity."

47

THE STORY OF YINGYING

(*Yingying Zhuan*)

鶯鶯傳

Yuan Zhen

元稹

The Story of Yingying (Yingying Zhuan), *which was written between 803–806* C.E., *is also referred to as* An Encounter with an Immortal (Huizhenji) *due to the title of the thirty couplets close to the end of the story. The author Yuan Zhen (779–831* C.E.*) presented this autobiographical tale of an illicit relationship between a scholar and an innocent young woman in order to warn men of the vice of lust. The story gained much popularity during its time and continues to evoke many responses from later scholars and writers, the most well-known of which are Dong Jieyuan's medley* (Chugongdiao), *the* Western Chamber Romance *in the Song dynasty, and the* Romance of the Western Chamber (Xixiangji) *by the master playwright, Wang Shifu, in the Yuan dynasty.*

Yingying is one of the first rebellious women in Chinese fiction. Although raised and educated under the Confucian ethical code for women, Yingying first breaks the precept on filial piety by choosing a man on her own. Yet her biggest mistake is her violation of the law of chastity, the moral paradigm for all females. At the end, Yingying, our tragic heroine, accepts Zhang's abandonment, putting all the blame on herself. Throughout the story, the reader watches a young and courageous woman trying to pursue her happiness only to be defeated by a prejudiced and patriarchal society.

Fatima Wu

During the Zhenyuan period (785–804 C.E.) there lived a young man named Zhang. He was agreeable and refined—and good-looking—

From James R. Hightower, "Yuan Chen and the Story of Ying-ying," *Harvard Journal of Asiatic Studies* 33 (1973): 93–103. Reprinted by permission of the *Harvard Journal of Asiatic Studies* and James R. Hightower.

but firm and self-contained, and capable of no improper act. When his companions included him in one of their parties, the others would all be brawling as though they would never get enough, but Zhang would just watch tolerantly without ever taking part. In this way he had gotten to be twenty-two years old without ever having had relations with a woman. When asked about this by his friends, he explained, "Deng Tuzi[1] was no lover, but a lecher. I am the true lover—I just never happened to meet the right girl. How do I know this? Because all things of outstanding beauty never fail to make a permanent impression on me. This shows I am not without feelings." His friends took note of what he said.

Not long afterward Zhang was traveling in Pu, where he lodged a few miles east of the city in a monastery called the Temple of Universal Salvation. It happened that a widowed Mrs. Cui had also stopped there on her way back to Chang'an. She had been born a Zheng; Zhang's mother had been a Zheng, and when they worked out their common ancestry, this Mrs. Cui turned out to be a rather distant aunt on his mother's side.

This year Hun Zhen died in Pu, and the eunuch Ding Wenya proved unpopular with the troops, who took advantage of the mourning period to mutiny. They plundered the citizens of Pu, and Mrs. Cui, in a strange place with all her slaves and chattels, was terrified, having no one to turn to. Before the mutiny Zhang had made friends with some of the officers in Pu, and now he requested a detachment of soldiers to protect the Cui family. As a result, they all escaped harm. In about ten days the Imperial Commissioner of Enquiry Du Que arrived with the full power of the throne and restored order among the troops.

Out of gratitude to Zhang for the favor he had done her family, Mrs. Cui invited him to a banquet in the central hall. She addressed him, "Your widowed aunt with her helpless children would never have been able to escape alive from these rioting soldiers. It is no ordinary favor you have done us; it is rather as though you had given my son and daughter their lives, and I want to introduce them to you as their elder brother so that they can express their thanks." She summoned her son Huanlang, a very attractive child of ten or so. Then she called her daughter, "Come out and pay your respects to your brother, who saved your life." There was a delay; then word was brought that she was indisposed and asked to be excused. Her mother exclaimed in

---

[1] A well-known lecher.

anger, "Your brother Zhang saved your life. You would be a slave if it were not for him—how can you give yourself airs?"

After a while she appeared, wearing an everyday dress and no makeup on her smooth face, except for a remaining spot of rouge. Her hair coils straggled down to touch her eyebrows. Her beauty was extraordinary, so radiant it took the breath away. Startled, Zhang gave her a deep bow as she sat down beside her mother. Because she had been forced to come out against her will, she looked angrily straight ahead, as though unable to endure the company. Zhang asked her age. Mrs. Cui said, "From the seventh month of the fifth year of the reigning emperor to the present twenty-first year, it is just sixteen years."

Zhang tried to make conversation with her, but she would not respond, and he had to leave after the meal was over. From this time on Zhang was infatuated, but he had no way to make his feelings known to her. She had a maid named Hongniang with whom Zhang had managed to exchange greetings several times, and finally he took the occasion to tell her how he felt. Not surprisingly, the maid was alarmed and fled in confusion. Zhang was sorry he had said anything, and when she returned the next day he made shamefaced apologies without repeating his request. The maid said, "Sir, what you said is something I would not dare repeat to my mistress or let anyone else know about it. But you know well who Miss Cui's relatives are; why don't you ask for her hand in marriage, as you are entitled to do because of the favor you did them."

Zhang said, "From my earliest years I have never been one to make an improper connection. Whenever I have found myself in the company of young women, I would not even look at them, and it never occurred to me that I would be trapped in any such way. But the other day at the dinner I was hardly able to control myself, and in the days since, I walk without knowing where I am going and eat without hunger—I am afraid I cannot last out another day. If I were to go through a regular matchmaker, taking three months and more for the exchange of betrothal presents and names and birth dates—you might just as well look for me among the dried fish in the shop. Can't you tell me what to do?"

The maid replied, "Miss Cui is so very strict that not even her elders could suggest anything improper to her. It would be hard for someone in my position to say such a thing. But I have noticed she writes a lot. She is always reciting poetry to herself and is moved by it for a long time after. You might see if you could seduce her with a love poem. That is the only way I can think of."

Zhang was delighted, and on the spot he composed two stanzas of Spring Verses that he handed over to her. That evening Hongniang came back with a note on colored paper for him, saying, "By Miss Cui's instructions."

The title of her poem was "Bright Moon on the Night of the Fifteenth":

I await the moon in the western chamber
Where the breeze comes through the half-opened door.
Sweeping the wall the flower shadows move:
I imagine it is my lover who comes.

Zhang understood the message: that day was the fourteenth of the second month, and an apricot tree was in bloom next to the wall east of the Cuis' courtyard. It would be possible to climb it.

On the night of the fifteenth Zhang used the tree as a ladder to get over the wall. When he came to the western chamber, the door was ajar. Inside, Hongniang was asleep on a bed. He awakened her, and she asked, frightened, "How did you get here?"

"Miss Cui's letter told me to come," he said, not quite accurately. "You go tell her I am here."

In a minute Hongniang was back, "She's coming! She's coming!"

Zhang was both happy and nervous, convinced that success was his. Then Miss Cui appeared in formal dress, with a serious face, and began to upbraid him, "You did us a great kindness when you saved our lives, and that is why my mother entrusted my young brother and myself to you. Why then did you get my silly maid to bring me that filthy poem? You began by doing a good deed in preserving me from the hands of ravishers, and you end by seeking to ravish me. You substitute seduction for rape—is there any great difference? My first impulse was to keep quiet about it, but that would have been to condone your wrongdoing, and not right. If I told my mother, it would amount to ingratitude, and the consequences would be unfortunate. I thought of having a servant convey my disapproval, but feared she would not get it right. Then I thought of writing a short message to state my case, but was afraid it would only put you on your guard. So finally, I composed those vulgar lines to make sure you would come here. It was an improper thing to do, and of course I feel ashamed. But I hope that you will keep within the bounds of decency and commit no outrage."

As she finished speaking, she turned on her heel and left him. For some time Zhang stood, dumbfounded. Then he went back over the wall to his quarters, all hope gone.

A few nights later Zhang was sleeping alone by the veranda when someone shook him awake. Startled, he rose up to see Hongniang standing there, a coverlet and pillow in her arms. She patted him and said, "She is coming! She is coming! Why are you sleeping?" And she spread the quilt and put the pillow beside his. As she left, Zhang sat up straight and rubbed his eyes. For some time it seemed as though he were still dreaming, but nonetheless he waited dutifully. Then there was Hongniang again, with Miss Cui leaning on her arm. She was shy and yielding, and appeared almost not to have the strength to move her limbs. The contrast with her stiff formality at their last encounter was complete.

This evening was the night of the eighteenth, and the slanting rays of the moon cast a soft light over half the bed. Zhang felt a kind of floating lightness and wondered whether this was an immortal who visited him, not someone from the world of men. After a while the temple bell sounded. Daybreak was near. As Hongniang urged her to leave, she wept softly and clung to him. Hongniang helped her up, and they left. The whole time she had not spoken a single word. With the first light of dawn Zhang got up, wondering, was it a dream? But the perfume still lingered, and as it got lighter he could see on his arm traces of her makeup and the teardrops sparkling still on the mat.

For some ten days afterwards there was no word from her. Zhang composed a poem of sixty lines called "An Encounter with an Immortal," which he had not yet completed when Hongniang happened by; he gave it to her for her mistress. After that she let him see her again, and for nearly a month he would join her in what her poem had called the "western chamber," slipping out at dawn and returning stealthily at night. Zhang once asked what her mother thought about the situation. She said, "She knows there is nothing she can do about it, and so she hopes you will regularize things."

Before long Zhang was about to go to Chang'an, and he let Miss Cui know his intentions in a poem. She made no objections at all, but the look of pain on her face was very touching. On the eve of his departure he was unable to see her again. Then Zhang went off to the west. A few months later he again made a trip to Pu and stayed several months with Miss Cui.

She was a very good calligrapher and wrote poetry, but though he kept begging to see her work, she would never show it. Zhang wrote poems for her, challenging her to match them, but she paid them little attention. The thing that made her unusual was that, although she excelled in the arts, she always acted as though she were ignorant, and although she was quick and clever in speaking, she would seldom indulge in repartee. She loved Zhang very much, but would never say so in words. At the time she was subject to moods of profound melancholy, but she never let on. She seldom showed on her face the emotions she felt. On one occasion she was playing her cither alone at night. She did not know Zhang was listening, and the music was full of sadness. As soon as he spoke, she stopped and would play no more. This made him all the more infatuated with her.

Some time later Zhang had to go west again for the scheduled examinations. It was the eve of his departure, and though he had said nothing about what it involved, he sat sighing unhappily at her side. Miss Cui had guessed that he was going to leave for good. Her manner was respectful, but she spoke deliberately and in a low voice, "To seduce someone and then abandon her is perfectly natural, and it would be presumptuous of me to resent it. It would be an act of charity on your part if, having first seduced me, you were to go through with it and fulfill your oath of lifelong devotion. But in either case, what is there to be so upset about in this trip? However, I see you are not happy and I have no way to cheer you up. You have praised my cither playing, and in the past I have been embarrassed to play for you. Now that you are going away, I shall do what you so often requested."

She had them prepare her cither and started to play the prelude to the "The Rainbow Robe and Feather Skirt." After a few notes, her playing grew wild with grief until the piece was no longer recognizable. Everyone was reduced to tears, and Miss Cui abruptly stopped playing, put down the cither, and ran back to her mother's room with tears streaming down her face. She did not come back.

The next morning Zhang went away. The following year he stayed on in the capital, having failed the examinations. He wrote a letter to Miss Cui to reassure her, and her reply read roughly as follows:

"I have read your letter with its message of consolation, and it filled my childish heart with mingled grief and joy. In addition you sent me a box of ornaments to adorn my hair and a stick of pomade to make my lips smooth. It was most kind of you; but for whom am I to make myself attractive? As I look at these presents my breast is filled with sorrow.

"Your letter said that you will stay on in the capital to pursue your studies, and of course you need quiet and the facilities there to make progress. Still it is hard on the person left alone in the far-off place. But such is my fate, and I should not complain. Since last fall I have been listless and without hope. In company I can force myself to talk and smile, but come evening I always shed tears in the solitude of my own room. Even in my sleep I often sob, yearning for the absent one. Or I am in your arms for a moment as it used to be, but before the secret meeting is done I am awake and heartbroken. The bed seems still warm beside me, but the one I love is far away.

"Since you said goodbye the new year has come. In the spring Chang'an is a city of pleasure with the chance for love everywhere. I am truly fortunate that you have not forgotten me and that your affection is not worn out. Loving you as I do, I have no way of repaying you, except to be true to our vow of lifelong fidelity.

"Our first meeting was at the banquet, as cousins. Then you persuaded my maid to inform me of your love; and I was unable to keep my childish heart firm. You made advances, like that other poet, Sima Xiangru;[2] I failed to repulse them as the girl did who threw her shuttle. When I offered myself in your bed, you treated me with the greatest kindness, and I supposed, in my innocence, that I could always depend on you. How could I have foreseen that our encounter could not possibly lead to something definite, that having disgraced myself by coming to you, there was no further chance of serving you openly as a wife? To the end of my days this will be a lasting regret— I must hide my sighs and be silent. If you, out of kindness, would condescend to fulfill my selfish wish, though it came on my dying day, it would seem a new lease of life. But if, as a man of the world, you curtail your feelings, sacrificing the lesser to the more important, and look on this connection as shameful, so that your solemn vow becomes dispensable, still my true love will not vanish though my bones decay and my frame dissolve: in wind and dew it will seek out the ground you walk on. My love in life and death is told in this. I weep as I write, for feelings I cannot express. Take care of yourself, a thousand times over, take care of your dear self.

"This bracelet of jade is something I wore as a child: I send it to serve as a gentleman's belt pendant. Like jade may you be invariably firm and tender; like a bracelet may there be no break between what came before and what is to follow. Here are also a skein of tangled thread and a tea roller of mottled bamboo. These things have no intrinsic value, but they are to signify that I want you to be true as jade, and your love to endure unbroken as a bracelet. The spots on the bamboo are like the marks of my tears, and my unhappy thoughts are as tangled as the thread: these objects are symbols of my feelings and tokens for all time of my love. Our hearts are close, though our

---

[2] A poet who fell in love with a rich man's daughter.

bodies are far apart and there is no time I can expect to see you. But where the hidden desires are strong enough, there will be a meeting of spirits. Take care of yourself, a thousand times over. The springtime wind is often chill; eat well for your health's sake. Be circumspect and careful, and do not think too often of my unworthy person."

Zhang showed her letter to his friends, and in that way word of the affair got around. One of them, Yang Juyuan, a skillful poet wrote a quatrain on "Young Miss Cui."

> For clear purity jade cannot equal his complexion,
> On the iris in the inner court snow begins to melt.
> A romantic young man filled with thoughts of love.
> A letter from the Xiao girl, brokenhearted.

Yuan Zhen of Henan wrote a continuation of Zhang's poem, "Encounter with an Immortal," also in thirty couplets:

> Faint moonbeams pierce the curtained window,
> Fireflies glimmer across the blue sky.
> The far horizon begins now to pale,
> Dwarf trees gradually turn darker green.
> A dragon song crosses the court bamboo,
> A phoenix air brushes the well-side tree.
> The silken robe trails through the thin mist,
> The pendant circles tinkle in the light breeze.
> The accredited envoy accompanies Xi wang mu,
> From the cloud's center comes Jade Boy.
> Late at night everyone is quiet,
> At daybreak the rain drizzles.
> Pearl radiance shines on her decorated sandals,
> Flower glow shows off the embroidered skirt.
> Jasper hairpin: a walking colored phoenix.
> Gauze shawl: embracing vermilion rainbow.
> She says she comes from Jasper Flower Bank
> And is going to pay court at Green Jade Palace.
> On an outing north of Luoyang's wall
> By chance he came to the house east of Song Yu's.
> His dalliance she reject a bit at first,
> But her yielding love already is disclosed.
> Lowered locks put in motion cicada shadows,
> Returning steps raise jade dust.
> Her face turns to let flow flower snow

As she climbs into bed, silk covers in her arms.
Love birds in a neck-entwining dance,
Kingfishers in a conjugal cage.
Eyebrows, out of shyness, contracted;
Lip rouge, from the warmth, melted.
Her breath is pure: fragrance of orchid buds;
Her skin is smooth: richness of jade flesh.
No strength, too limp to lift a wrist;
Many charms, as she likes to draw herself together.
Sweat runs: pearly drop by drop;
Hair in disorder: black luxuriance.
Just as they rejoice in the meeting of a lifetime,
They suddenly hear that the night is over.
There is no time for lingering;
It is hard to give up the wish to embrace.
Her comely face shows the sorrow she feels.
With fragrant words they swear eternal love.
She gives him a bracelet to plight their troth,
He ties a lovers' knot as sign their hearts are one.
Tear-borne powder runs before the clear mirror,
Around the flickering lamp are nighttime insects.
Moonlight is still softly shining
As the rising sun gradually dawns.
Riding on a wild goose she returns to the Luo River,
Blowing a flute he ascends Mount Sung.
His clothes are fragrant still with the musk perfume,
The pillow is slippery yet with the red traces.
Thick thick, the grass grows on the dyke;
Floating floating, the tumbleweed yearns for the isle.
Her plain cither plays the Resentful Crane Song;
In the clear Milky Way she looks for the returning wild
     goose.
The sea is broad and truly hard to cross;
The sky is high and not easy to traverse.
The moving cloud is nowhere to be found—
Xiao Shi stays in his chamber.

All of Zhang's friends who heard of the affair marveled at it, but Zhang had determined on his own course of action. Yuan Zhen was especially close to him and so was in a position to ask him for an explanation. Zhang said, "It is a general rule that those women endowed by Heaven with great beauty invariably destroy themselves or destroy someone else. If this Cui woman were to meet someone with wealth and position, she would use the favor her charms gain her to be cloud and rain or dragon or monster—I can't imagine what she might turn into. Of old, Emperor Xin of the Shang and King You of the Zhou were brought low by women, in armies were scattered, their persons butchered, and down to the present day their names are the objects of ridicule. I have no inner strength to withstand this evil influence. That is why I have resolutely suppressed my love."

At this statement everyone present sighed deeply.

Over a year later Cui was married, and Zhang for his part had taken a wife. Happening to pass through the town where she was living, he asked permission of her husband to see her, as a cousin. The husband spoke to her, but Cui refused to appear. Zhang's feelings of hurt showed on his face, and she was told about it. She secretly sent him a poem:

> Emaciated, I have lost my looks,
> Tossing and turning, too weary to leave my bed.
> It's not because of others I am ashamed to rise,
> For you I am haggard and before you ashamed.

She never did appear. Some days later when Zhang was about to leave, she sent another poem of farewell:

> Cast off and abandoned, what can I say now,
> Whom you loved so briefly long ago?
> Any love you had then for me
> Will do for the one you have now.

After this he never heard any more about her. His contemporaries for the most part conceded that Zhang had done well to rectify his mistake. I have often mentioned it among friends so that, forewarned, they might avoid doing such a thing, or if they did, that they might not be led astray by it. In the ninth month of a year in the Zhenyuan period (785–804 C.E.) when an official, Li Shen, was passing the night in my house in Jing'an Street, the conversation touched on the subject. He found it most extraordinary and composed a "Song of Yingying" to commemorate the affair. Cui's child-name was Yingying, and Li Shen used it for his poem.

48

THE STORY OF MISS LI
(*Li Wa Zhuan*)
李娃傳
Bo Xingjian
白行簡

In contrast to the tragic figure of Yingying, the prostitute Li Wa in The Story of
Miss Li *(Li Wa zhuan), written in 795* C.E., *enjoys a happy marriage and
success in her life. The author, Bo Xingjian (d. 826* C.E.*), the brother of the famous
Tang poet, Bo Juyi,[1] chooses a prostitute as the central character in his story in order
to give an emphatic lesson to all women: if a base woman can do it, all females must.
From a money-hungry and fickle-hearted woman, Li turns into the most understanding, generous, and altruistic companion to her lover. She has not only helped to
nourish him back to health, but she has also brought him to success and fame. For her
hard work and good intention, she was finally accepted by her father-in-law, given a
title by the emperor, and rewarded by heaven, as manifested by the magic toadstools
and white swallows found near her abode. Her overwhelming success was made
possible, of course, only by her adherence to the Confucian ethical code of chastity,
obedience, and self-sacrifice.*

Fatima Wu

Miss Li, ennobled with the title "Lady of Jianguo," was once a prostitute in Chang'an. The devotion of her conduct was so remarkable
that I have thought it worthwhile to record her story. In the Tianbao
era[2] there was a certain nobleman, Governor of Changzhou and Lord

---

From *More Translations from the Chinese*, translated by Arthur Waley (New York: Alfred A.
Knopf, 1919).

[1] See *Examination Essays (Panbacui)*, footnote 1 p. 341, for information on Bo Juyi.

[2] 742–756 C.E.

of Rongyang, whose name and surname I will omit. He was a man
of great wealth and highly esteemed by all. He had passed his
fiftieth year and had a son who was close on twenty, a boy who in
literary talent outstripped all his companions. His father was proud
of him and had great hopes for his future. "This," he would say, "is the
'thousand league colt' of our family." When the time came for the lad
to compete at the Provincial Examinations, his father gave him fine
clothes and a handsome coach with richly caparisoned horses for the
journey; and to provide his expense at the Capital, he gave him a large
sum of money, saying, "I am sure that your talent is such that you
will succeed at the fist attempt; but I am giving you two years' supply,
that you may pursue your career free from all anxiety." The young man
was also quite confident and saw himself getting the first place as
clearly as he saw the palm of his own hand.

Starting from Piling he reached Chang'an in a few weeks and took
a house in the Buzheng quarter. One day he was coming back from
a visit to the Eastern Market. He entered the City by the eastern gate
of Pingkang and was going to visit a friend who lived in the southwestern part of the town. When he reached the Mingke Bend, he saw
a house of which the gate and courtyard were rather narrow; but the
house was stately and stood well back from the road. One of the
double doors was open, and at it stood a lady, attended by her maidservant. She was of exquisite, bewitching beauty, such as the world
has seldom produced.

When he saw her, the young man unconsciously reined in his horse
and hesitated. Unable to leave the spot, he purposely let his whip fall
to the ground and waited for his servant to pick it up, all the time
staring at the lady in the doorway. She too was staring and met his
gaze with a look that seemed to be an answer to his admiration. But
in the end he went away without daring to speak to her.

But he could not put the thought of her out of his mind and
secretly begged those of his friends who were most expert in the pleasures of Chang'an to tell him what they knew of the girl. He learnt
from them that the house belonged to a low and unprincipled woman
named Li. When he asked what chance he had of winning the daughter, they answered: "The woman Li is possessed of considerable property, for her previous dealings have been with wealthy and aristocratic
families, from whom she has received enormous sums. Unless you are
willing to spend many thousand pounds, the daughter will have
nothing to do with you."

The young man answered: "All I care about is winning her. I do
not mind if she costs a million pounds." The next day he set out in

his best clothes, with many servants riding behind him, and knocked at the door of Mrs. Li's house. Immediately a pageboy drew the bolt. The young man asked, "Can you tell me whose house this is?" The boy did not answer, but ran back into the house and called out at the top of his voice, "Here is the gentleman who dropped his whip the other day!"

Miss Li was evidently very much pleased. He heard her saying, "Be sure not to let him go away. I am just going to do my hair and change my clothes; I will be back in a minute." The young man, in high spirits, followed the pageboy into the house. A white-haired old lady was going upstairs, whom he took to be the girl's mother. Bowing low, the young man addressed her as follows: "I am told that you have a vacant plot of land, which you would be willing to let as building-ground. Is that true?" The old lady answered, "I am afraid the site is too mean and confined; it would not be quite suitable for a gentleman's house. I should not like to offer it to you." She then took him into the guest room, which was a very handsome one, and asked him to be seated, saying, "I have a daughter who has little either of beauty or accomplishment, but she is fond of seeing strangers. I should like you to meet her."

So saying, she called for her daughter, who presently entered. Her eyes sparkled with such fire, her arms were so dazzling white, and there was in her movements such an exquisite grace that the young man could only leap to his feet in confusion and did not dare raise his eyes. When their salutations were over, he began to make a few remarks about the weather, and realized as he did so that her beauty was of a kind he had never encountered before.

They sat down again. Tea was made and wine poured out. The vessels used were spotlessly clean. He lingered till the day was almost over; the curfew-drum sounded its four beats. The old lady asked if he lived far away. He answered untruthfully, "Several leagues beyond Yanping Gate," hoping that they would ask him to stay. The old lady said, "The drum has sounded. You will have to go back at once, unless you mean to break the law."

The young man answered, "I was being so agreeably entertained that I did not notice how rapidly the day had fled. My house is a long way off and in the city I have no friends or relations. What am I to do?" Miss Li then interposed, saying, "If you can forgive the meanness of our poor home, what harm would there be in your spending the night with us?" He looked doubtfully at the girl's mother, but met with no discouragement.

Calling his servants, he gave them money and told them to buy provisions for the night. But the girl laughingly stopped him, saying,

"That is not the way guests are entertained. Our humble house will provide for your wants tonight, if you are willing to partake of our simple fare and defer your bounty to another occasion." He tried to refuse, but in the end she would not allow him to, and they all moved to the western hall. The curtains, screens, blinds, and couches were of dazzling splendor; while the toilet boxes, rugs, and pillows were of the utmost elegance. Candles were lighted and an excellent supper was served.

After supper the old lady retired, leaving the lovers engaged in the liveliest conversation, laughing and chattering completely at their ease.

After a while the young man said: "I passed your house the other day and you happened to be standing at the door. And after that, I could think of nothing but you; whether I lay down to rest or sat down to eat, I could not stop thinking of you." She laughed and answered: "It was just the same with me." He said: "You must know that I did not come today to look for building-land. I came hoping that you would fulfil my lifelong desire; but I was not sure how you would welcome me. What—"

He had not finished speaking when the old woman came back and asked what they were saying. When they told her, she laughed and said, "Has not Mencius written that 'the relationship between men and women is the groundwork of society'? When lovers are agreed, not even the mandate of a parent will deter them. But my daughter is of humble birth. Are you sure that she is fit to 'present pillow and mat' to a great man?"

He came down from the dais and, bowing low, begged that she would accept him as her slave. Henceforward the old lady regarded him as her son-in-law; they drank heavily together and finally parted. Next morning he had all his boxes and bags brought round to Mrs. Li's house and settled there permanently. Henceforward he shut himself up with his mistress and none of his friends ever heard of him. He consorted only with actors and dancers and low people of that kind, passing the time in wild sports and wanton feasting. In about a year his money, property, servants, and horses were all gone.

For some time the old lady's manner towards him had been growing rapidly colder, but his mistress remained as devoted as ever. One day she said to him, "We have been together a year, but I am still not with child. They say that the spirit of the Bamboo Grove answers a woman's prayers as surely as an echo. Let us go to his temple and offer a libation."

The young man, not suspecting any plot, was delighted to take her to the temple, and having pawned his coat to buy sweet wine for the libation, he went with her and performed the ceremony of prayer. They stayed one night at the temple and came back the next day. Whipping up their donkey, they soon arrived at the north gate of the Pingkang quarter. At this point his mistress turned to him and said, "My aunt's house is in a turning just near here. How would it be if we were to go there and rest for a little?"

He drove on as she directed him, and they had not gone more than a hundred paces, when he saw the entrance to a spacious carriage drive. A servant who belonged to the place came out and stopped the cart, saying, "This is the entrance." The young man got down and was met by some one who came out and asked who they were. When told that it was Miss Li, he went back and announced her. Presently a married lady came out who seemed to be about forty. She greeted him, saying, "Has my niece arrived?" Miss Li then got out of the cart and her aunt said to her: "Why have you not been to see me for so long?" At which they looked at one another and laughed. Then Miss Li introduced him to her aunt, and when that was over they all went into a side garden near the Western Halberd Gate. In the middle of the garden was a pagoda, and round it grew bamboo and trees of every variety, while ponds and summer-houses added to its air of seclusion. He asked Miss Li if this were her aunt's estate; she laughed, but did not answer and spoke of something else.

Tea of excellent quality was served; but when they had been drinking it for a little while, a messenger came galloping up on a huge Fergana horse, saying that Miss Li's mother had suddenly been taken very ill and had already lost consciousness, so that they had better come back as quickly as possible.

Miss Li said to her aunt: "I am very upset. I think I had better take the horse and ride on ahead. Then I will send it back, and you and my husband can come along later." The young man was anxious to go with her, but the aunt and her servants engaged him in conversation, flourishing their hands in front of him and preventing him from leaving the garden. The aunt said to him: "No doubt my sister is dead by this time. You and I ought to discuss together what can be done to help with the expenses of the burial. What is the use of running off like that? Stay here and help me to make a plan for the funeral and mourning ceremonies."

It grew late; but the messenger had not returned. The aunt said: "I am surprised he has not come back with the horse. You had better go there on foot as quickly as possible and see what has happened. I will come on later."

The young man set out on foot for Mrs. Li's house. When he got
there he found the gate firmly bolted, locked, and sealed. Astounded,
he questioned the neighbors, who told him that the house had only
been let to Mrs. Li and that, the lease having expired, the landlord
had now resumed possession. The old lady, they said, had gone to live
elsewhere. They did not know her new address.

At first he thought of hurrying back to Xuanyang and questioning the aunt; but he found it was too late for him to get there. So he
pawned some of his clothes, and, with the proceeds, bought himself
supper and hired a bed. But he was too angry and distressed to sleep,
and did not once close his eyes from dusk till dawn. Early in the
morning he dragged himself away and went to the "aunt's house." He
knocked on the door repeatedly, but it was breakfast time and no one
answered. At last, when he had shouted several times at the top of his
voice, a footman walked majestically to the door. The young man nervously mentioned the aunt's name and asked whether she was at home.
The footman replied: "No one of that name here." "But she lived
here yesterday evening," the young man protested. "Why are you
trying to deceive me? If she does not live here, who *does* the house
belong to?" The footman answered: "This is the residence of His
Excellency Mr. Cui. I believe that yesterday some persons hired a
corner of the grounds. I understand they wished to entertain a cousin
who was coming from a distance. But they were gone before
nightfall."

The young man, perplexed and puzzled to the point of madness,
was absolutely at a loss what to do next. The best he could think of
was to go to the quarters in Buzheng, where he had installed himself
when he first arrived at Chang'an. The landlord was sympathetic and
offered to feed him. But the young man was much too upset to eat,
and having fasted for three days fell seriously ill. He rapidly grew
worse, and the landlord, fearing he would not recover, had him moved
straight to the undertaker's shop. In a short time the whole of the
undertaker's staff was collected round him, offering sympathy and
bringing him food. Gradually he got better and was able to walk with
a stick.

The undertaker now hired him by the day to hold up the curtains
of fine cloth, by which he earned just enough to support himself. In
a few months he grew quite strong again, but whenever he heard the
mourners' doleful songs, in which they regretted that they could not
change places with the corpse, burst into violent fits of sobbing, and
shed streams of tears over which they lost all control, then he would
go home and imitate their performance.

Being a man of intelligence, he very soon mastered the art and finally became the most expert mourner in Chang'an. It happened that there were two undertakers at this time between whom there was a great rivalry. The undertaker of the east turned out magnificent hearses, and in this respect his superiority could not be contested. But the mourners he provided were somewhat inferior. Hearing of our young man's skill, he offered him a large sum for his services. The eastern undertaker's supporters, who were familiar with the repertoire of his company, secretly taught the young man several fresh tunes and showed him how to fit the words to them. The lessons went on for several weeks, without anyone being allowed to know of it. At the end of that time the two undertakers agreed to hold a competitive exhibition of their wares in Tianmen Street. The loser was to forfeit 50,000 cash to cover the cost of the refreshments provided before the exhibition. An agreement was then drawn up and duly signed by witnesses.

A crowd of several thousand people collected to watch the competition. The mayor of the quarter got wind of the proceedings and told the chief of police. The chief of police told the governor of the city. Very soon all the gentlemen of Chang'an were hurrying to the spot and every house in the town was empty. The exhibition lasted from dawn to midday. Coaches, hearses, and all kinds of funeral trappings were successively displayed, but the undertaker of the west could establish no superiority. Filled with shame, he set up a platform in the south corner of the square. Presently a man with a long beard came forward, carrying a hand-bell and attended by several assistants. He wagged his beard, raised his eyebrows, folded his arms across his chest, and bowed. Then, mounting the platform, he sang "The Dirge of the White Horse." When it was over, confident of an easy victory, he glared round him, as if to imply that his opponents had all vanished. He was applauded on every side and was himself convinced that his talents were a unique product of the age and could not possibly be called into question.

After a while the undertaker of the east put together some benches in the north corner of the square, and a young man in a black hat came forward, attended by five assistants and carrying a bunch of hearse-plumes in his hand. It was the young man of our story.

He adjusted his clothes, looked timidly up and down, and then cleared his throat and began his tune with an air of great diffidence.

He sang the dirge "Dew on the Garlic." His voice rose so shrill and clear that "its echoes shook the forest trees." Before he had finished the first verse, all who heard were sobbing and hiding their tears.

When the performance was over, everyone made fun of the western undertaker, and he was so much put out that he immediately removed his exhibits and retired from the contest. The audience was amazed by the collapse of the western undertaker and could not imagine where his rival had procured so remarkable a singer.

It happened that the emperor had recently issued an order commanding the governors of outside provinces to confer with him at the capital at least once a year.

At this time, the young man's father, who was governor of Changzhou, had recently arrived at the capital to make his report. Hearing of the competition, he and some of his colleagues discarded their official robes and insignia and slipped away to join the crowd. With them was an old servant, who was the husband of the young man's foster-nurse. Recognizing his foster-son's way of moving and speaking, he was on the point of accosting him, but not daring to do so, he stooped, weeping silently. The father asked him why he was crying, and the servant replied, "Sir, the young man who is singing reminds me of your lost son." The father answered: "My son became the prey of robbers, because I gave him too much money. This cannot be he." So saying, he also began to weep and, leaving the crowd, returned to his lodging.

But the old servant went about among the members of the troupe, asking who it was that had just sung with such skill. They all told him it was the son of such a one; and when he asked the young man's own name, that too was unfamiliar, for he was living under an alias. The old servant was so much puzzled that he determined to put the matter to test for himself. But when the young man saw his old friend walking towards him, he winced, turned away his face, and tried to hide in the crowd. The old man followed him and catching his sleeve said: "Surely it is you!" Then they embraced and wept. Presently they went back together to his father's lodging. But his father abused him, saying: "Your conduct has disgraced the family. How dare you show your face again?" So saying, he took him out of the house and led him to the ground between the Qujiang Pond and the Apricot Gardens. Here he stripped him naked and thrashed him with his horsewhip, till the young man succumbed to the pain and collapsed. The father then left him and went away.

But the young man's singing master had told some of his friends to watch what happened to him. When they saw him stretched inanimate on the ground, they came back and told other members of the troupe.

The news occasioned universal lamentation, and two men were dispatched with a reed mat to cover up the body. When they got there they found his heart still warm, and when they held him in an upright posture for some time, his breathing recommenced. So they carried him home between them and administered liquid food through a reed-pipe. Next morning, he recovered consciousness; but after several months he was still unable to move his hands and feet. Moreover, the sores left by his thrashing festered in so disgusting a manner that his friends found him too troublesome, and one night deposited him in the middle of the road. However, the passersby, harrowed by his condition, never failed to throw him scraps of food.

So copious was his diet that in three months he recovered sufficiently to hobble with a stick. Clad in a linen coat—which was knotted together in several hundred places, so that it looked as tattered as a quail's tail—and carrying a broken saucer in his hand, he now went about the idle quarters of the town, earning his living as a professional beggar.

Autumn had now turned to winter. He spent his nights in public lavatories and his days haunting the markets and booths.

One day when it was snowing hard, hunger and cold had driven him into the streets. His beggar's cry was full of woe, and all who heard it were heartrent. But the snow was so heavy that hardly a house had its outer door open, and the streets were empty.

When he reached the eastern gate of Anyi, about the seventh or eighth turning north of the Xunli Wall, there was a house with the double-doors half open.

It was the house where Miss Li was then living, but the young man did not know.

He stood before the door, wailing loud and long.

Hunger and cold had given such a piteous accent to his cry that none could have listened unmoved.

Miss Li heard it from her room and at once said to her servant, "That is so-and-so. I know his voice." She flew to the door and was horrified to see her old lover standing before her so emaciated by hunger and disfigured by sores that he scarcely seemed human. "Can it be you?" she said. But the young man was so overcome by bewilderment and excitement that he could not speak, and only moved his lips noiselessly.

She threw her arms round his neck, then wrapped him in her own embroidered jacket and led him to the parlor. Here, with quavering voice, she reproached herself, saying, "It is my doing that you have been brought to this pass." And with these words she swooned.

Her mother came running up in great excitement, asking who had arrived. Miss Li, recovering herself, said who it was. The old woman cried out in rage: "Send him away! What did you bring him in here for?"

But Miss Li looked up at her defiantly and said: "Not so! This is the son of a noble house. Once he rode in grand coaches and wore golden trappings on his coat. But when he came to our house, he soon lost all he had; and then we plotted together and left him destitute. Our conduct has indeed been inhuman! We have ruined his career and robbed him even of his place in the category of human relationships. For the love of father and son is implanted by Heaven; yet we have hardened his father's heart, so that he beat him with a stick and left him on the ground.

"Everyone in the land knows that it is I who have reduced him to his present plight. The Court is full of his kinsmen. Someday one of them will come into power. Then an inquiry will be set afoot, and disaster will overtake us. And since we have flouted Heaven and defied the laws of humanity, neither spirits nor divinities will be on our side. Let us not wantonly incur a further retribution!

"I have lived as your daughter for twenty years. Reckoning what I have cost you in that time, I find it must be close on a thousand pieces of gold. You are now aged sixty, so that by the price of twenty more years' food and clothing, I can buy my freedom. I intend to live separately with this young man. We will not go far away; I shall see to it that we are near enough to pay our respects to you both morning and evening."

The "mother" saw that she was not to be gainsaid and fell in with the arrangement. When she had paid her ransom, Miss Li had a hundred pieces of gold left over, and with them she hired a vacant room, five doors away. Here she gave the young man a bath, changed his clothes, fed him with hot soup to relax his stomach, and later fattened him up with cheese and milk.

In a few weeks she began to place before him all the choice delicacies of land and sea; and she clothed him with cap, shoes, and stockings of the finest quality. In a short time he began gradually to put on flesh, and by the end of the year, he had entirely recovered his former health.

One day Miss Li said to him: "Now your limbs are stout again and your will strong! Sometimes, when deeply pondering in silent sorrow, I wonder to myself how much you remember of your old literary studies?" He thought and answered: "Of ten parts I remember two or three."

Miss Li then ordered the carriage to be made ready and the young man followed her on horseback. When they reached the classical bookshop at the side gate south of the Flag-tower, she made him choose all the books he wanted, till she had laid out a hundred pieces of gold. Then she packed them in the cart and drove home. She now made him dismiss all other thoughts from his mind and apply himself only to study. All the evening he toiled at his books, with Miss Li at his side, and they did not retire till midnight. If ever she found that he was too tired to work, she made him lay down his classics and write a poem or an ode.

In two years he had thoroughly mastered his subjects and was admired by all the scholars of the realm. He said to Miss Li, "Now, surely, I am ready for the examiners!" But she would not let him compete and made him revise all he had learnt, to prepare for the "hundredth battle." At the end of the third year she said, "Now you may go." He went in for the examination and passed at the first attempt. His reputation spread rapidly through the examination rooms, and even older men, when they saw his compositions, were filled with admiration and respect and sought his friendship.

But Miss Li would not let him make friends with them, saying, "Wait a little longer! Nowadays when a bachelor of arts has passed his examination, he thinks himself fit to hold the most advantageous posts at Court and to win a universal reputation. But your unfortunate conduct and disreputable past put you at a disadvantage beside your fellow scholars. You must 'grind, temper, and sharpen' your attainments, that you may secure a second victory. Then you will be able to match yourself against famous scholars and contend with the illustrious."

The young man accordingly increased his efforts and enhanced his value. That year it happened that the emperor had decreed a special examination for the selection of candidates of unusual merit from all parts of the Empire. The young man competed, and came out at the top in the "censorial essay." He was offered the post of Army Inspector at Chengdu Fu. The officers who were to escort him were all previous friends.

When he was about to take up his post, Miss Li said to him, "Now that you are restored to your proper station in life, I will not be a burden to you. Let me go back and look after the old lady till she dies. You must ally yourself with some lady of noble lineage, who will be worthy to carry the sacrificial dishes in your Ancestral Hall. Do not injure your prospects by an unequal union. Good bye, for now I must leave you."

The young man burst into tears and threatened to kill himself if she left him, but she obstinately refused to go with him. He begged her passionately not to desert him, and she at last consented to go with him across the river as far as Jianmen.[3] Before he had started out again, a proclamation arrived announcing that the young man's father, who had been Governor of Changzhou, had been appointed Governor of Chengdu and Intendant of the Jiannan Circuit. The next morning the father arrived, and the young man sent in his card and waited upon him at the posting station. His father did not recognize him, but the card bore the names of the young man's father and grandfather, with their ranks and titles. When he read these, he was astounded, and bidding his son mount the steps he caressed him and wept. After a while he said, "Now we two are father and son once more," and bade him tell his story. When he heard of the young man's adventures, he was amazed. Presently he asked, "And where is Miss Li?" He replied, "She came with me as far as here, but now she is going back again."

"I cannot allow it," the father said. The next day he ordered a carriage for his son and sent him to report himself at Chengdu; but he detained Miss Li at Jianmen, found her suitable lodging, and ordered a matchmaker to perform the initial ceremonies for uniting the two families and to accomplish the six rites of welcome. The young man came back from Chengdu, and they were duly married. In the years that followed their marriage, Miss Li showed herself to be a devoted wife and competent housekeeper, and was beloved by all her relations.

Some years later both the young man's parents died, and in his mourning observances he showed unusual piety. As a mark of divine favor, magic toadstools grew on the roof of his mourning hut,[4] each stem bearing three plants. The report of his virtue reached even the emperor's ears. Moreover a number of white swallows nested in the beams of his roof, an omen that so impressed the emperor that he raised his rank immediately.

When the three years of mourning were over, he was successively promoted to various distinguished posts, and in the course of ten years was Governor of several provinces. Miss Li was given the fief of Jianguo, with the title "The Lady of Jianguo."

---

[3] The "Sword-gate" commands the pass that leads into Sichuan from the north.

[4] See *The Record of Rites*, XXXII, Section 3. On returning from his father's burial a son must not enter the house; he should live in an "outhouse," mourning for his father's absence.

He had four sons who all held high rank. Even the least successful of them became Governor of Taiyuan, and his brothers all married into great families, so that his good fortune both in public and private life was without parallel. How strange that we should find in the conduct of a prostitute a degree of constancy rarely equaled even by the heroines of history! Surely the story is one that cannot but provoke a sigh!

My great-uncle was Governor of Jinzhou; subsequently he joined the Ministry of Finance and became Inspector of Waterways, and finally Inspector of Roads. In all these three offices he had Miss Li's husband as his colleague, so that her story was well known to him in every particular. During the Zhengyuan period[5] I was sitting one day with Li Gongzuo[6] of Longhai; we fell to talking of wives who had distinguished themselves by remarkable conduct. I told him the story of Miss Li. He listened with rapt attention, and when it was over asked me to write it down for him. So I took up my brush, wetted the hairs, and made this rough outline of the story.

> [*Dated*] *autumn, eighth month of the year Yihai,* (795 C.E.),
> *written by Bo Xingjian of Taiyuan.*

---

[5] 785–805 C.E.

[6] A writer.

49

PRECEPTS FOR FAMILY LIFE
(Jiafan)
家范
Sima Guang
司馬光

Precepts for Family Life (Jiafan) *is a Song dynasty manual on interpersonal ethics within the family. It also takes up various aspects of household management. In the book, Sima Guang (1019–1086 C.E.), a pivotal figure in the development of Neo-Confucianism, provides advice to a Song audience by recalling and reinforcing the knowledge of family and gender that he believes had been established in the Confucian classics.* Precepts for Family Life *thus represents the efforts of Song scholars toward reviving Confucianism.*

In the selections presented here, Sima Guang discourses on the nature of the family and the conduct proper to daughters and wives. His effort to restore Confucian teaching reveals all the strengths and weaknesses of scholasticism in any intellectual tradition. The need for systematic exposition seems to require a proliferation of rules and increasingly detailed applications to the minutiae of ordinary living. This seems a far cry from the original Confucian emphasis on the cultivation of virtues that could be relied upon to determine appropriate behavior. The rules so determined seem increasingly restrictive of whatever discretion a woman might have over her own actions. On the other hand, Sima Guang's Confucian restoration does specifically entail the renewal of a commitment to the education of women. Though the education he calls for may also be unduly restrictive, it does require that women be taught The Book of Filial Piety, The Analects, The Book of Odes, *and* The Record of Rites. *Thus, they, too, can acquire the same training as the legendary women of old who are said to have had "history books on their left and illustrations of exemplary women on their right" in order to develop themselves in "womanly virtue." Literacy's potential for liberating women, in Sima Guang's scheme of things, is, of course, over-*

Translated by Ping Yao.

ridden by an appeal to the cosmic principles of Heaven and Earth, Yang and Yin,
that are used here to identify propriety as such with female submissiveness.

Ping Yao

Managing a Family *(zhijia)*

Yan Ying of the Qi State said: "A ruler should be moral, and a subject
dutiful; a father should be benevolent, and a son filial; an older brother
should be loving, and a younger brother respectful; a husband should
be amiable, and a wife gentle; a mother-in-law should be kind, and a
daughter-in-law submissive. These are the rules of propriety." Indeed,
the ideal rules for proper conduct can be made more explicit: a ruler
is moral and consistent, and a subject is dutiful and loyal; a father is
benevolent and educates his children, and a son is filial and amenable;
an older brother is loving and friendly, and a younger brother is
respectful and obedient; a husband is amiable and righteous, and a
wife is gentle and proper; a mother-in-law is kind and understanding,
a daughter-in-law is submissive and restrained.

The most important thing in managing a family is observing the
rules of proper conduct, and the essence of these rules is the separation of male and female. Therefore a person who manages a family
should make implementing the rules a priority. Men and women
should not sit together, nor share clothes hangers, towels, or combs.
Men and women should have no direct physical contact when giving
or receiving things. Wives and their brothers-in-law should not greet
each other. Concubines who give have given birth to children should
not wash underclothes. Discussions occurring in the outer quarters
should not be passed on to the inner quarters and vice versa. Once a
girl is engaged to be married, she should wear a colorful ribbon. She
should not enter the outer quarters unless for serious matters. When
married sisters and daughters return home for a visit, they should not
sit with their brothers on the same mat, nor share with them the same
set of eating utensils.

Without a matchmaker, a man and a woman should not be familiar with each other's names. They should not contact each other before
accepting each other's engagement presents. The families should publicly announce the wedding date in writing; make offerings to appease
the spirits; and prepare banquets and invite neighbors, friends, and
relatives. These confirm the importance of the separation of men and
women.

In addition, under no circumstances except at sacrifices and funerals, should a man and a woman directly pass a vessel to one another. If they have to, then the woman should put the vessel into a bucket. If no bucket is available, then both of them should sit down, and the vessel should be picked up by the other after it has been put down on the floor. The inner and outer quarters should share neither a well, nor a washroom. The inner and outer quarters should not use the same set of bedding or borrow things and containers from each other. When a man comes to the inner quarters, he should not whistle or make excessive gestures. When he walks around at night, a man should hold a candle. Without a candle, he should not make any move. When a woman leaves the inner quarters, she should have her face covered. When she walks around at night, she should hold a candle. Without a candle, she should not make any move. On the streets, men should walk on the right side and women on the left side.

Furthermore, once they reach the age of seven, boys and girls should not share a bed or eat at the same table. When a boy is ten years old, he should be educated by a teacher and live in the outer quarters. When a girl is ten years old, she should not leave the household. In addition, women should not leave the gate when greeting and saying farewell to guests. Women should not cross the threshold into the streets even when they see their brothers.

Daughter (nü)

Cao Dagu's *Lessons for Women*[1] says: Gentlemen nowadays only educate their sons, teaching them ancient classics and biographies. Don't such gentlemen realize that if serving a husband is absolutely important, women's knowing proper conduct is entirely necessary? Won't daughters be unequipped to be proper wives and mothers if a family only teaches boys and not also girls? *The Record of Rites* stipulates: a child of eight years old should be taught reading; a child of ten years old should have the aspiration of learning. Why can't we apply this rule also to girls' education?

In general, "womanly virtue" does not necessarily mean to have outstanding talents or intelligence; "womanly speech" does not necessarily mean to be sharp and argumentative; "womanly appearance" does not necessarily require being born pretty and attractive; and "womanly

---

[1] Cao Dagu is the title name of Ban Zhao. See pp. 177–188 for the full text of *Lessons for Women*.

work" does not necessarily require the best needlework.[2] Womanly virtue means being pure and peaceful, being chaste and orderly, conducting oneself properly, and avoiding shameful things. Womanly speech means selecting words carefully, avoiding bad language, speaking only when it is appropriate, and not annoying anyone. Womanly appearance means washing off dirty things around her, wearing fresh and neat clothes, taking baths regularly, and keeping her body clean. Womanly work means concentrating on weaving, avoiding merrymaking, cleaning, and preparing wine and food to entertain the guests.

The above are the four most important and indispensable female virtues. However, it is rather easy to do these things as long as a woman keeps them in mind. If a person does not study, he or she will not know proper conduct and its meaning; if a person does not know the proper actions and their meanings, he or she cannot distinguish good from bad and right from wrong. Therefore, even if a person committed a horrible crime, he or she will not realize it was wrong; and even if disaster and disgrace are imminent, he or she will not realize the danger. If it is absolutely necessary for everyone to learn, why should men and women be different in this matter?

Therefore, before a girl is married, she should read *The Book of Filial Piety*, the *Analects of Confucius*, *The Book of Odes*, and *The Record of Rites*. She should understand the general ideas contained in these books. In terms of womanly work, she can learn weaving, sewing, and cooking. As to embroidery, singing, and playing music instruments, not all of these are suitable for a girl to learn. Virtuous women of ancient times all enjoyed learning. They always had history books on their left and illustrations of exemplary women on their right. They used these books to admonish themselves.

Wife (*qi*)

The Great Historian[3] said: The Xia dynasty rose from the Tu Mountain, but because of Mei Xi, King Jie was disposed.[4] The Shang

---

[2] "Womanly virtue," "womanly speech," "womanly appearance," and "womanly work" are the four female virtues advocated by Ban Zhao in her *Lessons for Women* (see pp. 177–188).

[3] The Great Historian is Sima Qian (145 B.C.E.–?) of the Han dynasty. He wrote the *Historical Record*, the first Chinese history book.

[4] According to Sima Qian's *Historical Record*, the Xia dynasty, the first Chinese dynasty, ruled China from the twenty-first century B.C.E. to the sixteenth century B.C.E. King Jie

dynasty grew strong with the help of the Yourong clan, but King Zhou ended up being killed because he favored Da Ji.[5] The rise of the Zhou dynasty was due to Youjiang and Daren's virtues, but King You was captured by the barbarians because of his sexual indulgence with Baosi.[6] That is why *The Classic of Changes* stresses the concept of *yin* and *yang*, and *The Book of Odes* begins with the poem, "The Osprey's Cry," for the relationship between husband and wife is the essence of humanity.[7] Among all the rules of propriety, marriage should be the one most carefully observed. For when the music is harmonious, the four seasons are in right order; and the *yin-yang* combination is the principle of the universe. How can we not be vigilant?

As a wife of a man, a woman should have six virtues: first, be gentle; second, clean; third, not jealous; fourth, frugal; fifth, restrained; and six, diligent. A husband is like the heaven and a wife is like the earth; a husband is like the sun and a wife is like the moon; a husband is *yang* and a wife is *yin*. Heaven symbolizes superiority and highness, and earth symbolizes inferiority and lowliness. The sun does not wax and wane, while the moon changes between being full and declining. *Yang* is responsible for creating things, while *yin* is responsible for helping in such creation. Therefore, women should regard being gentle and submissive as the highest virtue, and should not take pride in being aggressive and argumentative.

---

was the last ruler of the Xia. He was deposed due to his obsession with his lover, Mei Xi.

[5] Zhou was the last ruler of the Shang dynasty (ca. 1600–1045 B.C.E.). Da Ji was his concubine.

[6] King You was the last ruler of the Western Zhou dynasty (1045–771 B.C.E.). Baosi was said to be a beautiful woman presented to King You by a barbarian tribe. See pp. 149–161 for the stories of Baosi in *Biographies of Women*.

[7] See pp. 4–24 for more selections from *The Book of Odes* and pp. 25–45 for *The Classic of Changes*.

50

TANG POEMS FOR
MY BELOVED WIFE
(Sanqian beihuai)

三遣悲懷

Yuan Zhen

元積

The poems with the title Sanqian beihuai (Three times trying to disperse sorrows) were written by Yuan Zhen (779–831 C.E.) after his wife Wei Cong died in 809 C.E. at the age of 26. A few allusions in the poems need explanation. Lord Xie refers to Xie An, a fourth-century C.E. leading statesman, who was known to favor his youngest niece, Xie Daoyun, above all his relatives on account of her literary talent. This allusion hints at both the prominence of Wei Cong's family and her own cultivation. Pan Yue (247–300 C.E.) was the first poet who mourned the death of his wife. Deng You fled to the south after the Jin dynasty collapsed in 316 C.E.; as he was able to save only one child from the turmoil, he took with him his nephew instead of his own son. Wei Cong bore altogether five children, but only one daughter survived. The pawning of the golden hairpin is a topos representing the lengths to which the loyal wife of a poor but hospitable man will go in order to enable him to entertain his visitors.

Pei-yi Wu

1

Lord Xie was most fond of his youngest daughter,
Who, ever since she married a poor scholar, had gone through
   a hundred woes.
Noticing that I had very little to wear, she searched to the
   bottom of the grass box.

Translated by Pei-yi Wu.

On the way to the wine shop I begged her for money: she
   took off her golden hairpin.
Wild plants we ate, and beanstalks were a luxury.
Short of firewood, she waited for leaves falling off the old
   elms.
With my salary now exceeding a hundred thousand cash,
I shall have for you, finally, sacrifice and libation as well as a
   Buddhist service.

2

We used to speak playfully of what to do if one of us were
   gone.
Now everything we said is emerging right before my eyes.
All your clothes are about to be given away.
But I still cannot bear to open your sewing case.
Our servants I treat with compassion, remembering your
   kindness to them.
Money is given to them because you told me to in my
   dreams.
I know only too well that such sadness befalls everyone,
Only as an impoverished couple we had shared so many
   sorrows.

3

When I have a moment to sit down I grieve for you as well as
   for myself.
How much longer am I going to be in this world?
Like Deng You I am approaching fifty without a son;
Isn't it futile to imitate Pan Yue in writing poems to mourn a
   lost wife?
I shall be buried next to you, but what can we share other
   than a dark tomb?
To meet again in a future life is even less certain.
The only thing I can do is repay your many careworn days
With my long sleepless nights.

51

THE SONG OF LASTING REGRET

(Changhen ge)

長恨歌

Bo Juyi

白居易

As all students of the Tang—as well as most students of other periods of Chinese history and literature—are well aware, "The Song of Lasting Regret" (Changhen ge) is the famous poet Bo Juyi's (772–846 C.E.) romanticized retelling of the notorious love affair between the great emperor Li Longji (r. 712–756 C.E., posthumously known as Xuan Zong) and Yang Yuhuan, the lady raised by him in 742 C.E. to the high rank of "Precious Consort" (guifei).

    The emperor's infatuation with Lady Yang and his virtual abandonment of governmental affairs (first to the dictatorial Li Linfu, who held sway as Minister of State until 752 C.E., and then to the equally grasping Yang Guozhong, a distant cousin of Lady Yang) have long been regarded in both official and popular history as the main factors leading to the ruin of Xuan Zong's long reign and the near destruction of the dynasty itself. The effective instrument of overthrow was, of course, the Sogdian-Turkic general known by the sinicized name An Lushan, who, as a personal favorite of both the emperor and his consort, gradually accumulated supreme military power in the northeast border region and, in December 755 C.E., turned his troops against the government. By July of 756, the rebel forces were in position to overrun the capital city, Chang'an. In the face of this imminent threat, the emperor and his immediate entourage and military guard fled the capital in the early morning of July 14, intending to take refuge in Shu (present-day Sichuan) in the southwest, where Yang Guozhong had built up a private stronghold and sphere of influence. The next day, at the Mawei post-station (located some thirty miles west of the capital), the imperial troops killed Yang Guozhong and refused to move on unless the emperor put Lady Yang to death as well. Xuan Zong was compelled to appease the soldiers, and

From Paul W. Kroll, "Po Chü-i's Song of Lasting Regret: A New Translation," *T'ang Studies* 8–9 (1990–1991): 97–105. Reprinted by permission of Paul W. Kroll.

Lady Yang submitted to being strangled to death with a cord wielded by Gao Lishi, chief eunuch and the emperor's oldest confidant. After this event the emperor moved on to sanctuary in Shu, while the heir-apparent (Li Heng, posthumously known as Su Zong, r. 756–762 C.E.) broke off with a contingent of soldiers from the main party to proceed northwest and organize a base of loyalist resistance against the rebels. Shortly thereafter, Li Heng proclaimed himself emperor; Xuan Zong had no choice but to acknowledge his now emeritus status. About a year and a half later, Chang'an was retaken by Tang forces, and Su Zong invited the old emperor to return to the capital, where he would live out his remaining years in sad remembrance of earlier glories. But it would not be until 763 C.E. that the rebellion begun by An Lushan would be fully quelled. When the state was again, finally, unified, and the forty-four-year reign of Xuan Zong—unprecedented in its splendor—was but a memory, it seemed to most that a great turning point in history had been passed. Notwithstanding more serious political and military causes for the disaster, that a reign of such magnificence could end with such a crash confirmed most members of the tradition-ally misogynist mandarinate in the view that the root cause of the debacle was lodged in the emperor's shameful relationship with the Precious Consort Yang.

This is the view adopted by Bo Juyi in his poem. But Bo is as interested in the sentimental side of the tale as he is in its political implications. Indeed, in his telling it is primarily a love story—one which he allows himself license to embroider, at times, with incidents contrary to fact (such as the trampling of Lady Yang under the army's horses and the emperor's reduced entourage passing by Mount Emei) as well as the insertion of scenes of pure fantasy (the Daoist adept's visit to Lady Yang's ethe-real essence in the isles of the immortals and his conversation with her there).

The poem was written early in 807 C.E. and was originally supplemented with a more historically accurate prose recitation of events, the "Tale of the Song of Lasting Regret," by Bo's friend Chen Hong. Composed in 120 heptasyllabic lines, the poem is organized in a series of vignettes set forth in rhyming couplets and in quatrains (the latter with an AABA rhyme scheme); these short, lilting units are framed by octets (rhyming AABACADA) at the beginning and the end of the poem. Rhyme changes in the original are indicated as stanza breaks in the translation here.

The narrative divides into six major sections: I (lines 1–32), telling of Lady Yang's captivation of the sensually sated emperor, his first view of her as she emerged naked from the hot springs at the imperial resort, their growing passion and her com-plete monopolization of the emperor's attention, the advancement of her relatives, and the extended revels over which she presided—until the arrival of An Lushan's rebel forces; II (lines 33–42), the imperial flight from the capital city and the forced exe-cution of Lady Yang at Mawei Slope, exacted by the army as the price for accompa-nying the emperor further; III (lines 43–50), the emperor's progress into safe exile in Sichuan, darkened by the loss of his love; IV (lines 51–56), Xuanzong's tearful halt at the spot where Lady Yang was killed, during his return journey in the winter of 757–758 C.E. to Chang'an upon its recapture from the rebels; V (lines 57–74),

Xuan Zong's lonesome and mournful existence amidst the palace environs that are heavy with memories of the beautiful past; and VI (lines 75–120), the quest of a Daoist adept, at the retired emperor's bidding, to find the soul of his beloved, the adept's discovery of her in the magic isle of Penglai, her sorrow-stricken recognition of the gulf that now separates her from Xuan Zong, and her consigning to the Daoist both physical and verbal tokens of her affection for Xuan Zong, to serve as pledges to the emperor of her continual remembrance of him and her hope that they will ultimately, beyond this life, be joined again. The final section comprises more than a third of the entire poem and is clearly the focus of Bo Juyi's most inventive—and most melodramatic—genius.

Paul W. Kroll

Monarch of Han, he doted on beauty, yearned for a
    bewitching temptress;
Through the dominions of his sway, for many years he sought
    but did not find her.
There was in the family of Yang a maiden just then reaching
    fullness,
Raised in the women's quarters protected, unacquainted yet   4
    with others.
Heaven had given her a ravishing form, impossible for her to
    hide,
And one morning she was chosen for placement at the side of
    the sovereign king.
When she glanced behind with a single smile, a hundred
    seductions were quickened;
All the powdered and painted ones in the Six Palaces now   8
    seemed without beauty of face.

In the coolness of springtime, she was permitted to bathe in
    the Huaqing pools,
Where the slickening waters of the hot springs washed over
    her firm flesh.
Supported as she rose by a waiting-maid, she was so delicate,
    listless:
This was the moment when first she acceded to His favor and   12
    beneficence.

Cloud-swept tresses, flowery features, quivering hair-pendants
    of gold,

And behind the warmth of the lotus-bloom drapings, they
   passed the springtime nights—
Springtime nights so grievously brief, as the sun rose again
   high!
16 From this time onward the sovereign king no longer held early
    court.

Taken with pleasure, she attended on the feasts, continuing
   without let;
Springtime followed springtime outing, evening after evening
   she controlled.

Of the comely beauties of the rear palace, there were three
   thousand persons,
20 And preferments and affection for all three thousand were
    placed on her alone.
In her golden room, with makeup perfect, the Delicate One
   serves for the night;
In a tower of jade, with the feast concluded, drunkenness
   befits love in spring.

Her sisters and brothers, older or younger, all were enfeoffed
   with land;
24 The most enviable brilliance and glory quickened their
    doorways and gates.
Then it came to pass, throughout the empire, that the hearts
   of fathers and mothers
No longer valued the birth of a son but valued the birth of
   daughters.

The high sites of Mount Li's palace reached into clouds in
   the blue,
28 And transcendent music, wafted on the wind, was heard there
    everywhere.

Measured songs, languorous dancing merged with sound of
   strings and bamboo,
As the sovereign King looked on all day long, never getting
   enough . . .
Until, out of Yuyang, horse-borne war-drums came, shaking
   the earth,
32 To dismay and smash the melody of "Rainbow Skirts and
    Feathered Vestments."

■■

By the nine-layered walls and watchtowers, dust and smoke
   arose,
And a thousand chariots, ten thousand riders moved off to
   the southwest.

The halcyon-plumed banners jounced and joggled along,
   moving and stopping again,
As they went forth westward from the metropolis' gates,   36
   something more than a hundred *li*.
And then the Six Armies would go no farther—there was no
   other recourse
But the fluently curved moth-eyebrows must die before the
   horses.

Floriform filigrees were strewn on the ground, to be retrieved
   by no one,
Halcyon tail feathers, an aigrette of gold, and hairpins made   40
   of jade.
The sovereign king covered his face—he could not save her;
When he looked back, it was with tears of blood that
   mingled in their flow.

■■

Yellowish grit spreads and scatters, as the wind blows drear
   and doleful;
Cloudy walkways turn and twist, climbing Saber Gallery's   44
   heights.
Below Mount Emei there are very few men who pass by;
Lightless now are the pennons and flags in the sun's dimmer
   aura.

Waters of Shu's streams deepest blue, the mountains of Shu
   are green—
For the Paragon, the Ruler, dawn to dawn, night upon night,   48
   his feelings:
Seeing the moon from his transient palace—a sight that tears
   at his heart;
Hearing small bells in the evening rain—a sound that stabs
   his insides.

■■

Heaven revolves, the days roll on, and the dragon carriage was
    turned around;
52 Having reached the spot, faltering he halted, unable to leave it
    again.
But amidst that muddy earth, below Mawei Slope,
Her jade countenance was not to be seen—just a place of
    empty death.

Sovereign and servants beheld each other, cloaks wet from
    weeping;
56 And, looking east, to the metropolis' gates, let their horses
    take them homeward.

Returned home now, and the ponds, the pools, all were as
    before—
The lotuses of Grand Ichor Pool, the willows by the Night-
    Is-Young Palace.

The lotus blossoms resemble her face, the willow branches
    her eyebrows;
60 Confronted with this, would it be possible that his tears
    should not fall?
From the day that peach and plum flowers open, in the
    springtime breezes,
Until the leaves of the "we-together" tree are shed in the
    autumn rain . . .

The West Palace and the Southern Interior were rife with
    autumn grasses,
64 And fallen leaves covered the steps, their red not swept away.
The artistes once young, of the Pear Garden, have hair gone
    newly white;
The Pepper Room attendants and their budding nymphs are
    become aged now.

Fireflies flit through the hall-room at dusk, as he yearns in
    desolation;
68 When all the wick of his lone lamp is used, sleep still fails to
    come.

Ever later, more dilatory, sound the watch-drum and bell in
    the lengthening nights;
Fitfully sparkling, the River of Stars streams onward to the
    dawn-flushed sky.

The roof-tiles, paired as love-ducks, grow chilled, and flowers
    of frost grow thick;
The halcyon-plumed coverlet is cold—whom would he share   72
    it with?
Dim-distanced, far-faded, are the living from the dead, parted
    more than a year ago;
Neither her soul nor her spirit have ever yet come into his
    dreams.

■■

A Daoist adept from Linqiong, a visitor to the Hongdu Gate,
Could use the perfection of his essential being to contact   76
    souls and spirits.
Because of his broodings the sovereign king, tossing and
    turning, still yearned.
So he set to task this adept of formulas, to search for her
    sedulously.

Cleaving the clouds, driving the ethers, fleeting as a
    lightning-flash,
Ascending the heavens, entering into the earth, he sought her   80
    out everywhere.
On high he traversed the sky's cyan drop-off, and below to
    the Yellow Springs;
In both places, to the limits of vision, she was nowhere to be
    seen.

Of a sudden he heard rumor then of a transcendent
    mountain in the sea,
A mountain resting in void and nullity, amidst the vaporous   84
    seemings.

High buildings and galleries shimmer there brightly, and five-
    colored clouds mount up;
In the midst of this, relaxed and unhurried, were hosts of
    tender sylphs.

And in their midst was one, known as Greatest Perfection,
88   Whose snow-white skin and flower-like features appeared to
      resemble *hers*.

In the western wing of the gatehouse of gold, he knocked at
      the jade bolting,
In turn setting in motion Little Jade who made report to
      Doubly Completed.
When word was told of the Son of Heaven's envoy, from the
      House of Han,
92   Then, within the nine-flowered drapings, her dreaming spirit
      startled.

She searched for her cloak, pushed pillow aside, arose, walked
      forth distractedly;
Door-screens of pearl, partitions of silver, she opened out
      one after another.
With her cloud-chignon half-mussed to one side, newly
      awakened from sleep,
96   With flowered cap set awry, down she came to the ceremonial
      hall.

Her sylphine sleeves, puffed by a breeze, were lifted, flared
      and fluttering,
Just the same as in the dance of "Rainbow Skirts and
      Feathered Vestments."
But her jade countenance looked bleak, forlorn, crisscrossed
      with tears—
100   A single branch of pear blossom, in springtime laden with
      rain.

Restraining her feelings, focusing her gaze, she asked her
      sovereign king's indulgence:
"Once we were parted, both voice and face were lost to
      limitless vagueness.
There, within Zhaoyang Basilica, affection and favor were cut
      short,
104   While here in Penglai's palaces, the days and months have
      lengthened.

Turning my head and looking down to the sites of the mortal
      sphere,

I can no longer see Chang'an, what I see is dust and fog.
Let me take up these familiar old objects to attest to my deep
　love:
The filigree case, the two-pronged hairpin of gold, I entrust　　108
　to you to take back.

Of the hairpin but one leg remains, and one leaf-fold of the
　case;
The hairpin is broken in its yellow gold, and the case's filigree
　halved.
But if only his heart is as enduring as the filigree and the
　gold,
Above in heaven, or amidst men, we shall surely see each　　112
　other."

As the envoy was to depart, she entrusted poignantly to him
　words as well,
Words in which there was a vow that only two hearts would
　know:
"On the seventh day of the seventh month, in the Hall of
　Protracted Life,
At the night's mid-point, when we spoke alone, with no one　　116
　else around—
'In heaven, would that we might become birds of coupled
　wings!
On earth, would that we might be trees of intertwining limbs!
　. . .'"
Heaven is lasting, earth long-standing, but there is a season
　for their end;
This regret stretches on and farther, with no ending time.　　120

Notes for a Minimalist Reading

L. 1　In the opening line, Bo Juyi adopts the convention—often used by Tang
poets when writing of contemporary political matters—that he is speaking of
the first great Chinese imperium, the Han. As will, however, be obvious, the poet
does not adhere closely to this convention throughout. "Bewitching temptress"
is literally "state-toppler" (*qing guo*), i.e., a beauty for whom one would lose everything, a classical Helen.

L. 8　The "Six Palaces" are the dwellings of the imperial concubines.

L. 9   The Huaqing (Floriate Clear) Palace on Mount Li, some fifteen miles east of Chang'an, included several hot springs. Xuan Zong was particularly fond of this imperial retreat. He had the buildings, grounds, and pools refurbished, and removed there with Lady Yang and necessary court officials at increasingly frequent intervals during the later years of his reign. See also lines 28–29.

L. 19   The "rear palace" indicates the women's quarters, whose numerous maidens are now wholly neglected by the emperor for whom Lady Yang is the only woman that exists.

L. 21   The "Delicate One" (*jiao*) figures Lady Yang in the person of Ajiao, beloved of Emperor Wu of Han (Han Wudi) in his youth and about whom he once said, "If I could have Ajiao, I should have a room of gold made in which to treasure her."

L. 23   Besides Yang Guozhong, other relatives of Lady Yang, including most conspicuously three of her sisters, received lavish conferments and marks of favor from the emperor.

L. 31   Yuyang, about 70 miles east of present-day Beijing, was An Lushan's headquarters.

L. 32   "Rainbow Skirts and Feathered Vestments" (*Nishang yüyi*) was the new name given by Xuan Zong to an exotic Serindian melody that he re-scored and to which Lady Yang danced in a costume made to resemble the fairy garments of moon maidens. (According to one tradition, the emperor brought the melody back with him from a mystical voyage to the moon.)

L. 34   The emperor and his personal retinue are fleeing the capital.

L. 38   The "fluently curved moth-eyebrows" are of course those of Lady Yang.

L. 44   Saber Gallery (Jian ge) is the name of the lofty pass that connects the territory of Qin (in which Chang'an is located) with that of Shu.

L. 45   Mount Emei about 100 miles southwest of Chengdu, is the most important mountain in Sichuan and was officially ennobled in Tang times for its supernatural potency. Although Xuan Zong's route to safety in Chengdu did not take him past Emei, the poet suggests that even as far distant as this the imperial splendor is now eclipsed.

LL. 49–50   The sight of the moon pains him because he remembers other nights when he and Lady Yang enjoyed it together, just as he recalls the music she used to play as he hears the plaintive sound of little bells tinkling in the rain under the eaves of a roof.

L. 51   The time is about a year and a half after the flight, in January of 758 C.E.

L. 58   Both the Grand Ichor Pool (Taiyi chi) and the Night-Is-Young Palace (Weiyang gong) were famous Han-time sites. The House of Tang had its own Taiyi chi within the grounds of the emperor's Palace of Great Light (Daming gong).

L. 62   The "we-together" tree is the wutong (*Sterculia platanifolia*). Its name is homophonous with the phrase "we together," and the falling of its leaves in the autumn rain suggests to Xuan Zong the extinction of the love he once shared.

L. 63 The West Palace and the Southern Interior, referring respectively to the Ganlu dian (Sweet Springs Hall) in the "Palace City" and the Xingqing gong ("Palace of Ascendant Felicity") near Chang'an's east market ward, were residences assigned by Su Zong to the retired emperor. He was not permitted to take up residence again in the grander compound of the Daming gong.

L. 65 The Pear Garden had housed Xuan Zong's group of private musicians in the years of his glory and pleasure.

L. 66 The Pepper Room refers to the dwelling of the chief consort.

L. 70 The "River of Stars" is our Milky Way.

L. 75 Linqiong is in Sichuan. The Hongdu Gate is a Han dynasty designation for one of the capital portals.

L. 81 The "cyan drop-off" (*biluo*) indicated the distant deep-blue reaches of the sky, and more specifically—to Daoist initiates—the region of Biluo kongge dafouli in the Heaven of Nascent Azure. The "Yellow Springs" (*huangquan*) is the traditional Chinese underworld destination of one's *po* or carnal (earth-bound) souls.

L. 87 "Greatest Perfection" (Taizhen) was the religious name adopted by Lady Yang when she briefly took orders as a Daoist priestess, prior to being recognized with a formal title as sharer of Xuan Zong's bed. Yang Yuhuan had originally been the wife of Xuan Zong's eighteenth son, Li Mao, Prince Shou. Her short period as a Daoist priestess, while not entirely a sham (Xuan Zong was intimately interested in Daoist teachings), served to "purify" her for attachment to the emperor.

L. 90 "Little Jade" (Xiaoyu) and "Doubly Completed" (Shuangcheng) are Taizhen's maids. The latter is known in Daoist tradition as an attendant of the goddess Xiwangmu; the former was the beautiful daughter of King Fuchai (r. 495–473 B.C.E.) of the ancient state of Wu.

L. 96 The "flowered cap" is that worn by Daoist priests and priestesses.

L. 103 The Zhaoyang ("Splendid Sunshine") Basilica was one of the halls occupied by imperial consorts during the Han.

L. 115 The Hall of Protracted Life (Changsheng dian) was part of the Huaqing complex on Mount Li.

52

SONG POEMS FOR DAUGHTERS
思念女兒

The following selections present images of daughters from four poets of the Song dynasty (960–1279 C.E.). Each poet expresses a father's affectionate longing for his children, especially his daughters. In the first poem, Chen Shidao (1053–1102 C.E.) recalls with great poignancy the forced breakup of his family due to poverty. He has sent his wife and three children to live in her father's house, where at least they will find food, clothing, and shelter. The second poet, Lu You (1125–1209 C.E.), daydreams of children whom he may yet care for. Although the poem has its speaker dismissing the dream as a distraction, the epitaph that Lu You wrote to commemorate the death of his daughter reveals the wintry desolation of his heart now that she is gone. In the third poem, penned by the Song statesman Ouyang Xiu (1007–1072 C.E.), the death of a favored daughter—only eight years old—prompts a vivid recollection of her refreshing presence in the ordinariness of his daily comings and goings. Finally, Wen Tienxiang (1236–1283 C.E.) worries about the safety of his family, especially his beloved daughters, now that he has been captured and imprisoned by the Mongols who were soon to crush the last Song resistance to their rule. Taken together these brief poems enrich our images of women by providing us with some balance in our understanding of what it meant to be a daughter, as well as a loving father, during the Song dynasty.

Pei-yi Wu

Chen Shidao (1053–1102 C.E.)

My daughter was just old enough to have her hair tied,
Yet she already knew the sadness of parting.
Using me as a pillow she refused to get up

For fear that getting up she would have to let me go.
The older son was just learning to talk.
Unused to adult ceremonies, he had to struggle with his
clothes
When he took formal leave of me, saying: "Father, I am
going now."
How can I ever bear to recall these words?
The younger son was still in swaddling clothes.
He was carried by his mother when they left.
His cry is still ringing in my ears:
Can anyone else understand how I feel?

Lu You (1125–1209 C.E.)

Dreaming of Children
In my dream I had a little son and a little daughter,
For whom I felt boundless love.
I took them to doctors whenever there was anything wrong;
I bored every visitor with the tales of their cleverness.
The morning rooster suddenly woke me up:
How can my love be there still?
Life is but a web of entanglements—
With a laugh I free myself of these fetters.

Epitaph for My Daughter
By a deserted hill and over a desolate ravine,
Amid frost and dew and surrounded by thorns and brush,
Lies my hapless daughter in a solitary grave.
No neighbor is seen in any direction.
When she was alive she never left the house.
In her death she is abandoned in a place like this.

Ouyang Xiu (1007–1072 C.E.)

In the evening when I came home she would welcome me
with a big smile.
In the morning when I was leaving she would pull me by my
jacket.

The instant after she jumped into my arms she would dash
away.

Wen Tianxiang (1236–1283 C.E.)

Daughters I have two, both bright and sweet.
The older one loved to practice calligraphy
While the younger recited lessons sonorously.
When a sudden blast of the north wind darkened the
    noonday sun
The pair of white jades were abandoned by the roadside.
The nest lost, young swallows flitted in the autumn chill.
Who will protect the girls, taken north with their mother?

53

THE CI OF SHUYÜ

(Shuyüci)

漱玉詞

Li Qingzhao

李清照

In the Northern Song period (960–1127 C.E.) there emerged in China an out-standing female ci[1] or lyric poet, Li Qingzhao (ca. 1081–ca. 1151 C.E.), also known as Yian Jushi.[2] Being born from a family of intellectuals, she was well read in the Classics. With her exceptional gift in rhetoric and poetry, Li became one of the greatest ci poets of China, male or female. Her work on the ci is considered on a par with if not better than those of the other major Song poets such as Su Shi, Liu Yong, Ouyang Xiu, and Huang Tingjian. Her only work extant today is the Shuyüci, which contains fifty-four complete ci poems and three incomplete ones, fol-lowed by eight narrative and conventional poems. The collection is concluded by two essays: the first is her famous Theory on Ci (Cilun), and the second is entitled Postscript to a Record of Gold and Stone (Jinshilu houxu).[3]

Li's ci poems are characterized by her talent in giving simple daily words a poetic significance. In other words, she is able to compose innovative poetic expressions by using combinations of common words. The dominant topic of her poems explores lone-liness and sorrow due to separation or death. They are the genuine feelings and roman-tic expressions of a Chinese woman in her quiet boudoir thinking of her distant

---

Translated by Fatima Wu.

[1] The term *ci* is used to mean both a lyric poet and a lyric poem.

[2] *Yian* can be translated as "easy and peaceful," and *Jushi* is an honorific term for a lay Buddhist.

[3] Contemporary records show that there was more than one edition of *Shuyüci* available during Li's lifetime. There was at least one edition that carried six volumes, another with five, and one even three. During the Qing dynasty (1644–1912 C.E.), other editions appeared. The fifty-four *ci* poems we have now are a collection of all Li's *ci* poems that are available today. The *Jinshilu* is a reference book on antique stone carvings and metal wine containers edited by Li's husband, Zhao Mingcheng.

husband or lover. Her ci poems reflect the epitome of parting sorrow in all Chinese women through the centuries.

Li's husband Zhao Mingcheng plays a central role in his wife's ci composition. Because of their mutual interests in poetry, painting, antiques, and literary criticism, the couple enjoyed much happiness and pleasure in their married life. When Li was in her late forties, her husband died and her life took a drastic change. Her lingering grief over this loss can be detected in many of her works. The two ci poems selected here were supposedly written when Li and her husband were parted from one another; it is also possible that the second one was composed after Zhao's death.

Fatima Wu

Like a Dream (Ru mengling)
Who will sit here with me by the lighted window?
Together with my shadow, there are two.
When the candlelight goes out for the night,
Even the shadow abandons me!
There is nothing . . .
There is nothing else but
A desolate being like me!

Spring in Wuling[4] (Wuling chun)
The wind has carried off any lingering fragrance.
The flower season is finished.
The day is drawing to a close.
I am too weary to comb my hair.
Objects are still in their place,
But the person is not.
Nothing matters anymore.
Tears flow before I can speak.

I heard that Spring at Shuangxi River[5] still offers its
    pleasures.
I would float on a small boat.
But I fear that the skeletal skiff at Shuangxi
Would not be able to carry such a heavy load of sorrow!

---

[4] In the Song dynasty, Wuling was the name of a county in Hunan Province. Here it is used as a name of the *ci* pattern or the pattern of a poem.

[5] *Shuangxi* literally means two rivers. The Shuangxi River is a meeting point of the waters from the Yongkang and Dongyang harbors in the Zhejiang province.

54

CLASSIC FOR GIRLS
(Nüerjing)
女兒經

The Classic for Girls (Nüerjing) *was a popular text among common Chinese women throughout later Chinese history. Although its original author and the time of composition is unknown, the text included here seems to be partly from the Song dynasty (960–1279 C.E.) and partly from the Ming dynasty (1368–1644 C.E.). Although a text from the Ming period clearly is beyond the scope of this collection, it is included here for two reasons. First, it illustrates how cultural values and customs that were originally developed by the elite came to be known among the masses; second, and related to the first, its poetic form made it particularly useful for educating illiterate women, since its rhymes were easy to memorize. Thus the* Nüerjing *not only confirms the fact that elite values cultivated in earlier times were disseminated among ordinary women but also suggests how they were disseminated. Considered historically, the work is comparable to another text, the* Classic for Boys (Sanzijing). *Both were written in rhymes composed of three Chinese characters per line so that they would be very easy to memorize and cite, even for those young people who could also read and write.*

This work, similar to other materials selected in this volume, evokes the proper behavior for women and urges the cultivation of womanly virtues. Its content is traditional and adds nothing substantially new to the expectations that society imposed upon women. Though Chinese tradition held that these were a natural and inevitable expression of the eternal Dao, *texts such as the* Nüerjing *allow us to understand the constructed nature of gender roles and the importance of popular education for persuading women to adhere to them.*

Robin R. Wang

This instruction for my sisters
I have called the *Nüerjing*.

From Isaac Taylor Headland, "Classic for Girls," *The Chinese Recorder and Missionary Journal* 26:12 (Dec. 1895): 554–560.

All its precepts you should practice, all its sentences should
    sing.
You should rise from bed as early in the morning as the sun,
Nor retire at evening's closing till your work is wholly done.

Then by wrapping in a towel
So that clean your hair may keep,
You should early take your brushes and should neatly dust
    and sweep.
Pay particular attention that the dust may not arise,
Clean your own apartments neatly, and 'twill glad your
    parents' eyes.

Then your hair comb smooth and shiny,
And your face no dirt should show.
To your needlework and cooking very early you should go,
And embroider well the pheasant and the phoenix and the
    drake.
Idle visits to your neighbors you should very seldom make.

Though the Changs may all be perfect,
And the Lis imperfect be,
Their perfection or their failings you should never deign to
    see.
And your relatives and neighbors, if on you they ever call,
With politeness entertain them, and converse with one and
    all.

Don't say "Father's sister's ugly,
But my mother's sister's good,"
Though your neighbors thus discuss them, you most surely
    never should.
And as long as you're a maiden, you at home should always
    stay,
And be very, very careful, of whatever you may say.

When the day is dead and buried,
And the moon is very small,
As a maiden in the darkness you should never walk at all.
If to go is necessary, you should summon as a guide,
A good servant with a lantern, who will linger by your side.

Let your laugh be never boisterous,
Nor converse in noisy way,
Lest your neighbors all about you hear whatever you may say.

Then be dignified in walking, and be orderly in gait,
Never lean against a door-post, but when standing stand up
    straight.

From Seven till Twenty

When the wheel of life's at seven,
You should study woman's ways.
Leave your bed when day is breaking, early thus begin the
    days.
Comb your tresses smooth and shiny, keep yourself both
    clean and neat,
Bind your "lilies"[1] tight and tidy, never go upon the street.

When the wheel's at eight or over,
While you gradually grow,
Both your old and younger brothers you should intimately
    know,
And while peacefully partaking of the tea and rice and wine,
About eating much or little never quarrel while you dine.

When the wheel at ten is turning,
You should never idle be,
To the making of their clothing and the mending you should
    see;
Your position should be daily sitting at your mother's feet,
Nor excepting on an errand should you go upon the street.

When the wheel has turned eleven,
You have grown to womanhood,
And all culinary matters should be clearly understood.
If for fancy-work from cooking you can save some precious
    hours,
You should spend them in embroid'ring ornamental leaves and
    flowers.

When the wheel has turned to thirteen,
You propriety should prize,
When your presence people enter you politely should arise;
Toward your aunts, your father's sisters, and his younger
    brothers' wives,

---

[1] The small feet of a woman.

You should not neglect your manners from the nearness of
  your lives.

When the wheel has turned to fifteen,
Or when twenty years have past,
As a girl with home and kindred these will surely be your last;
While expert in all employments that compose a woman's life,
You should study as a daughter all the duties of a wife.

A Wife's Virtues

First, though not the most important,
Is that filial you should be.
Filial piety and honor heaven naturally will see,
For the favor of your parents is as deep as earth and heaven;
You should recompense their kindness just as long as life is a
  given.

Then respect your elder brothers,
And your elder brothers' wives,
For disturbance has no foothold in a home where virtue
  thrives.
For a girl possessed of virtue, when no jealous thoughts can
  come
To her well-developed nature, is the jewel of the home.

Then a third important virtue
Is to save the rice and flour,
For economy in trifles such as oil and salt has power.
When provisions are abundant think of when they will be
  scant,
And prepare in time of plenty for a future time of want.

You should well prepare the cooking,
Be the food however plain,
And be able in receiving to politely entertain.
Things when first they come to market, though you purchase,
  do not eat,
But your own and husband's parents with such dainties you
  may treat.

It is also quite important—
Listen, girls, to what I mean—
That your old or new-made garments all be scrupulously
  clean;

For if, diligent and tidy, you yourself do not neglect,
Who of relatives and neighbors such a one does not respect?

If again I may advise you,
'Tis that evil thoughts are sin.
Love no other one's possessions, covet not a single pin,
If you slight your neighbor-duties and their love you do not
  prize,
You, your parents, and your brothers, all will utterly despise.

Then a meek and lowly temper
Is restriction number seven.
Your relation to your husband is the same as earth to heaven.
Where the hen announces morning there the home will be
  destroyed;
You from lack of woman's virtue neighbor's scorn cannot
  avoid.

This the eighth you may rely on,
By you all it should be known,
If you diligently manage you can make a happy home.
As a filial son will never house and home from parents' tear,
So a wife her wedding garments should not always wish to
  wear.

Ninth, a girl should prize her virtue,
And of goodness never tire,
For a jade that's pure and flawless, who does not with joy
  admire?
Anciently a girl was guarded, from her virtue would not part,
Pure as diamond was her body, firm as iron was her heart.

Tenth and last that I would offer
Is, be cautious all your life.
Once you marry 'tis forever, once you may become a wife;
Three dependencies, four virtues, let them all be perfect: then
Who can say that amongst our women, there are no "superior
  men"?

The Three Dependencies

"Girls are difficult to manage."
This is often said as true.
So from youth till grown to teach them is the best that we
  can do.

If she disregards instruction and refuses to be good,
Husband's parents will abuse her, as indeed they often should.

Girls have three on whom dependent
All their lives they must expect:
While at home to follow father, who a husband will select,
With her husband live in concord from the day that she is
    wed,
And her son's directions follow if her husband should be dead.

The Four Virtues

There are four important virtues,
I will one by one rehearse them that your minds they may
    impress.
First like lady T'sao be perfect, and your happiness secure,
Who in virtue and deportment and in words and work was
    pure.

First of all a woman's virtues
Is a chaste and honest heart,
Of which modesty and goodness and decorum form a part.
If in motion, or if resting, a becoming way is chief,
You should guard against an error as you guard against a
    thief.

In your personal appearance
You should ever take delight,
Ne'er depend upon cosmetics, whether they be red or white.
Comb and bathe at proper seasons; all the dirt remove with
    care;
In the washing of your clothing no exertion should you spare.

Of the virtues of a woman,
Conversation is the third,
By your friends 'tis often better to be seen than to be heard.
But to speak at proper seasons will incur no one's disdain
And one fit word o'er a thousand will the victory often gain.

Fourth, the duties of women,
Know that drawing and embroidering is not all of woman's
    work;
You should labor at your spinning all the time you have to
    spare,
And the flavorings for cooking you should constantly prepare.

Duties Toward Others

As the favor of your parents
Is as great as heaven's joy,
To be filial to your parents you should all your strength
    employ;
As Ti-Ying that filial maiden, who, her father's life to save,
By presenting a petition to him thus rescued from the grave.

All your father's elder brothers,
And his younger brothers too,
Are your intimate relations, the same bone and flesh as you;
You should with care expression utter that would break the
    family chain,
Thus denoting you forget those who in youth did you
    maintain.

To the wives of these your uncles,
Old and younger just the same,
If unfilial in your girlhood you will surely be to blame.
Though they manifest no anger, if you thus unfilial prove,
All your faults will be detected, you will lose your neighbor's
    love.

You should honor elder brothers,
And their wives you should respect,
Nor should treat them badly, hoping you your parents will
    protect.
All the members of your household should in peace and quiet
    dwell,
Then no wrangling nor disturbance will your disagreements
    tell.

With the families of your neighbors,
Whether Zhang or whether Li,
Let your intercourse exhibit fellowship and harmony.
Do not constantly require that your wishes they indulge,
Do not carry idle gossip and their secrets thus divulge.

Reasons for Certain Customs

Have you ever learned the reason
Why your ears should punctured be?
It's that you may never listen to the talk of Zhang and Li.

444

Part Five: Tang and Song

True, the holes were made for earrings that your face may be
    refined,
But the other better reason you should always keep in mind.

At your throat you wear a button,
It should teach you as a guide
That you never should, while walking, turn your head from
    side to side.
And the layers of your clothing have a lesson for you too,
They should decorate your body as the clouds adorn Mount
    Wu.

Then a woman's upper garment
And her skirt should teach again,
That, though living with her husband, she is on a different
    plain.
She should follow and be humble that it ne'er be said by men,
That "the morning there is published by the crowing of the
    hen."[2]

Have you ever learned the reason
For the binding of your feet?
It's from fear that will be easy to go out upon the street.
It is not that they are handsome when thus like a crooked
    bow
That ten thousand wraps and bindings are bound around
    them so.

Duties As a Wife

As a wife to husband's parents
You should filial be and good,
Nor should suffer imperfection in their clothing or their
    food.
Be submissive to their orders, all their wants anticipate,
That, because his wife is idle they your husband may not
    hate.

Be submissive to your husband,
Nor his wishes e'er neglect.
First of all in this submission is his parents to respect.

---

[2] This may mean that the woman (the hen) has overstepped her boundaries and is inappropriately taking on a man's (i.e., the rooster's) role.

Economical and active you should ever strive to be,
Nor complain that Zhang has nothing, and that few are poor
  as Li.

With his brothers' wives be peaceful,
And his sisters all respect,
And affectionately treat them, nor their company neglect.
Let not sisterly affection be by servants' stories killed,
Nor with smiles your face be covered while with hate your
  heart is filled.

Though your husband may be wealthy,
You should never be profuse,
There should always be a limit to the things you eat and use.
If your husband should be needy you should gladly share the
  same,
Being diligent and thrifty, and no other people to blame.

For your guests arrange in order,
Both your table and your dress;
Be not stingy in providing, nor yet lavish to excess.
Ne'er in treatment of your callers over-closely count the cost,
But if lavish in expenses all your wealth will soon be lost.

Duties As a Mother

Of prenatal education, be attentive as a mother,
For the influence is mutual of each upon the other.
Whether walking, standing, sitting, or reclining, have a rule,
They in eating and in drinking have a care yourself to school.

Ne'er by fondness spoil your offspring,
Whether they be girls or boys,
By indulgence soon their tempers you will utterly destroy.
Tho' in youth it matters little, yet the time will surely come,
When your offspring are indifferent to themselves and to
  their homes.

When he grows to years of boyhood
Then a teacher call at once,
Who will books and manners teach him that he may not be a
  dunce.
Lazy habits in his study will good people all annoy,
And his indolence the prospects of his future life destroy.

For your daughter in her girlhood,
To learn fancy-work is best,
Ne'er allow her to be idle, lolling to the east or west.
If in youth you do not teach her, when full-grown 'twill be
    too late,
When she marries it will bring her only shame, disgrace, and
    hate.

When your son arrives at manhood,
Then a wife for him secure,
Never mind about her parents, whether they be rich or poor.
If the maiden have but virtue, if the maiden have but health,
She will manage well her household, she will bring her
    husband wealth.

When your daughter weds she then is
To her husband's family brought;
To be frugal in the household she by parents should be
    taught.
To his parents, as a daughter, she should kind and filial be,
And submissive to her husband, to his home should gladly
    see.

If your sons, when you are aged,
Other people's daughters wed,
If impartially you treat them they will easily be led.
Don't because the one is wealthy and the other one is poor,
Treat the one as though a goddess and the other as a boor.

And the children of your children,
Boys or girls no matter which,
You should love them as your jewels, whether they be poor or
    they be rich.
To your neighbors be a neighbor that no person may declare,
That you love your kindred only, but for others do not care.

Thus we end the Girl's Classic;
You should learn it part by part,
And should practice it and keep it always living in your heart.
If you learn but do not heed it you will simply be, of course,
Though arrayed in woman's garments, as a cow or as a horse.

SUGGESTED READINGS

Bapat, P. V. *Change of Sex in Buddhist Literature*. Benares: Motilal Banarsidass, 1957.

Bernhardt, Kathryn. "Women and Property in China." In *Law, Society, and Culture in China*. Stanford: Stanford University Press, 1999.

Black, Alison Harley. "Gender and Cosmology in Chinese Correlative Thinking." In *Gender and Religion: On the Complexity of Symbols*. Boston: Beacon Press, 1989.

Brownell, Susan, and Jeffrey Waserstrom, eds. *Chinese Femininities/Chinese Masculinities: A Reader*. Berkeley: University of California Press, 2002.

Cahill, Suzanne. *Transcendence and Divine Passion: The Queen Mother of the West in Medieval China*. Stanford: Stanford University Press, 1993.

Chang, Kang-i Sun, and Haun Saussy, eds. *Women Writers of Traditional China: An Anthology of Poetry and Criticism*. Stanford: Stanford University Press, 1999.

Chen, Dongyuan. *History of Chinese Women's Life*. Beijing: Shangwu, 1937.

Cheng, Lucie, Charlotte Furth, and Hon-ming Yip, eds. *Women in China: Bibliography of Available English Language Materials*. Berkeley: Institute of East Asian Studies, 1984.

Ebrey, Patricia. *Confucianism and Family Rituals in Imperial China*. Princeton: Princeton University Press, 1991.

———. *The Inner Quarter: Marriage and the Lives of Chinese Women in the Sung Period*. Berkeley: University of California Press, 1993.

Ebrey, Patricia, and Rubie Watson. *Marriage and Inequality in Chinese Society*. Berkeley: University of California Press, 1991.

Elvin, Mark. "Female Virtue and the State in China." *Past and Present* 104 (1984).

Englert, Siegfried, and Roderich Ptak. "Nan-tzu, or Why Heaven Did Not Crush Confucius." *Journal of the American Oriental Society* 106 no. 4 (1986): 679–686.

Furth, Charlotte. *A Flourishing Yin: Gender in China's Medical History*. Berkeley: University of California Press, 1999.

Gilmartin, Christina K., ed. *Engendering China: Women, Culture, and the State*. Harvard Contemporary China Series 10. Cambridge, MA: Harvard University Press, 1994.

Goldin, Paul R. "The Motif of the Woman in the Doorway and Related Imagery in Traditional Chinese Funerary Art." *Journal of the American Oriental Society* 121 no. 4 (2001): 539–548.

———. *The Culture of Sex in Ancient China*. Honolulu: University of Hawaii Press, 2002.

Guisso, Richard W. "Thunder Over the Lake: The Five Classics and the Perception of Woman in Early China." In *Women in China: Current Directions in the Historical Scholarship*, Richard W. Guisso and Stanley Johannesen, eds. New York: Philo Press, 1983.

Guisso, Richard W., and Stanley Johannesen, eds. "Women in China: Current Directions in Historical Scholarship." In *Historical Reflections: Directions 3*. Youngstown, NY: Philo, 1981.

Harper, Donald. "The Sexual Arts of Ancient China as Described in a Manuscript of the Second Century B.C." *Harvard Journal of Asiatic Studies* 47 no. 2 (1987): 539–593.

Henry, Eric. "The Social Significance of Nudity in Early China." *Fashion Theory* 3 no. 4 (1999): 475–486.

Hinsch, Bret. *Women in Early Imperial China*. Lanham, MD: Rowman and Littlefield, 2002.

Horner, I. B. *Women under Primitive Buddhism*. 1930 (London: George Routledge). Reprint, Delhi: Motilal Banarsidass, 1975.

Hu Shi. "Women's Place in Chinese History." In *Chinese Women through Chinese Eyes*, Yu-ning, Li, ed. Armonk, NY: M.E. Sharpe, 1997.

Jackson, Beverly. *Splendid Slippers: A Thousand Years of an Erotic Tradition*. Berkeley: Ten Speed, 1997.

Ko, Dorothy. *Every Step a Lotus: Shoes for Bound Feet*. Berkeley: University of California Press, 2001.

Kristeva, Julia. *About Chinese Women*. Translated by Anita Barrows. New York: Urizen, 1997.

Lee, Lily Xiao Hong. *The Virtue of Yin: Studies of Chinese Women*. Sydney: Wild Peony, 1994.

Levy, Howard S. *Chinese Footbinding: The History of a Curious Erotic Custom*. New York: W. Rawls, 1996.

Levy, Howard S., and Akira Ishihara. *The Tao of Sex: The Essence of Medical Prescriptions (Ishimpô)*. 3rd edition. Lower Lake, CA: Integral, 1989.

Li, Chenyang, ed. *The Sage and the Second Sex: Confucianism, Ethics, and Gender*. Chicago and La Salle, IL: Open Court, 2000.

Li, Ling, and Keith McMahon. "The Contents and Terminology of the Mawangdui Texts on the Arts of the Bedchamber." *Early China* 17 (1992): 145–185.

Li, Wai-yee. *Enchantment and Disenchantment: Love and Illusion in Chinese Literature*. Princeton: Princeton University Press, 1993.

Mann, Susan, and Yu-yin Cheng, eds. *Under Confucian Eyes: Writings on Gender in Chinese History*. Berkeley: University of California Press, 2001.

Mou, Sherry J. *Gentlemen's Prescriptions for Women's Lives: A Thousand Years of Biographies of Chinese Women.* Eastgate. Armonk, NY: M.E. Sharpe, 2002.

Pao-Ch'ang, Shih, ed. *Lives of the Nuns: Biographies of Chinese Buddhist Nuns from the Fourth to Sixth Centuries: A Translation of the Pi-Ch'Iu-Ni Chuan.* Translated by Kathryn Ann Tsai. Honolulu: University of Hawaii Press, 1994.

Paul, Diana Y. *Women in Buddhism: Images of the Feminine in Mahayana Tradition.* 1979 (Berkeley: Asian Humanities Press). Reprint, Berkeley: University of California Press, 1985.

Raphals, Lisa. *Sharing the Light: Representations of Women and Virtue in Early China.* SUNY Series in Chinese Philosophy and Culture. Albany, NY: SUNY Press, 1998.

———. "Arguments by Women in Early Chinese Texts." *Nan Nü* 3 no. 2 (2001): 157–195.

Rouzer, Paul F. Articulated Ladies: *Gender and Male Community in Early Chinese Texts, Harvard-Yenching Institute Monograph Series 53.* Cambridge, MA: Harvard University, 2001.

Stone, Charles R. (forthcoming). *The Fountainhead of Chinese Erotica.* Honolulu: University of Hawaii Press.

Swann, Nancy Lee. *Pan Chao: Foremost Woman Scholar of China.* Ann Arbor: University of Michigan Press, 2001.

Tung, Jowen R. *Fables for the Patriarchs: Gender Politics in Tang Discourse.* Lanham, MD: Rowman and Littlefield, 2000.

Ueki, M. *Gender Equality in Buddhism.* New York: Peter Lang Publications, 2001.

Van Gulik, R. H. *Sexual Life in Ancient China: A Preliminary Survey of Chinese Sex and Society from ca. 1500 B.C. till 1644 A.D.* Leiden: E.J. Brill, 1961.

Watson, Rubie S., and Patricia Buckley Ebrey, eds. "Marriage and Inequality in Chinese Society." In *Studies on China 12.* Berkeley: University of California Press, 1991.

Wei, Karen T. "Women in China: A Selected and Annotated Bibliography." In *Bibliographies and Indexes in Women's Studies 1.* Westport, CT: Greenwood, 1984.